SOCIAL DEMOCRACY

The Enemy Within

Harpal Brar

Also by the same author

PERESTROIKA - The Complete Collapse of Revisionism
ISBN 1-874613-01-X [pbk]   ISBN 1-874613-00-1 [hbk]

TROTSKYISM OR LENINISM ?
ISBN 1-874613-02-8 [pbk]   ISBN 1-874613-03-6 [hbk]

First published in Great Britain
by Harpal Brar, London, 1995

Copyright Harpal Brar 1995

ISBN 1-874613-04-4 [pbk]
ISBN 1-874613-05-2 [hbk]

Printed in India
by Progressive Printers
Delhi 110095
India

All Harpal Brar publications are available from
E.J.Rule, 14 Featherstone Road, Southall, Middx. UB2 5AA (UK)
Cheques payable to 'E.J.Rule', please.

Dedicated to
Frederick Engels

Co-founder of scientific socialism, who through his writing rendered an undying service to the British working class, and whose analysis of the conditions of the working class has been key to a Marxist understanding of the development of social democracy in Britain

In commemoration of 100th Anniversary of his death

Contents

	page
Preface	(i)
Postscript to Preface	(xiv)

Part One
SOCIAL DEMOCRACY & THE ATTITUDE OF THE PROLETARIAT TOWARDS IT ... 1

Historical Conditions Preceding the Birth of the Labour Party ... 3

Organisational Breach between labour and the Liberal Party - Formation of the Labour Party ... 16

Lenin's Advice to British Communists and the Reasons Therefor ... 38

Labour Comes Out Unmistakably as the Third Capitalist Party ... 53

Labour Since the Second World War ... 71

Trendy-Troto 'left' - a fig-leaf for Social Democracy ... 82

Embellishment of Social Democracy by the Revisionists of the CPB ... 95

NCP's Capitulation to Social Democracy ... 105

Part Two
ON THE REVISIONISTS' & TROTSKYITES' BETRAYAL OF THE MARXIAN TEACHING ON THE STATE ... 137

The Marxian Teaching on the State ... 139

The Revisionist CPGB and the Slogan: "A General Election to kick out the Tories and to elect a Labour Government committed to left policies" ... 149

Trotskyites and the Slogan: "A General Election to kick out the Tories and to elect a Labour Government committed to left policies"   172

Part Three

THE COAL STRIKE OF 1984 - 85   191

Tories seeking confrontation with the miners   193

Government & NCB declare class war on the miners   195

May Day Resolution - Support the miners   201

111 days of the Coal Strike   205

Resolutely support the miners - fight the enemy within   213

TUC Conference must support the NUM - Dockers open second front   220

Miners poised for a historic victory - signs of disintegration & panic in the bourgeois camp   227

The NUM strike and the renegade Jimmy Reid   233

Contempt of court proceedings against the NUM   243

Mr. Steel's humbug on democracy   245

NUM strike - a fight to the finish   246

Whose Libyan connection?   251

Time for labour movement to redeem its IOUs - NCB's back-to-work abysmal failure   255

Hammer blows of the miners' strike hit home - pound collapses   265

NUM calls off the Coal Strike on a defiant note   272

The British Coal Strike of 1984-85   274

Facts and figures   283

Scabs out to form a bosses' union   284

Hands off Arthur Scargill and Peter Heathfield   287

Only mass mobilisation can win victory - fight shoulder to shoulder with the miners	291
Support the miners - fight this deliberate industrial vandalism	297

Part Four

SOCIAL DEMOCRACY & OTHER ECONOMIC STRUGGLES	309
The People's March for Jobs	311
TUC Betrayal of hospital workers	315
TUC leaders capitulate to Tory Government	319
Support the NGA - smash the bourgeois offensive against the trade-union movement	323
NGA dispute drowns in legal cretinism	326
Liverpool showdown - the collapse of Trotskyite dreams of 'socialism in one city'	333
Wapping - unions confronted	349
Wapping - frenzied violence of the bourgeoisie	354
Attempts to terrorise teachers	360

Part Five

SOCIAL DEMOCRACY & IMPERIALIST WAR, AGGRESSION AND OCCUPATION	363
Support the National Liberation Struggle of the Irish people	365
Hands off the Falklands - Las Malvinas Argentinas	383
London demonstrations show British people opposed to Gulf War	389

APPENDIX

Scargill nails bourgeois lies	397

Lalkar interviews Malcolm Pitt, 6th October, 1984	403
Kent NUM leader's speech to IWF Rally	410
Lessons of the NUM Strike (Malcolm Pitt talks to Lalkar)	414
Miners' Strike of 1984-85 - Malcolm Pitt sums up	419
Can the Labour Party bring us our economic salvation?	423
Bibliography	431
Index	435

PREFACE

With some honourable exceptions, what passes for the revolutionary left in Britain regards the Labour Party (the representative of social democracy in Britain) as a party of the British working class with the potential to unify the British proletariat in its struggle for social emancipation, maintaining that Labour can be an instrument for the attainment of socialism in Britain. The present writer, however, is of the opposite view, maintaining that Labour never has been, is not now, and will never in the future be, a party of the British proletariat; that it was formed to defend the interests of the privileged upper stratum (at the time composed of skilled workers organised in craft unions, which at the time embraced a tiny minority of the workforce) of the working class; that since the privileged position of this upper stratum - this aristocracy of labour - depended on the loot from the Empire and the extraction of imperialist superprofits from abroad, Labour from its inception was committed to the defence of the British Empire and British imperialism alike - for it could not defend the one (the privileges of the labour aristocracy) without defending the other (British imperialism); that, therefore, Labour has, throughout its existence, as its record over nearly a century amply proves, been an imperialist party - a *"bourgeois labour party"*, to use Engels' remarkably profound expression. The task I set myself in this book is to prove, by reference to irrefutable evidence, both historical and contemporary, the correctness of this assertion and to make this truth known among the lower stratum, the vast masses, of the British proletariat, whose interests the Labour Party has never championed in the past and does not champion now. The Labour Party has always defended the interests of British imperialism and of the privileged sections of the working class - the labour aristocracy. The composition of this labour aristocracy has undergone a remarkable change over several decades, but the labour aristocracy as such remains. If in former times it was composed of skilled craft workers, today it consists largely of skilled white-collar workers, administrators, labour and trade-union functionaries, and those in supervisory and managerial positions. But what this new labour aristocracy shares with the old labour aristocracy is its total contempt for the poor, the deprived and the downtrodden at home and abroad, its total disregard for the plight of the most disadvantaged and most cruelly exploited sections of the population here in Britain or in the rest of the world. And this, for the simple reason that such destitution - the existence of a "functional underclass", to use Galbraith's terminology, is a necessary condition for the maintenance of its privileged and parasitic existence, which explains its philistinism, the depth of its vilest subservience to, and its contemptible sycophancy in the service of, the imperialist bourgeoisie.

Secondly it is my task in this book to prove the continuing validity of the Leninist thesis concerning the very profound economic connection between imperialism and opportunism in the labour movement. Imperialism engenders a split in the working class, for it has singled out a handful of exceptionally rich and powerful states who plunder the whole world and who are able to use a portion of the superprofits thus derived to bribe the labour leaders and the upper stratum of the working class. "This stratum of bourgeoisified workers, or the 'labour aristocracy', *who are quite philistine in their mode of life, in the size of their earnings and in their entire outlook, ... is the principal* **social** *... prop of the bourgeoisie. For they are the real* **agents of the bourgeoisie in the working-class movement***, the labour lieutenants of the capitalist class, real channels of reformism and chauvinism."* (Lenin, Preface to the French and German editions of *Imperialism, the highest stage of capitalism*).

The chief function of this bribed, and therefore opportunist, stratum is to act as the watchdogs of capitalism and the corrupters of the labour movement. On the basis of its monopoly profits, and the bribing of its labour aristocracy, the bourgeoisie of each imperialist country long ago begot, nurtured and secured for itself a bourgeois labour party. The British bourgeoisie, since monopoly developed much earlier in Britain than elsewhere, was the first to secure such a party. The Labour Party was precisely such a *"bourgeois labour party."* It is, as it always has been, a party of opportunism and social chauvinism, which is totally alien to the revolutionary proletariat, and unless a determined ruthless struggle is waged against this party, it is pointless and hypocritical cant to talk about the struggle against imperialism, about Marxism-Leninism, about the socialist labour movement, or about proletarian revolution.

Historical facts fully confirm that in the entire history of British capitalism there has been a split in the working class, apart from two brief periods during which British capitalism, while sustaining the privileged position of the upper stratum of the working class, was nevertheless able to provide adequate living standards to the mass of the working class. These exceptional periods were, first, the years 1848-1868, that is, from the defeat of the Chartist movement to nearly the close of the seventh decade of the 19th century, when Britain possessed the largest Empire and enjoyed complete monopoly in the world market and could, therefore, rightly be described as 'the workshop of the world'. During these years Britain was not just the biggest act in town, it was the only act - it was the town. This monopoly position yielded enormous profits to the British ruling class, thus enabling it to treat the working class rather more leniently. Because of these exceptional circumstances, after the defeat of Chartism, there existed no party to defend the interests of the working class - not even that of its privileged upper stratum, which found it satisfactory to safeguard its interests through craft unions and in alliance with the bourgeois Liberal Party - the lib-lab alliance. From the 1870s, Britain's monopoly position was increasingly under challenge, especially from Germany and the United States of America, and by 1890 this monopoly was gone forever. With the disappearance of this monopoly, the British bourgeoisie could no longer afford its earlier leniency, and was thus forced to attack the living standards of the working class, including those of its upper stratum. Finding itself under attack from its former ally (the liberal bourgeoisie), and being no longer able to defend its interests through the Liberal Party, the labour aristocracy effected the first **organisational** breach in the hitherto existing notorious lib-lab alliance, with the formation in 1893 of the Independent Labour Party (ILP), and subsequently the Labour Representation Committee in 1900, which from 1906 began to be referred to as the Labour Party. However, this organisational breach in no way affected its lib-lab politics, which have continued up to the present day.

Secondly, the 30 years following the end of the Second World War (1945-1975), when post-war conditions of boom produced the Keynesian consensus, leading to the reconstruction of British imperialism at the expense of the increased exploitation and oppression of the colonial peoples, the institution of the National Health Service, universal benefits, full employment and a rising standard of living for the entire working class.

Just as the successful challenge to Britain's monopoly position in the last quarter of the 19th century put an end to the consensus of that period, likewise the deteriorating condition of British imperialism - its relative decline in comparison with its rival imperialist powers - has caused the breakdown of the Keynesian consensus, and with it the end to full employment, universal benefits and the National Health Service, at least in its hitherto existing form. No longer can British imperialism sustain the privileged conditions of the upper stratum of the working class and the petty bourgeoisie while at the same time providing an adequate, let alone a rising, standard of living for the vast masses of the working class. From now on, as indeed has been the case since the end of the 1970s, the privileged conditions of the former can only be maintained at the expense of the increased exploitation, poverty and misery of the latter. What was considered unthinkable not so long ago is already happening. Every one of the gains of the post-war period (gains which the Trotskyite and revisionist coteries of renegades still continue dementedly to attribute to the 'socialist' Attlee government) - full employment, universal benefits, the National Health Service - is under attack.

The result is an increase in poverty, a widening of the gap between rich and poor, and an intensification in the split in the working class. The recently published *Inquiry into income and wealth* by the Joseph Rowntree Foundation bears eloquent testimony to this phenomenon. This report, in its analysis of wage trends over a period of 18 years, covering the last 2 years of Labour government and the subsequent 16 years of Conservative administration, says:

"After 1977 the gap between low wages and high wages grew, the experiences of three parts of the distribution diverged; wages for the lowest paid hardly changed, and by 1992 were lower in real terms than in 1975; median wages grew by 35 per cent; but high wages grew by 50 per cent."

Commenting on the accentuation of this trend with the onset of the Thatcher administration in 1979, the report states:

"[O]ver the period 1979 to 1992 the poorest 20-30 per cent of the population failed to benefit from economic growth, in contrast to the rest of the post-war period, when all groups benefited during times of rising living standards."

From 1979 to 1992 there was a massive transfer of wealth from the poor to the rich. During these years, while the average income after housing costs rose by 36%, this only served to hide the fact that whereas the earning of the upper 10% went up by 60%, those of the bottom 10% went down by 17% in real terms. The report says that an increasing ratio of the working class are now earning less than £127 per week - a mere half of the average household income - with a particular concentration of poverty among black people:

"Since 1977 the proportion of the population with less than half the average income has more than trebled from 7 to 24 per cent."

And: *"Ethnic minority incomes tend to be lower than those of the rest of the population. Whereas only 18 per cent of the population classified by survey interviewers as 'white' was in the poorest fifth of the whole population, more than a third of the 'non-white' population was in the poorest fifth. ... you are twice as likely to be poor if you are black than if you are white."*

Council estates are increasingly becoming the dumping grounds for the poorest sections of the population:

"In the 1960s and early 1970s fewer than half of the individuals living in council housing were in the poorest 40 per cent of the population; by 1991 the proportion was three-quarters."

The report goes on to highlight the fast-deteriorating employment prospects for the young, linking these prospects to educational success at school and at higher levels of education. In the circumstances of the continued decline of British imperialism, the erosion of its manufacturing base, with the resultant bleak employment prospects, the government's education policy is tailor-made to produce not just the successful ones needed by capital for its self-expansion, but also the unsuccessful fated for the ranks of the bottom one-third, surrounded by conditions of dire, unrelenting and absolute poverty, shut up in deprived/problem working-class estates attending problem schools starved of resources.

Yet the so-called 'left', grouped in various Trotskyist (both inside and outside of the Labour Party) and revisionist organisations, these *"philistines in nightcaps"*, to use Lenin's very apt expression, possessed of an inordinate amount of inept pedantry, and imbued with a spirit of servility to the bourgeoisie, continue to deny the existence of the above split in the working class. The denial of this split is absolutely essential to their support for the Labour Party as the party of the entire working class, for the recognition of the split in the working class cannot fail to force on them also the recognition that Labour represents the interests of British imperialism and of the privileged layers of the working class. In denying this split, these ignorant country yokels also deny, albeit implicitly, the imperialist character of British capitalism. Just as the contemptible scoundrelly gentry of the Labour Party, cringing before the bourgeoisie, adapt every line of their programme to the requirements of British imperialism and that of the labour aristocracy and the petty bourgeoisie, in the same measure our Troto-revisionist 'left', which fancies itself to be revolutionary, increasingly cringing before social democracy, adapting itself to bourgeois parliamentarism, adjusts itself to the imperialist Labour Party and the latter's electoral requirements. Treating history and reality like Gogol's Petrushka, our representatives of lackey science that they are, our 'left', continue chanting the *mantra* that the Labour Party is a mass party of the British working class. Their stance, their scorn for historical facts, their disdain for reality, is distinguished by such a *"sweet naiveté, which would be touching in a child but is repulsive in a person who has not yet been officially certified as feeble-minded,"* to use Lenin's observation apropos Kautsky.

The entire history of bourgeois democracy shows that bourgeois democrats have always practised deception and trickery on the masses. They have always advanced, and still advance, all manner of slogans in order to trick the proletariat. The Labour Party is no exception. Throughout its existence it has advanced demagogic slogans to hoodwink the proletariat, to lull to sleep the Simple Simons among the socialists, while serving imperialism single-mindedly. The task of the socialists, therefore, is not to be satisfied with the slogans, with idealistic or charlatan phrases, but to get to class reality and test the sincerity of those putting forward the slogans - to compare their words with their **deeds**.

Today, however, the continuing relative decline of British imperialism is increasingly forcing the bourgeois democrats, including those of the Labour Party, to shed much of the sloganising and to confront the mass of the working class with hideous class reality in the form of an assault on the gains of the post-war period. During the past 25 years, the manufacturing workforce has been nearly halved (down from 8 million to 4.5 million), while the number of those employed in banking and insurance has nearly trebled. Between 1979 and 1989 alone, while investment in banking services went up by 125%, investment in manufacturing over the same period went up by a mere 13%. No wonder then that during those ten years employment in banking and financial services went up by over one million. In 1992, manufacturing output was 1% above that of 1979, while manufacturing investment was actually below that of 1979. Within manufacturing itself, one in ten manufacturing jobs are accounted for by the manufacture of armaments. Eleven of the top twenty British companies are involved in the manufacture of armaments. With such an erosion of its manufacturing base, and with such heavy reliance on the manufacture of the merchandise of death, how is British imperialism able to support the increasing proportion of the population involved in unproductive labour - the vast parasitic layers who produce no wealth, no surplus value? The answer, in the m n, must be found in the export of capital and the earnings from it. For instance, in 1990, Britain's overseas earnings from capital invested abroad were close to £26 billion, which represented 36% of all profit made in Britain in that year. With such a high proportion of the profits of British imperialism dependent on the export of capital, one can see why banking (the City) and militarism have assumed such monstrously gigantic dimensions.

In these conditions, if British imperialism is to continue its parasitic existence (and it can have no other existence), if it is to continue to provide privileged conditions for the petty bourgeoisie and the labour aristocracy, every government policy must be subordinated to the interests of the robber barons of finance capital; every military adventure abroad must be fully and enthusiastically supported in order to make sure of the continued flow of tribute from abroad. The support given by all bourgeois parties, including Labour, to the genocidal war against Iraq is but one of the scores of examples one could cite in this connection.

Notwithstanding the extraction of superprofits from abroad, the inexorable relative decline of British imperialism continues apace on all fronts - industrial, financial and political. British finance capital has come under severe pressure from German and Japanese finance capital and Tokyo is increasingly replacing London as the global financial centre. Without question, British capital is fighting hard, and, figures suggest with some degree of success, to maintain its parasitic privileged position. Between 1986 and 1990, its overseas investments ran at the rate of approximately $28 bn. *per annum*. Although 1991 witnessed a sharp decline to $17 bn. in these investments, the following years saw a steady recovery. In 1992 Britain's investments rose to $20 bn., in 1993 to $27 bn., and in 1994 to $30 bn. - the latter figure made her the second largest overseas investor (after the US, which invested $58 bn. abroad in the same year) in 1994. These figures do not, however, detract from the general trend of the decline of British monopoly capital taken over a long period of time, particularly in the light of the erosion of its manufacturing base. What they do reveal is that in the crowded global market, each imperialist power is fighting for space, for a place in the sun - a most ruthless war with no holds barred; and that the City, this symbol of British finance capital, with 3 centuries of cunning and experience behind it, will be no pushover; that Britain is still a major player in this fight for a global carve-up. The problem, however, is that even success in this field only serves to further its deepening crisis. On the one hand, the greater the investment abroad, the greater the inflow of superprofits. On the other hand, the greater the investment abroad, the less the investment at home, with the resultant further erosion of the manufacturing base, more closures at home, more unemployment and a further exacerbation of the crisis of overproduction. The gap between domestic investment in manufacturing and investment abroad is increasing year by year in favour of foreign investment. While direct overseas investment in 1980 was the equivalent of 113% of the domestic investment in manufacture, it rose to 250% in 1985 and 370% in

1989, before coming down to 164% in 1990. These figures, which reveal the truly parasitic character of British capitalism, do not include bank loans and portfolio investment, in comparison with which the direct investment figures assume a rather dwarfish look. If, for instance, between 1980 and 1986, direct overseas investment amounted to £46 bn., portfolio investment was £75 bn., and bank loans £200 bn.

Consequent upon the erosion of Britain's manufacturing base, it is confronted with a huge balance of trade deficit on manufactured goods (currently running at the rate of £20 billion a year). The problem is further exacerbated by the dramatic decline in North Sea oil revenues, which are but a meagre proportion of their peak in the early and mid-1980s. The continuing slump, with the consequent rise in unemployment (currently just under 3 million even according to the much-massaged official figures), has sent the Public Sector Borrowing Requirement (PSBR) soaring sky high and constantly rising further still.

Faced with this, the worst post-war crisis, British imperialism is intensifying its attack on the poorer section of the working class. Nearly half of all employees in Britain earn less than the European Decency Threshold, and with the bourgeoisie now bent on dismemberment, if not the dismantlement, of the National Health Service, and the abolition of universal benefits, we are poised for a massive increase in poverty and the widening of the split in the working class. Increasingly the 'contented majority' is turning into a minority, and for the first time since the end of the war, the overwhelming majority of the working class are being sucked into the abyss of absolute poverty, hopelessness and misery.

Labour will not give voice to, it will not represent, this vast mass of the destitute. Labour has lost four elections in succession for the reason that the privileged stratum of the working class deserted to the Tories. To win, Labour needs, in addition to the votes of the lower proletarian stratum, the electoral support of the upper stratum as well as a section of the petty bourgeoisie. Since, as a result of the breakdown of the Keynesian consensus, it is no longer possible for it to reconcile the interests of the labour aristocracy and of the lower stratum, Labour has, after each election defeat, moved away, distanced itself, from the lower layers - wooing the upper layers and the petty bourgeoisie has become its main concern. Labour lost the 1992 election because its commitment to a mild increase in spending on the National Health Service (£1 bn.) and education (£600 million) proved unacceptable to the petty-bourgeois and the upper stratum of the working class. As a result, Labour has dropped all such commitments.

The present-day Labour Party has moved so much to the right that the bewildered Tories are forever accusing the Labour Party of stealing their clothes. And that arch-reactionary union-buster, media mogul Rupert Murdoch, has gone on record as saying that *"I can imagine myself supporting the British Labour leader, Tony Blair."* Only a few weeks ago, Tony Blair travelled, in fittingly servile fashion, to Australia's (all expenses paid, courtesy Mr Rupert Murdoch) Hayman Island, off the Queensland coast, to speak, and explain Labour's policy to Murdoch's media executives at a Conference organised by Murdoch's News International. In characteristic fashion, he delivered a vacuous speech, the contents of which do not concern us, if for no other reason than that it was devoid of all content except for a cringing plea, worded in suitably servile language, to be accepted as a faithful lackey of imperialism by one of the most ruthless monopoly capitalists. The important point to note is that Blair, who even on bourgeois admission and by bourgeois standards is no more than a third class mediocrity, was introduced at the above conference by Murdoch himself as one of the *"most outstanding political leaders in the world today."* This reminds one of the following observation made by Marx apropos John Stuart Mill:

"On the level plain, simple mounds look like hills; and the imbecile flatness of the present bourgeoisie is to be measured by the altitude of its great intellects" - and by its leaders, we might add!

As this preface is being written, Blair, in response to criticism from within his own Party - including from the veteran right-winger Hattersley, who for years acted as hatchetman for that windbag Kinnock (who stabbed the miners in the back) - to the effect that he was forgetting the poor and that Labour under his leadership has no definable ideological bearing, has responded by saying that he was unashamedly wooing the votes of the 'middle class' and that he had no need to apologise for that.

In spite of this, the Trotskyite counter-revolutionaries and the revisionist renegades alike, while professing to be revolutionaries, are still harping on the theme of kicking the Tories out and electing a Labour government under pressure to implement socialist policies. This merely goes to show that the Trotskyite/revisionist gentry are but the 'left' wing of social democracy and are themselves saturated through and through with the filthy social-democratic culture of corruption, making them oblivious to the plight of the poor at home and abroad, and the objects of whose main concern too are the upper stratum of the working class together with the petty bourgeoisie.

In the conditions in which, being let down by, and disgruntled with, Tories and Labour alike, a significant minority of the working class is abstaining from voting at elections (notwithstanding the media blitz inviting them to take part in this great 'democratic' exercise), regarding them as a charade and a contest between two indistinguishable bourgeois parties with almost identical programmes, the Vote Labour campaign of the 'left' carries the additional risk of directing this disgruntled section of the working class into the arms of various fascist organisations who do assert in their propaganda that Labour and Tory are as good (or bad) as each other, and who do make demagogic anti-capitalist noises - all, of course, in the service of crisis-ridden imperialism.

Labour does not even support the economic, trade-union, struggles of the working class, let alone the question of the social emancipation of the proletariat. The trade-union leadership, composed by and large of the privileged upper stratum of the working class, is increasingly moving away from the collective representation of the working class to concentrate on the provision of personal services which can only benefit those enjoying higher-than-average incomes. This same leadership fears like the plague any action which might transcend the boundaries of Draconian anti-working class legislation put on the statute book by the bourgeoisie through its parliament over the last 15 years. Most significant industrial struggles have collapsed in the face of police violence, or drowned under the weight of legal cretinism or been simply betrayed by the TUC leadership. One exception to this was the heroic coal strike of 1984-5. During this year-long strike, the miners, led by the most courageous, the most militant and most incorruptible leadership, carried the torch of struggle on behalf of the entire working class against unemployment and for better conditions, and challenged the power of capital to treat workers as so much disposable trash. In doing so they revived all that is noble, heroic and self-sacrificing - the spirit of collectivism - in the long history of the struggle of the British proletariat. But, by the same act, they roused the frenzy of the bourgeoisie, the Furies of private interest. More than that, they roused the wrath of the Labour and TUC leaderships, who feared like death the miners' victory, for by their example the miners threatened to infect other sections of the working class with a spirit of defiance and rebellion against the dictates of monopoly capitalism. So the Labour/TUC leadership joined forces with the Thatcher government, the National Coal Board, the police and intelligence services, the judiciary, the bourgeois media, and the blacklegs from the Nottinghamshire coalfields, in order to isolate and defeat the miners. In the end this 'exotic' range of forced arrayed against the miners proved too much; the miners, deserted by other sections of the working class, thanks to the treachery of social democracy, were starved and beaten - literally beaten - back to work.

In view of this, it is perfectly clear that Labour, far from being the mass party of the working class (as the Troto-revisionist outfits, these contemptible scoundrelly renegades to socialism, would have us believe), is, on the contrary, the party of imperialism and a privileged stratum of the working class, which supports imperialism to the hilt, for its privileges and conditions of existence depend on the extraction of superprofits from abroad and the intensified exploitation of the vast lower layers of the proletariat at home. The task of the communists - revolutionary Marxist-Leninists - is to recognise the split in the working class, to fight against the *"bourgeois labour party,"* and *"to go down **lower** and **deeper**, to the real masses,"* for *"this is the meaning and the whole content of the struggle against opportunism."* It is the task of revolutionaries to *"explain to the masses the inevitability and the necessity of breaking with opportunism, to educate them for revolution by a merciless struggle against opportunism"* and to unmask *"the hideousness of National-Liberal-Labour politics and not to cover them up,"* for this is the only Marxist-Leninist line to be followed in the British, as well as the world, proletarian movement. (All quotations in this paragraph are from Lenin's pamphlet, *Imperialism and the Split in Socialism*).

Under attack, the vast masses of the working class are bound to fight back. It is the job of the communists to organise them outside of, and in opposition to, social democracy. This is not a job that can be trusted to the 'left' wing of social democracy, to wit, the Trotskyite and revisionist gentry, who are marked by a staggering accumulation of corruption and filth through decades of opportunism and compromise with social democracy, and whose objects of concern, too, are the privileged sections of the working class and the petty-bourgeois strata. It is a job that can only be accomplished by making a definite break with the ideology and organisational forms of social democracy. Marxist-Leninists alone are capable of accomplishing this task. They can do it - they must do it. The formation of a truly Marxist-Leninist party in Britain would be a first, and very important step, in the accomplishment of this historic task.

Now a few words about the contents of this book.

Part One traces the formation of the Labour Party and its record in government as well as in opposition. It is not, nor is it intended to be, a history of the Labour Party; it merely concentrates on the most significant economic and political questions and events, at home and abroad, with which British imperial policy had to grapple - and Labour's attitude towards the same. On every important questions Labour's view was identical with the views of the British ruling class.

Part Two deals with the distortions by the revisionists and Trotskyites of the Marxian teaching on the question of the state. This is essential for demolishing the illusion that socialism can be secured through parliament by electing a Labour government *"committed to socialist policies,"* or a Labour government *"under pressure to implement socialist policies,"* without the need for a proletarian revolution - without smashing the bourgeois state machine and establishing the dictatorship of the proletariat.

Part Three is a running commentary on the historic coal strike of 1984-5, revealing on the one hand the moral regeneration of the working-class movement which that strike helped to bring about, and on the other hand the hideous class reality of capitalist society, which inflicted such horrific violence, misery and starvation on the miners and their families, as well as the truly revolting nature of social democracy, which joined the forces of the imperialist state to defeat the miners, just as it had done nearly six decades earlier to defeat the General Strike of 1926.

Part Four deals with some other significant economic struggles over the last 15 years which have been lost thanks again to the treachery of the Labour Party-TUC leadership.

Part Five touches upon the question of imperialist war and imperialist occupation of other people's land; in particular it deals with the question of the six counties of Ireland in connection with the hunger strike, in which British imperialism, with the total and unreserved support of the Labour Party, claimed the lives of Bobby Sands and his comrades by denying them the political status they claimed and so richly deserved. Like other bourgeois parties, the ossified Labour Party, too, could see nothing in the Irish patriots other than simple 'terrorists' - totally ignoring the terror practised by the British state on the Irish people over so many centuries.

The final part is an **Appendix**, to which are consigned statements of, speeches by, and interviews with, miners' leaders, for they give the reader the flavour of the ideas, the moods, the spirit of collectivism, which permeates those who stand up and fight for the interests of the working class, something which sets them apart from the run-of-the-mill insipid, law abiding and servile lackeys of social democracy. The Appendix also includes the article *Can the Labour Party bring us our economic salvation*, for it unmasks the absurdity behind the idea that with the election of a Labour government (and without bothering to get rid of capitalism) we shall somehow quite painlessly get rid of all our economic difficulties, ranging from unemployment to run-down social services, homelessness and poverty. This article, as well as three others, two appearing in Part Four, under the titles *Liverpool Showdown - the collapse of the Trotskyite dreams of 'socialism in one city'* and *Attempts to terrorise teachers* respectively, and the third appearing in Part Five entitled *London demonstrations show British people opposed to Gulf war*, were written by my comrade and friend Ella Rule. The rest were written by me in the form of articles for *Lalkar*, the paper of the Indian Workers' Association (GB). The dates of their publication are indicated at the beginning of each article. There is one exception to this: the material contained in Part Two, concerning distortions of the Marxian teaching on the state, appeared originally as a pamphlet which I was instructed by the Association of Communist Workers (ACW) to write on the latter's behalf, in connection with the general election of 1974.

I take this opportunity to thank my close comrades and collaborators, without whose unstinting support - ideological, political, material and technical - this book would have been a near impossibility. I acknowledge with gratitude the help generously given to me by Trevor Rayne, discussions with whom concerning the significance of some of the statistical data used in this book I found invaluable. I also wish to put on record the fact that the Indian Workers' Association (GB), although a mass organisation of workers of Indian origin, and not a party, has throughout its long existence supported proletarian-revolutionary and working-class struggles, as well as the national-liberation and anti-imperialist movements the world over. Its stance has been genuinely proletarian and internationalist, of which working people could be justly proud, and from which many claiming to be revolutionary could learn a great deal. For my own part, the Indian Workers' Association (GB)'s steadfastly internationalist outlook has been a tremendous source of strength and has helped me sustain my bearings in some difficult times. The Indian Workers' Association (GB) must share the credit for all in this book which is creditworthy while, needless to say, the blame for any weaknesses is entirely my own.

Harpal Brar,
5th August, 1995

Post Script to Preface

As we are about to go to print, newly released papers at the Public Records Office show that the Attlee government, that darling of the Trotskyite, revisionist and Labour 'left', set up a covert anti-communist unit, allegedly in response to the *"developing communist threat to the whole fabric of Western civilisation,* [i.e., imperialism]". This unit was known as the Information Research Department (IRD). Among others, highly placed Labour politicians and TUC leaders, including Attlee, Christopher Mayhew, Denis Healey and Vic Feather, were used by the IRD to disseminate misinformation on the former USSR, the East European People's Democracies, and against the communist parties of the West, notably those of Britain, France and Italy. Bertrand Russell, the philosopher, and poet Stephen Spender also acted as willing tools in the IRD's anti-communist drive. These papers reveal that Healey, who at the time was the Secretary of the Labour Party's International Department, supplied the IRD with the names of social-democrat émigrés from Czechoslovakia and Hungary for use in this campaign. The documents reveal the Labour Party to be even more reactionary, rabidly anti-Soviet to the point of stupidity, than the anti-communist diehards manning the IRD, for in January 1949 the IRD commented on the anti-Soviet leaflets in the Labour Party's *Talking Points* series suggesting changes. In this connection, the *Guardian* of Friday 18 August says: *"Ironically, Mr Watson* [of the IRD] *told Mr Healey that Labour's criticism of Stalin's Russia, and support of the US, was exaggerated, and suggested changes. For example, the Labour leaflet wrongly claimed that the US had offered to surrender control of its atom bomb to a 'world authority'".*

A senior Foreign Office official, Christopher Warner, told his colleagues:

"We are under rigid instructions that it must not become general, public, knowledge that HMG are themselves conducting anti-communist propaganda. The papers prepared by IRD ... have a covering slip emphasising that although they may be given to people who will be interested, they must be given quite unofficially."

Staffed by 300 officials, the IRD channelled most of its misinformation through ministerial statements, the ever so 'objective' BBC, the press and British diplomatic missions abroad.

In one of its earlier reports, the IRD claimed that the CPGB had *"bored its way into the structures of British trade unionism,"* that it had a membership of 39,000 and two MPs, adding: *"One of the characteristics of the British is their distrust for and laziness in politics. The communists have seized on this weakness.*

"Activity in agitation, support of grievances, consequent election as shop stewards, tireless attendance at meetings, pre-arranged block voting - these and other methods have gained them control."

Interviewed on the day these revelations came to public light (i.e., 17 August 1995), Healey, who was a member of the CPGB during his days as a student at Oxford, said that it was his job as Labour's international secretary to fight communism because *"Russia was deluging the world with anti-capitalist propaganda."*

Writing on page 9 of the same issue of the *Guardian*, Stephen Dorril, an anti-communist who is nevertheless an opponent of secrecy, says that on the prompting of the IRD, *"Alleged communist front groups were attacked and conferences disrupted. Material was handed over to trade union anti-communist fronts such as the Industrial Research Information Service and Common Cause. Trade union and senior Labour Party officials were in receipt of briefings which, in the case of Labour, formed the backbone of its Proscribed List of organisations and was influential in the selection of candidates."* (The puppet masters).

Instead of attributing Labour's conduct to its anti-communist and pro-imperialist stance (presumably because he is in agreement with this stance), Mr Dorril concludes his article with the following apology for Labour and a lamentation that Labour shows no signs of wanting to reform the secret state:

"The reality is that the members of the 'secret state' have always been extremely successful at manipulating the Labour Party. Labour MPs know very little about the workings of the security services and invariably leave matters to the officials.

"The pity is that the Blair team appears to be heading in the same direction with not, as far as can be seen, a policy on reforming the secret state."

No, Mr Dorril! Labour is not as innocent as you make it out to be; it is not as ignorant of the workings of the security services as you imagine it to be. It never had any dearth of quite sophisticated figures well versed in the art of anti-communism. If Labour has throughout co-operated with the security forces, it has mainly been due to its hatred of anything working class; and if Labour is heading in the same direction, it is because it wants to, and knows how to, protect this outmoded system of production - capitalism.

None of the above revelations come to us as a surprise, for in our view nothing better can be expected from an imperialist party such as Labour. But the Troto-revisionist 'left' will doubtless find some excuse for all this and carry on, with intensified vigour, its campaign for kicking the Tories out and the election of a Labour government under pressure to implement socialist policies - and to work for affliation to the Labour Party!

BBC an MI6 Front

We communists have always known that the BBC is one of the most important propaganda arms of British imperialism. Now the bourgeoisie is obliged to go beyond this and admit that the real controllers of BBC policy are not the pompous and inflated journalistic fraternity but the British state's security services. The following article, written for the *Guardian* of 18 August 1995, in connection with the release of papers by the Public Records Office, by Seumas Milne and Richard Norton-Taylor, tells the story so well that we reproduce it here in full:

"A notable casualty of the decision to set up a covert anti-communist propaganda unit was the fragile independence of the BBC, which allowed itself to be manipulated by the IRD after broadcasting executives were told co-operation was essential to stem the advance of communism in Europe.

"Shortly after the IRD was created in 1948, Ralph Murray, its first head, set out the unit's broadcasting policy: 'Our situation is now such that it seems essential that we should approach the BBC and cause them, by persuasion if possible, to undertake such programme developments as might help us.'

"It was agreed to ask the BBC to include 'a speaker on labour affairs, a labour correspondent, a trade union quarter-hour' in foreign broadcasts to *'allow us to put over our own view'* to working class audiences. If the BBC accepted, he went on, *'it would automatically follow that they would echo the developments of policy expressed in government statements.'*

"A meeting was held in February 1948 between Murray, a senior FO official, and Major General Sir Ian Jacob, director of the BBC Overseas Service, at which the IRD's 'scheme of priorities' was 'approved'. Sir Ian asked for five copies of everything the IRD produced and arranged for members of the FO

unit to discuss co-operation with BBC controllers.

"The IRD was not only concerned about overseas broadcasts. Sir Maurice Peterson, the British ambassador in Moscow, complained to Christopher Warner, the FO official overseeing the propaganda unit, early in 1948 about a Home Service broadcast regarded as 'soft' on Soviet communism. The programme had talked 'nonsense' about the availability of women's hairdressing in Moscow, failed to make clear that many flats were communal and wrongly implied that central heating was reliable.

"*'It is not much good our planning anti-communist psychological warfare if we are going to let communist-inspired drivel of this kind into the inmost fortress of the BBC,'* thundered Sir Maurice.

"IRD gave advice to the BBC about propaganda broadcasts to the Soviet Union itself. In a memo to Jacob, one IRD official warned: *'Phrases like "the Kremlin" in a hostile context should never be used. The Kremlin is an evocative symbol to most Russians. Wicked things done in Poland, Korea, etc. should not be attributed to 'Russian imperialism' but to an international conspiracy of oppression using Russian troops. Russian revolutionary anniversaries should be make the occasion for references to Trotsky, Zinoviev, Bukharin and other "close friends of Lenin".'*

"This was not the first time the BBC became a tool of government foreign policy; it had been overtly directed by the government during the war, and papers disclosed yesterday clearly show it intended to use the corporation in the event of another 'emergency'.

"And while the IRD was subverting the BBC at home, British intelligence was secretly running an influential Arabic radio station. Senior BBC staff connived in the government's decision to convert the station into an open propaganda weapon.

"The radio station, *Sharq-al-Adna,* had the cover of a commercial station, transmitting anti-Israel commentary and readings of the Koran interspersed with music. During the Suez crisis it became the Voice of Britain, broadcasting propaganda with sanitised BBC newS bulletins. Sir Ian, now BBC director general, went along with the idea.

"But not all staff were compliant. A cabinet committee recorded at the time Whitehall's frustration with some BBC staff *'so obsessed by the notion of neutrality'.* The government threatened deep cuts in BBC grants." *(BBC was conscripted into MI6's anti-communist crusade).*

The Unit was supposed to have been abolished in 1977, but, knowing what we do from Mr Milne's book, *The Enemy Within*, that is hardly to be believed. Under another name, a similar unit continues its dirty work today, as it did during the NUM Coal Strike in 1984-5.

Part One

Social democracy and The Attitude of the Proletariat Towards it

"The fact is that 'bourgeois labour parties', as a political phenomenon, have been formed in ALL the advanced capitalist countries and unless a determined ruthless struggle is conducted against these parties all along the line ... it is useless talking about the struggle against imperialism, about Marxism, or about the socialist labour movement".

Lenin (Imperialism and the Split in Socialism)

Part One

Social democracy
and

Towards it

Historical Conditions Preceding the Birth of the Labour Party

Introduction

Ever since the foundation of the Communist Party of Great Britain (CPGB) in 1920, the question of the attitude of Communists to the Labour Party (the main party of social democracy in this country) has aroused much passion and heated controversy. Once again this issue has come to the fore consequent, first, upon the collapse of the erstwhile Soviet Union and the People's Democracies of Eastern Europe and the tremendous changes in the balance of world forces wrought by this collapse. The liquidation of the former CPSU and the disintegration of the USSR has given rise to two contradictory trends. On the one hand, under the impact of triumphant imperialist propaganda which represents the collapse of the USSR as the final collapse of communism, of Marxism-Leninism, it has brought in its train colossal renegacy and a dreary deluge of gloom and doom. In the aftermath of the counter-revolution in Eastern Europe, a number of parties, hitherto at least nominally communist, have liquidated themselves and openly embraced the counter-revolutionary ideology of social democracy, renounced Marxism-Leninism and declared the Great October Socialist Revolution to have been *"a mistake of historic proportions."* On the other hand, the same collapse is making it possible for an increasing number of proletarians to realise clearly the terrible consequences of social-democratic departures (for that is what revisionism is in its essence) from Marxism-Leninism. They are increasingly realising how the wholesale revision, and downright distortion, of Marxism-Leninism in the field of political economy, philosophy and class struggle, that was committed by the CPSU under the influence of Khrushchevite revisionism ever since the 20th Party Congress in 1956, have, over a period of more than three decades, led to the restoration of capitalism in the land of the Soviets, the land of Lenin, the land of once triumphant socialism; they are increasingly becoming aware how the same USSR, which beat the armies of 14 imperialist countries and their stooges during the war of intervention (which followed the successful October revolution) and which during the Second World War broke the back of the Nazi war machine how this same USSR collapsed so ignominiously under the impact of revisionism.

Secondly, the changes within the Labour Party over a long period of time, culminating in the accession of Tony Blair to its leadership, and the decisions of the last Labour Party Conference (held in Blackpool's Winter Palace from 3 to 7 October, 1994), have helped to push this question to the top of the agenda.

Communists can no longer, if they ever could, avoid discussing this question, and reaching conclusions on the basis of a sober, serious and all sided consideration of the facts, discarding dogmatism, opportunism and sectarianism alike. This debate must be frank and fearless, yet comradely, for what is at stake is the very existence in this country of the ideology of the modern proletariat and its organisational form, namely, Marxism-Leninism and a Marxist-Leninist party. Moreover, this question is relevant not just in this country, for in every other country too the revolutionary proletariat is faced with the same question of its attitude to its 'own' social democracy. By way of our contribution to this debate and to the resolution of this extremely important question, we present our views in this series of articles.

We state at the very outset that, in our considered judgment, there is absolutely no basis now, if ever there was during a much earlier period, for maintaining the stance of supporting the Labour Party, of working for the election of a Labour Government 'committed to socialist policies'.

What follows is a substantiation of this viewpoint of ours. In order to do justice to this issue, it is important to remind ourselves in the first instance of the historical circumstances and the conditions prevailing in Britain prior to, as well as immediately preceding, the birth of the Labour Party . This is rendered particularly necessary by the fact that young entrants into the proletarian movement are by and large ignorant of this history and those from the older generation (at least the majority of them), having learnt their labour history in diverse revisionist and Trotskyist outfits, have an extremely distorted, onesided and opportunist view of this history.

Historical background since the defeat of Chartism - Rise of the 'labour aristocracy'

After the final defeat of the Chartist movement in 1848, there followed a period during which British capitalism had at its disposal not only a vast colonial empire but also a monopoly in the world market. The rapid expansion of industry consequent upon the above, enabled British capitalism to ease the condition of the working class. Between 1850 and 1875, wages rose considerably, by almost a third. The major beneficiary of this rise was doubtless the labour aristocracy, consisting of skilled workers and craftsmen - these constituting between 10% and 15% of the working class. Their weekly wages were nearly double those of unskilled workers. This privileged stratum, increasingly assuming the leadership of the working class and turning its back on Chartism (which was undoubtedly revolutionary for its time), got on with the job of building craft unions designed to protect their trade and craft privileges in order to better the conditions for the sale of the labour power of their members within the conditions of capitalism. Let alone working for the abolition of the wages system, this upper stratum increasingly acquired a stake in this system, became infected with bourgeois respectability and a downright contempt for the mass of the working class, the vast majority constituting the unskilled workers. Engels describes the then prevalent narrow craft outlook and bourgeois respectability, especially of the upper stratum of the working class, in these vivid terms:

"The most repulsive thing here is bourgeois 'respectability' bred into the bones of the workers. The social division of society into innumerable gradations, each recognised without question, each with its own pride but also inborn respect for its 'betters' and 'superiors', is so firmly established that the bourgeois find it pretty easy to get their bait accepted..." (Letter to Sorge, 7 December 1889).

Tail end of the Liberal Party

In these circumstances it is hardly to be surprised at that no workingclass party arose which had the ability and willingness to represent the interests of that class. In an article dated 22 February, 1874, on *The English Elections*, Engels captures the depressing political scene, characterised by corruption and the sickening bourgeois respectability of the 'labour leaders':

"As regards the workers it must be stated, to begin with, that no separate political working-class party has existed in England since the downfall of the Chartist Party ... *This is understandable in a country in which the working class has shared more than anywhere else in the advantages of the immense expansion of its large-scale industry. Nor could it have been otherwise in an England that ruled the world market ...*

"Whenever the workers lately took part in general politics in particular organisations, they did so almost exclusively as the extreme left wing of the 'great Liberal Party'" (Marx & Engels, *On Britain*, Moscow, 1953, p.466).

Even after the Electoral Reform Act of 1867 had *"opened the door of Parliament to at least 60 working-class candidates,"* continues Engels, *"in order to get into Parliament, the 'labour leaders' had recourse, in the first place, to the votes and money of the bourgeoisie and only in the second place to the votes of the workers themselves. But by doing so they ceased to be workers' candidates and turned themselves into bourgeois candidates. They did not appeal to the working-class party that still had to be formed but to the bourgeois 'great liberal party'"* (ibid, pp.467-68)

Earlier in the same article, Engels remarked that the " ... shortest way would have been to proceed at once to form anew a strong workers' party with a definite programme, and the best political programme they could wish for was the People's Charter. *But the Chartists' name was in bad odour with the bourgeoisie precisely because theirs had been an outspoken proletarian party, and so, rather than continue the glorious tradition of the Chartists, the 'labour leaders' preferred to deal with their aristocratic friends and be 'respectable', which in England means acting like a **bourgeois**."(ibid, p.467)*

Four years later, in his letter to W.Liebknecht dated 11 Feb 1878, Marx expresses his total disgust at the demoralisation of the English working class by the period of corruption and the venality of the trade-union leaders:

*"The English working class had been gradually becoming more and more deeply demoralised by the period of corruption since 1848 and had at last got to the point when it was nothing more than the tail end of the Great Liberal Party, i.e., of its **oppressors**, the capitalists. Its direction had passed completely into the hands of the venal trade-union leaders and professional agitators. These fellows shouted and howled behind the Gladstones ... and the whole gang of factory owners ... **in majorem gloriam** [to the greater glory] of the tsar as the emancipator of nations, while they never raised a finger for their own brothers in South Wales, condemned by the mine-owners to die of starvation. Wretches!"(ibid, p.516).*

On 30 August, 1883, Engels, in a letter to Bebel, writes, *inter alia:* "Do not on any account whatever let yourself be bamboozled into thinking that there is a real proletarian movement going on here. I know Liebnecht is trying to delude himself and all the world about this, but it is not the case."

So, how are we to explain the opportunism and the venality of the 'labour leaders' of that time? How are we to explain the phenomenon of the non-existence of a *"strong workers' party with a definite programme"*? The answer must be sought in the British monopoly of the world market, and the connection between that monopoly and opportunism in the British workingclass movement.

British monopoly of the world market and its effects on the working class

One cannot even **begin** to understand the history of the labour movement in this country without acknowledging the effects on the working class of the monopoly exercised by the British bourgeoisie in the field of colonies and the world market throughout the 19th century. From the superprofits resulting from this monopoly, the British bourgeoisie was able successfully to bribe and corrupt a significant minority (an *"aristocracy of labour"* composed of skilled workers grouped in craft unions) of the working class, thus causing on the one hand a split between the working class masses (the lower proletarian stratum) and, on the other hand, this bribed, corrupt and opportunistic upper stratum (the aristocracy of labour), whose leaders constantly deserted to the side of the bourgeoisie and were directly or indirectly in their pay. Marx and Engels, who from 1852 to 1892 traced this phenomenon, this connection between monopoly and the rise of opportunism among the privileged sections of the working class, earned the hatred of these scoundrels for branding them as traitors to the working class.

"It must be observed," remarked Lenin *àpropos* the question under discussion, *"that in Great Britain the tendency of imperialism to divide the workers in this way, to encourage opportunism among them, and cause temporary decay in the working class movement, revealed itself much earlier than the end of the 19th and the beginning of the 20th centuries; for two important features of imperialism were observed in Great Britain in the middle of the 19th century, viz., vast colonial possessions, and a monopolist position in the world markets. Marx and Engels systematically traced this relation between opportunism in the labour movement and the imperialistic features of British capitalism for decades."* (Imperialism the Highest Stage of Capitalism).

Bourgeoisification of the working-class movement

This systematic treatment, referred to by Lenin, these pronouncements by Marx and Engels, are extremely instructive for anyone desiring to gain an understanding of the material (economic) basis of opportunism in the British working-class movement. We now turn to some of the most important pronouncements of Marxism in this regard over a period of several decades.

On 7 October 1858, Engels wrote to Marx: *"The English proletariat is actually becoming more and more bourgeois, so that this most bourgeois of all nations is apparently aiming ultimately at the possession of a bourgeois aristocracy and a bourgeois proletariat as well as a bourgeoisie. Of course, this is to a certain extent justifiable for a nation which is exploiting the whole world."* (*op cit*, pp.491-92).

Nearly a quarter of a century later, in a letter dated 11 August, 1881, Engels speaks of *"the worst type of British trade unions, which allow themselves to be led by men who have been bought by the capitalists, or at least are in their pay."*

Further, in a letter to Kautsky dated 12 September, 1882, Engels wrote: *"You ask me what the English workers think of colonial policy? Exactly the same as they think about politics in general, the same as what the bourgeois think. There is no working class party here, there are only Conservatives and Liberal Radicals, and the workers gaily share the feast of England's monopoly of the world market and the colonies"* (*ibid*, p.514).

Bourgeois respectability

Disgusted by the spirit of bourgeois respectability with which the British working class had become infected, Engels, in his letter to Sorge dated 7 December 1889, complains bitterly *"the most repulsive thing here is the bourgeois 'respectability' ... I am not at all sure, for instance, that John Burns is not secretly prouder of his popularity with Cardinal Manning, the Lord Mayor and the bourgeoisie in general than of his popularity with his own class. ... Even Tom Mann, whom I regard as the finest of them, is fond of mentioning that he will be lunching with the Lord Mayor. If one compares this with the French, one can see what a revolution is good for, after all."* (*ibid*, pp.522-23).

In March 1891 Engels refers to the old skilled unions as *"rich and therefore cowardly;"* and, six months later, exulting at the unsuccessful attempt of the TUC to reverse the decision of the Congress the year before to campaign for an 8-hour day, he says: *"The old unions, with the textile workers at their head, had exerted all their strength towards overthrowing the 8-hour decision of 1890. They came to grief ... and the bourgeois papers recognise the defeat of the **bourgeois labour party**."* (Letter,14.9.91,cited in *Imperialism and the Split Split in Socialism*, Lenin,1916) (Engels' emphasis).

Commenting on these profound pronouncements of Marxism, Lenin says: *"Here are clearly indicated the causes and effects.*

"The causes are:

"(1) The exploitation of the whole world by this country [i.e., Britain].

"(2) Its monopolist position in the world market.

"(3) Its colonial monopoly.

"The effects are:

"(1) A section of the British proletariat becomes bourgeois.

"(2) A section of the proletariat permits itself to be led by people who are bought by the bourgeoisie, or at least are in their pay." (Imperialism, the Highest Stage of Capitalism).

Engels publicly expressed these ideas, repeated for decades, in his preface to the second edition of his Condition of the Working Class in England. In this preface, written in 1892, he speaks of the *"privileged minority"* of workers as opposed to the *"great bulk of the workers"*. *"A small privileged protected minority"* of the working class, writes Engels, *"permanently benefited"* from the exceptionally privileged position of England during 1848-68, whereas *"the great mass had, at least, a temporary share now and then."* This is why he says: *"The truth is this: during the period of England's industrial monopoly the English working class have, to a certain extent, shared in the benefits of the monopoly. These benefits were very unequally parcelled out among them; the privileged minority pocketed most, but even the great mass had, at least, a temporary share now and then. And that is the reason why, since the dying out of Owenism, there has been no socialism in England."* With the end of English monopoly already in sight, Engels expresses himself in the following optimistic terms:

"With the breakdown of that monopoly, the English working class will lose its privileged position, it will find itself generally, the privileged minority not excepted, on a level with its fellow workers abroad. And that is the reason why there will be socialism again in England."

New Unionism.

And Engels had good reason to be optimistic, witnessing as he was the revival of the East End of London, which had become the home of 'New Unionism', that is to say, of the organisation of the great mass of unskilled workers. The new unions, says Engels, were *"essentially different in charac-*

ter" from the old unions in that, unlike the latter, they " ... *were founded at a time when the faith in the eternity of the wages system was severely shaken; their founders and promoters were Socialists either consciously or by feeling; the masses, whose adhesion gave them strength, were rough, neglected, looked down upon by the workingclass aristocracy; but they had this immense advantage, that **their minds were virgin soil**, entirely free from the inherited 'respectable' bourgeois prejudices which hampered the brains of the better situated 'old' unionists..*"

He contrasts these New Unionists with the representatives of old unionism, that is, *"those people who are forgiven their being members of the workingclass because they themselves would like to drown their quality of being workers in the ocean of their liberalism."*

And so exhilarated was Engels at this development as to declare with his characteristic youthful joy that *" ... for all the faults committed* [by the East Enders] *in the past, present and future, the revival of the East End of London remains one of the most fruitful facts of this fin de siècle, and glad and proud I am to have lived to see it."*

Why Engel's optimism was shortlived

In addition to the emergence of imperialism (monopoly capitalism), which Marx and Engels did not live to witness, and of which much more anon, two things happened to disprove Engels' optimism.

First, although Britain's industrial monopoly had disappeared by the end of the 19th century owing to powerful competition from the US, Germany and France, its colonial empire was larger than that of its rivals, and larger than ever as a result of new acquisitions in the last two decades of the century, especially during the scramble for Africa. The empire acted as a shock absorber against the rough and tumble of the competition from its rivals. Not only did the empire provide ample opportunity for direct, undisguised, straightforward plunder, it represented a source of cheap raw materials and an avenue of extremely lucrative investment, i.e., export of capital.

The relative decline of British industry, its relative lack of competitiveness, were bound to, and actually did, express themselves in a declining rate of profit on investment at home, thus forcing British capitalism to look for profitable investment abroad. And the empire provided a ready-made arena for such investment, resulting in vast overseas capital accumulation. There was a dramatic rise in the accumulation of overseas investment as a percentage of GNP.

Robert Clough in his *Labour - A Party Fit for Imperialism*, has this to say in this regard:

> "Accumulated overseas investment rose as a percentage of GNP from 73 per cent in 1870 to 139 per cent in 1890, and 164 per cent in 1910, by which time it amounted to a third of domestic capital investment ... Nabudere estimates that the years 1870 to 1913 saw a capital export of £2,400 million yielding a net income of £4,100 million, and that Britain was able to finance new investment out of the return on the old investment." (pp. 16-17).

Robert Clough reproduces from Nabudere's *The Political Economy of Imperialism*, the following table representing British accumulated capital abroad:

\<Accumulated capital abroad\>	
Year	£ 000,000
1870	692
1880	1,189
1890	1,935
1900	2,397
1910	3,371
1913	3,990

Furthermore, British imperialism continued to exercise a maritime monopoly, as well as a monopoly in the area of finance and insurance, which resulted in an ever-rising increment in invisible earnings. By the year 1913, invisible earnings from abroad as a percentage of GNP equalled gross private trading profits, the figures being 13.6% and 14.2% respectively.

During this whole period from 1879 to 1913, characterised as it was by the relative decline of Britain as an industrial power and the disappearance of its industrial monopoly, the trade deficit (visible trade) was nullified by the surplus on invisible earnings, thanks to the possession by Britain of a vast colonial empire. Thus, notwithstanding the disappearance of the British industrial monopoly, her ruling class was in a position, thanks to her colonial monopoly and earnings from investment abroad, shipping, insurance and financial services, to maintain its labour aristocracy in the conditions to which the latter had become accustomed in the period of Britain's industrial monopoly. Real wages rose throughout the period from 1879 to 1900. It goes without saying that the chief beneficiary of such rises was the upper stratum (the labour aristocracy) composed of skilled workers, whose weekly average earnings of 40 shillings compared rather favourably with the miserable wage of 20-25 shillings for unskilled workers, and 15 shillings for female and agricultural workers. In 1911 it required a minimum of 30 shillings for a family to maintain an adequate existence, yet 5 million out of a total of 8 million male manual workers earned on average only 22 shillings a week. In his 1905 study *Riches and Poverty*, Sir Leo Chiozza-Money concludes that 33 million out of 43 million people in Britain lived in poverty, and 13 million of these 33 million in destitution. Thus there is no question but that while benefits of the empire flowed in the direction of the labour aristocracy, the lives of the vast masses (the lower proletarian stratum) presented a picture of poverty and destitution. In view of the petty-bourgeois conditions of existence of the labour aristocracy, who had assumed the leadership of the working class, it is not surprising that the period under discussion was marked by demoralisation of the working class, by the corruption and venality of the trade-union leaders, the absence of a working-class party and political stagnation. Robert Clough correctly remarks: *"This period [1870-1900] was one of political stagnation. British imperialism could still afford to make concessions to labour aristocracy, in return for which it expected, and usually got, social peace." (ibid. p.21).*

There were the odd exceptions of course, one of them being New Unionism, i.e., the organisation of the great mass of the unskilled workers, a development on which Engels had pinned so much hope and of which he had spoken so enthusiastically.

This brings us to the **second reason** as to why Engels' optimism proved so short-lived. The New Unions, far from being helped by the old unions, actually had to contend, owing to the latter's domination by the labour aristocracy with its narrow craft outlook, bourgeois respectability and Lib-Lab politics, with their hostility. Such was the ferocity with which the combined forces of the bourgeoisie and its agents in the working-class movement, the labour aristocracy, attacked the New Unions, that the latter came to lose most of their membership within a period of 3 years. If their membership was 300,000 in 1890, by 1896 it had dwindled to a mere 80,000. If in 1890 the New Unions represented a quarter of TUC membership, by 1900 they were a mere 10% of it. Moreover, under pressure from the ruling class, the leadership of the New Unions, unable to resist the prevailing climate of bourgeois corruption, itself began to follow in the footsteps of the political and organisational *modus operandi* of the old craft unions even to the extent of refusing to recruit unskilled and casual workers.

Development of Marxian analysis by Lenin

But neither Marx nor Engels lived to see the emergence of imperialism. Instead of England's monopoly disappearing in the conditions of imperialism, it merely gave way to a monopoly of a handful of financially rich and powerful countries. It fell to Lenin to apply and to develop further the Marxist analysis in the conditions of the epoch of imperialism and inter-imperialist rivalries. Arguing against Kautsky, this is how Lenin describes the change from the situation in which England alone enjoyed a monopoly to that in which a handful of powerful and rich countries, including England, managed to develop monopoly.

"*Imperialism is monopoly capitalism. Every cartel, trust and syndicate, every gigantic bank, is monopoly. Superprofit has not disappeared, it has remained. The exploitation of all other countries by one, financially rich, country has remained and become more intense. A handful of rich countries ... have developed monopoly to vast proportions, obtain superprofits amounting to hundreds of millions, even billions, 'ride on the backs' of hundreds and hundreds of millions of the populations of foreign countries, fight among each other for the division of the particularly rich, particularly fat and particularly easy spoils.*" (*Imperialism and the Split in the Socialist Movement*, October 1916).

In the same article, Lenin develops in the following terms the Marxist analysis of the connection between monopoly and the growth of opportunism among a significant minority of the working class, the 'upper stratum', the 'aristocracy of labour', of a given country, and resultant split in the working class:

"*The bourgeoisie of a 'Great' imperialist Power is **economically in a position** to bribe the upper sections of 'its' workers by devoting for this purpose one or two hundred million francs a year since its **superprofits** amount perhaps to a billion.*"

Every Imperialist power bribes its Labour Aristocracy and Crushes the Lower Stratum

When the English industrial and colonial monopoly gave way to the monopoly of a handful of imperialist countries, each one of these Great Imperialist Powers was in a position to bribe the upper stratum of workers in their countries: *"Formerly the working class of **one** country could be bribed and corrupted,"* said Lenin, but now *"every imperialist 'Great' Power can and does bribe **smaller** (compared with 1848-68 in England) strata of the 'labour aristocracy'"*. Seizing upon Engels' remarkably apt expression, Lenin continues: *"Formerly a 'bourgeois labour party', to use Engels' remarkably profound expression, could be formed only in one country because it alone enjoyed a monopoly, and enjoyed it for a long period. Now the 'bourgeois labour party' is inevitable and typical for **all** the imperialist countries."* (ibid)

While monopoly permits of a handful of the upper strata being bribed, it at the same time more than ever oppresses, crushes, ruins and tortures the masses of the proletariat and the semi-proletariat through high prices, hunger, deprivation, homelessness and the misfortune of the imperialist wars. Contrasting these two tendencies, the opportunists to the increasingly oppressed masses, Lenin goes on to state:

"The history of the labour movement will from now on inevitably develop as the history of the struggle between these two tendencies: for the first [opportunist] *tendency is not accidental, it is 'founded' on economics. The bourgeoisie has already begotten, nurtured, secured for itself 'bourgeois labour parties' of social chauvinists in **all** countries ... The important thing is that the economic desertion of a stratum of the labour aristocracy to the side of the bourgeoisie has matured and become an accomplished fact. And this economic fact, this change in the relations between classes, will find political expression in one form or another without much 'difficulty'"*. (ibid)

Split irrevocable and the need to break with opportunism

By way of emphasising the irrevocability of this split, Lenin goes on to say: *"The social chauvinist or (what is the same thing) opportunist **tendency** can neither disappear nor 'return' to the revolutionary proletariat."*

And further, underlining the inextricability of the fight against imperialism and the fight against opportunism, he continues: *"The fact is that 'bourgeois labour parties', as a political phenomenon, have been formed in **all** the ad-*

SOCIAL DEMOCRACY &
THE ATTITUDE OF THE PROLETARIAT TOWARDS IT

vanced capitalist countries and unless a determined ruthless struggle is conducted against these parties all along the line ... it is useless talking about the struggle against imperialism, about Marxism, or about the socialist labour movement" (ibid).

Furthermore, says Lenin, in this struggle, "Engels draws a distinction between the 'bourgeois labour party' of the *old trade unions, the privileged minority* and the *'lowest mass'*, the real majority, and he appeals to the latter who are not infected by 'bourgeois respectability'. This is the essence of Marxist tactics!" (ibid).

Stating that the opportunists and social chauvinists represent only a minority, he goes on: "*And it is therefore our duty, if we wish to remain socialists, to go down **lower** and **deeper**, to the real masses. This is the whole meaning and whole purport of the struggle against opportunism.* By exposing the fact that the opportunists and social chauvinists are in reality betraying and selling the interests of the masses, that they are defending the temporary privileges of a minority of the workers, that they are the vehicles of bourgeois ideas and influences, that they are really allies and agents of the bourgeoisie, we teach the masses their true political interests, to fight for socialism and for the revolution ...

"The only Marxist line in the world labour movement is to explain to the masses the inevitability and necessity of breaking with opportunism, to educate them for revolution by waging a relentless struggle against opportunism, to utilise the experience of the war for the purpose of exposing all the vileness of national liberal-labour politics, and not of concealing it." (Ibid.)

Accusing the Kautskyites of "*fawning on the opportunists, who are alien to the proletariat as a class, who are the servants, the agents of the bourgeoisie and the vehicles of its influence,*" he goes on to stress that " ... unless the labour movement rids itself of them, it will remain **a bourgeois labour movement**." (Ibid).

LALKAR March/April 1995

II

Organisational breach between labour and the Liberal Party

- Formation of the Labour Party

Although, as pointed out earlier, the privileged workers continued to act as the tail end - an extreme radical wing - of the Liberal Party right up to the end of the ninth decade of the last century, the early 1890s witnessed a change in this state of affairs. The first organisational breach in this hitherto existing alliance - between the Liberal Party and labour - took place in 1893 with the founding of the Independent Labour Party (ILP). This breach was the direct result of stiff foreign competition, in the face of which the liberal bourgeoisie, which was dominantly represented in the textile and mining industries, proved to be just as ruthless as the Tories. The defeat inflicted by the employers during the 1892 strike in the textile industry played the role of a catalyst in the formation of the ILP. The founding conference of the ILP (1893) left no one in doubt that its leadership, in particular Keir Hardie, who was the moving spirit behind the formation of the ILP, though in favour of the **organisational** independence, was not in favour of the political independence of the ILP.

In other words, in the sphere of politics, the Lib-Lab alliance was to continue undisturbed. It was precisely for this reason that the founding conference refused to call the new party 'Socialist Labour Party'. Instead it was to be called the 'Independent Labour Party' on the flimsy excuse that the party had to appeal to the mass of workers and not merely to socialists. Translated into ordinary language, the masses to whom the ILP appealed, and who comprised its constituency, were none other than the upper stratum of the workers, organised in craft unions, characterised by a narrow outlook, bourgeois respectability and a contempt for socialism. This is how Lenin describes this stratum, and its political representative - the ILP.

"... the petty bourgeois craft spirit that prevails among this aristocracy of labour, which has divorced itself from its class, has followed the Liberals, and

contemptuously sneers at socialism as a 'utopia'. *The Independent Labour Party is precisely the party of Liberal-Labour politics. It is quite justly said that this party is* 'independent' *only of socialism, and very dependent indeed upon liberalism" ('Liberal-Labour Policy',* Oct 1912, CW Vol. 18, p.360).

Further, in his article *'Exposure of British Opportunists'*, written in July 1913, Lenin, by reference to the then recently-held parliamentary by-election in Leicester, gives a detailed and vivid account of ILP's opportunism, its alliance with, and dependence on, Liberalism. Leicester, like a few others, was a two-member constituency, but, these constituencies were, says Lenin, *"... particularly favourable for concluding a tacit bloc (alliance) between the socialists and the Liberals. ... It was precisely in such constituencies that the prominent leaders of the so-called Independent (independent of socialism, but dependent on liberalism) Labour Party were elected. Keir Hardie, Philip Snowden and Ramsay MacDonald, the leaders of the Independent Labour Party, were elected in such constituencies.*

"And in these constituencies, the Liberals who are predominant, advise the electors to give one vote for the Socialists and one for the Liberals, that is of course, if the Socialist is a 'reasonable', 'moderate', 'independent' and not an irreconcilable Social-Democrat [this was written before the First World War when Social-Democracy stood by revolutionary Marxism-Leninism] *whom the English Liberals and liquidators no less than the Russian, abuse as being anarcho-syndicalists.*

*"What actually takes place, therefore, is the conclusion of an alliance between the Liberals and the moderate, opportunist Socialists. Actually, the English 'independents' (for whom our **liquidators** have such tender feelings)* **depend** *on the Liberals. The conduct of 'independents' in the English Parliament constantly confirms this dependence"* (CW, Vol.19, pp.272-73)

Lenin, having given an account of how the opportunists of the ILP, hand in glove with the bourgeois Liberal Party, conspired successfully in the defeat of the revolutionary socialist Hartley, concludes:

*"Class-conscious workers in various countries often adopt a 'tolerant' attitude toward the British ILP. This is a great mistake. The **betrayal** of the workers' cause in Leicester by the ILP is no accident, but the result of the **entire** opportunist policy of the Independent Labour Party. The sympathies of all **real** social-democrats should be with those who are determinedly combating the Liberal corruption of the workers by the Independent Labour Party in Britain" (ibid).*

Important role of Fabian opportunism

Since the most important leaders of the ILP, such as Keir Hardie and Ramsay MacDonald, were prominent Fabians, it is not surprising that the Fabian Society should have played such a significant role in providing, first the ILP, and subsequently the Labour Party, with detailed facts, policies, programmes and theories. Formed in 1884, always small in numbers, primarily educational, this organisation of middle-class socialists, stuffed full with careerists and intellectuals *par excellence*, was characterised by its love of municipal socialism, contempt for the working class, hatred of class struggle, and therefore of Marxism, and for it socialism was but an extension of bourgeois liberalism. In three letters written between September 1892 and November 1893, by way of settling accounts with the Fabians, Engels gives the following, never to be forgotten, characterisation of this gentry. In his letter to Kautsky (September 4, 1892), Engels writes:

*"You see something unfinished in the Fabian Society. On the contrary, this crowd is only **too** finished: a clique of bourgeois 'socialists' of diverse calibres, from careerists to sentimental socialists and philanthropists, united only by their fear of the threatening rule of the workers and doing all in their power to spike this danger by making **their own** leadership secure, the leadership exercised by the 'eddicated'. If afterwards they admit a few workers into their central board in order that they may play ... the role of a constantly outvoted minority, this should not deceive anyone.*

"The means employed by the Fabian Society are just the same as those of the corrupt parliamentary politicians: money, intrigue, careerism. ... These people are immersed up to their necks in the intrigues of the Liberal Party, hold Liberal Party jobs, as for instance Sidney Webb. ... These gentry do everything that the workers have to be warned against" (op cit, pp.530-31).

In his letter to Sorge (January 18, 1893), Engels returns to the subject, saying:

"The Fabians here in London are a gang of careerists who have understanding enough to realise the inevitability of the social revolution; but not trusting this gigantic task to the crude proletariat alone, they are gracious enough to stand at the head of it. Their fundamental principle is fear of revolution. They are 'intellectuals' par excellence. Their socialism is municipal socialism; the municipality and not the nation should, at first, at any rate, take over the means of production. They depict their socialism as an extreme but in-

evitable consequence of bourgeois liberalism. Hence their tactics: not to wage determined struggle against the Liberals as opponents, but to push them towards socialist conclusions, i.e., to hoodwink them, to permeate liberalism with socialism, not to put up Socialist candidates against the Liberals but to foist them on the Liberals, i.e., to get them elected by deception. ... But, of course, they fail to understand that in doing so they are either lied to and deceived themselves or else misrepresent socialism.

"Besides a lot of rubbish, the Fabians have published several good works of a propagandist nature, in fact the best of the kind which the English have produced. But as soon as they get on to their specific tactics of hushing up the class struggle it all turns putrid. Because of the class struggle, they fanatically hate Marx and all of us.

"The Fabians, of course, have many bourgeois adherents and that is why they have lots of money. ...

"These people have, of course, many bourgeois adherents, and therefore money" (ibid, pp.532-33).

Towards the end of 1893, in a further letter to Sorge, Engels describes the *volte face* of the Fabian Society on the question of the independent activity of the working class, and its conversion to the idea of a separate workers' party, thus:

"These gentlemen, after having declared for years that the emancipation of the working class can only be accomplished through the Great Liberal Party, after having decried all independent election activity of the workers in respect to Liberal candidates also as disguised Toryism and after having proclaimed the permeation of the Liberal Party by socialist principles as the sole life task of the Socialists, now declare that the Liberals are traitors, that nothing can be done with them and that in the next elections the workers should put up candidates of their own, regardless of Liberals or Tories. ... It is a complete admission of sins committed by these overweening bourgeois, who would graciously deign to emancipate the proletariat from above if it would only be sensible enough to realise that such a raw, uneducated mass cannot alone emancipate itself and cannot achieve anything except by the grace of these clever lawyers, writers and sentimental old women" (ibid, p.534).

The last two letters were written following the formation of the ILP. Engels' expectation that some good may come out of the organisational independence of the working class in Britain was not justified by the ILP, whose activities very soon assumed a decidedly opportunist and anti-Socialist character. *"It is quite justly said"*, to repeat Lenin's just remark, *"that this party is 'independent' only of Socialism, but very dependent indeed on Liberalism"*.

Anyone who would doubt the veracity of the observations of Engels or Lenin on the Fabians, let him find out the truth through the Fabian's mouth. In 1895, Beatrice Webb expressed her contempt of the working class thus: *"Judging from our knowledge of the labour movement we can expect no leader from the working class. Our only hope is in permeating the young middle-class man"* (Quoted in J.Callaghan, *'Socialism in Britain'*, p.37).

And further: *"What can we hope from these myriads of deficient minds and deformed bodies that swarm our great cities - what can we hope but brutality, madness and crime"* (Quoted in Cliff and Gluckstein, *'The Labour Party - a Marxist History'*, p.18).

Formation of Labour Party: opportunism continues unabated

Although the ILP was thoroughly opportunist in character, immersed in Lib-Lab politics, and in no way opposed to the political alliance with the Liberal Party, it nonetheless encountered hostility on the part of the old unions who did their best, by a series of bureaucratic measures, ranging from the adoption of the block vote to ending trades council representation (solely because the ILP dominated smaller unions and trades councils), to isolate it. The economic reality, however, was inexorably making it impossible to preserve the Lib-Lab alliance, as that alliance no longer could guarantee the privileged status of the upper stratum of the working class. Faced with stiff competition from abroad, British capitalism, throughout the last decade of the 19th century, forced on the unions several confrontations, inflicting bitter defeats on the latter. In the face of this sobering reality, at its 1899 Congress, the TUC felt obliged to decide in favour of convening a conference to form a Labour Representation Committee (LRC). The said Conference took place in February 1990 and was attended by 65 delegates representing unions with a combined membership of 568,000, as well as by representatives of political organisations such as the ILP, the Fabian Society and the Social Democratic Federation (SDF). The Conference had little difficulty in rejecting the SDF formulation that the new organisation ought to be a *"party organisation separate from the capitalist parties based upon a recognition of class war"*. Instead, it went on to accept, by a majority of 102 votes against 3, the motion worded by Keir Hardie to the effect that *"this Conference is in favour of working-class opinion being represented in the House of Commons by men sympathetic with the aims and demands of the labour movement"*.

SOCIAL DEMOCRACY &
THE ATTITUDE OF THE PROLETARIAT TOWARDS IT

From the very outset, not only was the LRC intended to be a parliamentary body, first and foremost, it also excluded nine-tenths of the working class, formed as it was by the craft unions to protect their interests, in and outside of parliament, better than was possible under the old Lib-Lab alliance, now rendered obsolete by the changed economic reality. In 1882, only 1.5 million, out of a total workforce of 14 million, belonged to any trade union, and even fewer (less than a million) belonged to unions affiliated to the TUC. This ratio of the trade-union membership to the total workforce hardly underwent any change until just before the commencement of the First World War. The unions which set up the LRC were overwhelmingly the organisations of the aristocracy of labour. At the time of the setting up of the LRC, out of a total of 10 million unskilled workers, a mere 100,000 were organised in trade unions. What is more, at a time when the majority of the workers had no vote (in addition to women not having a vote, there was no universal male suffrage either), the electorate, which was to be the constituency of the LRC, was largely drawn from the upper privileged stratum of the working class.

The turn of the century brought with it such a decline in the competitiveness of British capitalism as to threaten the conditions of life even of the upper stratum of the British working class. Unemployment among members of the unions (remember that unionisation was mainly confined to the skilled upper layer) rose from 2.5 per cent to 8 per cent in the first decade of the 20th century, while wages fell by 6 per cent during the same period. To these deteriorating conditions, the response of the unions was the same as that of the present-day trade-union leadership (with the honourable exception of Scargill and the NUM) to the attack of Thatcherism. Strikes fell, this being further reinforced by the removal of trade-union immunity for strike action consequent upon the 1901 Taff Vale judgement[1].

In the face of these attacks, during this entire decade, the LRC and from 1906 the Labour Party (as the LRC came to be called from this year) continued, as is clear from Lenin's observations cited above, to act as the tail end of the

---

1   This is a reference to the case of **Taff Vale Railway Co. v. Amalgamated Society of Railway Servants** decided by the House of Lords (the highest court of appeal in the UK) in 1901. This case decided the union could be sued by the employers with a view to the latter recovering compensation for damages caused by industrial action. The effects of this House of Lords decision were to some extent reversed by Parliament passing the Trade Disputes Act of 1906, see especially its section 4.

Liberal Party by concluding secret electoral pacts with the latter, with not the slightest attempt at political independence. In parliament, the Labour Party, which by 1910 had nearly 40 MPs and held the balance, acted merely as an adjunct to the Liberal Party, refusing to oppose the latter on the pretext that such action would result in the fall of the Government and its replacement by the Tories (does not it sound topical!).

This Parliamentary opportunism of Labour is captured by Lenin in his article *'Debates in Britain on Liberal Labour Policy'* (October 1912), in which he reviews the 20th Annual Conference of the ILP, held at Merthyr on May 27 and 28, 1912, especially commenting upon the debate at that Conference on the parliamentary policy of Labour. Jowett, MP, moved a resolution against supporting the Liberals. Conway, who seconded the resolution, said: *"The average worker is asking the question whether the Labour Party in Parliament has a view of its own. ... A feeling is growing in the country that the Labour Party is simply a wing of the Liberal Party".*

McLachlan, who supported Jowett, had this to say: *"What are the interests of a political party? Are the interests of the party merely to be served by retaining men in the House of Commons? If the interests of the party are to be considered, then the men and women who are outside Parliament have as much right to be considered as the men in Parliament. As a socialist organisation we should try to give effect to our principles in our political activities"* (Quoted by Lenin, CW Vol.18, p.363).

McLachlan went on to say: *"Even if we lost every seat in the House through upholding our principles, it would do more good than attempts to coax a Liberal Government to make concessions"* (ibid, p.364).

The entire leadership of the ILP, including Keir Hardie and Philip Snowden, both MPs, opposed Jowett's resolution. Snowden, *"one of the most rabid opportunists, wriggled like an eel"* (Lenin, *ibid*) and said that if Labour did not take into consideration the consequences of voting in parliament on the fortunes of the government, such a *"policy would necessitate repeated General Elections and nothing is more irritating to the public than such contests. ... Politics means compromise"* (ibid). Needless to say, Jowett's resolution was thrown out by a majority of 195 against, with 73 in it its favour. And Labour's reward for its political subordination during this period to the Liberal Party? Crumbs in the form of the Trade Disputes Act 1906, which did away with the Taff Vale Judgement by restoring trade-union immunity for industrial strikes.

In the same article, Lenin makes an observation, which is of great interest to us concerning the composition of the Labour Party. *"It should be observed"*, says Lenin, *"that the Parliamentary Labour Party consists **not only** of ILP MPs, but also of MPs sponsored by trade unions. These call themselves Labour MPs and Labour Party members, and **do not belong** to the ILP. The British opportunists have succeeded in doing what the opportunists in other countries are frequently inclined to do, namely, in combining opportunist 'socialist' MPs with MPs of allegedly non-party trade unions. The notorious 'broad labour party', of which certain Mensheviks spoke in Russia in 1906-7, has materialised in Britain ..."* (ibid, p.361).

These words of Lenin need to be especially memorised for we shall frequently meet with the opportunist argument that the Labour Party is a 'broad workers' party', a 'Party of the working class', and so on and so forth. It is clear, however, that Lenin regards such views as liquidationist and treats them with utter contempt.

Sharpening Struggle and Labour's Response

The four years before the war witnessed a rise in the working-class movement, with marked resistance to the capitalist offensive. Millions of workers took to strike action. The seamen and dockers' strike of 1911, and that of the railwaymen and miners in 1912, marked a high point in the development of the working-class movement. The Labour Party earned notoriety for itself by its total condemnation of the rising militant strike movement. J.R.Clynes declared at the 1914 Labour Party Conference: *"too many strikes caused a sense of disgust, of being a nuisance to the community"* (Quoted in R.Miliband, *'Parliamentary Socialism'*, p.38).

War and Labour

The only time that a significant section of the British labour aristocracy came close to adopting a stance opposed to British Imperialism was during the Boer War. Under the influence of radical liberals, representing industrial capital, a large section of the labour aristocracy opposed the war as one waged by financiers for the control of the goldfields of the Rand and the Kimberley diamond mines. Following the lead of the Liberal J.A.Hobson, the ILP opposed this war. Keir Hardie denounced the Boer war as *"a capitalists' war, begotten by capitalists' money, lied into being by a perjured mercenary press, and fathered by unscrupulous politicians, themselves the merest tools of the capitalists"* (Quoted in B.Porter, *Critics of Empire - British Radical Attitudes to Imperialism in Africa 1895-1914*, p.128).

Forgetting about the fate of the overwhelming majority of the population of South Africa, namely, its indigenous colonised black people, Hardie went on to say: *"As Socialists our sympathies are bound to be with the Boers"* (ibid).

Hardie was not alone in this. Most of those in the British labour aristocracy who opposed the war cared not a fig for the oppressed black majority in South Africa.

Moreover, not only was the labour aristocracy split right in the middle, its ideological leadership, the Fabian Society, stood solidly on the side of British Imperialism. To give the reader a flavour of the sickeningly hypocritical and twisted imperialist logic, allegedly in the name of socialism, we reproduce the following quotations from the leading Fabians, and prominent Labour Party leaders, of the day.

In his pamphlet *'Fabianism and Empire'*, G.B.Shaw, having stated that the Fabians aimed at the *"effective social organisation of the Empire"*, went on to reason thus: *"The notion that a nation has a right to do what it pleases with its own territory, without reference to the interests of the rest of the world, is no more tenable from the international socialist point of view ... than the notion that a landlord has a right to do what he likes with his estate without reference to the interests of his neighbours"* (Porter, *ibid*, pp.116-17).

Ramsay MacDonald was even more candid, declaring that *"so far as the underlying spirit of imperialism is a frank acceptance of national duty exercised beyond the nation's political frontiers"*, it *"cannot be condemned"*, for *"the compulsion to expand and to assume world responsibility is worthy at its origin"*. And further: *"The question of Empire cannot be decided on first principles, so far as this country is concerned. We have a history, and it is an Imperial one"*. (Porter, pp.185-86 and p.189).

A more benign attitude towards British Imperialism would be hard to find. In view of this it is hardly to be surprised at that at the 1907 Stuttgart Congress of the Second International, MacDonald should find himself on the side of the 'socialist' opportunists supporting 'socialist colonialism'.

At a much later date, in 1921, in his *'Labour and the New World'* (hasn't the title got a strange resemblance to the contemporary 'New World Order'!), Snowden, by reference to China, was to assert the existence of *"inexorable limits to the right of self-determination"*, consequent upon which limits, China had no right to deprive *"the rest of the world* [read British Imperialism -HB] *of access to her material resources"*, and conclude, in language not dissimilar to that used by Shaw (see above):

"*By no moral right may the ownership and control of the natural and material resources of a territory* [unless of course such territory was under the ownership and control of British Imperialism - HB] *be regarded as the absolute monopoly of the people* [unless they are British, is the implicit assumption again - HB] *who happen to be settled there"* (P.Snowden, *'Labour and the New World',* p.289).

The Boer war was to prove to be the solitary occasion on which a fairly large section of the labour aristocracy took a position in opposition to British Imperialism. And, in the words of Robert Clough, *"The Radical Liberals created the space for this in their denunciation of British financiers. It was however their swansong. The growth of banking capital and its merging with industrial capital was already undermining the Liberal Party as the representative of manufacturing industry. The future of the Radicals lay in an alliance with the labour aristocracy, but in conditions where British Imperialism's colonial monopoly would be increasingly under challenge. In these circumstances, neither could afford themselves the luxury of such demonstrations of opposition; their privileged position was mortgaged to British Imperialism"* (*op cit*, pp.42-43).

Their attitude to the First World War was to prove this.

First World War

Long before the First World War broke out, socialists of all countries, at the time grouped in the Second International, recognised that war was an inevitable concomitant of capitalism, that the then coming war was an imperialist war waged by two groups of giant monopoly capitalist coalitions, not in the interests of freedom, but for the re-division of the world - colonies, markets and overseas investment - and strangulation of small nations; that therefore it was the duty of the socialists in all the belligerent countries to oppose such a war by refusing to vote for war credits and mobilising the workers of all countries against such a war. Thus in 1910, a whole four years before the war broke out, the Copenhagen Congress of the Second International resolved that socialists in parliament should vote against war credits. At the time of the Balkan War of 1912, the Basle World Congress of the Second International declared that the workers of all countries considered it a crime to shoot one another for the sake of increasing the profits of the capitalists. That is what they said in their resolutions.

But when, with the outbreak of the imperialist war, time came to put into effect these resolutions, the leaders and parties of the Second International, with the sole honourable exception of Lenin's Bolshevik Party, proved to be traitors, betrayers of the proletariat and servitors of the bourgeoisie. Instead of opposing war, they became the supporters of this imperialist butchery. On August 4th 1914, the German Social-Democrats in parliament voted for the war credits. So did the overwhelming majority of the socialists in France, Great Britain and many other countries. As a result, the Second International ceased to exist; it broke up into separate social-chauvinist parties - each warring against the other. Adopting a social-chauvinist position, and betraying the proletariat, the leaders of socialist parties became defenders of the fatherland, i.e., the defenders of their respective imperialist bourgeoisie, for to *"a Great Power 'defence of the fatherland' means defence of the right to share in the plundering of foreign countries"* (Lenin, *'The Collapse of the Second International'*, May-June 1915).

In a series of articles and pamphlets written during the war, Lenin exposed the treachery, the falsity and the hypocrisy of the slogan of defence of the fatherland in **that particular** war. He insisted on the recognition of *"the necessity of an historical study of each war"* (*Socialism and War*), and the recognition of the distinction between just and unjust wars, wars of national liberation and imperialist wars for the oppression. exploitation and strangulation of nations and for the division of the booty and the re-division of colonies.

War is the Continuation of Politics by Other Means

Following Clausewitz, whom he justly described as *"one of the profoundest writers on military questions"*, Lenin insisted that *'war is politics continued by other (i.e. forcible) means"*. Every war, he insisted, must be analysed by the point of its substance: *"... if the 'substance' of a war is, for example, the overthrow of alien oppression ... then such a war is progressive as far as the oppressed state or nation is concerned. If, however, the 'substance' of a war is re-division of colonies, division of booty, plunder of foreign lands (and such is the war of 1914-16), then all talk of defending the fatherland is* 'sheer deception of the people'.

"How, then can we disclose and define the substance of a war? War is the continuation of policy. Consequently, we must examine the policy pursued prior to the war, the policy that led to and brought about the war. If it was an imperialist policy, i.e., one designed to safeguard the interests of finance capital and rob and oppress colonies and foreign countries, then the war stemming from that policy is imperialist. If it was a national-liberation policy, i.e., one

expressive of the mass movement against national oppression, then the war stemming from that policy is a war of national liberation.

"The philistine does not realise that war is 'the continuation of policy', and consequently limits himself to the formula that 'the enemy has attacked us', 'the enemy has invaded by country', *without stopping to think what issues are at stake in the war, which classes are waging it, and with what political objects. ...*

"For the philistine the important thing is where the armies stand, who is winning at the moment. For the Marxist the important thing is what issues are at stake in this war, during which first one, then the other army may be on top.

"What is the present war being fought over? ... England, France and Russia are fighting to keep the colonies they have seized. ... Germany is fighting to take over these colonies. ... The real nature of the present war is not national but imperialist ... it is not being fought to enable one side to overthrow national oppression, which the other side is trying to maintain. It is a war between two groups of oppressors, between two freebooters over the division of the booty, over who shall rob Turkey and the colonies.

"The social-chauvinists plead self-determination in order to present this war as a national war. There is only one correct way of combating them: we must show that the war is being fought not to liberate nations, but to determine which of the great robbers will oppress more nations" ('A Caricature of Marxism and Imperialist Economism', Aug-Oct 1916, CW.Vol 23, pp.28).

In the same article, Lenin goes on to expose Kautsky's betrayal of the proletariat, his renunciation of Marxism, of revolution and of proletarian internationalism, by counterposing Kautsky the Marxist (pre-war) to Kautsky the social-chauvinist (after the war began) thus:

"Up to the 1914-16 War Karl Kautsky was a Marxist and his major writings and statements will always remain models of Marxism. On August 26th, 1910, he wrote in Die Neue Zeit, *in reference to the imminent war:*

"'In a war between Germany and England the issue is not democracy, but world domination, i.e., exploitation of the world. That is not an issue on which social-democrats can side with the exploiters of their nation'!

"There you have an excellent Marxist formulation, one that fully coincides with our own and fully exposes the present-day Kautsky, who has turned from Marxism to the defence of social chauvinism. ... It is a formulation that clearly brings out the principles underlying the Marxist attitude towards war. War is

the continuation of policy. ... 'World Domination' is, to put it briefly, the substance of imperialist policy, of which imperialist war is the continuation. Rejection of the 'defence of the fatherland' in a democratic war, i.e., rejecting participation in such a war, is an absurdity that has nothing in common with Marxism. To embellish imperialist war by applying to it the concept of 'defence of the fatherland', i.e., by presenting it as a democratic war, is to deceive the workers and side with the reactionary bourgeoisie" (ibid).

Lenin rightly insisted that *"whoever justifies participation in this imperialist war perpetuates imperialist oppression of nations. Whoever seeks to use the present difficulties of the governments in order to fight for a social revolution is fighting for the real freedom of really all nations, a freedom that can be realised only under socialism"* ('Socialism and War', August 1915).

In regard to the six imperialist powers, England, France, Russia, Germany, Japan and the USA, and by reference to the most incontrovertible figures, showing that between 1876 and 1914, the six 'great' nations grabbed 25,000,000 square kilometres, i.e., a territory two and a half times the size of Europe; that these six nations held enslaved more than a half-billion (523,000,000) of colonial people; that for every four inhabitants of the 'great' nations, there are five inhabitants in 'their' colonies, Lenin goes on to say:

"Everybody knows that the colonies were conquered by fire and sword, that the colonial populations are treated in a barbarous fashion, that they are exploited in a thousand ways. ... The Anglo-French bourgeoisie is deceiving the people when it says that it wages war for the freedom of peoples, including Belgium; in reality, it wages war for the sake of holding on to the colonies which it has stolen on a large scale. The German Imperialists would free Belgium, etc., forthwith, were the English and French willing to share with them the colonies on the basis of 'justice'. It is a peculiarity of the present situation that the fate of the colonies is being decided by war on the continent. From the standpoint of bourgeois justice ... Germany could unquestionably have a just claim against England and France, because it has been 'wronged' as far as its share of colonies is concerned, because its enemies are oppressing more nations than Germany. ... Germany itself, however, is waging war, not for the liberation, but for the oppression of nations. It is not the business of Socialists to help the younger and stronger robber (Germany) to rob the older and fatter bandits, but the Socialists must utilise the struggle between the bandits to overthrow all of them. For this reason the Socialists must tell the people the truth, namely, that this war is in three senses a war of slave-holders for the strength-

ening of the worst kind of slavery. It is a war, first, for the strengthening of colonial slavery by means of a more 'equitable' division of the colonies and more 'team work' in their exploitation; it is, secondly, a war for the strengthening of the oppression of minority nationalities inside the 'great' nations ..., third, it is a war for the strengthening and prolongation of wage slavery, the proletariat being divided and subdued while the capitalists are gaining through war profits, through fanning national prejudices and deepening the reaction, which has raised its head in all countries, even in the freest and republican" (ibid CW.Vol.21, p.303).

At the end of May 1917, just four months before the October Revolution, in his lecture on war entitled *'War and Revolution'*, Lenin returns to the topic insisting that one must never forget *"the class character of the war; why the war broke out; the classes that are waging it; the historical and historico-economic conditions that gave rise to it"*, for *"war is a continuation of politics by other means. Every war is inseparably connected with the political system which gave rise to it. The politics which a certain country, a certain class, pursued for a long period before the war, are inevitably pursued by that very same class during the war; it merely changes its form of action"* (pp.398 & 400).

Continues Lenin: *"War is a continuation of politics by other means. When the French revolutionary citizens and revolutionary peasants, at the end of the eighteenth century, after overthrowing the monarchy by revolutionary means, established a democratic republic, and having settled their accounts with their monarch also settled accounts in a revolutionary manner with their landlords - these revolutionary class politics could not but shake the rest of autocratic, tsarist, monarchist, semi-feudal Europe to its foundations. And the inevitable continuation of these politics of the victorious revolutionary class in France was war, in which, pitted against the revolutionary class were all the monarchist countries of Europe, which formed their notorious coalition, and waged a counter-revolutionary war against France"* (ibid).

By way of a refutation of the attempts on the part of the capitalist press to read into the First World war a historical meaning which it could not, and did not, possess, Lenin goes on to make this observation regarding the first imperialist war:

"Today, however, we are confronted, .. by two groups of capitalist powers ... the politics of which for a number of decades consisted of unceasing economic rivalry for world supremacy, to strangle small nationalities, to secure ... tenfold profits for bank capital, which has enmeshed the whole world in the

chains of its influence.

"... On the one hand there is England, a state which owns a great part of the globe; the wealthiest state in the world; which created this wealth, not so much by the labour of its workers as by the exploitation of vast colonies, by the vast power of the English banks which, constituting a numerically insignificant group of three, four or five giant banks, stand at the head of all other banks, controlling hundreds of billions of rubles, and controlling in such a way that we can say without exaggeration: there is not a spot on the whole globe that this capital has not laid its heavy hand on. ... By the end of the nineteenth and beginning of the twentieth centuries this capital had grown to such enormous proportions that its activities extended far beyond the frontiers of a single state and created a group of giant banks possessing incredible wealth. Pushing this insignificant number of banks to the front, it enmeshed the whole world in this net of hundreds of billions of rubles. This is the main thing in the economic policy of England and the economic policy of France ...

"On the other hand, opposed to this group, mainly Anglo-French, stand another group of capitalists, even more predatory and more piratical - a group which came to the capitalist banqueting table when all the places had been taken up, but which introduced into the struggle new methods of developing capitalist production, better technique, incomparable organisation, which transformed the old capitalism, the capitalism of the epoch of free competition, into the capitalism of gigantic trusts, syndicates and cartels. This group introduced the principle of state capitalist production, uniting the gigantic forces of capitalism with the gigantic forces of the state into one mechanism, and amalgamating tens of millions of people into a single organisation of state capitalism. *This is the economic history, this is the diplomatic history of a number of decades which ... alone provides the correct solution to the problem of war and leads us to the conclusion that the present war is also the product of the politics of the classes which are now at grips in this war; the politics of the two great giants who long before the war had enmeshed the whole world, all countries, in their nets of financial exploitation, and who before the war had economically divided the world among themselves. They had to come into collision because, from the point of view of capitalism, the redivision of this supremacy became inevitable.*

"The old division was based on the fact that for several hundreds of years England had crushed her competitors. ... By means of prolonged wars England, on the basis of her economic power, of her merchant capital, established

her unchallenged rule over the whole world. A new robber appeared. In 1871, a new capitalist power arose, which developed ever so much faster than England. ... This rapid development of German capitalism was the development of a young and strong robber, who came before the league of European Powers and said: 'You ruined Holland, you defeated France, you have taken half the world - please give us our share'.

"... this war is the continuation of the politics of annexations, that is, conquest, capitalist robbery, on both sides, on the part of both groups engaged in the war. Hence it is clear that the question as to which of these two robbers first drew the knife has no significance for us whatever. Take the history of the naval and military expenditure of both groups during the past decade, take the history of all the little wars they have waged before this big one - 'little' because, only a few Europeans died in those wars, but of the nations who were strangled, who from the European point of view were not even nations (Asiatics, Africans - are these nations?) hundreds of thousands died; the kind of war that was waged against them was as follows: they were unarmed, and they were shot down with machine-guns. Do you call that war? Why, strictly speaking, this is not war, and one may be permitted to forget about it. That is how they deceive the masses wholesale.

'This war is the continuation of the policy of conquest, the shooting down of whole nationalities, of incredible atrocities, which were committed by the Germans and English in Africa, by the English and Russians in Persia ... for which the German capitalists regard them as enemies. They said in effect: you are strong because you are rich! We are stronger than you, therefore we have the same 'sacred' right to rob as you have. This is what the real history of British and German finance capital for decades preceding the war amounts to .... This provides the key to an understanding of what the war is about" (War and Revolution, pp.402-6).

Elsewhere, Lenin makes a similar observation: "Comparing the 'continuation of the politics' of combating feudalism and absolutism - the politics of the bourgeoisie in its struggle for liberty - with the 'continuation of the politics' of a decrepit, i.e., imperialist, bourgeoisie, i.e., of a bourgeoisie which has plundered the entire world, a reactionary bourgeoisie which, in alliance with feudal landlords, attempts to crush the proletariat, means comparing chalk and cheese. It is like comparing the 'representatives of the bourgeoisie', Robespierre, Garibaldi and Zhelyabov, with such 'representatives of the bourgeoisie as Millerand, Salandra and Guchkov. One cannot be a Marxist *without feeling the deepest respect for the great bourgeois revolutionaries who had an historic right to speak for their respective bourgeois 'fatherlands', and, in the struggle against feudalism, led tens of millions of people in the new nations towards a civilised life. Neither can one be a Marxist without feeling contempt for the sophistry of Plekhanov and Kautsky, who speak of the 'defence of the fatherland' with regard to the throttling of Belgium by German imperialists, or with regard to the pact between the imperialists of Britain, France, Russia and Italy on the plundering of Austria and Turkey"* (Lenin, *The Collapse of the Second International*, May-June,1915, p.221).

Since the First World War was an imperialist war on both sides, as is conclusively proved by Lenin, and, indeed as it was recognised by the overwhelming majority of the socialists before the war broke out (as, for instance in the Basle Resolution of the Second International), how is one to explain the desertion, on such a vast scale, of the socialists of different countries to the side of their respective bourgeoisie? How is one to explain the conversion of socialists to social-chauvinists (socialism in words and chauvinism in deed) in complete betrayal of the interests of the international proletariat? The answer is to be found in opportunism, for *"Social-chauvinism is opportunism brought to its logical conclusions. ... Social-chauvinism is consummated opportunism"* (Lenin, *'Opportunism and the Collapse of the Second International*). *"Social-chauvinism's basic ideological and political content fully coincides with the foundations of opportunism. It is **one and the same** tendency. In the conditions of the war ..., opportunism leads to social-chauvinism. The idea of class collaboration is opportunism's main feature"* (Lenin, *ibid*, p.242). The war brought this idea to its logical conclusion with the betrayal of socialism by the most prominent representatives of the Second International, their desertion to the bourgeoisie, and their justification of an alliance between the socialists and the bourgeoisie.

The economic basis of opportunism and social-chauvinism is identical too. In Lenin's words: *"Chauvinism and opportunism in the labour movement have the same economic basis: the alliance between a numerically small upper stratum of the proletariat and the petty bourgeoisie - who get ... morsels of privileges of their 'own' national capital - against the masses of proletarians, the masses of the toilers and the oppressed in general"* (*ibid*, p.244).

And: *"Opportunism means sacrificing the fundamental interests of the masses to the temporary interests of an insignificant minority of the workers or, in other words, an alliance between a section of the workers and the bour-*

geoisie, directed against the mass of the proletariat. The war has made such an alliance particularly conspicuous and inescapable. Opportunism was engendered in the course of decades by the special features of the period of development of capitalism, when the comparatively peaceful and cultured life of a stratum of privileged working men 'bourgeoisified' them, gave them crumbs from the table of their national capitalists, and isolated them from the suffering, misery and revolutionary temper of the impoverished and ruined masses. The imperialist war is the direct continuation and culmination of this state of affairs, because it is a war for the privileges of the Great-Power nations, for the partition of colonies, and domination over other nations. To defend and strengthen their privileged position as a petty-bourgeois upper stratum or aristocracy (and bureaucracy) of the working class - such is the natural wartime continuation of petty-bourgeois opportunist hopes and the corresponding tactics, such is the economic foundation of present-day social-imperialism" (ibid, pp.242-43).

And finally, whereas before the first world war, opportunism was in its *"adolescent stage"*, with the outbreak of the war *"it grew to manhood and its 'innocence' and youth cannot be restored. An entire social stratum, consisting of parliamentarians, journalists, labour officials, privileged officer personnel, and certain strata of the proletariat, has sprung up and become* **amalgamated** *with its own national bourgeoisie, which has proved fully capable of appreciating and 'adapting' it"* (ibid, p.250).

If the first World War witnessed the most flagrant betrayal of their socialist convictions by the majority of the Social-Democratic parties of Europe, if it witnessed the complete victory of opportunism and the transformation of the Social-Democratic parties into national liberal-labour parties, in the case of the Labour Party in Britain no such transformation was necessary, for right from the outset, from the time of its formation, opportunism stood triumphant and Labour was never any thing other than a national Liberal-Labour Party - a level to which most of European Social-Democracy, hitherto revolutionary, sank with the outbreak of the war. This, among other factors explains, as we shall see shortly, the leading role that Labour came to occupy in the re-constituted post-war ranks of European Social-Democracy in the latter's counter-revolutionary struggle against Bolshevism and the Third International (The Comintern).

Literally on the eve of the war - two days before its outbreak - mammoth anti-war demonstrations took place in Britain, at which labour leaders not only denounced the then impending war but also, as per the official policy of the Second International, vowed to oppose it. Yet by 5th August, 35 out of 40 Labour Members of Parliament had gone over to the bourgeoisie, leaving behind five MPs belonging to the ILP, including Keir Hardie, Philip Snowden and Ramsay MacDonald. More than that. Shortly afterwards, Labour, declaring first an industrial, and then an electoral, truce, went on to act as a recruiting sergeant in this, the most dreadful slaughter of the international proletariat, in order to decide which group of the two imperialist robbers was to have what share of the booty. In a cynical and corrupt disregard of the hundreds of millions of people in the British Empire, suffering the worst kind of exploitation and abominable oppression, humiliation and infamies, denied the most elementary rights, jailed and tortured for demanding freedom from the jackboot of British colonialism, in a manifesto issued during the war Labour asserted:

"The victory of Germany would mean the death of democracy. ... Until the power that has pillaged and outraged Belgium and the Belgians, and plunged nearly the whole of Europe into the awful misery, suffering and horror of war is beaten there can be no peace" (Quoted in H.Tracey, *'The British Labour Party'*, p.105).

And again, in February 1915, a meeting of Allied Socialists, convened on Labour's initiative, with matchless hypocrisy and cynicism resolved:

"The invasion of Belgium and France by the German armies threatens the very existence of independent nationalities, and strikes a blow at all faith in treaties. In these circumstances a victory for German imperialism would be the defeat and destruction of democracy and liberty in Europe" (ibid).

As can be seen, Labour regarded a victory for German imperialism, not as defeat for British, French, Belgian and Russian Tsarist imperialism, but as *"the defeat and destruction of democracy and liberty in Europe"*. This at a time when these four countries possessed more than 80 per cent of the colonies, denying democracy and liberty to several hundred million colonial slaves, who far outnumbered the population of their colonial masters. Even the reference to liberty and democracy in Europe is utterly false, for while Britain denied freedom and democracy to the Irish, tsarist Russia denied it to a score of minority nationalities. Not for nothing did Lenin denounce tsarist Russia as a prison of nations and characterised it as a gendarme and hangman of the European revolutions. The labour leadership could not but have been well aware of all this. Therefore, its stance in defence of the interests of British imperialism flowed, not from ignorance, but from a deliberate desire to defend the privileges of the labour aristocracy, which privileges could not be defended without defending the empire and British imperialism. Nothing, no principles, no scruples, no qualms of conscience, no such trifles, were going to be allowed to stand in the way of its defence of these twin, and inextricable, interests. And if this defence required colonial slavery for hundreds of millions and the sanction of mass slaughter of the European, including British, workers in an imperialist war, Labour's hand was not to tremble at that.

Keir Hardie and Ramsay MacDonald soon became enthusiastic, not to say jingoistic supporters of British imperialism's war effort. The latter stated that: *"Victory must therefore be ours. England is not played out, her mission is not accomplished. ... The young men of the country ... must settle the immediate issue of victory. Let them do it in the spirit of the brave men who crowned our country with honour in the times that are gone"* (Quoted in Cliff and Gluckstein, *op cit*, p.21).

The distance that Keir Hardie had travelled since the days of his opposition to the Boer war, the dishonesty of the argument that he employs in justification of his support for the slaughter of the first imperialist world war, can best be gauged from the following remark of his:

"A nation at war must be united, especially when its existence is at stake. In such filibustering expeditions as our own Boer war ... where no national interest of any kind was involved, there were many occasions for diversity of opinion. ... With the boom of the enemy guns within earshot, the lads who have gone forth to fight their country's battles must not be disheartened by any discordant notes at home" (Quoted in Miliband, *op cit*, p.44).

The real meaning, the real content, of Labour's concept of democracy and liberty can perhaps be better perceived by reference to their attitude toward Irish freedom. When, taking advantage of the difficulty of the British government during the war, Irish people rose in the Easter rebellion of 1916 against British rule and proclaimed the Irish Republic, they faced nothing short of outright hostility and venomous denunciation on the part of the British Labour Party. *Socialist Review* and *Labour Leader*, both ILP publications, denounced the Easter Rebellion and warmly supported its suppression by armed force by the government, describing James Connolly, the foremost leader of the rebellion, as being *"criminally mistaken"*, whose execution the War Cabinet authorised following the suppression. When it was announced in the House of Commons that Connolly had been executed, Labour's Parliamentary leader, Arthur Henderson, led Labour MPs in a burst of applause by way of greeting this news item.

On the evening of the victory of British imperialism, in its *'Memorandum of War Aims'*, dated December 1917, and drafted by Sidney Webb, Labour made it abundantly clear that it was for the continued maintenance of the Empire and opposed to the right of self-determination of the subject peoples in the colonies, to whom it referred as *"non-adult races"*. *"Nobody contends"*, asserted the Labour Party in response to the peace proposals of the Bolshevik government in January 1918, *"that the black races can govern themselves...."* (Quoted in P.S.Gupta, *Imperialism and the British Labour Movement*, p.53).

Labour and Soviet Russia

It goes without saying that Labour was deeply hostile to the Bolshevik regime and to Soviet Russia. It tacitly supported the imperialist intervention, organised and led by British imperialism, against Soviet Russia. But the heroic defence of the revolution by the Russian masses and the Red Army combined with the stiff resistance by the masses of British workers who, in the aftermath of the war, were in a state of ferment, prevented the success of the intervention. Dockers, under the leadership of Harry Pollitt, on learning that the arms to be loaded on it were destined for use against the Red Army refused to load the *Jolly George* in April of 1920. That spelled the doom of the intervention and forced the British Government to put an end to it.

Through its efforts to reconstruct the Second International (the Berne International) and the formation of the Two-and-a-half International (Vienna), Labour did its dirtiest worst to isolate Soviet Russia and frustrate Lenin's attempts to form the Third International. The two opportunist outfits, the Second and the Two-and-a-half Internationals, merged in May 1923 to form the Labour and Socialist International (LSI) which has continued its counter-revolutionary work ever since. The collapse of the Second International following the outbreak of the first imperialist war, its break up into warring national factions, each supporting its own bourgeoisie, had the effect of putting the Labour Party, which had been an insignificant section of the Second International, into a predominant position in the conditions following the defeat of Germany and the victory of Britain in the war.

"The war and the disruption of international socialism", writes R.McKibbin, *"had landed the British Labour Party in a position it had not held before. Largely owing to the numerical strength - and the wealth - of the British trade unions, the Labour Party found itself willy-nilly the leading 'Allied' socialist*

party and the rock upon which European social democracy was already building its fortress against Bolshevism. Consequently, it appeared necessary to construct a political party appropriate to this industrial support" (R. McKibbin, *The Evolution of the Labour Party 1910-24*, p.91).

LALKAR May/June 1995

III

Lenin's Advice to British Communists and the Reasons Therefor

In the light of the foregoing, and knowing as he did the thoroughly opportunist nature of Labour, why did Lenin advise the British communists in early 1920 to support the Labour party; why did he advise the then newly formed Communist Party of Great Britain (CPGB) to even affiliate to the Labour Party?

First, the question of supporting the Labour Party. The concrete conditions in which Lenin gave his advice were characterised by the following facts:

(1) The British liberal bourgeoisie was abandoning the historical system of two parties of the exploiting class, a system which had hitherto been extremely advantageous to the exploiters, finding it necessary to unite their forces to fight the Labour Party;

(2) Although the leadership of the Labour Party was thoroughly bourgeois ('opportunist', 'social chauvinist', 'social-patriot' - these are the expressions frequently used by Lenin to characterise Labour leaders), there had as yet been no Labour Government and, therefore, the workers still had illusions in Labour;

(3) In the aftermath of the First World War there was great ferment in the British working class, for, as Lenin correctly noted, *"even in the purely Menshevik and utterly opportunist Independent Labour Party the masses are for Soviets"* (*'Left-Wing' Communism, an Infantile Disorder*);

(4) The British communists, who belonged to four separate organisations and had yet to unite themselves in a single party of the proletariat, found it hard to approach and get a hearing from the masses, who followed the Labour Party;

(5) The leadership of the Labour Party was afraid to secure power for itself, preferring instead a bloc with the Liberals.

In these concrete circumstances, Lenin, although being fully aware that *"the Hendersons, the Clynes, the MacDonalds and the Snowdens are hope-*

lessly reactionary ... that they want to take power in their own hands ..., that they want to 'rule' on the old bourgeois lines, and that when they do get into power they will unfailingly behave like the Scheidemanns and Noskes", nevertheless advised the British communists to unite in a single party, participate in parliamentary elections, give Labour some parliamentary support and reach a bloc with it. All this was, however, to be dependent on a condition precedent, namely, that the Communist Party *"retain complete liberty of agitation, propaganda and political activity, for without this latter condition, we cannot agree to a bloc, for it would be treachery; the British communists must absolutely insist on and secure* **complete liberty** *to expose the Hendersons and the Snowdens in the same way as ... the Russian Bolsheviks insisted on and secured it in relation to the Russian Hendersons and Snowdens, i.e., the Mensheviks"* (ibid, p.81).

Here is the thrust of Lenin's argument: *"... the majority of the workers in Great Britain still follow the lead of British Kerenskys or Scheidemanns and have* **yet had no experience** [my emphasis - HB] *of a government composed of these people, which experience was required in Russia and Germany to secure the mass passage of the workers to communism, ... the British communists* **should** *participate in parliamentary action, ... should from* **within** *Parliament, help the masses of the workers to see the results of a Henderson and Snowden government in practice, ... should help the Hendersons and Snowdens to defeat the combined forces of Lloyd George and Churchill"* (ibid, p.84).

And: *"... if we want* **the masses** *to follow us ..., we must, firstly, help Henderson or Snowden to beat Lloyd George and Churchill ...; secondly, we must help the majority of the working class to convince themselves by their own experience that we are right, that is, that Hendersons and Snowdens are absolutely unsuitable, that they are petty bourgeois and treacherous by nature, and that their bankruptcy is inevitable; thirdly, we must bring nearer the moment when,* **on the basis** *of the disappointment of the majority of the workers in Hendersons, it will be possible with serious chances of success to overthrow the government of Henderson at once ... "* (ibid, pp.85-86).

In view of the above, the Communist Party, says Lenin, should propose an election agreement to the Labour Party for a joint fight against the alliance of Lloyd George and the Conservatives, on the basis of the division of parliamentary seats *"in proportion to the number of votes cast by the workers for the Labour Party and the Communist Party (not at the elections, but in a special vote)"*, and on the basis of the retention by the Communist Party of *"***complete** *liberty of agitation, propaganda and political activity"* (ibid).

Whether or not the Labour Party consents to a bloc on these terms, the communists will be the gainers, for in the first case *"we shall carry our agitation among the masses ... and we shall not only help the Labour Party to establish its government more quickly, but also to help the masses to understand more quickly the communist propaganda that we shall carry on against the Hendersons **without any curtailment or omission** [last emphasis - HB]"* (ibid, pp.86-87).

But, what if the Hendersons and Snowdens reject a bloc on these terms? We shall still be the gainers, says Lenin, for *"we shall have at once shown the masses ... that the Hendersons prefer **their** close relations with the capitalists to the unity of all workers"* (ibid, p.87).

Such an electoral alliance, argues Lenin, would enable the communists, who found it *"hard to approach the masses and even to get a hearing from them"* not only to conduct propaganda in favour of the Soviets and the dictatorship of the proletariat, but also to explain that *"I want with my vote to support Henderson in the same way as a rope supports a hanged man - that the impending establishment of a government of Hendersons will ... bring the masses over to my side, and will hasten the political death of the Hendersons and the Snowdens just as was the case with their kindred spirits in Russia"* (ibid, p.88).

As to the question of affiliation of the Communist Party to the Labour Party, Lenin expressed himself in favour of such affiliation, but on the condition that the Communist Party *"can preserve its freedom of criticism and can pursue its own policy"* (Speech at the Second Congress of the Comintern, 23 July, 1920).

At the time the structure of the Labour Party was still such as to allow for this freedom. *"The British Socialist Party"*, says Lenin, *"can quite freely say that Henderson is a traitor and yet remain affiliated to the Labour Party"* (ibid).

Two weeks later, in yet another speech at the Second Congress of the Comintern, Lenin went on to elaborate his ideas by reference to the peculiar conditions surrounding the Labour Party, saying that the latter was *"not a political party in the ordinary sense of the word"*, that it was *"half trade-union and half political party"*, that it allowed *"sufficient liberty to all the political parties affiliated to it"*, that it allowed the British Socialist Party *"to remain in its ranks, ... to have its own organ of the press"* and openly criticise the leaders of the Labour Party as *"social-patriots and social-traitors"*. In these circumstances, concluded Lenin, it would be wrong for the communists not to affiliate as such a course would deprive them of the opportunity of exercising influence over a large section of the workers who still followed Labour (all remarks appearing in quotation marks above are from Lenin's speech at the Second Congress of the Comintern, delivered on 6 August 1920, pp.257-263).

CPGB's attempt at Affiliation to the Labour Party

Thus, as it can be seen, Lenin's observations were made in a particular, concrete, historical context. In the conditions then prevailing Lenin's advice was correct. That is why the newly formed Communist Party did its best to put that advice into effect. However, it takes two to tango, as the saying goes. Here briefly is the story of the attempt by the CPGB, soon after its formation, to gain affiliation to the Labour Party, and the latter's consistent and rabid anti-communism in refusing this affiliation.

Following Lenin's advice, the Communist Unity Convention, held in London on July 31st and August 1st, 1920, and which founded the CPGB, decided by a small majority in favour of affiliation to the Labour Party. In pursuance of this decision, the CPGB made its application for affiliation to the Labour Party in a letter dated August 10, 1920. There existed no constitutional reason why its application should be turned down by Labour, which had, after all, been a loose federation of affiliated bodies, embracing trade unions, individual members, and socialist societies. The latter, ILP being the largest, had their own press and programme and could argue their point of view within the Labour Party. Even the British Socialist Party (BSP), the openly Marxist predecessor of the CPGB, had been accepted as an affiliate. And yet the CPGB's successive applications were rejected by the Labour leadership and these rejections had been endorsed by the Labour Party's Annual Conferences in 1921, 1922, 1923 and 1924.

James Klugmann, commenting upon Labour's refusal to accept CPGB affiliation, particularly in view of the fact that the majority of the latter's membership had belonged to the BSP, correctly observes that although there *"was no formal reason, but there was a reason, and this was in a way a great compliment to the young Communist Party. The reason was the recognition by the right-wing leadership of the Labour Party and the affiliated trade unions - MacDonald, Henderson, Snowden, Clynes, etc. - that the Communist Party was to be something different from the old propagandist societies, that it would be capable of mobilising the workers for immediate struggles and for ideas of socialism, and that, ... it would be a major obstacle to their policy of reformism and class collaboration" (History of the Communist Party of Great Britain,* Vol.1, p.176, hereinafter 'Klugmann').

In September 1920, the month following the very first application of the newly-formed CPGB for affiliation to the Labour Party, the latter's National Executive Committee replied, declining the application on the grounds that the aims and objects of the Communist Party were not in accord with the Constitution, principles and programme of the Labour Party. The letter was signed by Arthur Henderson, Labour's Secretary at the time. From now on, the Labour leadership's familiar refrain, and excuse for refusing affiliation to the CPGB, was that the latter was *"dominated by Moscow"* and that it wished to pursue *"disruptive aims".*

Notwithstanding the Labour leadership's stance, there was strong rank-and-file pressure within Labour in favour of the acceptance of Communist affiliation. Bowing to this pressure, following the 1921 Annual Conference of the Labour Party, the Labour leadership agreed to a joint meeting with representatives of the CPGB. The only outcome of this meeting (held at the end of December 1921), at which Henderson tried unsuccessfully to divert the discussion away from Communist affiliation to one of parliamentary democracy versus *"Soviet Dictatorship",* was the agreement by Labour to submit a questionnaire to the CPGB. In this questionnaire, submitted at the beginning of 1922, and saturated through and through with anti-Communism, Labour raised four questions. First, whether the political line of the Communist Party and its affiliation to the Comintern was not incompatible with the objects of the Labour Party - *"the political, social and economic emancipation of the people by means of parliamentary democracy"*? Second, that it was *"a fundamental principle of the Labour Party to confine its operations to lawful means".* In view of its programme, its resolutions, its Constitution, and its affiliation to the Comintern, could the Communist Party claim to be consistent with this fundamental principle? Third, was not the pledge of the Communist candidates, when elected to parliament, to support the policy of the Communist Party in Parliament, incompatible with Labour's Constitution, which excluded the idea of such pledges? And, lastly, whether the CPGB proposed to become a *"loyal constituent of the Labour Party, conforming at all points with its Constitution and working for the promotion of its objects?"*

In mid-May 1922, the CPGB replied, dealing with all the points raised, but to no avail. Labour's Executive Committee considered this reply at the end of May, and resolved to recommend no change in existing policy. The issue was again referred to the Annual Conference of the Labour Party, which took place in Edinburgh on June 27-30, 1922. In opposing the affiliation, the miners' leader, Frank Hodges, in a reactionary vituperative and racist outburst, typical of the Labour leadership, accused the Communists of being *"the intellectual slaves of Moscow ... taking orders from the Asiatic mind"*. By a card vote, the Conference endorsed the decision of the Executive Committee by 3,086,000 to 261,000. The bloc vote was operating, as it almost always has done, in favour of the reactionary leadership. Frank Hodges, for instance, cast nearly a million votes against affiliation, even though everyone knew that from one-third to one-half of the miners would have voted in favour of affiliation.

In fact, the 1922 Conference, went further than just declining Communist affiliation. It amended the Party's rules by adding Clause 9, Section (b) - known as the Edinburgh eligibility clause - whereby delegates to local Labour Parties, or national or local Conferences of the Labour Party, were required individually to accept the Constitution and principles of the Labour Party, and no one was eligible to be a delegate who belonged to an organisation *"having for one of its objects the return to Parliament or to any Local Government Authority of a candidate or candidates other than such as have been approved as running in association with the Labour Party"*.

Under great pressure from its membership, the twenty-third Labour Party Conference, held in London at the end of June 1923, while still endorsing the Executive's decision to refuse affiliation to the Communist Party, decided to delete from its rules the Edinburgh 'eligibility clause', adopted only a year before.

But just over a year later, by which time the minority Labour Government having been in power for barely eight months was already in its death throws, the Labour Party's 24th Annual Conference, meeting on October 7, 1924 in London, decided not only to endorse the recommendation of the Executive Committee to refuse affiliation to the Communist Party, but also *"that no member of the Communist Party be eligible for endorsement as a Labour candidate for Parliament or any local authority"*. In a card vote the rejection of Communist Party affiliation was carried by 3,185,000 votes to 193,000; the rejection of Communists as Labour candidates by 2,456,000 to 654,000; and the resolution that no member of the Communist Party should be eligible for membership of the Labour Party was carried by the much narrower majority of 1,804,000 to 1,540,000 votes. Thus the door was finally closed to any direct Communist influence over the Labour Party. The Labour Party leadership, always anti-communist servitors of British imperialism, were particularly stung by the CPGB's consistent working-class criticism of the first Labour Government. Consequently they were determined to put a stop to communist influence and to prevent the CPGB from becoming the rallying centre of rising working-class protest against Labour's abject surrender to British monopoly capitalism. What is remarkable about this saga of the CPGB's battle for affiliation is the candid anti-communism and anti-Sovietism of the Labour leadership, making it only too plain that the Labour Party was a bourgeois party of class collaboration, in which there could be no place for any organisation or individual who stood for the interests of the proletariat. Again and again the point is repeated by the Labour leadership that whereas Labour *"seeks to achieve the Socialist Commonwealth by means of Parliamentary democracy ... the Communist Party seeks to achieve the 'dictatorship of the proletariat' by armed insurrection"* (Report of the Executive Committee, 1923-24, in *Report of the 24th Annual Conference of the Labour Party*, pp.38-40).

Labour becomes indistinguishable from the Liberals

There is nothing surprising about the above attitude of the Labour Party towards communism in general, and the question of communist affiliation in particular, for, if anything *"Right-wing domination of the Labour Party had been strengthened since the 1918 election, and anti-communism became part of its platform"* (Klugmann, *op cit,* p.186). This was shortly to be reflected in Labour's programme entitled *'International Peace and National Liberation'*, issued on the eve of the November 1922 election, the contents of which, with their support for imperial policy in India and Ireland, opposition to the withdrawal of British troops from Germany, and so on and so forth, made Labour indistinguishable from the Liberals and hardly distinguishable from the Tories. No wonder, the *New Statesman* of Oct 23, 1922, wrote that, *"on all questions of foreign policy and on nearly all questions of domestic policy, there is no serious division of opinion between the Liberals and the Labour Party".*

That old fox of the British bourgeoisie, Lloyd George, expressed his satisfaction, stating: *"whoever wins, there should be no detriment to the national interest from revolutionary measures ... "* (Electoral Address to the National Liberal Assembly, Oct 25, 1922).

Notwithstanding all this, the British ruling class feared substantial electoral advances by Labour. Why? The explanation is to be sought, not in the leadership, but in the pressure of its working-class supporters. In the end, this fear was to prove groundless, as was amply demonstrated by Labour when it formed its first administration at the beginning of 1924, following the Election of December 1923. In the 1922 Election, however, Labour, having polled 4.2 million votes, and won 142 seats (compared with 59 in December 1918), as against the Liberals' 117 seats, established itself as His Majesty's Official Opposition in the House of Commons - and a very loyal and servile one at that.

Even before the first Labour Government, Labour had given sufficient proof of its imperialist credentials on two questions so vital to British imperialism, namely, Ireland and India. On Ireland, Labour stood for an Irish Constituent Assembly subject to two provisos, that is, there must be protection for the minority and Ireland must not become a military or naval threat to Britain. Shorn of all euphemism, it stood for the partition of Ireland and the continued British military presence in that country.

As regards India, Labour stood for its continued subjugation. India was so important to British imperial interests, that she was rightly, and without any exaggeration, regarded as the jewel in the imperial crown. In his remarkable book, 'India Today', R.Palme Dutt, on the basis of irrefutable statistics, calculates that by 1913-14 India was worth £78 million per annum to Britain. Out of this total, £28 million was accounted for by British trade, manufacturing and shipping profits, the remainder represented income from British capital investments, which by this time stood at £500 million, and direct tribute in the form of home charges (£9 million a year at this time). To get an idea of the enormity of these sums, one has to realise that in present-day terms they represent £8 billion a year, if not more. By 1921-22, India was worth £146.5 million a year to Britain (*ibid*, pp.144-148). Labour was in no hurry to kill the goose, which accounted for such a lot of golden eggs in the imperial basket. In addition, India provided one million soldiers to help British imperialism defend 'democracy', which excluded, among others, the vast masses of India, against the onslaught of German imperialism - a war that cost the Indian tax-payer £300 million (£30 billion in today's terms).

Labour defended British imperialist interests in India, as it did elsewhere, for it could not defend its own privileges - privileges of the aristocracy of labour - without defending the empire. The defence of the former, was dependent upon, and required, the defence of the latter. As history was to prove, Labour would be prepared to commit any crime in the defence of these twin interests. No crime, no brutality, no infamy was to be too much in Labour's defence of these interests. 'Forgetful' of Britain's lack of a democratic mandate to rule India, in the 1918 General Election, Labour opposed full responsible government for India on the pretext that, as very few Indians understood the meaning and significance of the vote, the result would be to place the government in the hands of a tiny minority.

In the General Election of December 1923, Labour won 192 seats as against the Tories' 258. However, with the Liberals, who had won 157 seats, Labour held a majority in the House of Commons. With the Liberals agreeing to support a minority Labour Government, Labour formed its first ever administration. The very composition of the Cabinet gave a clue, if ever there was any doubt on this score, of things to follow. With MacDonald as Prime Minister and Foreign Secretary, Snowden as Chancellor of the Exchequer, Henderson at the Home Office and Thomas at the Colonial Office, the rabidly anti-communist, incurably anti-working class, and born lackeys of British imperialism were securely ensconced in the key departments of government. As to the rest, "... *fourteen members of the Labour Cabinet had served imperialism, directly or indirectly, in the capacity of members of previous government, departments of state, governors of colonies or diplomatic missionaries"* (Klugmann, *op cit*, p.251).

Philip Snowden himself most aptly painted this vivid picture of the composition of the first Labour Cabinet and the reassuring effect of its announcement on the bourgeoisie;

"The publication of the names of the Cabinet had a reassuring effect upon that section of public opinion which had been in terror about the advent of a Labour Government. The most timid Conservatives and the most frightened capitalists took heart from the presence in the Cabinet of men like Lord Parmoor, Lord Chelmsford and Lord Haldane; they could not believe that these men would be the instruments for carrying out the Socialist Revolution" (*An Autobiography*, Vol. II, p.607).

Absolutely correct! Further comment would be superfluous.

First Labour Government

Once in office, Labour got on with the job of defending British imperialism with an unprecedented zeal. Although before the Election, it had opposed the reparations regime imposed by the victors upon the vanquished through the Versailles Treaty, within two days of coming to office Labour, having made a hundred and eighty degree turn, had accepted it. The Labour Cabinet, stuffed full with labour aristocrats, racists and imperialists to their finger tips, very early on made known its brutal determination to defend the empire against revolutionary challenge from the subject peoples - by force if necessary. This is what the Labour Prime Minister, MacDonald, had to say in this regard:

"*I can see no hope in India if it becomes the arena of a struggle between constitutionalism and revolution. No party in Great Britain will be cowed by threats of force or by policies designed to bring Government to a standstill; and if any section in India are under the delusion that is not so, events will sadly disappoint them*" (Quoted in M.N.Roy, *Labour Monthly*, April 1924, p.207; also quoted by R.Palme Dutt, *Empire and War*, in Workers Weekly, 7th March 1924).

Within weeks of the formation of the Labour Government, on February 28, 1924, the Rt.Hon. J.H.Thomas, as this traitor to the cause of the working class had deservedly become, expressed, in a pious tone, on the question of the "*sacred trust of Empire*", the hope that "*it would be realised, when the time came for them to give up the seals of office, that they had not only been mindful of their responsibility, but had done nothing to weaken the position and prestige of this great Empire*" (Quoted in *Workers' Weekly*, March 7, 1924).

Three months later, Thomas reiterated that the Labour Government: "*intended above all else to hand to their successors one thing when they gave up the seals of office and that was the general recognition of the fact that they were proud and jealous of, and were prepared to maintain the Empire*" (*The Times*, May 16, 1924).

Sidney Olivier, a Fabian, and now in charge of the India Office, made his opposition to Indian self-rule in these flagrantly racist, smugly arrogant and imperialist terms: "*The programme of constitutional democracy ... was not native to India. ... It was impossible for the Indian people or Indian politicians to leap at once into the saddle and administer an ideal constitution. .. The right of British statesmen, public servants, merchants and industrialists to be in India today was the fact that they had made the India of today, and that no Home Rule or national movement could have been possible in India had it not been for their work*" (Quoted in M.N.Roy, *op cit*, p.209).

That this same worthy Fabian, who from 1907 to 1913 was the Governor of Jamaica, had scant regard for the dignity of the colonised peoples anywhere, is made patently clear by this remark of his: "*I have said that the West Indian negro is not fit for complete democratic citizenship in a Constitution of modern Parliamentary form, and I should certainly hold the same opinion with respect to any African native community*" (Quoted in F.Lee, *Fabianism and Colonialism - the life and thought of Lord Sidney Olivier*, p.117).

Nor was Olivier alone in these sentiments. The leading lights of the Fabian Society, the chief theoreticians of the Fabian Society, as well as of the ILP and Labour Party, the people who drafted Clause IV, the Webbs, were shockingly racist. In *Labour and the New Social Order*, written in 1918 by Sidney Webb, at a time when nearly 500 million people groaned under the heel of British colonialism, we find hypocritical characterisation of this vast colonial empire as a *"great Commonwealth"*, which could not be regarded as *"an Empire in the old sense, but a Britannic Alliance"*, for *"the maintenance and ... progressive development"* of which Labour stood firmly committed. The Webbs had already expressed their racist views in 1913 in the *New Statesman*, in terms even more blatant, in connection with the falling birth-rate among the whites:

"Into the scarcity thus created in particular districts, in particular sections of the labour market, or in particular social strata, there rush the offspring of the less thrifty, the less intellectual, the less foreseeing of races and classes - the unskilled casual labourers of our great cities, the races of Eastern or Southern Europe, the negroes, the Chinese - possibly resulting, as already in parts of the USA, in such a heterogeneous and mongrel population that democratic self-government, or even the effective application of the policy of a national minimum of civilised life, will become increasingly unattainable. If anything like this happens, it is difficult to avoid the melancholy conclusion that, in some cataclysm that it is impossible for us to foresee, that civilisation characteristic of the Western European races may go the way of half a dozen other civilisations that have within historic times preceded it; to be succeeded by a new social order developed by one or other of the coloured races, the negro, the kaffir or the Chinese " (Quoted in F.Lee, *op cit*, pp.189-90).

Almost the first act of the Labour Government was to stage a **political** trial - the notorious Cawnpore trial - in an endeavour to suppress the emerging, if still weak, Communist Party of India, which represented a mortal danger to British colonial rule and its imperialist interests in India. Eight leading Indian communists, including Dange, Muzaffer Ahmed, Shaukat Usmani and Das Gupta, were arrested and charged with attempting *"to use the workers' and peasants' associations to secure the complete separation of India from Great Britain, with such an economic programme as could easily appeal to ignorant people"*, and with conspiring *"to organise a working-class party in India, and so deprive the King of his Sovereignty"*. After the trial in an obscure District Court, four of them were sentenced to four years' imprisonment each, on the basis of the evidence of police agents. The only crime of the accused was that they were communists!

As regards the Middle East, the First Labour Government went on to further stabilise the gains secured by British Imperialism at the Versailles Conference, refusing at the same time to entertain the legitimate claims of Egypt over the Suez Canal. Within six months of the formation of the Labour Government, Iraqi tribal villages were being subjected to aerial bombardment on the instructions of Labour's Secretary of State for Air, Lord Manson. A few days earlier, in his reply to a question in the House of Commons on 30 June from Sir Samuel Hoare as to whether Labour's policy in Iraq was not identical with that of the previous Tory administration, the Under-Secretary for Air, Mr Leach, answered thus: *"I cannot honestly say we have made any change in the policy of the late Government"* (Quoted in *Workers' Weekly*, July 4, 1924).

With regard to China, the Labour Government supported the Canton Merchant Corps' rebellion (August-October 1924) against Dr Sun Yat-sen's nationalist Canton Government, which was striking revolutionary blows against warlordism, feudalism, comprador capitalism and foreign imperialism alike. Ostensibly organised under the leadership of Chen Lien-po, a comprador capitalist of the British-owned Hong Kong and Shanghai Bank, the real power of the 'Merchant Corps' was none other than British imperialism, or more correctly Labour imperialism of the First Labour Government.

From the beginning to the end, the imperialist record of the Labour Government was flawlessly consistent. In its final week in office before the General Election of October 9, 1924, which ousted it from office, the Labour Government authorised the Indian colonial administration to promulgate the notorious Bengal Special Ordinances, which gave the authorities arbitrary powers of indefinite internment or imprisonment by executive order, without specific accusation, trial or judicial sentence. All the major nationalist leaders of Bengal were arrested under these Ordinances. Perhaps the following quotation from J.R.Clynes could justly be used as an epitaph on the tomb, not only of the first, but also of each subsequent, Labour Government. Answering the accusation that British Labour had a disrupting influence in the Empire, he maintained that on the contrary:

"In the same period of years, no Conservative or Liberal Government has done more than we did to knit together the great Commonwealth of Nations which Britain calls her Empire. ... Far from wanting to lose our colonies, we are trying to keep them" (*Memoirs*, Vol II, 1924-37, pp.54-55).

Industrial Front

On the industrial front in Britain itself, all the major disputes in that short period involving railwaymen, shipyard workers, dockers, London traffic workers, workers at Wembley, miners, builders, etc. represent nothing but a succession of defeats or unsatisfactory settlements produced by the united front of the employers, the capitalist media, and the reactionary Labour leadership fully supported by the Labour Government.

To the normal threats and cajolery practised by all bourgeois governments in an attempt to seek resolution of industrial disputes to the satisfaction of the employers, now a new form of blackmail was introduced, namely, the damaging effects of any strike on the Labour Government. This combination of moral blackmail with the threat of the use of troops, sailors, police and the Emergency Powers Act (EPA), caused even the reactionary Ernest Bevin, during the February 1924 Dockers Strike, to declare:

"The Union had in mind in the latter stages of the negotiations the earnest appeal of the Prime Minister to make a just peace and an honourable settlement. I wish it had been a Tory Government in office. We would not have been frightened by their threats" (Quoted in *Workers' Weekly*, April 4, 1924).

The year 1924 had commenced amid a revival of working-class militancy and determination to halt and reverse the defeats and retreats of the previous years. The result, however, was a succession of defeats. James Klugmann correctly remarks: *"The employers' activities, the outcries of the press, the betrayal of right-wing trade-union leaders - this was nothing new. But what was new was that the workers, for the first time in Britain, saw Social Democracy in office. They saw a Labour Government denouncing their strikes, demanding that they return to work, supporting the employers on committee after committee, enquiry after enquiry, threatening them with the use of troops and blacklegs, invoking and even using the infamous EPA"* (op cit, p.265).

Following as it always did the reformist theory of the 'neutrality' of the capitalist state, it goes without saying that the Labour Government did not even attempt to make any changes in the departments of state, their composition or method of functioning. In regard to Ramsay MacDonald's conduct of the Foreign Office, a commentator justly remarked that he came, he saw, he was conquered. The obsequiousness with which the Labour ministers, including MacDonald, responded to the establishment, the awe with which they held it, is breathtaking. The role of the armed forces in strike-breaking, the use of the secret police against the labour movement and the Emergency Powers Act were left intact.

As early as the end of April 1924, the Government's abandonment of working-class interests in the internal, foreign and colonial spheres had become so manifestly clear that the Executive Committee of the CPGB felt obliged to issue a Manifesto entitled *'Future of the Labour Government - A Call to All Workers'*, in which it correctly stated: *"... In every direction the Labour Government has shown itself the servant of the bourgeoisie. ... Labour Cabinet Ministers have become the missionaries of a new imperialism. They brag of the glory of Empire. Armaments and coercion have become commonplace with them".*

The Labour Government having done its dirty work in the service of British imperialism, it was time for the ruling class to get rid of it on some pretext of the other. In connection with the withdrawal, under some pressure from the labour movement, of criminal proceedings against J.R.Campbell for incitement to mutiny, the Tories and Liberals joined forces to defeat the Government. On October 8, Sir Robert Horne moved a censure motion against the Government. A Liberal amendment, which called for the appointment of a Select Committee to investigate and report on the circumstances leading up to the withdrawal of proceedings against Campbell received 364 votes, while for the Tory censure motion there were 198. As MacDonald treated it as a question of confidence, the Government fell.

As the Election Manifesto of the CPGB for the October 1924 Election correctly stated, the Labour Government had been put into office to do the dirty work on behalf of British capitalism on issues of internal and external policy - a task which it performed in a manner most loyal and servile. Said the Manifesto:

"Sheltering behind the plea of being in a minority, it did exactly what a capitalist government might have done. It evicted unemployed, overawed strikes by threatening to use the Emergency Powers Act, arrested and spied on Communists, strengthened the Navy and Air Force, shot down and imprisoned workers and peasants in India, Mesopotamia, Sudan and Egypt. In its negotiations with Soviet Russia, it defended the interests of British capitalists, not of British workers. ... Worst of all, it carried through the infamous Dawes Report[1] ...".

In concluding this section, it must be said that for a short nine-month period, representing the entire life of the First Labour Government, these achievements in the service of British imperialism were no mean feat. In government, as out of government, Labour proved its fitness to govern on behalf of British imperialism. The exposure that Lenin had spoken of in 1920, thus took place during these nine months of 1924. By 1925, Labour's conversion to Empire Socialism was complete and irrevocable.

---

1   The Dawes Report was concerned with reparations to be paid by Germany for damage in the First World War.

IV

Labour Comes Out Unmistakably as the Third Capitalist Party

The General Strike 1926

After the fall of the first Labour Government, the most important issue to confront the British working class was the General Strike of 1926. The TUC leadership, against its own will, and most reluctantly, was forced to call the General Strike. For nine days, two million workers, at great personal expense and hardship, had downed tools, not in furtherance of their own interests, but in support of the miners who had been locked out for refusing to submit to a wage cut imposed by the employers. Just as the strike began to gain strength, the TUC leadership, in total betrayal of the working class, called it off, thus leaving the miners to battle on single-handedly for another seven months before hunger forced defeat on them. Meanwhile, in the aftermath of the General Strike, humiliatingly savage agreements were forced on the railwaymen, transport workers, printers and seamen on their return to work.

The General Strike failed because, first, the TUC and the Labour Party leadership refused to turn it into a political struggle; in fact the General Council of the TUC *"feared like the plague to admit the inseparable connection between the economic struggle and the political struggle"* (Stalin, *CW*, Vol.8, p.174). In direct contrast to this the Conservative Government, from the outset, correctly treated the general Strike as a fact of tremendous political importance, which could only be defeated by measures of a political character, that is, by invoking the authority of the crown and parliament, and by the mobilisation of the army and the police. Secondly, the General Strike failed because, far from seeking international support and solidarity, the TUC leadership spurned all such help from precisely such quarters as were the most genuine supporters of this gigantic strike of the British workers. Thus it was that the General Council refused to accept financial assistance from the workers of the USSR, who had, in response to the call of the All-Union Central Committee of Trade Unions (AUCCTU), made at the latter's meeting of May 5th, 1926, decided to contribute one-quarter of a day's earnings in support of the British workers. The same day, the AUCCTU, remitted 250,000 rubles to the British TUC General Council. Two days later, on May 7, the AUCCTU sent to the General Council two million rubles collected by the Soviet proletariat, only to be informed on May 9 of the General Council's decision to refuse acceptance of this assistance.

The spineless treachery of the TUC and Labour leadership was fully matched by the behaviour and actions of the Second International and the Amsterdam Federation of Trade Unions, who, while passing platonic resolutions in support of the Strike, refused to give any meaningful financial assistance to it. Only the equivocal conduct of these two bodies can explain the fact that all the trade unions of Europe and America donated a mere one-eighth of the amount which the Soviet proletariat found it possible to afford to the British proletariat. In addition, far from stopping the transport of coal, the Amsterdam Federation literally acted as a strike-breaker.

The British General Strike proved conclusively, if such proof was needed, that in any major confrontation between the proletariat and the bourgeoisie, between labour and capital, the trade union and Labour leadership would unfailingly betray the cause of the proletariat and desert to the side of the enemy. It proved conclusively, too, that international Social Democracy could always be relied upon to act as a reliable friend of international imperialism in the form of a Trojan horse within the working-class movement.

Lesson Drawn by TUC-Labour leadership from the General Strike

If the CPGB at the time correctly drew the above conclusion from the events of the General Strike, the lesson drawn by the TUC and Labour leaders from the same happenings was just to the opposite; namely, *'Never Again'* would they be party to such an enterprise which they had not wanted in the first place, and which they had called off at the earliest opportune moment. Only the cooperation of the workers with the capitalists, argued these traitors to the working class, in the reorganisation and rationalisation of industry, aimed at increased productivity, could ensure trade union recognition and higher wages. With the logic of servitors as their guide, the TUC leaders entered into discussions with an influential group of employers headed by Sir Alfred Mond, the founder of ICI, on questions such as rationalisation and of industrial strife, that is, on questions of redundancy, speed-up and wage cuts - all this at a time when Britain, like the rest of the capitalist world, was firmly and inexorably heading for the worst economic crisis it had ever experienced.

In the aftermath of the General Strike, for its part, the Labour Party too reaffirmed its faith in the gradual parliamentary road to socialism and determined never to take any kind of direct action. From now on, persuading the middle-class voter, rather than leading the working class, was to be higher still on its agenda. Not surprisingly, therefore, the Labour representatives on the Government (Blanesborough) Committee jointly signed a majority report, advocating cuts in unemployment benefit.

Communists an Obstacle

However, there was one chief obstacle to the pursuit of this policy of docility and class-collaboration by the TUC and Labour leadership, to wit, the Communist Party. Although at the end of 1926, the CPGB was still very young (6 years of age), with a membership of only 7,900, it enjoyed a disproportionately wide influence in the working-class movement, since it had initiated and led several important movements such as the Minority Movement (which acted as an instrument for trade-union activists to propagate militant policies) and the National Unemployed Workers' Committee Movement (which mobilised the unemployed with the slogan '*Work or Full Maintenance*'). In addition, there were 1,500 Communists inside the Labour Party as individual members of the latter. Communists could still be elected by their trade unions as delegates to the Labour organisations, including to the Annual Conference of the Labour Party. Thus the CPGB and the Communists, who acted as a magnet for attracting support from non-communist militant workers, including members of the Labour Party, were a terrible nuisance, to which the latter was determined to put a stop. So, to deal with this menace, while the Labour leaders got on with expelling the 'trouble-makers' from the Labour Party, the TUC General Council devoted its undivided attention to smashing the Minority Movement and to preventing the election of Communists to trade-union offices.

Although the decision to bar Communists from individual membership of the Labour Party had been taken at the 1924 Annual Conference of the Labour Party (and reaffirmed at the autumn 1925 Liverpool Conference) and the trade unions asked not to nominate Communists as delegates to Labour organisations, there were serious problems in the way of its implementation. For at the end of 1926, out of the CPGB's total membership of 7,900, as many as 1,544 were still individual members of the Labour Party, and another 242 were trade-union delegates to Labour organisations. In the aftermath of the General Strike, the Labour Party felt obliged to initiate a process of disaffiliation of all those local Labour parties who refused to expel those of their members who were also members of the Communist Party, with the result that between 1926 and 1929, as many as 27 such local organisations were declared illegal and replaced by 'official' parties. Herbert Morrison was the chief witch-hunter and the top of his hit-list was the Battersea Party which had the honourable distinction of selecting as their local MP Shapurji Saklatwala who, in addition to being a Communist, was the first Indian ever to enter the House of Commons. Battersea Party was disaffiliated and replaced by an 'official' party after the former, in defiance of Morrison's *diktat* that it expel its Communist members, had refused to do so. At the time Saklatwala made the apt observation that *"the people who have started rival Labour parties in Battersea are the very ones who are always complaining that the Communists are 'splitting the movement'. Here we have an example of the lengths to which the official clique are prepared to go in their efforts to show to the bosses that the Labour Party means no harm to them"* (Sunday Worker, 11 July, 1926).

Witch-Hunt Extended

Soon the campaign to expel Communists was extended to those who wanted to co-operate and work with the Communists, the latter being characterised by Morrison as *"elements it was not desirable to mix with"* (Quoted in Maureen Branson, *History of the Communist Party of Great Britain 1927-1941*, p.8). Scores of prominent Labour Party activists who associated with either the Left-Wing Movement, the Minority Movement or the International Class Prisoners' Aid, were expelled from the Labour Party. Undeterred by protests from its own radical members, at the 1928 Labour Party Annual Conference, its National Executive introduced a series of 'loyalty clauses' debarring trade unions from electing communists as delegates to Labour Party meetings - nationally or locally. From now on, not only Communists, but non-communist members of the Left-Wing Movement, were barred from sharing platforms at meetings convened by Labour Parties. In 1929, the Labour Party went on to elaborate these 'loyalty clauses' so as to exclude members of organisations 'ancillary or subsidiary' to the CPGB, followed shortly afterwards by an Executive circular listing seven such organisations: the Left-Wing Movement, the Minority Movement, the National Unemployed Workers' Committee Movement (NUWCM), the League Against Imperialism, Workers' International Relief, International Class War Prisoners' Aid, and Friends of Soviet Russia. As a result, no member of any of these organisations could either belong to the Labour Party or be elected as a delegate to Labour Party meetings.

TUC's Attempts at Crushing Working-Class Resistance

Simultaneously with the above happenings in the Labour Party, the TUC leadership got on with the task of smashing the Minority Movement (MM) which had been established at the initiative of the CPGB in 1924 for co-ordinating militant movements in a number of industries. It was affiliated to the Red International of Labour Unions (RILU), the latter having been founded in 1921 as a radical antidote to the class-collaborationist International Federation of Trade Unions. In a pre-1926 leaflet the Minority Movement declared: *"Most of the Unions today are supporters of the capitalist system. We hold that it is the duty of the Unions to stoutly resist the continuous encroachments of the Employing Class and aim definitely at the OVERTHROW OF THE CAPITALIST SYSTEM"* (quoted in *ibid*, p.11).

In view of this, it is not to be surprised at that the TUC General Secretary, Walter Citrine, hated the Minority Movement. In December 1927, in a series of articles, later to be issued as a pamphlet with the title *'Democracy or Disruption'*, he set out to attack the Minority Movement. Writing in the pages of the journal 'Labour', he argued that the trade-union movement should run *"in the direction of making the workers' organisations an integral part of the economic machinery of society"*, for to allow the trade unions to be used as instruments of social upheaval would be *"fatal to our hopes of ordered progress"*. In contrast, the Communists wanted *"to capture the trade-union movement and exploit it for a revolutionary subversive purpose"*, and the Minority Movement, under the leadership of the CPGB, had as its purpose *"to set the rank and file of the working-class movement in bitter opposition to its elected and responsible representatives"*. Taking due notice of Citrine's call, the Executives of several unions went on to bar Communists or Minority Movement members from holding office or being elected as delegates to Labour organisations.

In a parallel development, the TUC intensified its efforts to isolate the NUWCM. By the autumn of 1927, the TUC had severed its links with this body. In consequence of which the November 1927 Miners' March from South Wales to London, to draw attention to the appalling conditions of the unemployed miners, took place, with the Communist Wal Hannington as its chief marshall, in the teeth of bitter opposition on the part of the TUC. The TUC circulated local trades councils along the route not to organise reception and hospitality for the miners.

The 1928 Swansea TUC Congress confirmed the decision to outlaw the Minority Movement. After a persistent and shamelessly unprincipled attack, lasting two years, the leadership of the Labour Party and the TUC succeeded in hounding Communists and non-communist militants from the Labour Party and the trade unions.

External Policy: China

In the international arena, the Labour leadership supported with limitless zeal all the brutal and bloodthirsty actions of British Imperialism. When in August 1926, the British Navy subjected the Chinese town of Wanhsien, on the banks of the Yangtse, to bombardment, killing 500 people, MacDonald gave his party's full support, for which he received the grateful thanks of the Conservative Sir Austen Chamberlain. A few months later, the Shanghai strike of 1927, aimed at reclaiming foreign concessions in China, spread to Hankow and Canton, and developed into a full-scale insurrection. It was brutally suppressed by the traitorous Chiang-Kai-shek clique with the full support of British and Japanese troops. Tom Mann, on his return from a visit to China in 1927, expressed the anger of the Chinese masses at this imperialist aided and abetted massacre, which claimed the lives of hundreds of thousands of Chinese workers and peasants, in the following words:

"They [the Chinese people - HB] *have no illusions about the Chinese capitalists, but the greatest curse, they declare, is the foreign imperialists, and in this they are undoubtedly right; and of all the imperialist forces in China beyond any question Great Britain is the worst" (Labour Monthly,* August 1927).

And the actions of this the worst imperialist power had the wholehearted and unreserved support of the Labour Party.

External Policy: India

Towards the end of 1927, having rushed through Parliament the necessary enabling legislation, Lord Birkenhead, the Tory Secretary of State for India, set up the Simon Commission to review the progress of the Montague-Chelmsford reforms[1]. Although Indians had been excluded from the Commission, Mac-

---

1 The British enacted the Montague-Chelmsford Reforms in 1919 to attempt to counter the rising movement for national self-determination in India, following the inspiration of the 1917 Russian Revolution. The Reforms, along the lines of so-called 'Dyarchy' in the Provinces, or

Donald, over-ruling even the objections of Labour's NEC, secured the appointment of Clement Attlee and Steven Walsh (an odious imperialist) as Labour nominees on the Commission. This could not but inflame Indian opinion. Not surprisingly, therefore, the Simon Commission's arrival in India on Friday, 3 February 1928, was greeted by a general strike and mammoth demonstrations. With police firing on the demonstrators, wholesale arrests, the army parading in the streets of the principal cities, India was overnight turned into an armed camp. The Indian working class played the leading role in opposing the Simon Commission, displaying in the process a degree of political clarity not seen even in some advanced imperialist countries. Shapurji Saklatwala aptly observed, in his report for the *Sunday Worker* of 5 February 1928, that:

"It has been well-known for some time that the Commission would have a hostile reception from the Indian workers, who view it as the latest weapon of British imperialism. ... When the Bombay workers burned the effigy of MacDonald in the streets along with that of Lord Birkenhead and others, they showed that they viewed the Labour Party as nothing more or less than the willing hirelings of British imperialism" (Quoted in Sehri Saklatwala, *The Fifth Commandment*, pp.391-92).

Labour - the Third Capitalist Party

In the light of the conduct of the Labour Party in the years spanning the period between the first and the second Labour Governments, when Labour had stuck to a bi-partisan approach in the field of internal and external politics alike, when it had opposed every working-class mobilisation at home and supported with barely disguised glee every brutal imperialist suppression of the revolutionary national liberation movements abroad, notably in China and India, when it had tenaciously opposed all united action with the CPGB and made vicious use of 'loyalty clauses', bans and proscriptions against the Communists as a means of stifling all working-class mass movements, or avoiding any involvement with them, the CPGB was obliged to review its attitude towards the Labour Party. In particular, it had to answer three important questions. These were: First, should the CPGB, now being hounded out of the Labour Party and the trade unions, continue its struggle to stay inside it? Sec-

---

division of portfolios between British and Indian ministers, also attempted to create divisions within the Indian bourgeois-nationalist class.

ond, in the light of Labour's home and foreign policy and practice, should the Communist Party go on calling for the election of a Labour Government? Third, should the CPGB put up candidates now that the Communist candidates could no longer be adopted by local Labour parties?

Harry Pollitt and Palme Dutt, among others, led the fight for a reversal of the Party's line on all these issues, arguing that whereas in 1920 Labour's programme still incorporated many working-class demands and its constitution allowed affiliated organisations to have their own programmes and policy, by 1928 it had become a third capitalist party, had *"surrendered socialism"*; while its disciplinary measures made it impossible for affiliated partied to propagate their own programme. They therefore proposed that the CPGB discontinue its attempts to affiliate to the Labour Party, refuse to vote for Labour candidates unless the latter agreed to support the party's policy, and stand candidates against people like MacDonald and Henderson. Although representing, at the time, the minority of the Central Committee of the CPGB, the Pollitt-Dutt viewpoint won the day with some considerable help from the analysis of the European scene made by the Comintern. According to this analysis, being in the grip of a severe economic crisis and intensified competition, all the capitalist countries were pushing ahead at a furious pace with rationalisation, resulting in the growth of trusts and a tendency of the latter to merge with the state. The effects of this rationalisation and trustification on the working class manifested themselves in ruthless exploitation, closures of vast enterprises and chronic unemployment on an unprecedented scale. In most European countries Social-Democracy led the workers. While preaching socialism, everywhere the Social-Democratic parties were in reality collaborating with capitalism. Although several European countries had by then had the experience of Social-Democratic Governments, far from bringing socialism nearer, they had only served to strengthen capitalism and betray the working class.

Faced with this stark reality, the CPGB at its 1928 Congress justly denounced the Labour Party for having *"come out unmistakably as the third capitalist party"* - a characterisation to which the Trotskyite social-democrats of the SWP, Cliff and Gluckstein, take such a strong objection, dubbing it as the *"ultra-left insanity"* of the Communist party. On the eve of the 1929 General Election, the CPGB, in its pamphlet *'Class Against Class'* - the programme with which it entered that election - elaborated further on its 1928 statement. Declaring itself in favour of the dictatorship of the proletariat, the programme went on:

SOCIAL DEMOCRACY & THE ATITUDE OF THE PROLETARIAT TOWARDS IT

"The Communist Party ... enters the General Election ... to reveal to the working class the nature of the present crisis, to expose the sham of parliamentary democracy maintained by the Tories, Liberals and Labour alike. ... Three parties ... appeal to you in the name of the 'NATION' One party - the Communist Party - appeals to you in the name of the working class. No Party can serve two masters. No Party can serve the 'nation' so long as the nation is divided into two warring classes. ... No Party can serve the robbers and the robbed. ... The Communist Party is the Party of the workers, the oppressed" (p.7).

Having characterised the Labour Party as *"the third capitalist party"* (p.8) the programme goes on to explain the reason for the CPGB's changed attitude to it thus:

"The situation in 1929 is entirely different from that of the years prior to the General Strike and the Labour Government of 1924. In the years immediately after the war, the Labour Party, in spite of its anti-working class leaders, was forced by the pressure of the workers into action against the Tories and the Liberals, e.g., threatened general strike against war on Russia, repudiation of the Versailles Treaty. ... The Labour Party also had not yet become a closely-knit party with a single discipline. It was a federation ... offering facilities for criticism from within" (p.9).

And further:

"The Labour Government [of 1924 - HB] *exposed the Labour Party leadership completely. ... The 'minority' Labour Government was nothing more than a coalition with the Tories and Liberals. The Labour leaders 'led' the General Strike only to betray it in the face of the challenge of the state. The General Strike raised the question of power. The Labour Party leadership ... stood for capitalist power against working-class power, but from within. ... They developed the offensive against the Communist Party and the revolutionary workers who stood for working-class struggle for power. They tied the trade unions to the Tories and Liberals under the banner of Mondism and transformed the Labour Party from a federal organisation to a single party with a capitalist programme under the banner of 'Empire and Mondism'. It is now no longer possible for the Communist Party or the trade unions to bring pressure to bear on the Labour Party from within. It is a completely disciplined capitalist party"* (p.9).

In other words, with its accession to office, Labour had rid itself of its federal structure, and with it of all susceptibility to socialism and working-class influence.

In the preface which he provided for the first English edition of Lenin's writings on Britain (dated January 1934), Harry Pollitt was to go on to endorse the CPGB's above stance in the following words:

"Just now ... it is a common thing to hear certain 'left' leaders defending their support of the Labour Party and remaining affiliated to it on the ground that they are carrying out the advice given [by Lenin] *to the British communists in 1920.*

"They never dare to state to the workers, what the conditions were that Lenin attached to the application of the Communist Party for *affiliation to the Labour Party. Lenin insisted that it was only permissible to fight for this as long as there was no compromise on revolutionary principles, and with the fullest freedom of agitation and propaganda and criticism"*

He added that the section in the book dealing with Lenin's attitude on this question *"will reveal the unscrupulous opportunism of this school of 'Leftists', who precisely because of their 'left' language deceive the workers, and retard their coming to Communism. At the same time they will explain the political reasons why the reformist leaders of all kinds hate the insistence of the Communists upon freedom of criticism, the use of which so powerfully exposes the anti-working class policy of the reformist leaders and strengthens the workers in their fight against all their enemies".*

Thus it was that the CPGB, for the first time since its formation in 1920, came to the conclusion that the Labour Party had become a closely-knit third capitalist party with a single discipline, no longer susceptible to working-class influence; that it was, therefore, useless trying to work for the election of a Labour Government and equally useless trying to gain affiliation to the Labour Party. It was far better to build a real working class - communist - alternative. These decisions reached by the CPGB were correct, based as they were on sound economic and political analysis of the British reality and the attitude of the Labour Party to it. To describe these conclusions as *"ultra-insanity"* as do the ultra-social democrats, namely, the Trotskyites Cliff and Gluckstein, is to reveal one's incurable proclivity for social-democratic offal, verging on cretinism.

Although the CPGB was to revert in 1935 to its earlier policy of gaining affiliation to the Labour Party, there was little basis, in principle or in reality, for such a change of stance. And the Labour Party's rejection of the CPGB's application only made this all too painfully clear. After the General Election of

November 1935, which returned the National Government to office with a big majority under Stanley Baldwin, the CPGB applied for affiliation. In its formal application for affiliation, dated 25 November 1935, the CPGB pointed out that MacDonald, Snowden and Thomas, the most bitter opponents of communist affiliation had since gone over to the enemy camp; that the return of the National Government could only mean intensified oppression of the working class at home and support for Nazi Germany abroad, and that its defeat demanded united action. Besides, went on the CPGB, how could the Labour Party claim to represent the united front of the working class, if it excluded *"workers and organisations which hold the revolutionary standpoint"*.

In its communication of 27 January 1936, the NEC of the Labour Party rejected the CPGB's application stating that no circumstances had arisen as to justify a departure from the decision of 1922; that there was an *"irreconcilable"* hostility between the Labour Party's adherence to *"democracy"* and the Communist Party's commitment to *"dictatorship"*; that the advent of fascist dictatorships abroad was attributable to communist activities which had split the working class; that, since the Communist Party merely aimed at using the Labour Party facilities as an instrument for the propagation of communism, any weakening on the part of the Labour Party in the defence of democracy would only help the forces of reaction and hinder the victory of socialism in Britain.

Following this rejection, the CPGB launched a campaign for affiliation. By September 1936, more than 1,400 organisations (including 831 trade-union branches and 407 local Labour Party organisations) had passed resolutions in support of Communist affiliation. So alarmed were the TUC leaders that their 'Black Circulars' had failed to check the growth of communist influence, that in July 1936 the National Council of Labour - a body representing the TUC, the NEC of the Labour Party and the Parliamentary Labour Party (PLP) - had felt obliged to issue a document entitled *British Labour and Communism*, in which the by now familiar objections to Communist affiliation were reiterated. It was asserted in particular that Communist revolutionary activities had *"stimulated fascist and Nazi reaction in some countries with disastrous consequences"*. Not only was the victory of fascism attributed to the communists, but also an attempt was made to equate communism and fascism by presenting both as *"dictatorships"* whose aim was to destroy democracy so zealously guarded by the Labour Party.

Notwithstanding a vigorous campaign by the CPGB, the Labour Party Annual Conference in October 1936, rejected Communist affiliation by a majority of 1,728,000 against 592,000 votes. Hardly anything better could be expected from a rabidly anti-communist and staunchly imperialist party such as the Labour Party - a party which by 1933 had proscribed eleven organisations, including the Relief Committee for the Victims of German Fascism, for being *"ancillary or subsidiary to the Communist party"*. This meant that if a member of the Labour Party belonged to, or actively supported, such an organisation, or spoke from its platform, he could be expelled forthwith. And, any local Labour Party, unwise enough to send a delegate to attend the meetings of such an organisation, faced the threat of disaffiliation. Apart from the one mentioned immediately above, here are the names of the other proscribed organisations: The League Against Imperialism, Left-Wing Movement; Minority Movement; National Unemployed Workers Movement; Workers' International Relief; Friends of Soviet Russia; International Labour Defence; British Anti-War Council; European Workers Anti-Fascist Congress, and the National Charter Campaign Committee.

Labour Government 1929-31

That the CPGB's stance was correct was proved only too well by not only the conduct of the Labour Government of 1929-31, but also by that of every subsequent Labour Government in the sphere of internal and external policy alike.

From the General Election of 31st May 1929, the Labour Party, having received 37.1 per cent of the vote, emerged for the first time as the largest party in the House of Commons and formed the next government.

India and the Second Labour Government

In the wake of the near revolt of the Indian people, which greeted the arrival of the Simon Commission in India, British Imperialism, emboldened by a split in the Indian National Congress (caused entirely by Gandhi's moderate, dilatory, bourgeois tactics, which gave the Government until 31st December 1929 to accept the Congress demand for self-rule), struck, and, at one fell swoop, removed the entire working-class leadership of the Indian masses. The most prominent leaders of the working class, including the entire leadership of the Red Flag Union, were arrested and taken to Meerut for trial on the charge of *"attempting to deprive the King-Emperor of the sovereignty of India"*. Labour, in opposition, refused to support the demand for the release of the Meerut detainees. On coming to power in May 1929, Labour continued the policy of imperialist plunder and oppression, albeit with a veneer of socialist phrases.

Compelled by the Government's failure to respond to Gandhi's deadline of the end of December 1929, the latter was obliged to make a modicum of protest. So Gandhi, accompanied by a select group of his followers, led a march on Dandi by way of protest against the Government's monopoly of salt and as a prelude to his non-cooperation campaign. On 6 April 1930, as Gandhi made salt illegally, the Indian national movement, pent up for so long thanks to Gandhi's infuriatingly collaborationist tactics, burst forth like a volcanic eruption. Peasants in many areas refused to pay land revenue. Revolts broke out in many places. The North-West-Frontier town of Peshawar fell into the hands of the rebels. This is how R.Palme Dutt captures one scene in connection with the incidents in Peshawar:

"*Two platoons of the Second Battalion of the 18th Royal Garhwali Rifles, Hindu troops in the midst of a Moslem crowd, refused the order to fire, broke ranks, fraternised with the crowd, and a number handed over their arms. Immediately after this, the military and the police were withdrawn from Peshawar; from 25 April to 4 May the city was in the hands of the people*" (*India Today*, p.332).

The Government unleashed an unbridled reign of terror. The Simon Commission report of June 1930 made no meaningful concession, and thus served only to exacerbate Indian sentiment. In its endeavour to break the deadlock, the Labour Government of MacDonald convened a 'Round Table Conference', to which were invited, among others, several puppet rulers of the princely states. In return for MacDonald's vague statement about responsible self-government, which committed the Government to nothing, Gandhi was lured to persuade the Congress to call off its agitation and attend the Conference in London. In return the Government agreed to withdraw its ordinances and release 90,000 imprisoned during the previous ten months, except those guilty of 'violence' and 'incitement to violence'. Thus, under this formula, the Meerut detainees and the Garhwali soldiers were excluded from the amnesty - not to mention a group of brilliant Punjabi revolutionaries who were hanged immediately.

The Round Table farce was continued for a year in London, away from the grim reality of the Indian sub-continent where people suffered daily violence, humiliation, oppression and exploitation under the jackboot of British imperialism. No surprise then that a contemporary English revolutionary should have been driven to write:

"*Hanging, flogging, slaying, shooting and bombing attest the efforts of parasitic imperialism to cling to the body of its victim. The Round Table Con-*

ference beside these efforts is like the ceremonial mumblings of the priest that walks behind the hangman" (Robin Page Arnot, *Labour Monthly*, Sept.1930, p.530).

Just as the first (1924) Labour Government had supervised the Cawnpore trial against leading communists, so the second Labour Government saw to it that the rising Indian working-class movement was decapitated through the trial, on trumped-up charges, of leading working-class leaders and the long prison sentences doled out at Meerut. India was too important to British imperialism for its fate to be decided by Indians. And Labour saw to it that the interests of British imperialism were defended with an unprecedented zeal and determination, for on the defence of these interests depended the defence of the privileges of the aristocracy of labour, the upper stratum of the working class, represented by the Labour Party. There were impeccable reasons for the tenacity with which all governments representing British imperialism - Tory, Liberal and Labour - wanted to hold on to India. An issue of the *Manchester Guardian* in 1930 had occasion to refer to the material advantages which accrued to Britain from her Indian colony:

"There are two chief reasons why a self-regarding England may hesitate to relax her control over India. *The first is that her influence in the past depends partly upon her power to summon troops and to draw resources from India in time of need. ... The second is that Great Britain finds in India her best market, and she has one thousand million pounds of capital invested there"* (Quoted in R.Palme Dutt, *India Today*, p.497).

The suppression of the Indian liberation struggle of 1928-31 is the most shameful example of Labour's naked imperialism, for it eliminated the possibility of the Indian working class's leading role in this struggle, which from then on became the preserve of the Indian bourgeoisie, whose most representative spokesman was the Congress grouping led by Gandhi. In this regard one cannot but marvel at the wisdom contained in, and the prophetic nature of, the observation made by W.J.Brown, an ILP member of parliament in a debate in 1930:

"I venture to suggest that we should regard it as a cardinal feature of British policy to carry Gandhi with us, for if we do not, we have to face the alternative to Gandhi, and that is organised violence and revolutionary effort" (Quoted by Clemens Dutt, *Labour Monthly*, June 1930).

Brown's observation was fully confirmed by the biggest Indian industrialist and the chief patron of Gandhi, G.D.Birla, who wrote in his letter of 14

March 1932 to Sir Samuel Hoare, that: *"Gandhiji is the greatest force on the side of peace and order. He alone is responsible for keeping the left in India under check"* (Quoted in R.Palme Dutt, *India Today*).

As early as 2 March 1930, in his letter to Viceroy Irwin, Gandhi himself had, with disarming candour, proclaimed the fight on two fronts, not only against British rule, but also against the internal enemy in India. This conception of the fight on two fronts corresponded to the role of the Indian bourgeoisie, alarmed as it saw the ground slipping from beneath its feet with the growing conflict between the Raj and the masses, compelled to undertake the leadership of the struggle, despite the *"mad risk"* (Gandhi's phrase in his letter to the Viceroy), in order to hold it within bounds of 'reason', i.e. within bourgeois limits. This is what, inter alia, Gandhi wrote to the Viceroy:

"The party of violence is gaining ground and making itself felt. ... It is my purpose to set in motion that force (non-violence) as well against the organised force of the British rule as the unorganised violence force of the growing party of violence. *To sit still would be to give rein to both the forces above mentioned"* (quoted in *ibid*, p.329).

Of all the bourgeois politicians of their time, Gandhi and MacDonald were undoubtedly the most accomplished, shrewd, hypocritically dishonest and, above all, committed to the bourgeois property relations. They were therefore in the best position, if anyone was, to eliminate the leading role of the Indian working class - the 'party of violence' if you please - in the Indian liberation struggle, which leading role alone could have held the promise of the Indian liberation transcending the bounds of bourgeois rule. Alas, it must be admitted, they succeeded.

It is to be hoped that the reader will not regard the following penetrating description of Gandhi given by Palme Dutt as too much of a diversion from the subject.

Notwithstanding *"his personal idiosyncrasies, there was no question that he* [Gandhi - HB] *was the most subtle and experienced politician of the old group, with unrivalled mass prestige which world publicity had now enhanced as the greatest Indian figure; the ascetic defender of property in the name of the most religious and idealist principles of humanity and love of poverty; the invincible metaphysical-theological casuist who could justify and reconcile anything and everything in an astounding tangle of explanations and arguments which in a man of common clay might have been called dishonest quibbling, but in the great ones of the earth like MacDonald or Gandhi is recognised as a* higher plane of spiritual reasoning; the prophet who by his personal saintliness and selflessness could unlock the door to the hearts of the masses where the moderate bourgeois leaders could not hope for a hearing - and the best guarantee of the shipwreck of any mass movement which had the blessing of his association. This Jonah of revolution, this general of unbroken disasters was the mascot of the bourgeoisie in each wave of the developing Indian struggle. ... All hopes of the bourgeoisie (the hostile might say, the hopes of imperialism) were fixed on Gandhi *as the man to ride the waves, to unleash just enough of the mass movement in order to drive a successful bargain, and at the same time to save India from revolution" (India Today, p.*323).

In the Middle East - in Egypt, Iraq and Palestine - Labour continued its bi-partisan policy, namely, its total support for imperialist subjugation of the people of the Middle East. In fact, in regard to Palestine, Labour proved to be more pro-Zionist than any previous British Government. In August 1929, the MacDonald Government suppressed with unprecedented and ruthless brutality a general strike of Palestinian workers and a peasant revolt in the countryside against ceaseless Zionist expropriation of Arab land and increased Jewish immigration.

Thus, one can see that it was not without justification that *The Times* of 15 April, 1930, in this comment should have expressed such confidence in the imperialist credentials of the Labour Government:

"Every far-sighted view of our imperial interests, and of the hope of removing them altogether from party controversy, goes to show how important it is that a Labour government, and no other, should have the handling of the great external problems which are crowding upon us this year - the Naval Conference, the Imperial Conference, Egypt, and above all, India ".

Consequent upon MacDonald's defection, the second Labour Government fell in August 1931. In the autumn General Election, Labour's parliamentary strength was reduced to 52 seats. The General Election of the autumn of 1935 brought a partial recovery for Labour although it returned the National Government with a convincing majority. After 1931 Labour was to remain in opposition until 1940 when the Labour leadership accepted Churchill's invitation to join his war-time Coalition Cabinet. But, in or out of government, in power or in opposition - partisanship on questions of imperial policy at home and abroad continued to be the hallmark of Labour.

On a whole host of issues on the home front, ranging from the struggles of the unemployed and the hunger marchers to the resistance of the poor to means testing, cuts in benefits, and of the tenants to high rents, the fight against Mosley and his British Union of Fascists, the attitude of the Labour Party was characterised by its uncompromising hostility to anything that smacked of direct action in defence of the interests of the working class. Everywhere the Labour Party strove for conciliation, industrial peace and class collaboration. Hence its opposition to such movements as the Minority Movement (which united trade-union activists campaigning for more militant policies), the National Unemployed Workers' Committee Movement (which rallied the unemployed around the slogan 'work or full maintenance'), rank-and-file movements (of which the London Busmen were an outstanding example).

The chief target of Labour's witch hunt was undoubtedly the Communist Party, for the sole reason that it was the only organisation which truly represented the interests of the working class and led the latter, through a number of movements, in resisting the encroachments of capital, which exposed the class collaboration of the Labour Party and TUC leadership, which alone espoused the cause of liberation of the colonial people subjugated by British imperialism, and which alone fought for the defence of the socialist Soviet Union. The stubborn resistance of the Labour leadership to united action with the CPGB, and the bans and proscriptions imposed on Communists, were aimed at stifling mass movements and as a means of avoiding any involvement in them. The Hunger March in the autumn of 1936 against the means test illustrates this point very well indeed. The National Unemployed Workers Movement (NUWM), as the organiser of this March, invited the Labour Party to sponsor the March. The latter refused. The TUC for its part rejected the proposal for industrial action against the means test at its Plymouth Conference in 1936, with Citrine, TUC General Secretary, telling the delegates that it was not *"morally right"* for a section of the community to subvert the will of Parliament by such methods as direct action.

Notwithstanding Labour's opposition, the NUWM organised the March and the marchers' arrival was greeted by a crowd of 250,000 people in Hyde Park, a circumstance which compelled the leader of the PLP, Clement Attlee, to accept an invitation to speak at the rally in Hyde park.

In the international arena, Labour's main concern was the defence of British imperial interests, its vast colonial possessions, and the gigantic oil wealth of the Middle East. In 1940 it joined, without any qualms, the Churchill Cabinet, whose chief pre-occupation was the preservation of the Empire rather than the defeat of fascism. Churchill's persistent refusal to open a second front to

70 SOCIAL DEMOCRACY - THE ENEMY WITHIN

defeat Germany, while the USSR single-handedly fought the entire might of the German army for three whole years, had the full support of Clement Attlee and the rest of the Labour leadership.

V

Labour Since the Second World War

Labour Governments of 1945-51

The record of the Labour Party since the end of the Second World War is no better than its record prior to it. It has continued to furnish daily proof of its impeccable imperialist credentials and its total hostility to the interests of the overwhelming majority of the British working class, let alone the oppressed and super-exploited peoples of Asia, Africa and Latin-America.

The Attlee Governments of 1945-51, which have been portrayed by 'left' Labourites such as Tony Benn and Ken Livingstone, as well as their Trotskyite poodles from the SWP, Militant and such-like outfits, as shining examples of socialism, rested firmly on the twin pillars of alliance with US imperialism for a crusade against communism and the reconstruction of the war-torn British economy at the expense of the colonial peoples inhabiting the British Empire. With commendable candour, Bevin declared:

"I am not prepared to sacrifice the British Empire because I know that if the British Empire fell ... it would mean the standard of life of our constituents would fall considerably" (Quoted by R.Palme Dutt, *The Crisis of Britain*, p.80).

War had almost bankrupted British imperialism. To finance the war it had incurred an external debt of nearly £3,700 million (a sum huge for those days); it had also been forced to liquidate £1,000 million of foreign investment in order to pay for arms purchases from the United States. The resulting fall in invisible earnings, consequent upon the disposal of these foreign assets, meant that the big deficit on trade in visibles could no longer be made up. The problem was exacerbated further still by two factors. First in December 1945, US imperialism terminated the land-lease agreement which had enabled Britain to secure credit on favourable terms, thus forcing the latter to contract a loan of $3,750 million at market rates. Secondly, there was the question of Britain's trade deficit with the US, which at the time stood in the ratio of 5 to 1 in favour of the United States. To solve this problem of dollar scarcity and dollar indebtedness, the 'socialist' Attlee Government turned to the ruthless exploitation of the colonies, especially such high dollar earners as the Gold Coast (Ghana) and Malaya. Had it not been for the intensified exploitation of the colonies, the post-war reconstruction of the British economy would have been a far more hazardous affair, risking social unrest, perhaps even revolutionary upheavals, for it would have to have taken place by relying solely on the exploitation of the British working class. Thus the naked plunder of the colonial people helped to protect the British working class from the worst effects of British imperialism's post-war crisis and the difficulties of reconstruction. Not without reason has one writer stated that "...the Labour Government used the colonies to protect the British consumer from the high social price which continental countries were then paying for their post-war reconstruction. Consciously or not, this was to adopt 'social imperialism' *in an extreme form"* (Fieldhouse in R. Ovendale, ed., *The Foreign Policy of the Labour Governments 1945-51*, p.99).

Not without reason did Oliver Littleton, soon to become Colonial Secretary in the Conservative Government, observe tauntingly during the autumn 1951 Election Campaign that:

"The Government claims that the dependent territories were exploited in the past, but are not being exploited now. But in fact the Socialist Government seems to be the first government which has discovered how to exploit the colonies" (Quoted in R.Palme Dutt, *ibid*, p.270).

If the British worker got off relatively lightly, the colonial worker and peasant was not so lucky. Intensification of exploitation in the colonies brought in its train intensified resistance and revolt on the part of the peoples of the Empire against British imperialism. But the 'socialist' Attlee Government put down all such revolt with ruthless severity and extreme barbarity - all in the interests of solving the worst crisis of British imperialism at the expense of the colonial people. The 'socialist' Attlee Government had succeeded in reconstructing Britain's shattered economy, had delivered on the front of nationalisation, National Health Service and full employment - but at the cost of millions upon millions of colonial slaves, tens of thousands of whom died in the revolts put down with such barbarity by our 'socialist' government. And if after all this the Labour, Trotskyite and revisionist 'left' still applauds the achievements of the Attlee Government, this is solely to be explained by the fact that it represents the privileged sections of the working class, whose culture is thoroughly corrupt; that this 'left' is prepared to defend its privileges at any cost - and if this involves sacrificing the lives of millions of super-exploited workers and peasants abroad, so be it.

Attlee Government's 'Achievements'

Here briefly are the most important 'achievements' of Attlee's 'socialist' administration.

Labour played a significant role in the suppression of the Greek liberation struggle in the aftermath of the war. It helped restore French imperialist control over Indo-China. British troops, commanded by Major General Gracey, armed the defeated Japanese fascist and French quisling troops, paving the way for the return of French rule. It took the Vietnamese people another three decades of armed struggle and several millions of lives in brutal wars, waged first by French and then by US imperialism, before achieving reunification and liberation of their country, courtesy of the intervention organised by the 'socialist' Attlee Government at the behest of US imperialism. By similar methods, and at the cost of 40,000 Indonesian casualties, British troops, under General Christison, helped restore Dutch imperialism's rule in the East Indies.

In the Middle East, while refusing to withdraw troops from the Suez Canal, it endeavoured to install a whole host of puppet regimes to safeguard British imperialism's oil riches and almost went to war with Iran over the nationalisation, by the latter, of the Anglo-Iranian Oil Company. To protect Britain's high-yielding investments in rubber plantations and tin-mining, both noted for their dollar earnings, Labour, using the most medieval methods of torture, murder, head-hunting and collective punishment, launched a barbaric colonial war against the liberation struggle of the Malayan people. It was to be 12 years before British imperialism succeeded in imposing its will.

In 1949, Labour played an important role in helping US imperialism establish the war-mongering NATO (North Atlantic Treaty Organisation), and, shortly thereafter went on to give its full and unreserved support to US imperialism's genocidal war of aggression against the Korean people, which cost three million Korean lives - a war in which the Korean people, with Chinese and Soviet support, fought US imperialism and its partners in aggression to a bloody standstill. The British contingent, numbering 12,000, was the largest after that of the US. To this day the tragic partition of the Korean peninsula is a legacy of this dirty war in which the Attlee 'socialist' government played such a shameful role.

As for Africa, not a single country obtained independence from Labour.

With a view to safeguarding its investments in South Africa, it outlawed Chief Seretse Khama from the British protectorate of Bechuanaland. This had been demanded by the then newly-elected Nationalist Government which was to go on to institute the notorious *apartheid* system. Labour complied for it needed South African gold and South West African (Namibian) uranium for atomic weapons.

In view of the foregoing, it is impossible to disagree with the following observation of Robert Clough, *à propos* the Attlee Government:

"... *Labour never had to kill one British worker at home to rebuild British imperialism. But it had to kill untold thousands in the rest of the world, often with the enthusiastic support of its left-wing. Hence those who seek to show that Labour played a progressive role can only do so on the racist assumption that the lives of the colonial people are of far less importance than those of British workers*" (*Labour A Party Fit for Imperialism, op cit*, p.107).)

Record of the Wilson-Callaghan Governments

After thirteen years in opposition, Labour was back in power in 1964, with Harold Wilson as Prime Minister, on whose government so many people had placed high hopes. Their illusions were shattered within weeks of the Wilson Government coming into office. It soon became clear that his Government was to be no different from any previous Labour administration, that the pre-occupation of Labour now, as before, was the defence of the interests of British imperialism, without which defence Labour could not defend the interests of its own constituency, namely, the alliance of the labour aristocracy and a section of the middle class. But this defence required an attack on the majority of the working class in Britain and on hundreds of millions of workers and peasants in Africa, Asia and Latin America. Labour was ready and willing to do the filthy work. Here is a brief summary of Labour's shameful record.

The Wilson Government maintained full trade links with the *apartheid* Pretoria regime, supplying the latter with fighter bombers. At the end of 1966, Wilson offered Ian Smith, the Rhodesian rebel leader, terms which would have guaranteed white minority rule for decades to come. Ian Smith's regime turned out to be too stupid to accept those generous terms, thus laying the basis for its own destruction at the hands of the Zimbabwean liberation movement.

If Attlee's Government had restored French imperialism to Indo-China, Wilson's Government fully backed the genocidal war of aggression waged by US imperialism against the Vietnamese and other Indo-Chinese people. When, in the summer of 1965, the US started its Nazi-like bombing of north Viet Nam (the Democratic Republic of Viet Nam - the DRVN), with Hanoi and Haiphong as special targets, Wilson cabled his Government's support to President Lyndon Johnson in these racist terms:

"I wholly understand the deep concern you must feel at the need to do anything possible to reduce the losses of young Americans in and over Viet Nam. ... our reservations about this operation will not affect our continuing support for your policy over Viet Nam" (quoted by Robert Clough, *op cit*, pp.112-113).

Although Labour's 'left'-wing, too concerned with party unity, followed sheepishly in the wake of the Wilson Government, Bertrand Russell was so outraged by Labour's stance that he publicly tore up his membership card after making this statement:

"When I compare the horrors of the Viet Nam war with the election Manifesto of the Labour Government, I find myself confronted with the most shameful betrayal of modern times in this country. Hitler, at least, seldom professed humanity, but these men who now pollute the chairs of office professed, before the election, the most noble and lofty ideals of human brotherhood. ... I can no longer remain a member of this so-called 'Labour' Party, *and I am resigning after 51 years"* (Quoted *ibid,* p.113).

What a refreshing contrast Russell's above statement presents to the utterances of Labour's 'left' charlatans à la Ken Livingstone, who, having made such a din about Tory (sorry, Tony) Blair's success in removing Clause IV from Labour's Constitution, has finally and spinelessly, although not unexpectedly, made his peace with the following glowing tribute to the same Blair:

"... The legacy of Labour's compromisers and wafflers, from Wilson to Kinnock, was failure and defeat. The sense of relief when a competent, honest right-wing Labour leader finally appeared in the form of John Smith *was felt throughout the Party. We may therefore find to our surprise that Blair could yet deliver a Labour government of which socialists could be proud if he is prepared to take on the vested interests of the City.*

"If Blair does this he will win a place in history as the Prime Minister who transformed and modernised Britain. He would rank with Churchill and Attlee *as a truly great leader...."* (*The Guardian*, Monday, June 12, 1995, *'The right face for the 'job' "*).

Well, we know what pre-occupied Churchill and Attlee. Their pre-occupation was the defence of British imperialism and the reconstruction of the shattered British economy at the expense of the vast colonial masses. If there are 'socialists', and to our shame there are, who feel proud of the achievements of Churchill and Attlee, these are renegades from socialism who find it convenient to wear a 'socialist' mask to dupe the working class. It is precisely such kind of renegade 'socialists' who are limbering up to greet an expected Blair government with pride. Be it said in parenthesis, never was it the purpose of either Churchill, Attlee or any other British government *"to take on the vested interests of the City"*. On the contrary, for them it was an article of faith, and a fundamental principle of policy, to defend the vested interests of the City. A Blair government will be no different in this regard. Mr Livingstone, and he must know this, is indulging in the wildest of illusion-mongering in even suggesting that a Blair government might *"take on the vested interests of the City"*.

In regard to the struggle of the Irish people for national self-determination and for the unification of their forcibly divided and occupied country, Labour's attitude was impeccably hostile. In the face of the growing strength of the civil rights movement, and the inability of the Stormont semi-fascist statelet to crush this movement, the Labour Government sent troops to Ireland in 1969 to suppress the nationalists. In 1974 it put on the statute book the notorious Prevention of Terrorism Act (PTA) and presided over the Guildford 4 and Birmingham 6 trials, which since then have been exposed to be the most scandalous frame-ups of the 20th century which pass for British bourgeois justice. Between 1976 and 1979, it instituted a regime of terror in police stations in the 6 Counties, withdrew political status from Irish prisoners and established the H-Blocks.

Race Relations

In the area of race relations, Labour proved its racist credentials with effortless ease. In 1968, through a new Immigration Act, it took away the right of East African British passport holders, almost all Asian, to enter Britain. In 1969 new legislation, aimed at Asian women, barred women from bringing into Britain their fiancées and husbands. During 1974-79, the Labour Government presided over mass deportation of black workers (on average 200 black people awaited deportation every day) and carried out virginity tests on Asian women coming to Heathrow. Already gasping its last breath, the Callaghan Government sent 5,000 police to protect, in the name of 'free speech', a National Front meeting - allegedly an election rally, but to which black people were not allowed. The resulting police carnage left one dead (Blair Peach), 1,000 injured, 800 arrested and 342 tried on trumped-up charges.

Working-class struggles

As regard the working class and its struggle, Labour was as vicious as any Tory Government could be. The thrust of its policy was to drive working-class living-standards down through a host of devices such as productivity deals, statutory wage restraints, incomes policies and the notorious social contract, which justly came to be known as the social con-trick. Finding itself resisted on the industrial front, Labour published its 'In Place of Strife' in an effort to control strike activity. Working-class opposition forced the withdrawal of these Union-bashing proposals. This is how, at the time, *The Economist* evaluated the effects of the second stage of Labour's incomes policy:

"...the 7 per cent by which the past year's 10 per cent increase in earnings fell behind its 17 per cent increase in prices represents the biggest recorded fall in the average Briton's real disposable income for over a hundred years: worse than anything that happened in the 1930s" (Quoted in R.Clough, *op cit*, p.162).

All this was accompanied by a dramatic fall in state expenditure as a ratio of the GNP from 49.35 per cent in 1975 to 43.25 per cent in 1978; with its attendant harmful effect on the poorest sections of society.

The result of Labour's attacks on wide sections of the working class was the *'Winter of Discontent'* when, in the winter of 1978, poorly-paid council workers struck. In the General Election of the following summer, a combination of abstentions on the part of a sizeable section of the poorer workers and the defection from Labour to the Tories by a significant section of the skilled workers (C2 voters in the pollsters' terminology) brought the Tories to office under Margaret Thatcher's leadership.

Labour's record in Opposition

Since 1979, Labour has been in opposition. In the 1992 General Election it received its fourth consecutive defeat. Its response to each defeat has been to move further to the right in an effort to win the votes of the privileged layers of the working class and sections of the middle class (petty-bourgeosie) - portions of the population who determine the outcome of elections. As to the poorer sections, the deprived at home and abroad, they form no part of Labour's calculations. Here are a few examples of Labour's rabidly anti-working class and undeviatingly imperialist stance in opposition.

During the 1981 Hunger Strike in which ten Irish prisoners, including Bobby Sands, became martyrs in their fight for recognition as political prisoners, Labour supported the Government. This is not surprising since it was Labour which had deprived the Irish liberation fighters of that status in the first place. It beat the jingoistic war drum even more loudly than the Thatcherites during the Malvinas (Falklands) conflict and enthusiastically supported British imperialist participation in the Gulf war against Iraq. It confirmed its commitment to the war-mongering aggressive NATO alliance and to Britain's nuclear weapons.

At home, Labour made sure of its total condemnation of all and any resistance by the working class and the oppressed; it denounced in no uncertain terms the 1981 and 1985 revolts of the youth in inner city areas of Britain; it opposed all mobilisation against the hated poll tax.

However, during this period the NUM coal strike of 1984-85 was the single most significant battle, which brought to the fore not only the split within the working class (privileged upper layer, the labour aristocracy, versus the mass of the working people), but also made strikingly clear that Labour was on the side of the privileged layer, committed to the defence of the latter's interests, which in turn required the defence of the interests of British imperialism - it being economically impossible to defend one without defending the other. So, the Labour and Trade-Union leadership joined forces with the Coal Board, the Thatcher administration, the Nottinghamshire miners (who enjoyed conditions of relatively better job security and terms of service), the media, the police and even the intelligence services, to defeat this historic struggle. On top of the Nottinghamshire miners, who became willing hirelings of the Coal Board in the latter's attempts at defeating the strike, the Iron and Steel Trades Confederation (ISTC), abetted by Bill Sirs, co-operated with non-union labour to unload coal at Hunterston, thus keeping the Ravenscraig plant in commission for weeks. EEPTU, the power workers union, led by the notorious Hammond, too, decided against supporting the miners. Led Murray, the TUC General Secretary, did everything possible to sabotage any working-class action in support of the miners.

As for the scab-in-chief, to wit, Labour leader Neil Kinnock, with characteristic hypocrisy and double standards he condemned the miners for defending themselves against police violence. From the rostrum of the September 1984 TUC Congress he nauseatingly proclaimed:

"Violence, I do not have to tell this Congress ... disgusts union opinion and divides union attitudes ... and is alien to the temperament and intelligence of the British trade-union movement".

This self-proclaimed apostle of peace and non-violence had little difficulty in accepting daily police violence against the mining communities and pickets, let alone his enthusiastic support for the imperialist Gulf war against Iraq and the barbarity of the Zionist state of Israel against Palestinian and Lebanese people.

The year 1994, nine years after the defeat of the coal strike, saw the publication of *'The Enemy Within: MI5, Maxwell and the Scargill Affair'* (Verso 1994). In this excellent book, its author, Seumas Milne, reveals in great detail the powerful range of forces arrayed against the NUM, who succeeded in defeating the strikers, although they failed in breaking the NUM President, Arthur Scargill - a special target of their hate and slander campaign. According to Milne, in order to defeat the miners, Mrs Thatcher, who regarded the miners as *"the enemy within"*, not only employed thousands of police who subjected the miners to brutal violence and imposed an occupation regime in the mining villages, but also instituted a covert operation run by the MI5, the Special branch and the Government's spy centre, the GCHQ. For the Thatcherites, no dirty and mean trick was too low to stoop to, for as Milne rightly observes:

"As far as the Thatcherite faction in the Cabinet and their supporters in the security services were concerned, the NUM under Scargill's stewardship was the most serious domestic threat to state security in modern times. And they showed themselves prepared to encourage any and every method available - from the secret financing of strike-breakers to mass electronic surveillance, from the manipulation of agents provocateurs to attempts to 'fit up' miners' officials - in order to undermine or discredit the union and its leaders".

Milne reveals that Thatcher gave personal authorisation for a mass electronic surveillance operation, in which GCHQ and US National Security Agency facilities in Europe were used to trace miners' money. In co-ordinating the scabbing activities of the working miners, Thatcher utilised the services of the millionaire David Hart, who contributed his own money and raised half a million pounds from Lord Hanson, Sir Hector Laing and others - funds which were to be put at he disposal of the scabs for use in court actions to get the strike outlawed. The resultant fines and the NUM's refusal to pay put the latter 'in contempt' of court and its assets liable to sequestration.

"It was essential, Hart believed, that the miners should be forced to return to work without a settlement - which at the initiative of Kim Howells and others in the NUM's South Wales Area is what eventually happened" (ibid, p.270).

The Government employed the services of the former Chief Executive of the NUM, Roger Windsor, planted by MI5 to destabilise the NUM. Sent by the NUM to Libya during the strike to get the Libyan Government to stop oil exports to Britain, he insisted on personally meeting the Libyan leader, Gaddaffi, and embracing him in the glare of TV cameras - thus providing a heaven-sent propaganda gift to the Government and the bourgeois media.

Even after the strike was over, the Government's attempts to destroy Scargill, who in providing such courageous and principled leadership to his membership during the strike had come to richly deserve the hatred of the ruling class, continued. In 1990, the MI5, using Roger Windsor, who by then had departed from the NUM, approached the *Mirror* with a false story that Scargill and NUM Secretary, Peter Heathfield, had employed Libyan money to redeem their mortgages. Without the slightest attempt at verification, the *Mirror* paid £80,000 to Windsor and splashed the story across its pages, along with an editorial signed personally by Robert Maxwell, the owner of the *Mirror* since 1984 and a Labour supporter. Whilst Scargill and the Libyan money tale was a patent falsehood and shown to be so, it is pertinent, not to say ironical, that Maxwell embezzled £400 million of his employees' pension funds and committed hara-kiri, and Windsor is being proceeded against by the NUM in the French courts for the return of NUM money which he really did use to redeem his mortgage.

However, the most shameful section in Milne's book is that which treats the Labour Party's dirty tricks in defeating the NUM. Labour and TUC leadership hated Scargill and the NUM no less than did the Thatcherites. Not only had the Labour leadership known of the *Mirror* smear story in advance, but the active involvement of Kevin Baron, Labour's coal spokesman, and Kim Howells, former NUM employee and now MP, shows also that the smear campaign had its full endorsement. Representing as they did the spirit of resistance against the daily encroachments of capital, the miners and their leader presented a challenge to the Labour Party - this proven representative of the interests of the labour aristocracy and of British imperialism alike - no less than to the Tory Party. By their heroic resistance the miners were setting an eloquent example to other sections of the working class, an example which could not but rouse the fury of the parties of imperialism, Labour included.

As Milne so correctly remarks:

"The Scargill Affair depended on a coincidence of purpose between an exotic array of interests, foremost among which were the Thatcher administration and the Labour leadership" (p.24).

The coal strike has proven, except to the politically blind who will not see, that if the NUM were rightly regarded by British imperialism as *"the enemy within"*, the British proletariat has, for its part, every right, nay, every duty, to treat the Labour Party as *"the enemy within"*. Unless it learns to do so, it will see victory no more than it will see its ears.

VI

Trendy-Troto 'left' - A fig-leaf for social democracy

It is shameful to have to admit, but it is a sin to hide, that there still exist organisations, calling themselves communist, who are totally blind to the reality outline above, who still continue to regard the Labour Party as a party of the British working class, and who continue to call for electoral support for this party. What reasons can there be for this purblind gentry to adopt such an attitude towards a viciously anti-working class and pro-imperialist party that Labour has demonstrated itself to be ever since its inception?

Here are the argument put forward by them over decades in support of their stance - their reasons for supporting Labour. **First** that Lenin advised so; **second** that Clause IV of the Labour Party Constitution which COMMITTED Labour to *"common ownership of the means of production"*, somehow made it a socialist party; and **last** that it has links with the trade unions, which makes it not only a mass party of the British working class, but also susceptible to the influence of the masses who, it is alleged, control the unions and, therefore, indirectly the Labour Party.

Let us briefly refute these phoney arguments. As regards Lenin's advice, it has been amply shown earlier that Lenin gave his advice in a particular, concrete, historical context. Long after the conditions, which gave rise to Lenin's observations and advice, have disappeared, some comrades in the movement continue, mindlessly as it were, to put forward slogans learned by rote - and all in the name of Leninism. Lenin's advice was given at a time when there had not been a single Labour government as yet, and Lenin was correctly of the view that helping Labour to power would serve to expose Labour for what it really was, namely, a bourgeois Labour party. Since then there have been several Labour Governments and no one can be in doubt as to their record, as we have shown above, in defending the interests of British imperialism (and with it that of the labour aristocracy) at the expense of both the vast masses (the lower stratum) at home and hundreds of millions of oppressed peoples abroad.

Moreover, Lenin was prompted to give his advice at a time when the Labour Party was really a sort of loose federation which allowed other parties not only to be affiliated to it, but also to have their own programmes, press organs and complete freedom to criticise the Labour leadership. In fact, almost at the time of Lenin's speech in 1920, the Labour Party was well on the way to dispensing with this luxury by tightening up its organisation through its 1918 Constitution, with its much-trumpeted Clause IV, of which we shall speak later. Shortly after Lenin's speech, this condition too disappeared. Since then a whole number of Trotskyist groups adopted the tactics of entryism into the Labour Party allegedly to replace the right-wing leadership of this allegedly working-class party and get elected a Labour Government committed to socialist policies. The result, instead of getting Labour committed to socialism, has been either the periodical wholesale expulsion of the dim-witted Trotskyite renegades to socialism or their inevitable conversion to ordinary social democrats, reduced to justifying counter-revolutionary social democracy with a sprinkling of Marxian, or more often, and more fittingly, Trotskyist phrases. At the time of Lenin's speech, the British bourgeoisie viewed the Labour Party, even if mistakenly, with dread as a working-class party; that is why Lloyd George, the most consummate and skilful representative of the bourgeoisie, found it necessary to work for an alliance of the Liberals and Conservatives to defeat Labour. That ceased to be the case long ago. By the time of the election of the first Labour Government in 1924, the Labour Party had rightly earned the title of the third party of imperialism.

Clause IV

As to Clause IV, an assortment of Trotskyite and revisionist writers and organisations perceive it an expression of Marxian socialism, which must be defended, and which makes the Labour Party an anti-capitalist party deserving of working class and communist support. Cliff and Gluckstein have characterised it as an *"extraordinary transformation"*, a *"commitment to socialism"*, a *"minimal anti-capitalist position"*, which we must defend now. As a matter of fact, Clause IV has little to do with socialism. On the contrary it was an anti-communist provision born out of specific historical circumstances ushered in by the October Revolution in the aftermath of the First Imperialist World War. The October Revolution, by freeing subject peoples, by granting rights to working people, and by expropriating capitalists and landlords, had set a rather infectious example to the working class the world over - an example which in the conditions of ferment following the war stood every chance of being followed. With force alone the bourgeoisie could not hope to cope with this challenge. Labour needed much deceit and trickery to forestall such a development. Clause IV was the answer of the thoroughly imperialist and unashamedly racist leadership of the Labour Party.

Having emerged victorious from the war, it was but natural that British imperialism would assume the role of leading the counter-revolutionary crusade against Bolshevism. For such a risky enterprise the masses at home had to be at the very least pacified. The Labour Party was only too happy to give a helping hand. Through Clause IV, which it had no intention of taking seriously let alone implementing, the Labour leadership through Arthur Henderson and Sidney Webb, both imperialist and racist to the core and authors of Clause IV - in reality the latter was the one who drafted it - made vague promises to dupe and pacify the working class so as better to assist British imperialism in its counter-revolutionary vanguard role against Soviet Russia. Thus there is great truth in the observation of R.McKibbin, àpropos the 1918 Constitution with its Clause IV, that:

"The war and the disruption of international socialism had landed the British Labour Party in a position it had not held before. Largely owing to the numerical strength - and the wealth - of the British trade unions [and, the victory of British imperialism in the war, McKibbin ought to have added - HB], *the Labour Party found itself willy-nilly the leading 'Allied' socialist party and the rock upon which European social democracy was already building its fortress against Bolshevism. Consequently, it appeared necessary to construct a political party appropriate to this industrial support"* (*The Evolution of the Labour Party, op cit,* p.91).

Prior to the 1918 Constitution, Labour had neither local branches nor any provision for individual membership, it being a federation of trade unions and political parties and groupings. Such a structure was not sufficient in the conditions following the war. Labour needed to have a broader base of support. Not only did it need to attract middle-class socialists and disaffected radical liberals, but also the wider working-class layers. The latter, again a by-product of the war and the October Revolution, was to be crucial as it became clear that the British ruling class would no longer be able to resist working-class demands for widening the franchise. The post-war legislation finally conceded this demand by granting suffrage to men over 21 and women over 30, with the result that there was a dramatic increase in the electorate from 8.5 million in 1915 to 22 million in 1922. To appeal to poorer sections of the working class, soon to be franchised, to mobilise their support, Labour would need not only local branches but also a programme, albeit on paper. The 1918 Constitution, with individual membership, local branches, Clause IV and Union block votes, was Labour's answer to the situation emerging in the wake of the war. To make sure that the masses will have no input on questions of policy, the 1918 Constitution gave complete control, through the block vote, to Union bosses over the election of the National Executive Committee as well as Conference policy. Thus, what our trendy and imperialist 'left' regards as Labour's historic links with the masses in fact amounted to the creation of a rotten borough which handed control to a smug and exclusive coterie of Union barons, who have always acted in the past, and will do so in the future, in the defence of the interests of British imperialism, on which defence depends the defence of their own privileges and that of the upper stratum of the working class which they represent. All this is known even to our trendy-Troto 'left'. Hence the truly pitiful contortions, convolutions and downright convulsions they undergo in their attempts at justification of the unjustifiable, namely, their defence of the Labour Party. Here are a few examples.

'Socialist Outlook' Trots and social democracy

The Trotskyite social democrats of Socialist Outlook (formerly Socialist Challenge and before that IMG), terribly upset at the then impending removal of Clause IV from Labour's Constitution, wrote thus at the end of February, 1995:

"Tony Blair *has thrown the gauntlet. Ditching Clause Four is his big power play. He is attempting a profound shift* [is he really? - HB] *in the politics of the Labour Party*".

And further:

"*He is trying to reverse the working class nature of the Labour Party. He wants to change its identity*".

The reader may find it impossible to believe it, but in the very next paragraph the schizophrenic luminaries of Socialist Outlook go on to make this startling statement:

"*While the Party has never been a socialist Party and Clause Four is not a programme for socialism, the Clause does give voice to a completely different type of society* [as do many phrases in the bible, one might add - HB].

"*Blair wants it out because it challenges capitalism. He wants to remove all reference to socialism form British politics. This is why we must defend it*".

(Socialist Outlook, No.78, 25 Feb. 95, 'Clause Four Fight: What is at stake').

Reader, do you understand this hocus-pocus? How can any honest and sane person, possessed of the least logic and powers of reasoning, write such claptrap, such rigmarole? If the Labour Party has "never been a socialist party, and Clause Four *is not a programme for socialism"*, as we are told, is it not utter nonsense to talk about Blair *"attempting a profound shift in the politics of the Labour Party"*? Profound shift from what to what? A shift from capitalist politics to capitalist politics, from slightly disguised capitalist politics to open and avowedly capitalism politics, can be described as *"profound shift"* either by those who do not know the meaning of the word *"profound"*, or who have 'profoundly' lost their bearings - their marbles - or by those who are in the business of duping themselves and the masses by prettifying social democracy and portraying it in the brightest of colours and who are terribly upset now that Blair is making their job nearly impossible. We say nearly, for this dim-witted and corrupt petty-bourgeois gentry will doubtless find some other excuse to hang on to the stinking carcass that social democracy has been ever since the start of the First Imperialist World War. If the Labour Party *"has never been a socialist party, and Clause Four is not a programme for socialism"*, as we are told, how could it *"give voice to a completely different* [whatever this means - HB] *society"*, let alone *"challenge capitalism"*? Unless, of course, one believes that the only party that can *"challenge capitalism"* has to be a party which *"has never been a socialist party"* and whose set of aims *"is not a programme for socialism"*. In comparison with such nonsensical beliefs, the belief in virgin birth, holy spirit, reincarnation and such-like miracles sound almost sensible.

In the same issue, in an article entitled *'Why nationalisation is not enough'*, the same gentry, desirous of covering their total renegacy, write about the inadequacy of the wording of Clause IV. Having stated that this wording negates the *"self-activity of the working class"*, supercilious Trots that they are, they go on to utter the following profound pronouncement: "It is therefore hardly surprising that the authors of Clause IV, the Webbs, were such fervent admirers of Stalin *in the 1930s".*

The absurdity of this argument immediately reminds one of the Russian phrase: There is a bush in my garden and my Uncle is in Kiev. Yes, but what has one to do with the other. It is not Stalin who wrote Clause IV; it is not Stalin who is defending Clause IV or its authors or their imperialism and racism. It is the dim-witted Trotskyite renegades of a hundred and one varieties, the entryists of Socialist Outlook included, who are defending Clause IV. Could one not, at least with equal force, conclude that their defence of Clause IV is inextricably bound up with their admiration for its authors, the Webbs. And if in the 1930s, the Webbs, having visited the USSR, and having seen her gigantic achievements in socialist construction (which according to Trotskyism was simply impossible), were impressed by, and reported, these developments in a very large volume, this only testifies to a degree of belated honesty and integrity on their part from which the congenital liars and psychopaths of divers Trotskyite organisations could well learn something. Nor were the Webbs alone in this. Many a big capitalist could not fail to be impressed with the monumental achievements of socialism in the USSR, the only country in the 1930s to have had no unemployment and with continuously rising living and cultural standards, when the capitalist world, in the aftermath of the recession, could offer tens of millions of working people no other prospect than that of unemployment, the dole queue, hunger, homelessness and war. For self-assurance, for it does not convince any one else, they add further on:

"*As revolutionaries* [don't laugh - HB] *we do not believe that any Labour government has ever acted primarily in the interests of the working class ...*" and so on and so forth. This being the case, we seek forgiveness for asking the rude question: Will you, please, be kind enough to tell us why are you in the Labour Party and why are you forever calling upon the working class to support it? Since you will not answer this simple question directly and honestly, we have the right to draw the only conclusion. namely, that you are incurable social-democratic counter-revolutionaries.

In the same issue, in yet another article 'Blai*r follows in the footsteps of failure'*, Socialist Outlook describe Hugh Gaitskell's 1959 attempt to ditch Clause IV (*"an explicit renunciation of socialist aspiration"* - to use Socialist Outlook*'s* terminology). Without the least expenditure of intellectual energy, they declare *"Gaitskell was as Conservative as Blair. And this brought 15 years of failure to the Labour Party"*. Far from it. What had caused the defeat of the Labour Party in the 1951 Election and two subsequent elections had nothing to do with Labour's Conservatism or the attempt to get rid of Clause IV, which attempt was made a full 8 years after the defeat of 1951. These defeats and failures are to be explained by the fact that Labour's alliance with its middle-class supporters - an alliance produced by the peculiar conditions of the years immediately after the end of the Second World War - broke down. Although the working class voted in unprecedented numbers for it, Labour still lost because 2 million middle-class voters returned to the Tories in the conditions of post-war boom made possible by the Attlee Government's reconstruction of British capitalism on the backs, and at the expense, of millions of colonial slaves, of which we hear very little from these prettifiers of *"the most radical of Labour Governments - that of 1945"* (*'Why nationalisation is not enough, op cit*).

If Gaitskell's Conservatism "brought 15 years of failure to the Labour Party", then Harold Wilson's alleged radicalism made possible four election victories:

"Gaitskell's successor as leader, Harold Wilson, who described the attack on Clause IV as like 'taking Genesis out of the Bible', led Labour to four election victories with the Clause intact but largely ignored"

Obviously, Socialist Outlook have come up with a cheap and easy formula for ensuring Labour electoral successes: Keep Clause IV intact but ignore it, just as Harold Wilson did! It is a pity that Tony Blair cannot learn from Socialist Outlook. If the retention of Clause IV could guarantee Labour victories, then all the defeats Labour has suffered since 1918 are simply inexplicable, which they really are to the bird brains of Socialist Outlook and such-like 'socialist' practitioners of witchcraft. What Socialist Outlook and other camp followers of social democracy refuse to talk about is a split in the working class, between the privileged stratum, the bought-off section which, because of its economic position and privileges constantly sides with imperialism, on the one hand, and the broad masses of the proletariat, on the other hand. The privileged stratum do not desire any socialism or radicalism. Without their support no party can win an election here. It is precisely to appeal to them that the Labour Party is forever trimming its sails. Labour's massive defeat in the 1983 election, when, compared with the one in 1979, it lost 3 million votes and polled a mere 28 per cent of the vote, was caused by the increasing desertion of the upper layers of the working class from Labour. Being the beneficiaries of council house sales and privatisation, these sections deserted Labour in droves and voted for the Tories. A mere 34 per cent of the C2 voters (skilled workers) voted for Labour in 1983 - a debacle which produced the TUC's 'New Realism' and the election of Neil Kinnock as leader of the Labour Party. The following paragraph, taken from Neil Kinnock's leadership address, read for him by Robin Cook, makes it perfectly clear, except to the dullards of the Trotskyist/revisionist fraternity, which sections of the population his appeal is aimed at:

"...[W]e can only protect the disadvantaged in our society if we appeal to

those who are relatively advantaged. The apparent over-concentration of our energies and resources on these groups like the poor, the unemployed and the minorities - does a disservice both to them and to ourselves ... if we are to be of real use to the deprived and insecure we must have the support of those in more secure social circumstances - the home owners as well as the homeless, the stable family as well as the single parent, the confidently employed as well as the unemployed, the majority as well as the minorities".

Although Labour recovered some of its support among the skilled workers in the 1992 election (it received 42 per cent of the C2 vote), it was not enough to give victory, for just to scrape home Labour needed nearly 50 per cent of the votes of this section of the working class. Tony Blair is only following in the footsteps of Neil Kinnock in continuing to target his appeal to the ruling class as well as the privileged strata among the working class.

Let it be said in passing that Harold Wilson was no radical and his government's actions, outlined already, provide ample proof of this. It is Socialist Outlook who have failed to understand the significance of Harold Wilson's opposition to ditching Clause IV. He was opposed to taking it out not because he believed in it any more than he believed in Genesis, but rather because getting rid of it would gratuitously upset quite a few people. Since it was in the Constitution as a mere ritual, and nobody took the blindest bit of notice of it, one might as well vote for its retention.

And finally, with an eye on the then impending Special Conference of the Labour Party, at which Blair was to successfully get rid of Clause IV, Socialist Outlook concluded:

"Blair's repudiation of any socialist or radical politics make it clear that a Labour government led by him would follow MacDonald*'s example in 1931, and reserve its attacks for the working class while grovelling to big business and the middle class.*

"Although no socialist programme will be on the agenda of labour's special conference in April, a rejection of Blair's attack on Clause Four would offer an important first step in the fight to turn Labour back towards its roots in the working class and trade union movement".

Well, Blair has since then successfully got rid of Clause IV, and thus prevented Labour from taking *"an important first step in the fight to turn Labour back towards"* its alleged *"roots in the working class and trade union movement".* As of now it even looks as if he is likely to lead the next government, which most certainly *"would follow MacDonald's example in 1931, and re-*

serve its attacks for the working class while grovelling to big business and the middle class". Despite all this Socialist Outlook are still grovelling in the Labour Party, working for the election of a Labour government to kick the Tories out. What happened to the *"gauntlet"* thrown by Tony Blair with his announcement last October to get rid of Clause IV. Socialist Outlook have, instead of taking it up, simply run the gauntlet - being attacked by the bigwigs of social democracy on the one hand, and Marxist-Leninists on the other - a fate richly deserved by them.

We apologise to the reader for having spent so much time on, and given so much space to, such an insignificant Trotskyite organisation (sorry, a faction of the Labour Party) as Socialist Outlook. However this will serve to save time, as their position reflects, only more explicitly, the position of a few other organisations, whose views we shall record without much comment.

Spartacist Trots and Social Democracy

Workers Hammer, paper of the *Sparts*, which normally is so scathing, and justifiably so, of its sister Trotskyite organisations, falls into the same morass as these others. In its Jan/Feb. 1995 issue (No.144), it splashed the self-annihilatory headline "Benn/Scargill *peddle myth of Labour's 'socialist soul' - Oppose Blair's attack on Clause IV"*. With a headline like this it is not difficult to anticipate the content of the article that followed. On the one hand, it is stated correctly that "At best a statement of reformist parliamentary 'socialism', Clause IV (4) was penned in 1918 by the Fabian socialist Sydney Webb. Its purpose was to head off the palpable possibility of workers' rule spreading to Western Europe precipitated by the Russian Revolution. *In order to deceive the workers, the leaders of the Labour Party felt it necessary to have a 'pink' fig leaf. But the real essence of the Labour Party was parliamentary reformism"*.

On the other hand, we are told that *"Tony Blair and his crypto-SDP advisors are attacking Clause IV from the right, from an openly anti-working-class standpoint"*, that the *"Labour Party is riven by the contradiction between its working-class base and its pro-capitalist leadership. .. The fight over Clause IV ... reflects a class divide in the British labour movement"*, and that, therefore, the *"Revolutionaries have a side in this fight, against Tony Blair"*. Continues the *Workers Hammer*, *"The defeat of Blair's plan would put a big spanner in the Labour right-wing's works, and would widen and deepen the debate in the labour movement on the true nature of socialism, and the means necessary to achieve it. It would strengthen the prospects for working-class struggle to transcend the parliamentary dead-end of a future Labour government".*

If the purpose of Clause IV was, as is the correct assertion of *Workers Hammer*, *"to deceive the workers"* by providing *"a 'pink' fig leaf"* for Labour, God alone knows how the retention of this deception might help the British working class in the struggle for its social emancipation! If the presence of Clause IV in Labour's Constitution for all these 77 years has not served to *"widen and deepen the debate...."*, how would the defeat of Tony Blair help to *"strengthen the prospects for working-class struggle to transcend the parliamentary dead-end of a future Labour government"*? We are not initiated into the mysterious intricacies of this mechanism by the super-revolutionaries, to wit, the counter-revolutionary Trots, of *Workers Hammer*. The form of its expression may be different, but in essence their viewpoint is no different from that of Socialist Outlook, SWP and several other organisations.

This, however, does not prevent Workers Hammer from criticising Arthur Scargill, Tony Benn and the *"notoriously reformist Militant group"* for asserting that Clause IV *"is an unambiguous challenge to capitalism"* which *"represents the very soul of the Labour Party"*, for "the Labour Party *has never had, and never will have, a 'socialist road'"*. All the same we must *"oppose 100 per cent Blair's attack on Clause IV"*!

Again, criticising Scargill and Benn, Workers Hammer says that for them "'unity' of the Labour Party against the Tories, and a commitment to reformist parliamentarianism *takes precedence ... for Tony Benn, no less than Tony Blair, a Labour government administering capitalist Britain is the ultimate prize"*. This did not prevent them, back in 1982, from supporting Benn in the election for deputy-leadership of the Labour Party on the pretext of driving *"out the blatantly pro-imperialist CIA-connected right-wing and place Benn in a position where his ultra-reformist politics could be more effectively exposed and combated"* (Spartacist *Britain*, No.41, April 1982).

Whereas some of these charlatans maintain that Labour must be put at the head of a government so as to more effectively expose its anti-working class politics - many decades after the completion of that task - others, Spartacists among them, have now moved from the party, its programme and decades of practice, to individuals. This is not a Marxist-Leninist way of viewing and evaluating any social phenomenon, but a mockery of it.

When the Sparts talk about the *"working-class base"* of the Labour Party and contrast it with its *"pro-captialiast leadership"*, they forget, **first**, the following words of Lenin, spoken at the Second Congress of the Comintern in August 1920, *àpropos* the British Labour Party:

"Of course, for the most part the Labour Party consists of workers, but it does not logically follow from this that every workers' party which consists of workers is at the same time a 'political workers' party'; that depends upon who leads it, upon the content of its activities and of its political tactics. Only the latter determines whether it is really a political proletarian party. From this point of view, which is the only correct point of view, the Labour Party is not a political workers' party but a thoroughly bourgeois party, because, although it consists of workers, it is led by reactionaries, and the worst reactionaries at that ... ".

Secondly, their reference to the *"working-class base"* can either be an allusion to the membership of the Labour Party or its organisational links with the trade unions. We shall talk of the Unions later on. As regards the class composition of the Parliamentary Labour Party and individual membership, it has since the Second World War undergone a complete change. Already, of the 393 Labour MPs elected in 1945, there were 44 lawyers, 49 University lecturers, 15 doctors, 25 journalists and 18 businessmen. In his Report, Larry Whitty, the then General Secretary of the Labour Party, gave the following portrayal of Labour's membership:

"60 per cent of party members have a degree or equivalent higher educational qualification, compared to a national average of just 11 per cent. Labour Party members are twice a likely to be employed in the public sector as the private. 62 per cent of them read The Guardian, and only 25 per cent the Daily Mirror" (quoted in Cliff and Gluckstein, *op cit*, p.351).

Hardly an image of a party teeming with downtrodden proletarians rearing to smash capitalism but only held back by the *"blatantly pro-imperialist CIA-connected right wing leadership"*.

'Workers Power' Trots and Social Democracy

Workers Power is another insignificant anti-communist Trotskyite group, the product of expulsion from the IS (since then transfigured into SWP) for *"factionalism"*. On being expelled, it accused the IS of pursuing a "shameful chauvinist line on Ireland", and of "economism" - both charges being correct in our view. It too, in senseless Trotskyist fashion, calls for a "campaign against Blair" to *"force Labour to act in the workers' interests"* (*Workers Power*, Nov. 1994). These half a dozen Trots who comprise Workers Power would be better employed at a centre for training pigs to fly than being in the business of creating illusions that Labour might somehow be persuaded to act in the workers' interests.

SWP Trots and Social Democracy

Socialist Worker, paper of the Socialist Workers Party, the largest Trotskyist organisation and a divorced parent of Workers' Power, whimpered its support in defence of Clause IV thus:

"... we support all those fighting inside Labour and the Unions to defend Clause Four.

"The commitment to socialism will be invaluable in building in future resistance if we get a Blair government which, as seems certain, implements policies scarcely different to John Major's" (Socialist Worker, 25 Feb. 1995).

How the retention of Clause IV in Labour's Constitution might have proved *"invaluable in building resistance"* to a right-wing labour government led by Blair, when it failed to be such a valuable weapon against previous Labour governments which doubtless implemented anti-working class policies - on this *Socialist Worker* leaves its readers in total darkness. These counter-revolutionaries, who see in Clause IV a *"commitment to socialism"*, when, as shown above, in fact it was an anti-communist device to meet the revolutionary challenge of Bolshevism, and, having served that purpose, was of no further consequence, have the temerity to point an accusing finger at that great revolutionary, J.V.Stalin, for *"betraying the revolution"*. We understand, gentlemen, your problem! To cover your betrayal to the working class, to cover your flight and desertion to the camp of counter-revolutionary social democracy, you are obliged not only to embellish the latter but also to accuse and downgrade great revolutionaries who fought against the treachery of social democracy, including that of the Trotskyite variety, built real socialism (not the fictional one of Clause IV type which has your wholehearted support) and advanced the cause of world revolution by defeating Nazi Germany and extending the frontiers of socialism right up to and into central Europe. We understand, gentlemen, why you, being genetical reformists, hate the achievements of socialism in the former USSR and the man under whose leadership these momentous achievements took place, while at the same time lauding to the skies the deception of the working class that Clause IV undoubtedly was. You want to cover your reformist tracks, for, still harbouring revolutionary pretensions, you suffer from a guilty conscience. The tongue ever returns to the aching tooth, as the saying goes. In this duplicity you are only following, like myriads of other Trotskyist organisations, Trotsky himself, with whom ultra-revolutionary phrases were always meant to disguise his ultra-reactionary actions.

Earlier we were correctly told by the SWP's journal Socialist Review that "Clause 4 has never represented the triumph of the left in the Labour Party or the conversion of the Labour Party *to socialism. The people responsible for Clause 4 saw it as a way of STIFLING not promoting socialism"*. This, however, did not prevent the *Socialist Worker* from waxing hysterical in defence of this clause for *"stifling"* socialism and launching a campaign for its retention in the Labour Party Constitution. Nor did it prevent the *Socialist Review* from stating that *"we should resist with all our might"* Blair's attempt to jettison *"the illusion of its socialist past"*. Going to further depths of degeneration, it went on to say that even if this *"illusion"* - Clause IV - is got rid of, *"that won't mean that the Labour Party has become an openly capitalist party like the Tories and the Liberal Democrats"*. Oh no! The 'illusion' of Labour's socialism, with or without Clause IV, must be maintained at any cost, for otherwise the 'revolutionaries' of the SWP, that is, these incurable Trotskyist counter-revolutionaries, will be deprived of the fig leaf with which to cover their hideous nakedness and their support for, and alliance with, social democracy.

VII
Embellishment of Social Democracy by the Revisionists of the CPB

Stance of the Communist Party of Britain and the 'Morning Star'

The Communist Party of Britain's *Morning Star*, while running articles and speeches, notably those of Arthur Scargill, in defence of Clause IV, confines itself to a meaningless editorial in its 14 March 1995 issue. Entitled *"Still on the Agenda"*, the editorial moans that by taking "steps that are now being taken by Tony Blair" (*Morning Star*'s euphemism for the jettisoning of Clause IV), he "is busy trying to change the Labour Party *into an SDP-type party"*., of the type that Shirley Williams would have been very happy to be in. Thus the illusion is created that the Labour Party was something quite different from an SDP-type party before the question of ditching Clause IV was raised. The illusion is shattered by the leading article itself when, in the next but one paragraph, it goes on to say:

"*It* [the attempt to change Labour into an SDP-type party - HB] is the logical outcome of the crisis of right-wing reformism. *This aimed to secure reforms within capitalism without challenging its power structure"*.

This means, if it means anything at all, that the Labour Party has always been an *"SDP-type party"* for it has always stood for securing *"reforms within capitalism without challenging its power structure"*. That being the case, the attempts to change it into something which it has always been can only be described as a fruitless waste of time.

The editorial correctly goes on to say that British imperialism is no longer in a position to *"make various reforms and concessions"*, for in its global competition with its imperialist rivals, it is obliged to export capital, neglect investment at home, attack the welfare state, reduce taxation and attack *"trade union and democratic rights"* in order to *"blunt mass popular resistance to these attacks on living standards and the right to work* [the reference to right to work is totally incorrect for no such right exists under capitalism - HB]". Consequently, says the *Morning Star* (MS), *"the basis for right-wing reformism has ... collapsed, as it has gradually degenerated into open collaboration with capitalism"*. This can only mean that right-wing reformism, which has always been in control of the Labour Party, is now switching from a position of concealed collaboration with capitalism to that of open collaboration. Although, in our opinion, the collaboration of the Labour Party with British capitalism (the word imperialism, which the MS so studiously avoids, is a more apt expression) has always been fairly open, even on MS's premise the change is one of form rather than substance. Despite all this, the MS goes on to say that the "attempts to transform the Labour Party into an SDP [which it has been all along - HB] *carry the process to a qualitatively new stage"*! From an SDP-type Party to an SDP-type Party, from collaboration with capitalism to collaboration with capitalism - what a *"transformation"* and what a *"qualitatively new stage"*!! In any case, those who call themselves revolutionaries ought to be pleased that concealed collaboration with imperialism will now make way for open collaboration, for that will make the task of exposing this collaboration that much easier.

And what sort of conclusion does the MS draw from all this? Here it is:

"The very crisis of British capitalism ... leaves the working class only one way out of the problems which it now faces.

"It can only advance if it adopts policies which stand up to big business and bring about a shift in the balance of wealth and power in favour of working people.

"The struggle for public ownership under democratic control is therefore very much on the agenda - no matter what short-term successes Blair may have".

This is a formulation in new words of the time-worn and hollow revisionist formula of working to elect a Labour government committed to socialist policies. In the present political climate, this is tantamount to working for the election of a Blair government on the pretext that the labour movement can pressurise it to adopt socialist policies to benefit working people. And socialist policies merely dwindle down to *"public ownership"* and *"a shift in the balance of wealth and power in favour of working people"*, that is, reforms within capitalism to be effected by this shift of the balance of wealth and power, not a revolutionary reconstruction of society through the overthrow of capitalism and the establishment of the dictatorship of the proletariat. Any party putting forward such a programme can justly be characterised as a social democratic, or even an SDP-type, party. Such is the wretched degeneration of wretched revisionism.

As we have had the occasion to dwell on this aspect, i.e., of the vulgarisation of the teachings of Marxism on the question of the state (see page *** in this book), we shall say no more on this question.

Split in the Working Class

What the Communist Party of Britain (CPB), in common with many other organisations calling themselves 'communist' and ' revolutionary', will not talk about is the several-decades long split within the working class, between the privileged strata (the labour aristocracy), who have sold themselves to imperialism in return for their privileges, and who support imperialism to the hilt, on the one hand, and the lower stratum of the proletariat, the vast masses of the poor and the oppressed, on the other hand. In this they go completely against the word and spirit of Leninism, for the latter demands the recognition of the existence of the split which imperialism has engendered within its ranks. In his 'Notes on the Dictatorship of the Proletariat *in the Conditions Prevailing in England'*, Lenin argued against those who talked about the proletariat as a homogenous whole without any differentiation;

"The new and material, the concrete is brushed aside, but they keep on talking about the 'proletariat' in general ...", adding "the proletariat, not in general, not IN ABSTRACTO, but in the twentieth century, after the imperialist war, inevitably split from the upper stratum. Evasion of the concrete, deception by means of abstractions (dialectics *versus eclecticism)"* (*Lenin on Britain*, p.207).

Today, more than ever before, the very survival of British imperialism demands an unprecedented impoverishment of the working class - and this means the vast masses from lower layers. Ever since the breakdown of the Keynesian consensus (which was a product of the peculiar conditions of post-war boom, under which the privileged conditions of the middle class and the labour aristocracy could be ensured whilst providing a suitable standard of living for the vast masses of the working class) and the accession to office by Thatcher's Conservatives, this process of impoverishment has been going on. Today, the poorest 10 per cent of the population are 14 per cent worse off as compared with 1979, the year the Tories came into office. During the same period, the share of the national income of the poorest 40 per cent declined from 24 per cent to 17 per cent. A third of our children are growing up in poverty - this adds up to an enormous figure of 4 million. If one adds the two million pensioners to it, it totals up to 6 million. 47 per cent of all employees (10 million) earn less than the European Decency Threshold, with one million earning less than £2.50 an hour, of whom 300,000 earn under £1.50 an hour - the European Decency Threshold being £5.90 an hour presently. On the other hand, the labour aristocracy have benefited from the sale of council houses as well as privatisation and the purchase of shares.

The vast masses of the working class can no longer be provided with an adequate standard of living - only the privileged sections and the middle class can be, and this by further attacks on the poorer sections, who constitute the majority. Like the Tories, the Labour Party, too, stands for protecting the privileged at the expense of the poorer sections. It has adjusted every one of its policies to suit the needs of British imperialism and the privileged stratum among the working class. It will go into the next election with policies indistinguishable from that of the Tory Party on a whole array of issues ranging from anti-trade union legislation, NHS and education 'reforms', to defence, re-nationalisation of industries privatised in the last 16 years, benefits, pensions, minimum wage, student grants, tax and 'law and order'. The question, therefore, is whether the ruling class is to entrust the Tories or Labour with the job of accelerating the attack on the vast masses of the working class and on what has come to be known as the welfare state.

In these circumstances, to go on speaking about the proletariat in general, *in abstracto*, is merely to evade the concrete and urgent tasks of today and to practise deception on the masses by means of abstractions. The task today is not to launch campaigns in defence of Clause IV, or to discuss whether Labour, with or without Clause IV in its armoury, will act for the benefit of the working class, or bring socialism, or effect a fundamental shift in the balance of power and wealth in favour of the working class. No, the urgent task today is to recognise that both Tory and Labour are as determined as each other to attack and impoverish further the vast masses, the lower layers of the working class in the interests of the survival of British finance capitalism and the privileges of the middle class and the labour aristocracy. The task today for any organisation, claiming to represent the interests of the working class, is to make up its mind as which side of the fence it will stand - on the side of British imperialism and the privileged stratum or on the side of the vast masses from the lower stratum. And, lastly, the most urgent task today is to forge an organisation, a really revolutionary Marxist-Leninist party, as an instrument for leading the downtrodden lower layers in resisting the imperialist onslaught and the struggle for its social emancipation. Only such an approach to the reality unfolding before our eyes is a correct Marxist-Leninist approach.

Far-sighted Bourgeois Ideologues and Blinkered 'Socialists'

It is a matter of shame that while those claiming to be Marxists are shunning the Marxist method of approaching this extremely important question, some of the far-sighted ideologues of even the most reactionary sections of the bourgeoisie are adopting the Marxist approach, even perhaps without realising it and whilst entertaining a most burning hatred of Marxism and everything proletarian. In this instance, we cannot help citing almost fully an article in the *Sunday Telegraph* of 11 June 1995 by Peregrine Worsthorne, that reactionary but candid barometer of the thinking of the British bourgeoisie. He realises that the welfare state is shortly to be dismantled, but is filled *"with foreboding"* that today's ruling class and those charged with this task are guilty of the *"politics of provocation"*. What is required of today's ruling class, he says, is not even *"so much noblesse oblige as bourgeoisie oblige"*. Although, according to him, the Tories should be able to supply this, and he would rather that they did, new Labour, he states implicitly, is certainly able to. Here is Mr Worsthorne in his own words:

"Some of the hostility to the inordinate perks of Cedric Brown, the gas man, may be due to the politics of envy, as so many Tories alleged, but not by any means all of it. I don't think my own critical reaction, for example, is due to envy. Certainly I have never been envious of high earners before, or of unearned riches either, for that matter.

"What offends in Cedric Brown's case, and in others like it, is the brazenness of the greed, the complete disregard for the traditional masks usually adopted to disguise greed. It is almost as if Mr Brown was being greedy on principle, positively wanted to be seen with his snout in the trough; could not imagine any more proud posture.

"I am aware, of course, that the motive force for capitalism has to be greed, both personal and corporate. But in former times, at least in this country, it usually behoved the greedy to take into account the need to temper their greed with tact, discretion and a modicum of sensitivity. Not so Mr Brown who carries on being greedy with a puritanical zeal more often found among those serving God than Mammon.

"The timing, for example, was almost guaranteed to give maximum offence: announcing his perks in the midst of a gigantic lay-off of staff - which is rather as if some 1930s employer had chosen to drive through Jarrow in a

Rolls-Royce, smoking a fat cigar, on the very departure day of the hunger marchers. I am not saying that employers were less greedy in the 1930s than their counterparts in the 1990s. But they were certainly more restrained, or at any rate more prudent, as were the politicians. As I have said before in these columns, the then Prime Minister Stanley Baldwin *was the master of the phrase that turneth away wrath, and also of the healing touch.*

"*So in my view it is not the critics of Cedric Brown et al who are guilty of the politics of envy. It is rather the Cedric Browns et al who are guilty of the politics of provocation. Possibly the fault does not lie with the businessmen themselves, who may genuinely not know any better. More to blame is the capitalist culture out of which they spring; a culture so pro-business - or rather so anti-anti-business - that it positively encourages tycoons to feel they have a patriotic duty to be greedy, since any weakening in this regard would be a sign of ideological backsliding.*

"*In this new conservative culture any recognition that there might be an unacceptable face of capitalism is derided as a hangover from the anti-business culture of a bygone patrician age which nearly brought Britain to its knees. According to this view, an ungreedy businessman would be as unfit for command as would be a cowardly general. That is not the message coming from the CBI, which is much more circumspect. It is the message coming from what passes muster today as the conservative Right wing; even, until public hostility began to make itself felt, from Downing Street.*

"*It fills me with foreboding. For the next stage of capitalism is going to be too serious to be left to capitalist ideologues. Certainly their rigour was necessary for the battle against trade unionism and socialism, since without it there would have been no victory. But the struggle to dismantle the welfare state is going to require a much more sensitive and traditional political style. How could it be otherwise when the sacrifices called for will be so much greater and those affected so much more numerous? Of course a business culture based on greed will have a crucial economic part to play. But that won't solve the political problem of winning consent; consent, that is, for a degree of belt-tightening undreamt of in the post-war half century.*

"*For this to succeed there will need to be a much more inspirational style of leadership. Fair shares, equality of sacrifice, workers' rights - the wartime formula - clearly cannot be repeated in present circumstances since you cannot appeal to, in effect, the rhetoric of the welfare state while hell-bent on dismantling it.*

"So what is to be done? Nobody knows. The Asian capitalist systems don't much bother about consent. They rely instead on the smack of firm government, or worse. It may come to that for the Western democracies as well. But before that evil day, surely it would be worth at least making a determined effort to avoid all unnecessary provocations.

"Would it really be out of the question, for example, for today's economic top dogs to be asked to sacrifice their share options, or at any rate to avoid taking them up while engaged in making their workforces redundant? Would it be out of the question for today's political top dogs to be asked to make more of an effort to appear as determined to serve the public weal as to feather their own nests? Would it be out of the question for inequality to impress itself once again on the public mind as a spur to virtue among its beneficiaries rather than as a justification for vice among its victims?

"The value of exemplary, inspiring, touching, even noble behaviour in high places cannot be exaggerated. A little of this magic goes a long way. One imaginative, heartfelt gesture will often do more good, and be remembered longer, than a whole library of detailed legislation. Heaven knows, England would not be asking today's ruling class to lay down their lives; only to give up their share options and their sleaze: not so much 'noblesse oblige' as 'bourgeoisie oblige'.

"That, in effect, is what new Labour, shorn of its socialism [he means the socialist-sounding terminology of Clause IV - HB] amounts to. Old conservatism, drawing on its much deeper roots in this kind of soil, should have no difficulty, given the chance, trumping that trick" ('They lie because they have no clothes').

It must be admitted of Mr Worsthorne that, incurable reactionary weed though he may be, his clarity of thought puts the majority of our self-proclaimed communists and revolutionaries to shame.

Communist Liaison

Communist Liaison, a group in a kind of loose coalition with the CPB[1], says in its *Bulletin*:

---

1 As this book goes to the printers, the news has come that Communist Liaison has disbanded itself and advised its members to join the CPB.

"It is now clearer than ever that the 'modernisers' aim to 'modernise' the Labour Party *out of existence, and with it prospects for social change*".

On the contrary, the *"prospects for social change"*, and one beneficial to the working class, will only brighten up with *"the Labour Party out of existence"*. That there are communists who dread the day when the Labour Party will no longer exist, only tells one of the dubious nature of such communists.

Tony Benn Persists in Illusion-mongering

'Left'-wing MP, Tony Benn, the darling of the revisionist and Trotskyite groups and organisations, of whom Paul Foot of the SWP wrote after the 1980 Labour Party Conference that *"there can hardly have been a socialist in Britain who did not feel warmth and solidarity for Tony Benn"*, spread the illusion about Labour's socialist credentials with these words:

"I am never going to commit myself to a competitive market economy. The idea that the Labour Party was brought into being to support capitalism and run it better is absurd" ('Defend Clause 4, *Defend Socialism*' Newsletter, Issue no.1).

Well, if Mr Benn is never going to commit himself to a competitive market economy, what has he been doing all these years in the Labour Party? He was, after all a Minister in Harold Wilson's government, during which time he managed not merely to lend a helping hand in an attempt to make Britain's economy more competitive, but also to do some pretty nasty things, which only renegade socialists, overcome by *"warmth and solidarity with Tony Benn"* and throwing to the wind the very basic principles of socialism, can forget. Not only was Mr Benn a member of the Cabinet which presided over growing investment in, and increasing trade links with, *apartheid* South Africa, he also personally signed a contract with Rio Tinto Zinc for unlawful extraction of 7,500 tons of uranium from the Rossing mine in South West Africa (Namibia now), then under South African illegal occupation. Despite this, nobody in CND or in 'left' circles ever questioned Mr Benn's 'socialist' and 'left' credentials. It was during the same period that the government, whose integral part he was and which he never quit in protest, gave its support to the barbaric US war of aggression against the Vietnamese people. That this same gentleman should spread illusions about the Labour Party and its alleged socialism is perfectly understandable.

Arthur Scargill

What is far less comprehensible is that a man like Arthur Scargill, with his courageous and dedicated record of service to the British working class, with his own bitter experience of the Labour Party, especially during the Coal Strike of 1984/85, with his integrity and intelligence, should find himself in the camp of the third-class social-democrat, Trotksyite and revisionist fraternity, whose business it has always been to spread illusions about social democracy among the workers. It is painful to have to report the following remarks of the NUM President:

"... I don't want to see merely nationalised industries. I want to see the Labour Party win political change. I want to see the introduction of the common ownership of the means of production, distribution and exchange" ('Defend Clause 4, *Defend Socialism*' Newsletter, Issue no.1).

In the middle of February of this year, speaking to an audience of 200 people in Tony Blair's Sedgefield constituency, Arthur Scargill had this to say:

"Blair has declared war on socialism itself."

"Clause Four is what marks out the Labour Party from the other major political parties in Britain. Without Clause Four the Labour Party is indistinguishable from the Liberal Democrats *and the Tories.*

"I didn't join the party because I wanted to see Labour run the system better than the Tories, I joined it to destroy capitalism" (Reported in *Socialist Worker*, 25 Feb. 1995).

All we can say is that Blair is not the first Labour leader to declare war on socialism. That war was declared long ago by the very authors of Clause IV, Arthur Henderson and Sidney Webb, and Clause IV was a part and parcel of the declaration of that war on socialism and Bolshevism. If Mr Scargill joined the Labour Party *"to destroy capitalism"*, he has patently been the victim of a cruel deception all these years.

Mr Scargill went on to add: *"you can't have a competitive economy working on capitalist lines and at the same time hope to have an economy that works to meet the interests of the majority"* (*ibid*).

We find ourselves in complete agreement with this observation. If this is what Mr Scargill really wants, he will sooner or later, no matter how reluctantly, have to say good riddance to this stinking corpse called the Labour Party and help build a revolutionary party of the British proletariat which truly represents the interests of the British working class and gives genuine fraternal support to proletarian and liberation struggles abroad. Mr Scargill has the ability and the capacity for such a task, if only he were willing to undertake it. If he was to decide in favour of such an enterprise, his service to the struggle of the British working class for its social emancipation would be truly unforgettable.

It is no point in Mr Scargill asserting on the one hand, that *"It is essential that socialists understand that we cannot build a socialist system of society without destroying the corrupt capitalist system under which we live"* - a sentiment we fully share with him - and, on the other hand, go on to state that "In the face of despair we must reaffirm commitment and hope and build the fight back which will include electing a Labour government committed to taking power and implementing socialist policies - that means retaining and regaining Clause Four as a central plank of the Labour Party*'s Constitution"* (Arthur Scargill, *'Compromise will lead to betrayal'*, Morning Star, 22/3/95).

One thing or the other. Either we want to build socialism by destroying the corrupt capitalist system, in which case we don't want to be in the Labour Party, for it is as useless an instrument for social revolution as is, for instance, the Catholic Church for propagating the principles of dialectical and historical materialism; or we want to elect a Labour government *"committed to taking power and implementing socialist policies ..."*, in which case, whatever our terminology, we are merely looking for an excuse not to involve ourselves in the much more difficult, but also much more rewarding, business of destroying *"the corrupt capitalist system under which we live"*.

If retention of Clause IV were tantamount to the attainment of socialism and the destruction of capitalism, we would long since have been living in a workers' paradise. Labour's record, including the 77 years during which Clause IV remained enshrined in Labour's Constitution, is one of utter betrayal of the working class at home and abroad, and of total subservience to British imperialism, in the service of which there is not a crime it has not committed, and a crime that it will not commit. There is no point in reminding Arthur Scargill of all this, for he knows it only too well and has made extensive references to Labour's betrayals in the pamphlet from which we have quoted his remarks above.

VIII

NCP's Capitulation to Social Democracy

The prize for the most open (and therefore easy to expose), cringing, creepy, servile and shameful (for an organisation calling itself Marxist-Leninist) defence of, and capitulation to, social democracy must be handed to the New Communist Party (NCP). The NCP's stance on the question of its attitude to the Labour Party was elaborated in an article entitled *'Voting Labour - a communist strategy'* by George Davies and published in the organ of the NCP, the *New Worker*, dated 2 December 1994. Since then this article has been reproduced, and distributed, as an NCP document with a new title *"Why we should vote ... Labour!"* (hereinafter referred to as 'The document'). In view of this, its contents cannot be regarded as representing the views of its author alone; they are very much the views of the NCP. The same issue of the *New Worker*, in which this article/document appeared, also carried from Eric Trevett, the General Secretary of the NCP, an editorial statement entitled *"General Election Now!"* (hereinafter referred to as 'The statement'). We shall consider the document and the editorial statement together and bring to the reader's attention the arguments put forward by the NCP in justification of its position. As their position is not different in essence from that of the SWP and other Trotskyist outfits, or that of the CPB and other revisionist organisations, some of whom we have refuted above, very little comment would be necessary. Whatever has already been said in refutation of the arguments similar to those of the NCP which these others have put forward applies, naturally, equally to the NCP.

The document begins by emphasising, first, the profundity of the "economic crisis" and the deteriorating living conditions of the working class and, second, that the "Labour Party leadership, along with the TUC, *provides little or no IMMEDIATE prospect of struggle against the Government or the employers*" (our emphasis). The word *"immediate"* here serves for the NCP the purpose of the proverbial straw, by hanging on to which it hopes to prevent itself from drowning. Take away this word and the NCP's entire dream castle collapses like a house of cards.

Notwithstanding *"the Blair leadership's unseemly haste to dump Clause Four - and the speed with which John Monks [TUC General Secretary] has jumped into bed with Tory government ministers"*, there is, says the NCP, the undeniable *"commitment to oppose all this"*!! The question, however, is, *"on what basis such a fightback is to be conducted"*? The NCP's answer to this very important question is to ask anyone who would listen to it to vote Labour, get a Labour government - even a Blair (whom the editorial statement correctly regards as *"the employers' choice"*) government and put pressure on the latter to respond favourably to working-class struggles for jobs, homes, better education, a decent NHS, trade-union rights, etc. In the words of Eric Trevett's statement:

"We want the Tories brought down and replaced by Labour government elected under pressure to respond positively to the various struggles..."

If the Labour Party cannot be pressurised into adopting a pro-working class stance while it is still in opposition, the chances of the success of such pressures when Labour is in government are exactly nil. Besides, if the working-class movement is strong enough to successfully pressurise a bourgeois Labour government, its ability to pressurise bourgeois Tory governments is no less considerable. Whichever way we view it, the NCP's argument is a hollow mockery of Marxism-Leninism.

As if entertaining doubts about the enthusiasm even of the Labour Party activists for a Labour government, the statement continues: "We call on Labour Party activists to fight around the demands that the Tory government must go and that Clause Four must be defended ... We should agitate, formulate resolutions, and get up petitions at our places of work - around the simple call to kick the Tories out".

Well, what after? We are told in the same statement: *"Getting rid of the Tory government must be the immediate demand. But what will it be replaced by? The answer is a right-wing Labour government"*.

To its own question *"Will that be any better?"*, the statement clearly and frankly answers thus: *"For the working class, certainly. Pushing the Tories out of office will end their claimed mandate for the anti-working class offensive"*.

Since the Tories will be replaced by *"a right-wing Labour government"*, led by someone who, on NCP's own admission, is the *"employer's choice"*, with policies indistinguishable from that of the Tories, will not the election of such a government, while ending the Tories *"claimed mandate for the anti-working class offensive"*, by the same token, be tantamount to the conferment of exactly the same mandate on Labour? On this we are left completely in the dark. Obviously the NCP has either not got the capacity or willingness, to work out the logic of its own reasoning, which in itself is a rehash of the time-worn and meaningless slogans, mindlessly put forward by the revisionists and Trotskyites alike over the past three or so decades.

Without explaining why and how, the statement says: "The election of a Labour government, even a right-wing one, will raise the morale of the working class. It will raise its expectations and its demands in relation to wages, pensions and student grants, *and in relation to the restoration of democratic rights and local government powers"*. Not so long ago, we used to be lectured on by the trendy 'left' as to how the victory of the 'left'-wing, led by Tony Benn, in the Labour leadership election would do wonders to the morale and expectations of the working class. Now the NCP turns round and confidently asserts that this morale and these expectations can after all be raised just as much by the election of a Labour government with impeccably right-wing credentials.

Having given utterance to the above social-democratic cretinism, Eric Trevett remembers that he is supposed to be the leader of a party which swears by Marxism-Leninism. So, post haste, he adds by way of an afterthought, or simply as a ruse to cover up the NCP's rotten social-democratic position, the following:

"Of course the basic problem will still need to be addressed. The symptoms of the crisis - such as mass unemployment, job insecurity, the widening range of people affected by poverty ... - cannot be eliminated without eliminating capitalism".

Of course, in making this obviously correct statement, Eric Trevett shows remarkable *"forgetfulness"*, for in its editorial for a month earlier (4 November 1994) the *New Worker* stated: *"Labour must pledge to end unemployment"* and *"spell out to the electorate how it is going to do it"* (*'The Communist Agenda'*). Thus the illusion is created that capitalism, if managed by Labour, can after all eliminate unemployment. Either Eric does not read the *New Worker*, or the editor of the *New Worker* does not read Eric Trevett's statements, or the NCP suffers from a condition of unmitigated chaos where one hand does not know what the other hand is doing.

Ignoring Labour's imperialist and anti-working class record, in the same November issue we were informed that at election time, the working class *"will only rally to Labour if the traditional working-class policies of the Labour Party are upheld"*. Now, however, we are told that the right-wing Labour Party, shorn of its *"traditional working-class policies"* is electable after all.

But to return to the statement. Having stated that *"symptom of the crisis cannot be eliminated without eliminating capitalism"*, it continues:

"In the course of the struggle around the immediate demands, we must also build a revolutionary leadership. The immediate call to bring down the Tory government must be linked to the more profound preparation for revolution, working-class state power and socialism. Some say the time is not ripe for such ambitious prospects. ... capitalism has NOW [only now! - HB] *reached its obsolete state"*, Eric Trevett's statement concludes with these ringing words:

"The slave-owners and feudal landlords had to be deposed by force. The capitalist class is no different. This is why Lenin stated that the only truly class-conscious worker was he or she who understood the necessity for the dictatorship of the proletariat - *that is to say working-class state power*.

"That is what makes the New Communist Party different from the Communist Party of Britain. We are not looking for soft options or illusionary parliamentary roads to socialism. *We are communists in the mould of Lenin*.

"It is in the interests of the working class that our party is strengthened, and earns the right to be recognised as the revolutionary vanguard of the working class as it helps that class develop the capacity to achieve its emancipation from capitalist exploitation and oppression".

Sounds wonderful. The problem with it is that it is negated by what is stated prior to it, and which we have analysed above, and what comes every week in the *New Worker* and that which appears in the document, which is also the subject of analysis by us here.

But all these high-sounding words about the need to build a *"revolutionary leadership"*, making *"profound preparations for revolution"*, for deposing the capitalist class by force, and understanding *"the necessity for the dictatorship of the proletariat"*, turn out to be mere wretched phrases and the purest form of charlatanry when the NCP, as a matter of fact, is *"looking for soft options and illusory parliamentary roads to socialism"* by attempting to convince, against all historical evidence, and in flagrant violation of Leninism, that *"the Labour Party does not belong to the right wing. It belongs to the working class, and we need to reclaim it".*

These concluding words of its document fly in the face of historical truth, for the Labour Party has never been a party of the working class; it has never belonged to the working class; it has been, to use Lenin's apt terminology *"a bourgeois labour party"* of the type which the conditions of monopoly engendered first in Britain and subsequently in all the imperialist countries. Those, like the NCP, who want to *"reclaim"* it, merely express the desire to reclaim a *"bourgeois labour party"* for the working class. Moreover, they 'forget' Lenin's words that "the social chauvinist *or (what is the same thing) the opportunist tendency can neither disappear nor 'return'* [or be *"reclaimed"* by, to use NCP's terminology - HB] *to the revolutionary proletariat"*. Whereas Lenin, recognising the irrevocable split in the working class, between the privileged minority, on the one hand, and the vast masses, on the other, says: "The fact is that 'bourgeois labour parties', as a political phenomenon, have already been formed in all the advanced capitalist countries, and unless a determined ruthless struggle is conducted against these parties all along the line ... it is useless talking about the struggle against imperialism, about Marxism, *or about the socialist labour movement"* (*Imperialism and the Split in Socialism*).

The NCP, in typical Kautskyite fashion, endeavours to reconcile the proletariat to the *"bourgeois labour party"* instead of waging a ruthless determined struggle against it.

"Kautskyism does not represent an independent trend", says Lenin, *"since it has no roots in the masses or in the privileged stratum which has deserted to the side of the bourgeoisie. The danger of Kautskyism lies in that it utilises the ideology of the past in its efforts to reconcile the proletariat with the 'bourgeois labour party', to preserve the unity of the proletariat with that party and thereby to uphold its prestige..."* (*ibid*).

A little further down, criticising Kautsky's sophisms, and this criticism is directly applicable to the NCP and such-like groups and organisations, Lenin says:

"One of the most common sophisms of Kautsky is his reference to the 'masses'; we do not want to break away from the masses and mass organisations! But think how Engels approached this question. In the nineteenth century, the 'mass organisations' of the English trade unions were on the side of the bourgeois labour party. Marx and Engels did not conciliate with it on this ground, but exposed it. They did not forget, first that the trade union organisations directly embrace the MINORITY OF THE PROLETARIAT. In England, then, as in Germany *now, not more than one-fifth of the proletariat was organised. It cannot be seriously believed that it is possible to organise the majority of the proletariat under capitalism. Second - and this is the main point - it is not so much a question of how many members there are in an organisation, as what is the real, objective meaning of its policy: does this policy represent the masses? Does it serve the masses, i.e., the liberation of the masses from capitalism, or does it represent the interests of the minority, its conciliation with capitalism? The latter was true for England of the nineteenth century, it is true for Germany, etc., at the present time.*

"Engels draws a distinction between the 'bourgeois labour party' of the OLD trade unions, a privileged minority, and the 'great mass', the real majority. Engels appeals to the latter, which is not infected with 'bourgeois respectability'. This is the essence of Marxian tactics!" (ibid).

From all this, Lenin draws the conclusion: "*And it is our duty, therefore, if we wish to remain Socialists, to go down LOWER and DEEPER, to the real masses: this is the meaning and the whole content of the struggle against opportunism. Exposing the fact that the opportunists and social-chauvinists in reality betray and sell out the interests of the masses, that they defend the temporary privileges of a minority of workers, that they transmit bourgeois ideas and influences, that in practice they are the allies and agents of the bourgeoisie, we thereby teach the masses to understand their real political interests, to fight for socialism and revolution. ...*" (ibid).

Emphasising the necessity of breaking with opportunism, Lenin concludes: "*To explain to the masses the inevitability and the necessity of breaking with opportunism, to educate them for revolution by a merciless struggle against opportunism, ... unmasking the hideousness of National-Liberal-Labour politics and not to cover them up, is the only Marxian line to be followed in the world labour movement*" (ibid).

The NCP, which claims to be *"in the mould of Lenin"*, far from learning from the above profound pronouncements of Leninism, is, on the contrary, working overtime to do all that which is within its power to foster illusions in the Labour Party, *"to reconcile the proletariat with the 'bourgeois labour party', to preserve the unity of the proletariat with that party and thereby to uphold its prestige"*. Far from building an alternative revolutionary leadership, which it claims to be engaged in, the NCP is hindering the fulfilment of this the most important task of today by calling upon class-conscious workers not to down-play "*the historical role of the Labour Party and its potential to unify the working class"* (NCP document). This is nothing less than an attempt to foster the illusion that the Labour Party, this tried, tested and proven agent of British imperialism, has the *"potential to unify the working class"* in the interests of the working class and we must do nothing to hinder the realisation of that, its potential, which, moreover, accords with its *"historical role"* as such a unifying force!

Moreover, this is nothing less than an endorsement of the parliamentary road to socialism, albeit in a most indirect and subtle way, and a most vulgar distortion of the Marxian teaching on the state. Once again, as this question is dealt with elsewhere in this publication, it is not dealt with here. The criticisms made of other organisations in this regard apply equally to the NCP.

If this is so, would it not be the only logical thing for the NCP to call a special congress to discuss, and pass, a resolution for voluntary liquidation and ask its members to join the Labour Party, as has been done by diverse Trotskyite and revisionist groups on precisely the same grounds, namely, that *"the masses are in the Labour Party, we do not want to break with the masses, its leadership may be right-wing but the party belongs to the masses and we must reclaim the Party for the latter, that we must not down-play Labour's historical role and its potential for unifying the working class"*, and so on and so forth *ad nauseam*?

As if to leave no one in doubt about the NCP stance, the document adds: *"And why is it okay to work inside the trade unions - in which we have to contend with the right-wing all the time - but not inside the Labour Party* [the NCP ought to know the difference between a trade-union organisation and a political party - this is elementary - HB] *where we meet the same individuals and policies* [this does not prevent the NCP from stating in the same document a few paragraphs further down that the right-wing Labour leadership wants to sever the connection between the Labour Party and the trade unions because the latter are progressive and, therefore, a danger to its right-wing agenda! - HB]".

"Those who argue for a 'new party of labour' to be set up", says the NCP smugly, *"should be mindful of the words of J.F.Hodgson"* that *"... other people ... have got hold of the political movement of the workers, BECAUSE WE HAVE BEEN ABSENT"* (emphasis in original). In other words, the Labour Party is THE political movement of the British proletariat and we ought not to be absent from it, which is to say that we should be in the Labour Party to wrest control from the *"other people"* - the right-wing!

We fear that unless the comrades of the NCP retrace their steps and desist forthwith from this patently incorrect, and blatantly reactionary, line, they are in real danger of falling over the precipice into the abyss of social democracy, from which it will not be possible for us to *"reclaim"* them for the working class.

Far from building a revolutionary alternative, it opposes those who want to break with Labour and build a new party with a left-wing programme, for, argues the NCP, *"If the political will and resources exist to create such a party, then surely they can be used to change the disastrous and class-collaborationist stance of today's Labour Party"*. If this is not a call to disgruntled Labour Party members to stay put and call a call to others to join this imperialist party in order to *"change the ... class-collaborationist stance of today's Labour Party"*, we fail to understand what it is. While claiming to be "in the mould of Lenin", the NCP comrades, going completely against Leninism, which advocates the necessity of recognising the irrevocable split in the working class, and of the need to give it political and organisational form, are busy attempting *"to reconcile the proletariat with 'the bourgeois labour party', to preserve the unity of the proletariat with that party and thereby to uphold its prestige"*.

Far from building a revolutionary alternative, the NCP is interested merely in gaining affiliation to the Labour Party at any cost - and this, incidentally, it does by completely ignoring the long history of the CPGB's struggle (and it was a real struggle which mobilised hundreds of thousands of workers unlike the NCP's declamations) to gain affiliation to the Labour Party. The CPGB's attempts failed because, as shown above, the Labour Party, being a reactionary tool of British imperialism would never allow affiliation of revolutionary organisations. And to keep following along that rut is nothing short of self-delusion. In the NCP's own terminology: *"It seems rather strange that in 1994* [1995 now - HB] *we are having to restate what the Labour Party actually is, nearly a hundred years after its foundation"*!

Far from building a revolutionary alternative, which is inextricably bound up with destroying Labour's pernicious influence over the working class, the NCP fears like the plague the destruction of the Labour Party, for, to quote its document, *"arguing for the destruction of the Labour Party or 'refusing to vote for them' is counter-productive* [and] *... is also deeply reactionary"* as these two alternatives *shirk the responsibility of winning back* [sic!] *the Labour Party for the working class"* and therefore *"obvectively give in to the right-wing"*. Continues the document:

"And strangely, neither position puts forward any conception of fighting the bans and proscriptions enshrined in Labour Party rules against communists. Nor indeed does either stance consider campaigning for an understanding that communists, in alliance with the left, should conduct a campaign for affiliation to the Labour Party itself".

The logic of this argument is clear. Don't do anything that might lead to the destruction of the Labour Party; instead work hard, and in alliance with the left, conduct a campaign for affiliation to the Labour Party. Meanwhile do not do anything, as for instance standing candidates at elections, which might provide an excuse to the right-wing in the Labour Party to keep NCP out. It is a counsel of capitulation to social democracy all along the line.

Thus, whichever way one turns, one finds nothing but the NCP's touching concern for the health and preservation of this stinking corpse which is called the Labour Party; at every turn one finds the NCP's attempts to reconcile the proletariat to this stinking corpse by inculcating in it the illusion that this stinking corpse can not only be revived, but also made fragrant in the interests of the working class. All of this goes to show beyond reasonable doubt that the NCP, instead of making a serious attempt to build a revolutionary alternative organisation, with the intent, will and capacity to represent the true interests of the British proletariat and lead the latter in its struggle for socialism, for the dictatorship of the proletariat, is in reality fast reducing itself into a society for the preservation of the Labour Party. In view of all that has been said above, it is impossible to treat with anything other than derision the NCP claim that "we are communists in the mould of Lenin".

After all this, we do not know whether to admire the NCP more for its audacity or for its sense of humour when it asserts with great aplomb that it *"is in the interests of the working class that our party is strengthened* [so that it may work hard to strengthen the Labour Party? - HB] *and earns the right to be recognised as the revolutionary vanguard of the working class as it helps that class to develop the capacity to achieve its emancipation from capitalist exploitation and oppression".*

With its present attitude to the Labour Party, the NCP is more likely, and deservedly so, to win the right to be recognised as the tail-end of the former for the untiring services it (the NCP) is rendering in an attempt to tie the proletariat ever more firmly to the chariot of counter-revolutionary social-democracy. Whether prompted by courage, born out of ignorance and its own make-believe reality, or by its remarkable sense of humour, the above assertion of the NCP is bound to provoke Homeric laughter.

We, on the contrary, must explain to the masses that the position of working to preserve the Labour Party is the one which is *"counter-productive"* and *"also deeply reactionary"* from the point of view of the interests of the proletariat; that it is only by ignoring the interests of the proletariat and the tenets and injunctions of Marxism-Leninism alike that one can adopt the position taken by the NCP; and that in adopting this position, wittingly or otherwise, the NCP is serving the interests of the class whose interests are irreconcilably hostile to that of the British proletariat.

In pursuing this erroneous political line, the NCP goes further than any of the other organisations which we have had the opportunity to criticise in these pages. It opposes even the policy of standing candidates at elections, national or local, against official Labour Party candidates, first, because such a policy is not only *"sectarian and divisive, leading to confusion in the minds of the working class"*, but also *"deeply reactionary"*. Secondly, as the policy of standing candidates prevents, under Rule Three of the Labour Party Constitution, organisations doing so from gaining affiliation to the Labour Party, this policy, asserts the NCP, *"only assisted the right wing in keeping communists out"*.

We have already commented at length on the attempts of the CPGB to gain affiliation to the Labour Party, and on the latter's persistent refusal to accept communist affiliation. There is no need, therefore, to repeat those arguments here. We would merely add that the Rule Three of Labour Constitution is far more all-embracing in its anti-communist sweep than the NCP's interpretation of it would cause anyone to believe. Rule Three says that *"political organisations not affiliated to or associated under a national agreement with the Party on January 1, 1946, having their own programme, principles and policy for distinctive, separate propaganda, or possessing branches on the constituencies or engaged in the promotion of parliamentary or local government candidatures, or owing allegiance to any political organisation situated abroad, shall be ineligible for affiliation to the Party"*.

As can be seen, not only do organisations standing candidates in elections attract ineligibility for affiliation; so also do those with *"their own programme, principles and policy for distinctive, separate propaganda ... or owing allegiance to any political organisation situated abroad"*. Is the NCP proposing that revolutionaries stop having their programme, principles and policy, that they stop disseminating their distinctive, separate propaganda, so as not to assist the right wing in keeping communists out? If the NCP leadership as much as dared to say so openly, it would become not only an instant pariah in the communist movement but face a revolt on the part of its membership. And yet this is the remorseless logic of the document it has put forward; it is prepared to do anything to save the skin of the Labour Party and to gain affiliation to it. While an organisation still possesses even a modicum, even a tiny resolve, of communist principles, the Labour Party would never allow it affiliation. *"While the drooping flowers pine for love, the heartless brook carries on"*, so runs an old Chinese proverb. The Labour Party will continue to treat the NCP's wooing with complete and utter contempt. In order to be close to its beloved, in order for its love to be requited, the NCP must make a humiliating act of complete and unconditional surrender, admit the error of its ways, drop all pretence to independence and assertions of being the vanguard of the British working class, drop all allusions to Marxism-Leninism - in short tread the same path of apostasy that so many Trotskyites and revisionists have already traversed.

In its zeal to defend its bankrupt policy, the NCP even goes to the length of accusing the erstwhile CPGB of sectarianism for no other reason than the latter stood candidates at elections. In the language of the document;

'The position of the communist movement in Britain, from the foundation of the CPGB in 1921 up until 1977, was a sectarian one with regard to the Labour party and elections".

The NCP, which has difficulty mobilising 50 persons at a time, has the gall to criticise the CPGB for precisely those of its policies which were correct, revolutionary, and successful in rallying around it tens of thousands, even hundreds of thousands, of workers. There is a lot in the programme, the policies and tactics of the CPGB during the twenties and thirties of which revolutionaries today can be very proud, and from which they can learn a great deal, instead of snivelling and flippantly characterising the CPGB's position as sectarian, and as having assisted the right-wing in keeping communists out of the Labour Party.

If one of the excuses, used by the organisations criticised by us in the pages above, was, to use the terminology of the NCP document, *"its socialist constitution in the form of Clause Four"*, Labour has removed this fig leaf used so long by the trendy-Troto and revisionist 'left' for masking its capitulation to social democracy. This is the sequence of events in this regard.

Labour Ditches Clause IV

Tony Blair, the present Labour Party leader, set the tone, in his speech to the Labour Party Conference on Tuesday, 4th October 1994. Having stated that *"ours is a project of national renewal"*, he went on to urge the delegates to *"debate new ideas - new thinking - without fearing the taunt of betrayal"*, adding that there would be *"no more ditching, no more dumping"*. Making a particular point of rejecting "the socialism of Marx, or state control", he asserted that the restoration of the British economy *"won't be done by state control or by market dogma"*, but *"only ... by a dynamic market economy* [i.e. by market dogma] *based on partnership"* - whatever this means.

In an attempt to obscure his total and utter obsequiousness to monopoly capitalism he drowned the Conference with a torrent of meaningless, hypocritical and hollow rhetoric. Equating socialism with *"social partnership"*, he said that the new Britain would be built on *"opportunity, responsibility, fairness and trust"*. Following the time-hallowed custom of all bourgeois tricksters, Blair retracted every promise to working people no sooner than it had been made. Labour stood by its commitment to a minimum wage, he said, but it would be introduced *"flexibly and sensibly"*. No wonder, then, that the Conference in its resolution on this question failed to mention the sum of £4.15 an hour - that is, a mere half of the average earnings for an hour. Reiterating the Labour Party's commitment to full employment, a commitment which cannot be reconciled with its commitment to a *"dynamic market economy"* and its rejection of Marxian socialism, Mr Blair went on to dispel all illusions on this score by adding that full employment could not be achieved *"overnight"*, proposing instead "a national voluntary task force of young people given constructive tasks to do ... we will put welfare to work" - something the bourgeoisie has been demanding so insistently for years, and, which even the hated Tories have not dared to give effect to.

During the same speech he was extremely firm and sincere in his promises to monopoly capitalism - the only promises his party in government can be relied to keep. Anti-trade union legislation, passed during the decade-and-a-half of Conservative rule, would not be repealed, he said. Strike ballots will be kept intact. Public undertakings, privatised during the past 15 years by the Conservatives, will not be brought back into public ownership. Echoing the concerns of a section of the ruling class, he expressed a pious wish for the continued public ownership of the Post Office and the railways.

Acting according to his own advice that the Party should only promise what it can deliver, and by way of a pointer to what it can deliver to the working class, Blair, with a cynicism unprecedented even by bourgeois standards, ended up by making no promises. Instead he bombarded the Conference with a plethora of trivial constitutional proposals, such as the abolition of hereditary peerages, the enactment of a Bill of Rights and a Freedom of Information Act, and the establishment of a Scottish parliament and a Welsh assembly.

Most of all, and by way of a diversion from the misery and shame of his hour-long hollow speech, Mr Blair regaled the delegates by attacking Tory sleaze and corruption: *"Their time is up. Their philosophy is doomed. Their experiment is over. Their failure is clear. It is time to go"*. He went on to say that the Labour Party was once again *"the mainstream voice"*, representing the majority in British politics. Addressing himself especially to middle-class voters, he said: *"The Tories have betrayed you ... Labour is on your side"*.

The decisions of the 1994 Conference on all the important issues, ranging from the economy, unemployment and minimum wage to defence, education, trade-union legislation, social benefits and Ireland, reflected that which was demanded by Tony Blair in his speech. The notorious 'left' windbags and illusion-mongers such as Peter Hain, Tony Benn, Ken Livingstone and a few others, having made their customary growls, grovellingly fell in line. One felt sorry at the presence of such an upright, sincere and dignified figure as Arthur Scargill, the miners' leader, amidst such a disgusting gathering of hundreds of renegades and traitors to the cause of the British and the international proletariat. It was precisely the sincerity, steadfastness and fidelity to the working-class movement, so characteristic of Scargill, which made his presence in the Conference hall such a bizarre occurrence.

In order to give a *de jure* effect to that which had been there *de facto* for the previous 76 years, and in an attempt to break even the semblance of a connection between the Labour Party and what might be perceived as socialism by the bourgeoisie and the 'left'-wing of social democracy (the revisionists and Trotskyites) alike, Tony Blair announced from the rostrum of the conference hall his determination to get rid of Clause IV of the Labour Party Constitution, which committed the Party "to secure for the workers by hand or by brain the full fruits of their industry, and the most equitable distribution thereof that may be possible upon the basis of the common ownership *of the means of production, distribution and exchange, and the best obtainable system of popular administration and control of each industry or service"*.

Although two days later, on Thursday 6th October, the Conference, by a tiny majority, voted in favour of the motion (Composite 57) in support of Clause IV, Tony Blair and his supporters made all but clear, in fashion characteristic of bourgeois leaderships, that they will ignore this resolution and push ahead with plans to get rid of this embarrassment and electoral liability which is what Clause IV is to them, engaged as they are in a desperate attempt to win the voters belonging to the middle class and the well-off sections of the working class - the so-called C1s and C2s. The Labour Party must not only champion the interests of British monopoly capitalism and the labour aristocracy, which it has always done, but must also be seen to be doing so. As Clause IV obscures this perception, at least on the part of the dull-witted bourgeois, petty-bourgeois and labour aristocrats, it must be consigned to the grave and a cross put on it. Thinking (the programme) must catch up with practice; for far too long has it been allowed to lag behind practice. Even at the time the Clause was drafted and inserted in the Labour Party's programme in 1918, it was done not with the aim of bringing socialism but for keeping the trade unions, the Independent Labour Party (ILP), the syndicalists and pacifists all on board, as well as a diversion from the kind of public ownership ushered in by the Great Socialist October Revolution under the leadership of the Bolshevik Party. And since its inclusion in the Constitution of the Labour Party, Clause IV has been honoured by its breach rather than observance. The editorial in the *Economist* of 8th October 1994 explained rather well the motives behind Tony Blair's attempt to get rid of a provision which has been dead as a dodo in practice right from its inception. Said the *Economist*:

"... *If politics were entirely about substance, this* [i.e. dropping Clause IV - HB] *would mean nothing. Labour had no intention of putting Clause Four into practice. But in politics, symbols matter. Clause Four stands for Labour's intellectual debts to Marx, for its origins as a party of struggling proletarians, for the politics of protest and confrontation. It also stands for Labour's ability to lie to itself and the electorate - a tendency that Mr Blair explicitly named and denounced*".

Of course, we do not agree with the above formulation in so far as it implies that Tony Blair is opposed to either the Labour Party lying to itself or the electorate, through Clause IV or otherwise. The important thing, however, is that the dichotomy between the Labour Party's practice and Clause IV, which can be, as it has been, exploited by the Conservatives to scare voters from the middle class and upper layers of working class away from Labour by painting it as a socialist party bent upon taking into public ownership *"the means of production, distribution and exchange"*. Hence Tony Blair's insistence in his speech that the Labour Party *"requires a modern constitution that says what we are in terms that the public* [i.e. middle class and privileged layers of the working class, let alone the bourgeoisie - HB] *can understand"*.

Nor do we agree with the implication that the Labour Party was formed as a party of *"struggling proletarians"*, for in our view the Labour Party was formed by a small privileged stratum of the British working class - the labour aristocracy - in close alliance with a radical section of the middle class for the sole purpose of safeguarding their economic and political interests. Consequently, we assert, that the Labour Party is not, never has been, and never will be, a party of the British proletariat. Although this is the reality, the perception - partly the creation of the bourgeois and Tory propaganda machine, and partly of the radical wing of social democracy ranging from the revisionists to the hundred and one varieties of Trotskyism - persists which identifies Labour with the interests of the *"struggling proletarians"* and the *"politics of protest and confrontation"*. And it is this perception, this symbol, that Mr Blair and his party set out in 1994 to get rid of, and for which Mr Blair earned the accolades of the British imperialist print and electronic media. Even the most loyal Tory scandal sheets, with not a little hyperbole, compared him to Winston Churchill, that arch reactionary leader of British imperialism during the Second World War. The BBC's *Panorama* programme on the Monday following the Labour Party Conference (10th October 1994) was nothing short of a political broadcast on behalf of Tony Blair and the new-look Labour Party.

Even back in October 1994, there was not the slightest doubt that Tony Blair would be successful in dumping Clause IV. For all the noises made by those who opposed him at the Conference on this question, they ended the mutiny on their knees almost as soon as the Conference was over. On Saturday October 8th, Bill Morris, General Secretary of TGWU, the biggest affiliated union, which voted in favour of Clause IV, publicly backed the Labour leader's proposal, as did Robin Cook, the leading Shadow Cabinet sceptic. Welcoming the review, Bill Morris said:

"It gives this generation a chance - the first in over 70 years - to establish Labour's aims and values for the next century".

Peter Hain, Chairman of the allegedly left-wing Tribune group, stated: *"I think the majority mood is - let's seize the opportunity provided by this debate and consultation and achieve a clear commitment to public ownership, but not of the old state-socialist nationalisation model"*! One cannot fail to be astounded by the staggering ignorance of economics and political economy displayed in this remark made by the leader of a group, allegedly the guardian of socialist principles.

As soon as the 1994 Labour Conference was over, an assortment of illusion-mongers, always on the look-out for some excitement and diversionary activity away from the real task of building a truly proletarian party, set up a Campaign to Defend Clause Four, allegedly *"Labour's socialist soul"*. Nothing came of it in the end. Tony Blair received the endorsement of Labour's National Executive (at the latter's meeting on 13 March 1995) for dumping Clause IV by a majority of 21 against 3. A month later, a Special Conference of the Labour Party, attended by 1000 delegates, met on Saturday 29th April 1995 in Westminster Hall, and voted 65.23 per cent in favour of ditching Clause IV. The reaction of the 'left', who had vowed to fight to the death in the struggle to save Clause IV, was rather typified by the following remark of Rodney Bickerstaffe, leader of the public service workers' union - UNISON: *"I have difficulty keeping sight of the tail lights of the modernist juggernaut"*. Instead of picking up, as they had promised, the gauntlet thrown by the Labour leadership, the 'left', including the Trotskyite and revisionist 'left', have meekly submitted and are working hard and conscientiously to *"Kick the Tories out"* and replace it by a Tory Blair government. Only the NCP, ever hankering after illusions, and for want of something better to do, has found a way out of this dead end by declaring in the columns of its paper that a campaign must now be launched for the restoration of Clause IV to the Labour Party Constitution. This could surely keep the NCP busy for the rest of its life!

Labour's Connection with Trade Unions

Now we must deal with the third - and the last - excuse for the Trotskyite-revisionist 'left' supporting Labour, namely, that because of its connections with the unions, Labour is the mass party of the British working class, and that through the unions the 'left' can have a decisive say in the policy and conduct of the Labour Party - it being further asserted that the trade unions are the source of all that is progressive in the Labour Party. This argument is more fully developed by the NCP than any of the other organisations supporting Labour. We shall therefore take the NCP position as a basis of our analysis on this question. In its document the NCP states, that the right-wing in the Labour Party "has set itself the task of transforming Labour into a continental-style social democratic party - abandoning its socialist constitution in the form of Clause Four *and, more importantly, seeking to retain no ORGANISED links with the mass organisations of the working class* [in other words, the trade unions].

"The Labour Party was established to represent the interests of the trade unions in Parliament at the beginning of the century. The links between the trade unions and the parliamentary party *were established in struggle.*

"And while those links remain, the Labour Party can be rightly described as the mass party of the working class".

For a start, if the truth be known, it is continental social democracy which has, historically speaking, followed the trail blazed by the Labour Party. That this happened at the time of the start of the First World War, is known even to serious and honest bourgeois scholars, but somehow this simple truth has alluded the communists of the NCP.

Although it is undoubtedly true that the Labour Party was established by the trade unions to have their interests represented in Parliament, it is equally true, as we have already shown, that the trade unions at the time represented a privileged minority of the working class, the labour aristocracy (composed by and large of skilled craft workers). And it was this privileged aristocracy, who, hitherto in alliance with the Liberal Party and acting as an adjunct of the latter, finding that in the changed conditions the Liberal Party could no longer be trusted to safeguard their privileged position, effected an organisational breach with the Liberal Party by setting up the Labour Representation Committee, which in 1906 became the Labour Party. The overwhelming majority of the working class were outside of the trade unions and outside of the Labour Party; and neither the trade unions nor the Labour Party ever bothered much about the conditions of the lower layers of the working class. In 1982, out of a workforce of 14 million, a mere 1.5 million (less than 10 per cent) belonged to the trade unions. This remained the situation until almost the eve of the First World War. In the years following the First World War, trade unions represented but a fifth of the working class. Even in 1979, when trade union membership was at its peak, with 13 million members, the trade unions did not represent a majority of the working class. Since then their membership has shrunk to 7.5 million. Apart from this, as pointed out earlier, a party does not become a *"political workers' party"* just because it consists of workers. Whether a party *"is really a political proletarian party"* depends upon *"who leads it, upon the content of its activities and of its political tactics"*. "From this point of view, which is the only correct point of view, the Labour Party *is not a political workers' party but a thoroughly bourgeois party"* (Lenin, *op cit*).

And why for some years has *"the right-wing conducted a campaign ... for a weakening of links between the political and industrial wings"*? Because, says the NCP document: *"Those on the right have always been perfectly aware of the potential represented by the link between the political and industrial wings of the movement"*. Continues the document:

"After the debacle of the Callaghan *government of 1979 and its anti-working class stance - followed by the Tory election victory - the right wing began a serious offensive to break the organised link between the political and industrial wings"*.

And further: "What the right wing wanted was the removal of trade union *influence at the annual Labour Party conferences and in the selection of constituency candidates.*

"In other words, those organisations representing the overwhelming majority of organised workers are no longer to have any say in the creation and promotion of policy, let alone help to determine who should represent them in Parliament - *the very purpose the Labour Party was set up for.*

"From the point of view of the right, with its strategy of class collaboration, this removal is crucial if an assault on the socialist constitution of the Labour Party, enshrined in Clause Four, *is to be successful".*

The breaking of the formal links between the political and industrial wings, says the document, "is the Blair *leadership's real target and has always been so. Once the formal link between the political and industrial wings has been broken, then the road is clear for a complete surrender to the interests of the transnationals and their economic priorities.*

"But we can draw a positive conclusion from all this. If the right-wing fears the potential that unity of the two wings of the movement brings about, it is because they at least recognise it as a danger to its own agenda.

"Each year up until now, the Labour Party conference has repeatedly passed progressive economic and political resolutions, emanating essentially, from within the trade union movement, after discussion amongst its own members".

And *"If the right-wing recognises the strength of unity between the political and industrial wings, then so must we. And accordingly, we must fight at every level of the movement to preserve it.*

"The agenda of the ruling class is clear. It is one which seeks to remove the trade unions from all effective intervention in the economic and political affairs of the country.

"We should not try and assist it by down playing the historical role of the Labour Party *and its potential to unify the working class. ... ".*

And finally *"Today, the Blair leadership is on the brink of achieving what the right wing has failed to do over nearly a hundred years: to break the organisational unity of the working class.*

"Campaigning for the retention of Clause Four will be meaningless if it is divorced from an understanding that the unity of the political and industrial wings of the labour movement is paramount".

Every single sentence in these extensive quotations, reproduced immediately above from the NCP document, is either factually incorrect or politically wrong (if not downright reactionary), or both.

Firstly, it is not true that the trade unions represent the overwhelming majority of the workforce, for out of a workforce of 27 million less than a third (7.5 million) are in the trade unions - 7 million of these belong to unions affiliated to the TUC. The NCP would probably protest that it never said such a thing, as its document speaks of the *"organisations representing the overwhelming majority of the organised workers"*. However, unless given the interpretation that we, in a mood of kindliness and generosity, have given it, the sentence is a meaningless tautology, for it would simply mean that the majority of the trade unionists are represented in the trade unions!!

Secondly, as is the perennial fate of the NCP, it has got everything upside down with the assertion that for the right wing it is essential to break the formal link between the political and industrial wings *"if the assault on the socialist constitution of the Labour Party, enshrined in Clause Four, is to be successful"*! Well, the assault on the allegedly socialist constitution has been successfully accomplished without as yet breaking the links between the two wings of the Labour Party. What is more, the trade unions just as gleefully joined in this assault on 'socialism' by voting in favour of dumping Clause IV as did the other sections of the Labour Party.

Thirdly, displaying complete ignorance of the history of the labour movement or complete 'forgetfulness', the NCP asserts that the right wing needs to break the formal links between the political and industrial wings as a means of clearing the way for *"a complete surrender to the interests of the transnationals and their economic priorities"*. Even honest bourgeois scholars, let alone Marxist-Leninists, acknowledge that Labour made *"a complete surrender"* to British monopoly capitalism a very long time ago - again without in the least severing the link between the two wings, and at a time it was busy writing and incorporating the 'socialism' of Clause IV into its constitution. Has the NCP not heard of the betrayal of the General Strike of 1926 and of Mondism?

Fourthly, equally wrong is the assertion of the NCP that the Labour Party Conference has repeatedly passed progressive resolutions on economic and political questions and that these resolutions have emanated essentially from within the trade-union movement. We have fully demonstrated above that the TUC, whether under the stewardship of Citrine or any of his equally despicable successors, has never been less reactionary than the political wing on any really important issue of British imperial policy touching upon the really vital interests of British imperialism at home or abroad. We challenge the NCP to produce some evidence in substantiation of its viewpoint rather than a mere assertion, a repetition of the same assertion, and a vague reference to *"progressive economic and political resolutions"*. Whether it was the question of imperialist and colonial wars, of India or Ireland, the General Strike or the plight of the unemployed, the question of the attitude towards the Socialist Soviet Union or the war against fascism in Spain, Egyptian sovereignty over the Suez Canal or the Middle East oil riches, the fight against Mosley's fascists or the attitude to the CPGB, or the Coal Strike of 1984-5, the TUC was, without exception, at one with the Labour leadership, and both were always on the reactionary side. In view of this, the NCP must be living in a completely different world - in its own make believe reality - looking at an imaginary trade-union movement which is totally discordant with the real trade-union movement as is known to us and every serious and honest student of this question. Thus, it can be seen, the unity of the two wings - political and industrial - has presented no danger to the right-wing agenda, the vociferous assertions of the NCP to the contrary notwithstanding.

For our part, we too are against the neutrality of the trade-union movement; we too would like the trade-union movement to be guided by the political wing. The all too important question, however, is what must be the physiognomy of that political wing, what must be the programme, the policies and political tactics of that wing, and, who leads that wing? We too would like the British trade-union movement to have links with, and be guided by, a truly revolutionary party - a communist party - of the proletariat. However, thanks to the treachery of modern Khruschevite revisionism, no such party, unfortunately, exists in Britain today. Therefore, the most important task confronting British communists today is to exert every ounce of their energy in the fulfilment of this task, to devote themselves with single-minded determination to build such a revolutionary party, without which the British proletariat will not move a flea hop nearer the goal of its emancipation.

And this task, notwithstanding the NCP's distaste for the bitter truth, is inextricably linked with destroying the influence of the Labour Party over the working class, if not destroying this monstrosity itself. In severing links with the unions, objectively speaking, Tony Blair, no matter how base his motives, is acting in a far more revolutionary way than is the NCP, no matter how noble the latter's motives.

Instead of stressing this, the NCP preaches a peculiar mix of economism and social democraticism, and its political line may be described as one of economist-social democracy, or more accurately, social-democratic economism, which boils down to working for the preservation of social democracy (this *"mass party of the working class"*, whose *"historical role ... and potential to unify the working class"* one must now downplay, you see), whose industrial wing being more *"progressive"*, must guide its political wing.

Although claiming to be *"in the mould of Lenin"*, the NCP are clearly oblivious to the fact that the trade unions of their own accord can bring forth no other politics than trade union politics, which is precisely what economism is. And, in the NCP's dreamland scenario, if the industrial wing of the Labour Party was to have a determining influence on Labour Party policy, we would hardly fare any better, for the end result would be economism pure and simple, leading, to use Lenin's memorable phrase to *"a slavish cringing before spontaneity"*, the complete overwhelming of consciousness by spontaneity, and the strengthening of bourgeois ideology among the workers. This is the essence of trade union politics of which the NCP are so enamoured.

Trade Unions Today

Even from the narrow trade-union angle, the trade unions do not by any means present the idyllic picture painted of them by the NCP and such other worshippers of British trade unionism. The dramatic fall in the membership of trade unions since 1979, accompanied by changes in the composition of the workforce (away from manufacturing to banking, financial services, insurance, etc.[1]), the restructuring and amalgamation of the unions, have all produced a

---

1 Whereas the numbers of those employed in the mines, on the railways and in manufacturing have been falling steadily, those employed in banking, financial services and insurance have risen sharply. Those in the former category, fell from being 9.786 million in 1964 to 7.580 million in 1979 and 4.939 million in 1991; during the same period, those in the latter category rose from 3.699 million to 5.053 million and 6.740 million. Within the manufacturing sector itself, this period witnessed a shift in the pattern of employment away from manual jobs in

situation whereby the unions are more and more coming to resemble what they were at the end of the last century - representing not merely a minority of the working class but also its privileged layers alone.

Basing himself on the 1991 Labour Force Survey presented in the *Employment Gazette* of January 1993, Gavin Scott (see his article *'Whose Unions'* in FRFI June/July 1993) correctly concludes that "the trade unions are increasingly dominated, controlled and directed by a new labour aristocracy *of non-manual workers - a tiny minority of educated, managerial, professional and associated workers"*, that "the trade-union movement *does not represent women, the low-paid, part-time or temporary workers"*, let alone the unemployed. This is even more true now as trade union membership has fallen by a further million since then. The unions today embrace less than 30 per cent of the workforce (7.5 million out of a workforce of 27 million). The fall in trade union membership has been facilitated by the change in trade-union policy, whereby, instead of collective representation of the workforce, the unions are concentrating on the provision of personal services such as credit cards, private health, insurance and cheap holidays. As only those enjoying relatively high incomes can take advantage of these services, it is not surprising that the better off sections have become the focus of union activity. They have in fact become friendly societies, managing huge property portfolios amounting to hundreds of millions of pounds, run by a privileged and corrupt coterie, enjoying incomes and perks undreamt of by workers and which set them apart from, and in opposition to, the workers, and providing the above-enumerated services largely to the privileged layers of the working class.

To give the reader a glimpse of the chasm that divides the proletariat from the new labour aristocracy who run and control the unions, we shall resort to the information provided by the Certification Office for Trade unions and Employers' Association, to whom the unions are obliged by law to furnish, *inter alia*, information on salaries and perks awarded to union officials. Unless abso-

---

favour of white collar jobs. Whereas the white collar workers represented 23.1 per cent of the total manufacturing workforce in 1964, they had come to represent 28.6 per cent of the same by 1979. These changes could not but result in a change in the composition of the privileged strratum, which now consists in the main of white collar employees. This privileged stratum, of predominantly educated, salaried white collar workers grew in response to the expansion of the state and the service sector, and, more recently, in response to what has come to be called the information technology revolution.

lutely necessary, in order to avoid personalising the issue, we shall refrain from mentioning the names of the recipients of these huge salaries. We shall mention the total sum received by the head of the union concerned. Here, then, are the sums received annually by the Union bosses. Royal College of Nursing: £76,262; Association of Teachers and Lecturers: £71,860; National Union of Teachers: £65,126; National Communications Union: £53,241; Engineers and Managers Association: £59,887; MSF: £60,399; UNISON: £60,000; National Union of Mineworkers: £56,000 + car; National Association of Schoolmasters: £50,000; Institution of Professional Managers and Specialists: £57,331; Union of Communication Workers: £54,137; Inland Revenue Staff Federation: £55,367; General, Municipal and Boilermakers: £55,000; Banking, Insurance and Finance Union: £54,002; USDAW: £53,894; Royal College of Midwives: £49,724; RMT: £57,107; and TGWU £54,000

Clive Jenkins of MSF took early retirement in 1988 with a handshake of more than £200,000 from his union, which, according to a senior MSF official was *"strictly in accordance with his contract"*. His successor, Ken Gill, received a retirement package of £201,000 in 1992.

As to the political wing of *"this great movement of ours"*, to use Michael Foot's fatuous expression, we have the example of Mr Neil Kinnock, former leader of the Labour Party, who has been appointed as one of Britain's Commissioners on the Commission of the European Union; in this job he will enjoy a basic salary of £140,000 per annum, plus £21,000 for living abroad and a £6,000 entertainment allowance. In addition, he will be the beneficiary of a generous pension scheme, free life and health insurance, first class travel on business trips, a chauffeur-driven limousine, and relocation expenses for the move to Brussels. Meanwhile Mrs Kinnock, in her capacity as a Euro MP, will be able to supplement the family income with her modest salary of £31,687 and expenses totalling over £100,000.

The above figures, which by the standards of the budgets of working-class families are simply staggering, remind one of Lenin's penetrating observation concerning the economic basis of opportunism in the working-class movement. *"What is the economic basis of this world-historic phenomenon* [opportunism-HB]?", asks Lenin. And he answers this question thus:

"Precisely the parasitism and decay of capitalism which are characteristic of its highest historical stage of development, i.e., imperialism. ... Capitalism has now singled out a HANDFUL ... of exceptionally rich and powerful states which plunder the whole world simply by 'clipping coupons'. Capital exports yield an income of eight to ten billion francs per annum, at pre-war prices and according to pre-war bourgeois statistics. Now, of course, the yield is more.

"Obviously, out of such enormous SUPERPROFITS (since they are obtained over and above the profits which capitalists squeeze out of the workers of their 'own' country) it is POSSIBLE TO BRIBE the labour leaders and the upper stratum of the labour aristocracy. *And the capitalists of the 'advanced' countries are bribing them: they bribe them in a thousand different ways, direct and indirect, overt and covert.*

"This stratum of bourgeoisified workers, or the 'labour aristocracy', who are quite philistine in their mode of life, in the size of their earnings and in their entire outlook, is the principal prop of the Second International, and in our days, the principal SOCIAL (not military) PROP OF THE BOURGEOISIE. For they are the real AGENTS OF THE BOURGEOISIE IN THE WORKING-CLASS movement, the labour lieutenants of the capitalist class, real channels of reformism and chauvinism. In the civil war between the proletariat and the bourgeoisie they inevitably, and in no small numbers, take the side of the bourgeoisie, the 'Versaillese' against the 'Communards'.

"Unless the economic roots of this phenomenon are understood and its political and social significance is appreciated, not a step can be taken toward the solution of the practical problems of the Communist movement and of the impending social revolution.

"Imperialism is the eve of the social revolution of the proletariat. This has been confirmed since 1917 on a world-wide scale" (Lenin, Preface to the French and German Editions of *Imperialism, the Highest Stage of Capitalism*, 6 July 1920).

To return to the Labour Force Survey (LFS) and Scott's analysis of it. From its peak of 13 million in the late 1970s, union membership density (the proportion of workers belonging to a trade union) fell to 33 per cent in 1991 (8,488,000 members). That the fall in density was lower among the self-employed, is to be explained by *"the shift in union policy away from collective representation of the working class to provision of individual, personal, largely financial, services ..."* (Scott, *ibid*). Women, being by and large lower paid, have a lower density - 32 per cent as against 42 per cent among men. As for part-time workers, union density is extremely low - a mere 13 per cent among men and 23 per cent among women. In the public sector, men and women are equally represented as regards union membership, as is also true of banking and finance, indicating thus that "... there is little difference between union densities *of male and female full-time employees in industries where women account for a large proportion of total employment"* (*Employment Gazette*).

Density is much lower among young workers. In the age group 16 - 24 year-olds, the density is only 22 per cent, whereas among 35 year-olds it is 42 per cent. Among workers with a record of employment of ten or more years, membership density rises to 58 per cent.

There is also a definite link between union density and education. As for men employees, the highest density was among those possessing a higher qualification short of a degree (44 per cent) and A-level or equivalent (45 per cent), whereas it was only 33 per cent among those with one O-level or equivalent. As for female employees, density is 49 per cent in the case of degree holders and 64 per cent among those who have other higher education qualifications, whereas those with A-levels or lower qualifications have a membership density of less then 30 per cent. The concentration of highly qualified women in the teaching and health professions, where density is high, explains this phenomenon.

In its examination of the public sector (some of it privatised since then), the LFS revealed the ascendancy of highly qualified, professional, managerial and supervisory grades. The *Employment Gazette* (EG) says that the differences in union density *"between manufacturing and service industries are quite small; instead, the key factor appears to be public sector status ... all the industries where union density was above 50 per cent in 1991 are those where employment is largely or wholly in the public sector"*, adding that *"the levels of union density by occupation occur amongst certain occupations commonly associated with the public sector"*. Included among the latter are associate health professionals with a density of 74 per cent and teaching professionals with 70 per cent density.

Further, in the public sector, the non-manual workers are disproportionally represented in the unions:

"The most striking finding ... that other services, which includes national and local government, education and health, accounted for 40 per cent of trade union membership, whereas [this] *sector formed only 27 per cent of total employment"* (EG).

Union density among this group (of non-manual workers) has been rising since the end of the war. Whereas in 1948 a mere 23 per cent of non-manual workers belonged to a union, in 1991 a majority (53 per cent) held union membership. In the same period there was a reduction in the ratio of union members in manufacturing from 44 per cent to just 24 per cent. The traditional 'blue-collar' occupational groups accounted for less than 40 per cent of the total trade union membership in 1991 - a fact partly explained by changes in industry and also by *"the marked increases in union density that took pace during the 1970s amongst non-manual workers in manufacturing industry and amongst public sector workers"* (EG).

Significantly, the LFS underlines the link between managerial responsibility and union density: *"Union density was higher in 1991 amongst foremen/supervisors (46 per cent) than it was amongst people with no managerial or supervisory responsibilities"*.

The explanation for this is that managerial positions are most often held by those who have progressed from junior position and therefore *"they are likely to possess considerable seniority which ... is positively related to union membership"*.

Stressing the general nature of the phenomenon of the link between managerial responsibility and union density, the EG adds:

"Although density varies significantly by broad industrial classification, the relationship between union density for foremen/supervisors and union density for people with no managerial or supervisory responsibilities is broadly constant across industries".

The EG underscores this point by adding that *"... in 1991, over a third of all union members worked in managerial, professional or associate professional occupations"*.

Unlike the woolly assertions of the NCP and such other sentimental worshippers of British trade unionism, this official Labour Force Survey gives, it must be admitted, a true picture of Britain's modern labour aristocracy. It is this labour aristocracy (composed by and large of workers who are non-manual and well qualified, doing jobs of a managerial, supervisory or professional nature) who, with their control of the organisational structures, have a decisive influence over the character and conduct of the unions. It is the same labour aristocracy which, thanks to the organisational links between the Labour Party and the unions, represents the unions in the Labour Party, where the two wings - industrial and political - both representing privileged upper stratum and bourgeoisified sections of the working class, join hands and hatch conspiracies against the working class. Only the very blind can fail to see this.

Even the SWP Trotskyists, whose faith in, and worship of, all that is reactionary in British trade unionism, have been obliged to accept the link between grade and union organisation:

"... the massive rise in white-collar trade union membership over the past 40 years cannot simply be equated with a growth in unionisation of the lower more 'proletarian' grades. ... A study of union membership in a bank, an insurance company and a local council concludes ... in all three institutions the level of union organisation rose with grade level" (Alex Callinicos and Chris Harman, *'The Changing Working Class*, p.69).

Further, they are forced to recognise the employers' ability to undermine rank-and-file trade unionism through bribery of the militant workers. Citing the examaple of the CPSA, they remark that the *"attraction to some of the ablest militants of upward mobility and the continual turnover in staff presents a big obstacle to sustained rank-and-file organisation"* (p.72).

And further:

"... the most trade-union conscious white collar workers are those with greatest hopes of moving up the career ladder, eventually into jobs in which they will supervise other workers. This explains one of the central peculiarities of white-collar trade unionism: those who are most committed union activists, whose activity leads them to play a key role in union branches, are often those who end up in managerial positions" (p.78).

The SWP comes as close here to admitting as we shall ever get it to, that the British trade-union movement is dominated by a privileged stratum of workers, who, according to a study cited by Harman, *"exert a moderating influence"* and *"often drew attention to the constraints under which the management worked"*. *"One reason"*, confesses Harman, *"middle grades are paid more is to buy such support from them"*. Well spotted, Mr Harman.!

And, if in spite of the foregoing, the SWP continues to gawp in awe at all that is reactionary in the trade-union movement, it can only be that it represents a tiny layer of public sector workers, non-manual workers, whose fate is inextricably intertwined with the rest of the labour aristocracy who dominate and control the unions. The same, if to a lesser extent, is probably true of the NCP.

Conclusion

The Labour Force Survey has provided excellent new material in substantiation of Lenin's observation that: *"on the basis"* of imperialism, *"the political institutions of modern capitalism - press, parliament, associations, congresses, etc. - have created POLITICAL privileges and sops for the respect-*

ful meek, reformist and patriotic office employees and workers, corresponding to the economic privileges and sops. Lucrative and soft jobs in the government or on the war industries committees, in parliament and on diverse committees, on the editorial staffs of 'respectable', legally published newspapers or on the management councils of no less respectable and 'bourgeois law-abiding' trade unions - this is the bait by which the imperialist bourgeoisie attracts and rewards the representatives and supporters of the 'bourgeois labour parties'" (Lenin, *Imperialism and the Split in Socialism*, CW. Vol.23, p.117).

The Keynesian consensus produced by the post-war boom enabled imperialism to provide nearly full employment, the welfare state, and thus a fairly decent standard of life to the overwhelming majority of the working class. Now, however, the crisis of capitalism, which has been steadily deepening over the last three decades, has so undermined the economy that the Keynesian consensus can no longer be maintained. With the breakdown of this consensus, we are once again confronted with the reversion to the conditions of a deep split within the working class. On the one hand, a small but significant minority of privileged, self-seeking and reactionary workers - an aristocracy of labour - who are prepared to do imperialism's bidding to preserve their privileged position; on the other hand, the overwhelming majority of the working class, the lower layers, composed of the low-paid, the unemployed, the casual and part-time employees, a majority of women and of ethnic minorities. The essence of Marxian tactics is to recognise this split, to recognise that, *"... economically, the desertion of a stratum of the labour aristocracy to the bourgeoisie has matured and become an accomplished fact; and this economic fact, this shift in class relations, will find political form, in one shape or another, without any particular 'difficulty'"* (Lenin, *ibid*, p.116). It may be said, verily, that it is the essence of Marxian tactics to assist this shift in class relations to find political form, for "the social chauvinist or (what is the same thing) opportunist *TREND* can neither disappear nor 'return' to the revolutionary proletariat" (*ibid*).

It is the essence of Marxian tactics to recognise that *"unless a determined and relentless struggle is waged all along the line"* against the *"bourgois labour party"*, *"there can be no question of a struggle against imperialism, or of Marxism, or of a socialist labour movement."* (*ibid*).

In failing to recognise, in theory, let alone carry out in practice, the above tactics, in its fervent desire to hang on the coat tails of rotten social democracy, the NCP, no matter how loudly it proclaims itself to be *"in the mould of Lenin"* is daily furnishing proof of its Kautskyite character. The NCP sees socialism where it simply does not exist and never has existed. Because of the erstwhile Clause IV, it characterised Labour's Constitution as socialist. If Clause IV talked of the common ownership of the means of production, Clement Attlee, the right-winger, who helped start the Cold War against the USSR and did so much to restore imperialist rule in so many parts of the world, endorsed the following definition of socialism:

"The essentials of Socialism have been well stated by Bertrand Russell. 'Socialism means the common ownership of land and capital together with a democratic form of government. It involves production for use not profit, and distribution of the product either equally to all or, at any rate, with only such inequalities as are definitely in the public interest. It involves the abolition of all unearned wealth and of all private control over the means of livelihood of the workers. To be fully realised it must be international'" (*The Labour Party in Perspective* by Clement Attlee, Leader of the Labour Party).

We shall not quibble about Bertrand Russell's formulation, as that does not concern us here. The question, however, is this: Why did Attlee, this rabid anti-communist, endorse a definition which would allow *"production for use not profit"*, equality of distribution and the abolition of all *"unearned wealth and of all private control over the means of livelihood ..."*? The answer is that both at the time of the incorporation of Clause IV and at the time Attlee was writing, there was a strong communist movement internationally and in Britain, a great ferment in the working class with the ever-present danger that the working class might follow the dreaded Bolsheviks. So, to hoodwink the working class, social democrats everywhere, while acting to protect the interests of their respective imperialist bourgeoisie, paid lip service to socialism and swore by it - all in an attempt to undermine working class support for communism. This was particularly urgent as the Communist Party then was correctly teaching the workers that Labour as well as Conservatives and Liberals were all capitalist parties.

As Lenin correctly observed: "Wherever Marxism *is popular among the workers, this political trend* [social chauvinism - HB], this 'bourgeois labour party', will swear by the name of Marx. *It cannot be prohibited from doing this, just as a trading firm cannot be prohibited from using any label. ... It has always been the case in history that after the death of revolutionary leaders who were popular among the oppressed classes, their enemies have attempted to appropriate their names so as to deceive the oppressed classes"* (*op cit*, p.118).

Now we have no such movement, no such party, bringing this truth to the working class. On the contrary, the working class is being constantly lectured to by the likes of the NCP, the SWP and such-like 'revolutionary' organisations that the Labour Party is the *"mass party"* of the British working class, and that *"we must not downplay Labour's role to unify the working class"*. A better example of the behaviour of Tolstoy's fool, who went around wishing mourners at funeral processions many happy returns of the day, would be hard to find. In this situation, the Labour Party has no need to pay even lip-service to socialism. In addition, now that the Keynesian consensus has broken down, Labour is keen to woo the sections of the electorate which determine the outcome of the elections, namely, the rich as well as the privileged sections of the working class. Ever since its defeat in the 1979 election, Labour has been busy adapting its policies to suit the interests of these privileged sections. Each successive defeat at elections (1979, 1983, 1987 and 1992) has brought a further shift to the right in Labour's policy.

The position has been reached whereby "John Major faces a phenomenon unknown to his predecessors: a Labour leader who assails him from the Right. But can a Tory leader allow himself to be out-flanked from the Right by Labour? His only alternative is to take his party even further to the Right. In such circumstances new Labour becomes a catalyst for reactionary change, thus denying its raison d'être" (Jimmy Reid, *Sunday Telegraph*, 28 May 1995). It is difficult to disagree with the above remarks even if, or rather perhaps because, they are written by a renegade like Mr Reid.

Although its policy is now indistinguishable from that of the Tories, the Labour leadership, so as not to leave an iota of doubt in the minds of the privileged sections as to where Labour stands, and in order to win their electoral support, is busy getting rid of the symbols which might be perceived by the privileged as connecting Labour with socialism and the working class. It has successfully got rid of Clause IV. In all probability, it will sever its links, at least in the present form, with the trade unions. When that happens, the NCP, the SWP and such other guardians of working-class 'unity', these advocates of the *"link between the industrial and political wing"*, seeing the final fig-leaf for their support of Labour disappear, will cry foul murder. Our guess, however, is that they will still be working hard, good little social democrats that they are, to kick the Tories out and get elected a Labour government - even a right-wing Labour government - *"under pressure to carry out policies benefiting the working class"*.

The fact, however, is that Labour has never in the past organised or represented the interests of the proletarian masses, nor will it do so in the future. History, both recent and not so recent, teaches us that it is no part of Labour to represent or organise the poor, downtrodden, deprived and oppressed masses - at home or abroad. That honour, to represent the proletarian masses, belongs solely to a revolutionary vanguard party of the proletariat - a Marxist-Leninist party, which not merely claims to be in the mould of Lenin, but acts in a Leninist way too. As no such party exists in Britain at the moment, the most urgent task facing Marxist-Leninist groups and individuals is to devote themselves wholeheartedly and with grim determination to the creation of such a party - a task inextricably linked with a relentless exposure of, and fight against, this stinking corpse that is called the Labour Party. Let the genuine Marxist-Leninists rise to the occasion. When they do this, only then will they deserve to bear this honourable title.

136 SOCIAL DEMOCRACY - THE ENEMY WITHIN

Part Two

On the Revisionists' & Trotskyites' Betrayal of the Marxian Teaching on The State

How 'our' petty-bourgeois democrats with near-Marxian phraseology embellish parliamentary cretinism and social democracy.

"The struggle for the emancipation of the toiling masses from the influence of the bourgeoisie in general, and of the imperialist bourgeoisie in particular, is impossible without a struggle against opportunist prejudices concerning the 'state'."

V.I. LENIN

1
The Marxian Teaching on the State

A General Election to kick out the Tories and to elect a Labour Government committed to Socialism

For quite some time[1] the above slogan has been put forward, by some organisations calling themselves Marxist, by way of a 'solution' to the crisis of British Imperialism and a cure to the sufferings of the British working class, groaning under the increasing attacks of British monopoly capitalism. To be more specific, this slogan is put forward by the revisionist Communist Party of Great Britain (CPGB) and by the three main Trotskyite organisations — The International Socialists (IS)[2], the International Marxist Group (IMG)[3] and the former Socialist Labour League (SLL) now transformed, by the trick of a resolution and to the accompaniment of trumpet blowing and fanfare characteristic of it, into the Workers' Revolutionary Party (WRP)[4]. This slogan — *'A General Election to kick out the Tories and to elect a Labour Government committed to Socialism'* — is the stock in trade of the revisionist CPGB, but not of the CPGB alone. It will be shown that, 'revolutionary' phase-mongering notwithstanding, it is also the slogan of the above Trotskyite organisations. It will be shown during the course of this pamphlet that this slogan is opportunist and that in this instance there is nothing to choose between the revisionists and the Trotskyites; that they both are opportunists; that they are not Marxists but

---

1 This article was first published in 1974
2 Now the Socialist Workers Party (SWP)
3 Now a faction in the Labour Party, and bearing the name 'Socialist Outlook'
4 This organisation has since split into several, each of these splinters being as insignificant as the others.

petty-bourgeois democrats with near-Marxist phraseology; that they both betray the interests of the working class and serve the interests of the bourgeoisie by acting as the conductors of bourgeois influence into the proletariat; and that differences of opinion and battles of words between them are of no more importance that the usual jealousy between two department managers in the same store.

The content as well as the manner in which the above slogan is being advanced by the revisionists and Trotskyites constitute, in the light of all the concrete facts, a complete departure from Marxism-Leninism. Their slogan constitutes a wretchedly liberal distortion and a downright falsification of the Marxian teaching on the question of the tasks of proletarian revolution in relation to the state; it dupes the proletarian masses with the illusion that it is possible to introduce socialism through bourgeois parliamentarism; that the bourgeois 'Labour' Party can be the vehicle of socialism; and that there is no need to smash the bourgeois state machine.

In view of the above distortions of Marxism by the Revisionist-Trotskyite gang on the most fundamental question of all, namely the state, it has become necessary for the genuine Marxist-Leninists to once again enter into controversy with the opportunists on this question, to defend the Marxian teaching on the state against all opportunist attacks on it, and to preserve it from all distortion. The importance of defending and applying the Marxian teaching, and of fighting against opportunist prejudices, on the state can never be over-emphasised, for as Comrade Lenin said:

"The struggle for the emancipation of the toiling masses from the influence of the bourgeoisie in general, and of the imperialist bourgeoisie in particular, is impossible without a struggle against opportunist prejudices concerning the 'state'." (Lenin: Preface to the first edition of *The State and Revolution*

We shall therefore, start by looking at the Marxian teaching on the question of the State. Then we shall pass on to the questions of whether socialism can be introduced through the British bourgeois parliament, and whether the 'Labour' Party could be the vehicle of socialism. In dealing with each of these issues we shall be able to show concretely and palpably how the revisionists and Trotskyites are indulging in the distortion and vulgarisation of Marxism and a base renunciation of it in practice.

The Marxian Teaching on the State

The Marxian teaching on the state can be briefly summed up as follows:

1. That the state has **not** always existed and will **not** always exist; that it is a transitional historical category, which is the product and the manifestation of the <u>irreconcilability</u> of class antagonisms.

'The state is, therefore, by no means a power forced on society from without, just as little is it 'the reality of the ethical idea', 'the image and reality of reason', as Hegel maintains. Rather, it is a product of society at a certain stage of development, it is the admission that this society has become entangled in an insoluble contradiction within itself, that it is cleft into irreconcilable antagonisms which it is powerless to dispel. But in order that these antagonisms, classes with conflicting economic interests, might not consume themselves and society in sterile struggle, a power seemingly standing above society became necessary for the purpose of moderating the conflict, of keeping it within the bounds of 'order'; and this power, arisen out of society, but placing itself above it, and increasingly alienating itself from it, is the state.'' (Engels: *Origin of the Family, Private Property and the State*).

In other words the state arose because of the division of society into irreconcilably hostile classes — the exploiting and the exploited classes — which gave rise to the *"irreconcilable antagonisms" between these classes,* which antagonisms this society is *"powerless to dispel"*. The conflicting interests of the exploiting class, on the one hand, and that of the exploited classes, on the other hand, being <u>irreconcilable</u>, the exploiting class needed a state machine as an instrument for the exploitation and enslavement of the exploited and the oppressed class, which could not be held in subjugation without a special apparatus called the *"state"*. Wherever there exist irreconcilable class antagonisms, there exists the state; and conversely, the existence of the state proves the existence of <u>irreconcilable</u> class antagonisms. We shall see further on how our petty-bourgeois democrats with near-Marxist phraseology — the revisionists and the Trotskyites — distort Marxism on this point by spreading in <u>practice</u> the illusion that the irreconcilable class antagonisms in our society can be reconciled and socialism introduced through bourgeois parliamentarism without smashing the bourgeois state to smithereens.

2. **That in its struggle for emancipation, the proletariat also needs a state.**

The proletariat needs its own state for crushing the <u>inevitable</u> resistance of the bourgeoisie and in order to organise the economic reconstruction of society, in order to create the material and spiritual conditions, which will, in due course, lead to the elimination of classes and class antagonisms and to a completely communist society in which there will exist no state. As to why the proletariat needs a state, here is the explanation given by Marx and Engels in *The Communist Manifesto*:

"In depicting the most general phases of the development of the proletariat, we traced the more or less veiled civil war, raging within existing society, up to the point where that war breaks out into open revolution, *and where the violent overthrow of the bourgeoisie lays the foundation for the sway of the proletariat.*

"*We have seen above, that the first step in the revolution by the working class, is to raise the proletariat to the position of ruling class, to win the battle of democracy.*

"*The proletariat will use its political supremacy to wrest, by degrees, all capital from the bourgeoisie, to centralise all instruments of production in the hands of the State, i.e., of the proletariat organised as the ruling class; and to increase the total of productive forces as rapidly as possible.*"

Thus Marx and Engels define the proletarian state as *'the state, i.e., the proletariat organised as the ruling class".*

And what Lenin stated in his day on the opportunists' 'forgetfulness' of the above definition of state, applies equally to the present-day conditions, when opportunism (in the form of social democracy, revisionism and Trotskyism) is showing an equal disregard and 'forgetfulness' of this definition, Comrade Lenin castigates the opportunists in the following terms:

"*This definition of the state* ["the state, i.e., the proletariat organised as the ruling class" - HB] *has never been explained in the prevailing propaganda and agitation literature of the official Social-Democratic parties. More than that, it has been deliberately forgotten, for it is absolutely irreconcilable with reformism, and is a slap in the face of the common opportunist prejudices and philistine illusions about the 'peaceful development of democracy'.*" (*The State and Revolution*).

The opportunists of our own day - the revisionists and Trotskyites are so busy spreading *"opportunist prejudices and philistine illusions"* concerning the *"peaceful development of democracy"* that they have reduced the above *"supremely interesting"* definition of the state into one of the *"forgotten words"* of Marxism.

Thus it can be seen that the proletariat needs *"a state, i.e., the proletariat organised as the ruling class"*; it needs its own *"special form of organisation of violence against the bourgeoisie"*. How can such a state be created? Can it be created without first smashing, destroying, abolishing the state of the bourgeoisie? This leads us to the next point which contains the answer to this question.

3.That, whereas all previous revolutions (i.e. revolutions before the proletarian revolution) have perfected the state machine, the task of the proletarian revolution is to destroy, break, smash it.

And, it is of this conclusion that Marx is speaking, by way of summing up the experience of the French Revolution of 1848-51, in the following exposition of the subject:

"But the revolution is thoroughgoing. It is still journeying through purgatory. It does its work methodically. By December 2, 1851 [the day of Louis Bonaparte's coup d'état], *it had completed one half of its preparatory work; it is now completing the other half. First it perfected the parliamentary power, in order to be able to overthrow it. Now that it has attained this, it perfects the executive power, reduces it to its purest expression, isolates it, sets it up against itself, as the sole target, in order to concentrate all its forces of destruction against it* [my emphasis - HB]. *And when it has done this second half of its preliminary work, Europe will leap from its seat and exultantly exclaim: 'Well grubbed, old mole'!*

"This executive power with its enormous bureaucratic and military organisation, with its ingenious state machinery, embracing wide strata, with a host of officials numbering half a million, besides an army of another half million, this appalling parasitic body, which enmeshes the body of French society like a net and chokes all its pores, sprang up in the days of the absolute monarchy, with the decay of the feudal system, which it helped to hasten ...

"The first French Revolution, with its task of breaking all separate local, territorial, urban and provincial powers in order to create the civil unity of the nation, was bound to develop what the absolute monarchy had begun: centralisation, but at the same time the extent, the attributes and the number of agents of governmental power. Napoleon perfected this state machinery. The Legitimatist monarchy and the July monarchy added nothing but a greater division of labour. ... Finally, in its struggle against the revolution, the parliamentary republic found itself compelled to strengthen, along with the repressive meas-

ures, the resources and centralisation of governmental power. All revolutions perfected this machine instead of smashing it [my emphasis -- HB]. *The parties that contended in turn for domination regarded the possession of this huge state edifice as the principal spoils of the victor."* (Marx: *'The Eighteenth Brumaire of Louis Bonaparte'*).

The conclusion that suggests itself from the above profound analysis is simple and clear: All previous revolutions have *"perfected"* the state machine, the task of the proletarian revolution is to *"concentrate all its forces of destruction against it"*.

The truth of the above analysis was brilliantly borne out by the Paris Commune. Summing up the experience of the Paris Commune, Marx and Engels wrote:

*"**One thing especially was proved by the Commune, viz. that 'the working class cannot simply lay hold of the ready-made state machinery and wield it for its own purposes'.**"* [my emphasis - HB]

The above conclusion of Marx and Engels has been remarkably corroborated by every revolution - successful and unsuccessful (Chile is the latest example).

Marx and Engels regarded the above conclusion as being of such cardinal importance that they introduced it by way of a correction to the *'Communist Manifesto'*.

As if not to leave matters in doubt, on April 12, 1871 (at the time of the Commune, Marx had this to say in a letter to Kugelmann:

"If you look at the last chapter of my 'Eighteenth Brumaire', you will find that I say that the next attempt of the French Revolution will be no longer, as before, to transfer the bureaucratic-military machine from one hand to another, but to smash it, and this is the preliminary condition for every real people's revolution on the continent. And this is what our heroic Party comrades in Paris are attempting."

The essence of Marxian teaching on the tasks of the proletarian revolution in relation to the state is summed up in the expression *"to smash the bureaucratic-military machine"*. And it is precisely on this the most fundamental teaching of Marxism that the opportunist distortion is taking place. The revisionists of the CPGB and the Trotskyites are busy today whipping up support for the 'Labour' Party in order that the latter may *"peacefully"* and unobserved introduce socialism; these gentry have substituted the electoral victory of the bourgeois 'Labour' Party for the struggle *"to smash the bureaucratic-military machine"*; they are conducting themselves in accordance with the notorious Bernsteinian[1] formula: *"the movement is everything, the aim is nothing"*. This is where their unprincipled floundering on questions of theory, in particular their distortion and renunciation of the Marxian teaching on the tasks of the proletarian revolution in relation to the state, has led them.

Marxism teaches, and historical experience confirms, that the proletarian revolution cannot but *"concentrate all its forces of destruction"* against the bourgeois state, it cannot but set itself the aim not of perfecting the state machine, but of smashing and destroying it.

The revisionists and Trotskyites, however, ignore the teaching of Marxism and historical experience alike.

If the task of the proletariat during the revolution is to *"smash the bureaucratic-military machine"*, what must the proletariat put in its place after smashing this bureaucratic-military machine? It is to this question that Marxism gives the following answer.

4. That having *"smashed the bureaucratic-military machine"* the proletariat must establish its own state power i.e. the dictatorship of the proletariat - of the type of the Paris Commune.

"Between capitalist and communist society lies the period of the revolutionary transformation of the one into the other. There corresponds to this also a political transition period in which the state can be nothing but the revolutionary dictatorship of the proletariat". (Marx: *Critique of the Gotha Programme*).

The proletariat needs its own state - the dictatorship of the proletariat - for the *"entire historical period which separates capitalism from 'classless society', from communism"* (Lenin).

"The essence of Marxist teaching on the state has been mastered only by those who understand that the dictatorship of a single class is necessary not only for every class society in general, not only for the proletariat which has

---

1   Bersteinism - a trend in the international Social-Democratic movement hostile to Marxism, that arose in Germany at the end of the 19th century and took its name from the German Social-Democrat Eduard Bernstein. After Engel's death, Bernstein openly advocated revision of the revolutionary theory of Marx along reformist lines.

overthrown the bourgeoisie, but also for the entire historical period which separates capitalism from classless society', from Communism. The forms of bourgeois states are extremely varied, but their essence is the same; all these states, whatever their form, in the final analysis are inevitably the dictatorship of the bourgeoisie. The transition from capitalism to Communism certainly cannot but yield a tremendous abundance and variety of political forms, but the essence will invariably be the same; the dictatorship of the proletariat." (Lenin: *'The State and Revolution'*).

The dictatorship of the proletariat is necessary to make possible the *"expropriation of the expropriators"*, to crush the inevitable resistance, and attempts at restoration, of the former exploiting classes, to organise the economical reconstruction of society - in a word to prepare the material and spiritual conditions for the transference of society from the lower phase to the higher phase of Communism.

5. That the dictatorship of the proletariat will wither away, it will not be abolished.

The reason for this is that with the expropriation of the bourgeoisie, the elimination of class antagonisms, and the creation of the necessary conditions for a completely communist society, the reason for the very existence of the state, namely, the existence of irreconcilable class antagonisms, will disappear. Indeed, the dictatorship of the proletariat is from its very inception something less than a state; for this state is for the first time a state of the exploited majority and used in the interests of this majority for the forcible suppression of the exploiting (former exploiting, to be more precise) minority. And because it is a state of the majority, precisely for this reason it does not require the special apparatus that the exploiting classes needed to hold down the exploited majority in the interests of the exploiting minority. When the moment arrives when there is no class to be *"forcibly held down"*, the state withers away, leaving behind a completely Communist classless society, in which society prevails the formula: from each according to his ability, to each according to his needs.

"As soon as there is no longer any class of society to be held in subjection; as soon as, along with class domination and the struggle for individual existence based on the anarchy of production hitherto, the collisions and excesses arising from these have also been abolished, there is nothing more to be repressed which would make a special repressive force, a state, necessary. The first act in which the state really comes forward as the representative of society as a whole - the taking possession of the means of production in the name of society - is at the same time its last independent act as a state. The interference of the state power in social relations becomes superfluous in one sphere after another, and then ceases of itself. The government of persons is replaced by the administration of things and the direction of the processes of production. The state is not 'abolished', it withers away. It is from this standpoint that we must appraise the phrase 'free people's state' both its temporary justification for agitational purposes, and its ultimate scientific inadequacy - and also the demand of the so-called anarchists *that the state should be abolished overnight."* (Engels: *Anti-Duhring*)

It emerges from what has been said above that whereas the bourgeois state machine must be smashed, the dictatorship of the proletariat can only *"wither away".*

"Revolution alone can 'abolish' the bourgeois state. The state in general, i.e., the most complete democracy, can only 'wither away'." (Lenin: *'The State and Revolution'*).

The way the revisionists carry on one would think that it is not only the *"state in general"*, but also the bourgeois state that was going to *"wither away"*. The conduct of the Trotskyists over a number of decades reveals that these gentlemen believe on the one hand that the bourgeois state is going to *"wither away"*, and, on the other hand, that the proletarian state is *"abolished"*. That the Trotskyists share the revisionist *"superstitious reverence"* for the bourgeois state, that they harbour illusions regarding the bourgeois state *"withering away"*, that they are opposed to the smashing of the *"bureaucratic-military machine"*, will become fully clear from what follows. As with everything else, the Trotskyists have got an upside down view of the state. They never look at the world standing on their feet instead; they stand on their heads to view the world. No wonder they find the world upside down.

We may conclude this section with the following summary of Engels' views on the state:

"The state, then, has not existed from all eternity. There have been societies that did without it, that had no conception of the state and state power. At a certain stage of economic development, which was necessarily bound up with the cleavage of society into classes, the state became a necessity owing to this cleavage. We are now rapidly approaching a stage in the development of production at which the existence of these classes not only will have ceased to be a necessity, but will become a positive hindrance on production. They will fall as inevitably as they arose at an earlier stage. Along with them the state will in-

evitably fall. The society that will organise production on the basis of a free and equal association of the producers will put the whole machinery of state where it will then belong: into the Museum of Antiquities by the side of the spinning wheel and the bronze axe." (Engels: *Origin of the Family, Private Property and the State*.)

The above presentation, in summary form, constitutes the Marxian teaching on the state. This presentation claims to be no more than a summary, and, therefore, suffers from all those defects which are generally attendant upon summarised versions. The reader would therefore be well advised, in order to get a comprehensive and a clear picture of Marxian teaching on the state, to read (that is, if he has not already done so) the following works:

1. *'Manifesto of the Communist Party'* by Marx and Engels.
2. *'The Origin of the Family, Private Property and the State'* by Engels.
3. *'Critique of the Gotha Program'* by Marx.
4. *'Anti-Duhring'* by Engels.
5. *'The Eighteenth Brumaire of Louis Bonaparte'* by Marx
6. *'The Civil War in France'* by Marx
7. *'The State and Revolution'* by Lenin.

In the light of the above teaching of Marxism on the question of the state, let us examine the slogan, *"A General Election to kick out the Tories and to elect a Labour Government committed to socialism"*.

II

The Revisionist CPGB and the Slogan:

A GENERAL ELECTION TO KICK OUT THE TORIES AND TO ELECT A LABOUR GOVERNMENT COMMITTED TO LEFT POLICIES

- 'Socialism' through bourgeois Parliament with the aid of the bourgeois Labour Party

Can socialism be introduced through bourgeois Parliamentarism and without smashing the "bureaucratic-military machine"? No, it most certainly cannot. Can the bourgeois 'Labour' Party, which up to now has acted as an agency of imperialism in the working-class movement, be the vehicle of socialism? No, it cannot. But the essence of the above slogan is that it answers both these questions in the affirmative; and this is precisely why this slogan constitutes a liberal distortion of the teaching of Marxism, on the question of the state. Let us examine in detail this slogan and the arguments of those who put it forward, namely, the revisionists of the CPGB and the Trotskyists.

The Communist Party of Great Britain and the Slogan 'A General Election to Kick out the Tories'

The revisionists of the CPGB have been putting forward this slogan for quite some time. We reproduce below some of their formulations of this slogan:

"Clear the Tories out - a General Election now!

"We say, force a General Election, get rid of the Tory Government. But the election must mark a break with the past. Previous Labour Governments have failed because they have refused to stand up to big capitalist monopolies. We need a Labour Government committed to left policies which will start to shift

the balance of wealth and power in favour of the people.

"This means breaking the grip of right wing leaders who refuse to challenge capitalism and seek to hold back the struggle.

"But the forces are there ... to win a General Election and compel the next Labour Government to implement a comprehensive alternative to Tory policy. The decisions of the TUC, the Labour Party Conference and the Communist Party Congress provide the basis for such an alternative. We have outlined the main points in our programme to beat the crisis.

"We appeal to all ... to unite and fight for this now. It is a programme which would overcome the problems of today, and at the same time, it would open the way to socialism.

"Capitalism has had its day. No amount of tinkering by Tory or right wing Labour politicians can put it right. [Presumably, it means tinkering by 'left' 'Labour' and sham socialist politicians will put capitalism right! But more of it anon.]

"The Communist Party ... have made a vital contribution to the struggle against the Tory Government and the policies of collaboration with capitalism advocated by the right-wing Labour leaders ... ' [Taken from a document *'The Way Out of the Crisis, what the Communists propose'*, issued by the CPGB in December 1973.]

In a statement he made on 7 Feb 1974 (reported in the *'Morning Star'* of Feb 8 1974) on the forthcoming General Election, John Gollan, the General Secretary of the CPGB, had this to say:

"The British people should seize the chance to get rid of him [Heath] *and the whole gang which has brought such disasters upon us.*

"They should also demonstrate that they don't want a Labour Government like the last one, which compromised with big business and failed to fight for the people who elected it.

"This time the new Government must be committed to left policies which will put the burdens of the crisis on the rich who caused it, not on the workers.

"This means voting for Communist candidates wherever they are standing, and pressing Labour candidates to pledge themselves to support such policies.

"Let the labour movement, and all who stand for progress, rally, organise and act to drown the Tories in a massive and overwhelming vote for a pro-

gramme to solve the crisis, meet the demands of the working people and pensioners and to defend all democratic and trade union rights from Tory attacks."

The above two quotations, which we have cited at length in order not to be accused of distorting and misquoting our opponents, sum up the position of the CPGB and provide us with a wealth of information relating to the content of their slogan: *"Clear the Tories out, a General Election Now".* Nearly every sentence in the above two quotations is a gem, which contains a, disgraceful for a Communist, falsification and repudiation of the fundamental teachings of Marxism-Leninism. The sum total of their policy, as summed up in their statements quoted above, is to substitute the fight against the Tories for the fight against imperialism, and precisely for that reason constitutes a betrayal of the working class. Concretely their policy amounts to a complete break with Marxism-Leninism, because:-

1. **It creates the illusion that the British proletariat has no need to smash the 'bureaucratic-military machine' of the British bourgeoisie; that Socialism can be introduced by winning a majority in Parliament in elections held under the rule and supervision of the bourgeoisie.**

But the essence of bourgeois parliamentarism consists of deciding *"every few years which member of the ruling class is to repress and crush the people through Parliament"* (Lenin). And elections and universal suffrage under the rule of the bourgeoisie cannot but be the instruments of the rule of capital over wage labour. For as Engels remarks correctly, universal suffrage is *"the gauge of the maturity of the working class. It cannot and never will be anything more in the present day [i.e. bourgeois] state."*

But it is just this *"more"* that our petty-bourgeois philistines with near-Marxist phraseology - the revisionists and Trotskyites - expect and demand from universal suffrage.

As stated above, Marx, on the basis of the concrete historical experience of the French Revolution of 1848-51, came to the conclusion in 1852 that whereas all previous revolutions had perfected the state machine, the task of the proletarian revolution was to *"smash"* the *"bureaucratic-military machine"*. Marx and Engels throughout their lives taught this lesson to the proletariat. Since the death of Marx and Engels, their followers have repeatedly taught this lesson to the proletariat. This great teaching of Marxism - that the task of the proletariat during the revolution is to smash the *"bureaucratic-military machine"* - has been brilliantly borne out in practice. Yet, 122 years after Marxism began to teach this universal truth to the proletariat, some sham socialists - the revisionists and the Trotskyites who have the hypocrisy and the gall to describe themselves as Marxists - assert that the bourgeois state machine need not be smashed after all.

All that is necessary, they say, is to defeat the Tories, elect a Labour government *"committed to left policies"*, and, as a watertight guarantee that such a 'Labour' Government will keep its promise and put into effect its 'left policies', elect a few sham socialists as members of Parliament. By way of an embellishment of bourgeois parliamentarism, Mr Gollan, the General Secretary of the CPGB, says: *"... what's wrong with Parliament is that we are not in it."* (*Morning Star*, Saturday Feb 2 1974)

The slogan concerning the election of a 'left' 'Labour' Government committed to 'left' policies is opportunist inasmuch as it admits the possibility of the proletariat coming to power without destroying the state machine of the bourgeoisie. In other words, the very thing which Marx and Engels declared, in 1872, to be obsolete when they said: **"One thing especially was proved by the Commune viz., that 'the working class cannot simply lay hold of the ready-made state machinery, and wield it for its own purposes.'"** [my emphasis - HB]is now revived by our petty-bourgeois democrats as a real possibility. In doing so the petty-bourgeois democrats are engaged in the repudiation of revolution and in *"efforts to make capitalism look more attractive, an occupation in which all the reformists are engaged"* (Lenin).

It is obvious that the revisionists and Trotskyites are not Marxists but petty-bourgeois democrats, who have discarded the concept of achieving Socialism through the revolutionary overthrow of the bourgeoisie, and substituted for it the petty-bourgeois utopia of peaceful submission of the minority to the majority. Here is what Lenin had to say by way of characterisation of such petty-bourgeois democrats:

"The petty-bourgeois democrats, those sham socialists who have replaced class struggle by dreams of class harmony, *even pictured the socialist transformation in a dreamy fashion - not as the overthrow of the rule of the exploiting class, but as the peaceful submission of the minority to the majority which has become conscious of its aims. This petty-bourgeois utopia, which is inseparably connected with the idea of the state being above classes, led in practice to the betrayal of the interests of the toiling classes, as was shown, for example, by the history of the French revolutions of 1848 and 1871, and by the experience of 'Socialist' participation in bourgeois cabinets in England,*

France, Italy and other countries at the end of the nineteenth and the beginning of the twentieth centuries." (Lenin: *'State and Revolution'*)

2. It creates the illusion that the bourgeoisie can be disposed of, can be tricked out of power without a violent revolution which marks its overthrow.

The reasoning is that in Britain democratic traditions and respect for constitutional methods are so well-established that the bourgeoisie will never dare act in an unconstitutional way. But this constitutional cretinism, this *"superstitious reverence"* for the constitution, fails to take into account the class nature of the British Constitution; it fails to understand that the British Constitution is a bourgeois Constitution, which is designed to secure the rule of the bourgeoisie; that this is the spirit of the present Constitution, and, if this spirit could be carried out only by violating the letter of the Constitution, the bourgeoisie will have no hesitation. Our constitutional cretins fail to grasp the simple truth that there are times (times of revolutionary upheavals when the masses threaten the rule of capital) when the only way the bourgeoisie can carry out the spirit of the Constitution is by violating its letter; they are utterly incapable of understanding the essence of what Marx wrote about the construction (interpretation) of the French bourgeois Constitution, which is applicable to the interpretation of all bourgeois Constitutions. By way of an answer to the petty-bourgeois Ledru-Rollin, who believed that he could beat the National Assembly by means of the Constitution, Marx wrote: *"... the letter* [of the Constitution] *must be construed in its living meaning and the bourgeois meaning was its only meaning."* Let the petty-bourgeois Ledru-Rollins of today - the revisionists and Trotskyites - ponder over the great truth contained in the above sentence of Marx taken from his pamphlet *'Class Struggles in France'*!

History shows that the only people who suffer from this constitutional cretinism are the petty-bourgeois democrats. The bourgeoisie certainly do not suffer from this affliction. Ever since the French revolution of 1848, the bourgeoisie everywhere has given proof of the *"insane cruelties"* to which it will be driven once the working class presents a threat to the present bourgeois order of society. Rather than peacefully depart from the scene, the bourgeoisie will inevitably, on one pretext or the other, start a civil war to defend its class rule and privileges.

It is extremely instructive in this context to take note of what Engels had to say in his introduction to Marx's pamphlet *'The Civil War in France'* regarding the events immediately after the French Revolution of 1848, which led to the overthrow of the Louis Philippe monarchy and the establishment of the Republic. The Republic had been won with the help of the Parisian working class, which now had arms. Here is how Engels describes the situation just after the overthrow of the Louis Philippe monarchy:

"... *Louis Philippe vanished, and with him the franchise reform.* [which is all that the liberal bourgeois of the parliamentary opposition had been fighting for - HB]; *and in its place arose the republic, and indeed one which the victorious workers themselves designated as a 'social' republic. No one, however, was clear as to what this social republic was to imply; not even the workers themselves. But they now had arms and were a power in the state. Therefore, as soon as the bourgeois republicans in control felt something like firm ground under their feet, their first aim was to disarm the workers. This took place by driving them into the insurrection of June 1848 by direct breach of faith by open defiance and the attempt to banish the unemployed to a distant province. The Government had taken care to have an overwhelming superiority of force. After five days' heroic struggle, the workers were defeated. And then followed a blood-bath among the defenceless prisoners, the like of which has not been seen since the days of the civil wars which ushered in the downfall of the Roman republic. It was the first time that the bourgeoisie showed to what insane cruelties of revenge it will be goaded the moment the proletariat dares to take its stand against the bourgeoisie as a separate class, with its own interests and demands. And yet 1848 was only child's play compared with the frenzy of the bourgeoisie in 1871.*"

Since 1871 the bourgeoisie has repeatedly furnished eloquent testimony of the *"insane cruelties of revenge"* to which it has been, and to which it will be, goaded *"the moment the proletariat dares to take its stand against the bourgeoisie as a separate class ..."*.

In this connection we can recall the frenzy with which the international bourgeoisie waged a war of intervention against the young Soviet Republic for no other reason than that the proletariat in that country had dared take its stand as a separate class against the bourgeois order of society; we can recall the cold-blooded extermination of revolutionaries in Germany by the Fascist thugs; we can recall the campaigns of annihilation waged by the Chiang-Kai-Shek bandits with the aid of international imperialism against the liberation forces led by the Chinese working class; we recall the ferocity with which Nazi aggressors pillaged the USSR during the Second World War; we can recall the genocidal wars of aggression waged by US imperialism in Korea, Vietnam, Laos and Cambodia; we can recall the murder of about a million Indonesian revolutionaries by the Suharto Fascist clique; and we recall (that is, if there are those, like the revisionists and Trotskyites, who have already forgotten) the mass murder of the Chilean working class and revolutionaries by the Chilean Junta. And yet 1848 and 1871 were only *"child's play"* compared with the frenzy of the bourgeoisie in the examples enumerated in this paragraph.

Only the incurable philistines, who have *"superstitious reverence"* for bourgeois constitutionalism, and who kneel in prayer before this constitutionalism, can fail to draw from the historical experiences listed above the only possible conclusion, namely, that the *"bureaucratic-military machine"* of the bourgeoisie must be smashed. Only petty bourgeois renegades and philistines can behave the way that the revisionists and the Trotskyists do. Their behaviour reminds us of the pigeon who, on seeing a cat, shut its eyes and believed that the cat could not see it just because it could not see the cat. It realised too late that reality was quite different from what it had imagined it to be. The stupid pigeon paid with its life for its stupidity. The revisionists are precisely such stupid pigeons who cannot see reality; the only difference is that when the revisionists get influence over the masses and lead them to disaster, it is not just the revisionists, but also thousands of proletarians who are drowned in a blood bath, who are led to the slaughterhouse like sacrificial lambs. Chile furnishes the latest example of such stupidity of revisionism, of its constitutional cretinism and of the inevitable retribution that such cretinism was bound to meet.

The revisionists of Chile and Allende also believed in constitutionalism, they too had a *"superstitious reverence"* for the Chilean constitution and the Chilean state; they too believed that the Chilean armed-forces would respect the constitution and, they too believed that they could *"peacefully"*, without smashing the bourgeois state, introduce socialism. The naiveté of these gentlemen and the illusions they entertained on this score are evident from the following statements.

Here, for example is statement made in September 1973, (i.e., only a few weeks before the Allende Government was overthrown by the Chilean armed forces in a coup d'état which witnessed the massacre of thousands of proletarians and revolutionaries) by Luis Corvalán, General Secretary of the revisionist Chilean Communist Party.

"*Some reactionaries have begun to seek new ways to drive a wedge between the people and the armed forces, maintaining little less than we are intending to replace the professional army.*

"*No Sirs! We continue to support the absolutely professional character of the armed institutions. Their enemies appear not in the ranks of the people but in the reactionary camp*" (*Marxism Today*).

Allende's Popular Unity Government refused to arm the workers, even as late as June 1973 which had witnessed an attempted (but unsuccessful) coup. Allende stated categorically:

'*There will be no armed forces here other than those stipulated by the Constitution, that is to say, the Army, the Navy and the Air Force. I shall eliminate any others if they appear.*"

What happened?

A few weeks later Allende's "*Constitutional*" forces overthrew Allende's "*Constitutional*" Government by methods unconstitutional. Just before dying Allende appealed to the working class to arm itself. But it was too late. The Chilean bourgeoisie and imperialism were making preparations for striking a decisive blow while the petty-bourgeois democrats of the Popular Unity Government and those of the Communist Party of Chile went around the country giving lectures on the Chilean Constitution. The bourgeoisie struck through its armed forces, and when it did, a copy of the Chilean Constitution proved, as was to be expected, a very poor match indeed for the shells fired by the Chilean army.

The working class of Chile, indeed of all countries, can learn more about the Marxian teachings on the state from the negative example of the Fascist Chilean Junta than from the revisionists and such like petty-bourgeois philistines; the working class can learn from the Chilean experience the truth that "*a standing army and police are the chief instruments of state power*" (Lenin); that unless the proletariat smashes the bourgeois army and police - these "*chief instruments of the state power*" of the bourgeoisie - and creates its own army - a people's army - then it cannot escape the fate met by the Popular Unity Government. The Chilean bourgeoisie and imperialism are our great teachers by negative example; and, when the proletarians have mastered the lessons of the Chilean counter-revolution, then they will wipe off the face of the earth the rule of the bourgeoisie and of imperialism.

The revisionists of the CPGB, however, refuse to pay any heed to the experience of the Chilean counter revolution. Britain, they imply, is different. With almost imperialist chauvinism they imply that what happened in Chile can only happen in a backward country like Chile; that sort of thing could never happen in a civilised and advanced society such as Britain, for the democratic and constitutional traditions are very deep-rooted in Britain. But so are the traditions of the rule of the bourgeoisie. How do these gentlemen think the bourgeoisie will react to any attempt at doing away with such a deep-rooted tradition as the bourgeois rule? What this gentry fail to realise is that the British Constitution is a fig leaf of British Imperialism. How, then, can Socialism be established constitutionally? To assert that under the present Constitution Socialism can be established is to remove the fig leaf from imperialism, and to become oneself a screen for its nakedness. These gentlemen who put forward the miserable prattle about *"democratic"* and *"constitutional"* traditions of the British society should for a change pay heed to the following sound advice given by that genius of revolution, Lenin:

*"A democratic republic is the best possible political shell for capitalism, and, therefore, once capital has gained control of this very best shell (through the Palchinskys, Chernovs, Tseretelis and Co.[1]), it establishes its power so securely, so firmly, that no change, either of persons, of institutions, or of **parties** in the bourgeois democratic republic, can shake it."* (State and Revolution, my emphasis -HB)

It is not that the revisionists are not aware of the nature and role of the armed forces in our *"democratic"* and *"constitutional"* Britain. Here, for example, are a few paragraphs taken from a pamphlet *Time To Change Course*, by Jack Woddis, member of the Central Committee of the CPGB. As to the nature and training of the army, Mr Woddis writes:

"The upholders of the establishment are given all the facilities they require to mould the minds of the army men, to foster anti-democratic conceptions and influence them to regard civilian activities for the redress of grievances or for changing our society as dangerous heresies that must be repressed by force.

"At the same time, the members of the armed forces are denied demo-

---

[1] We might say through the Wilsons, Heaths, Barbers, Callaghans, Barbara Castles, Prentices, Foots and Co.

cratic freedoms, and are banned from participating in normal political activities or belonging to trade unions or political parties.

"The politics of preserving the status quo are dinned into the troops every day; but the politics of working for progressive change are disallowed."

As to the experience gained by the armed forces in dealing with *"political discontent"* in Northern Ireland, and, the usefulness of this experience for the ruling class in dealing with *"political discontent"* in Britain, Mr Woddis has this to say:

*"Involved as it is in military operations against urban fighters in Northern Ireland and in repressing sections of the civilian population, it [the army] is not only gaining experience in combating political discontent in that territory, but being trained and psychologically prepared so that, **if monopolies feel it necessary for the defence of their profits and their system, it could perform a similar role in keeping down the British people.**"* (My emphasis - HB).

What conclusion would and should a revolutionary draw from the above statements? That the bourgeois standing army, this *"chief instrument of the state power"* of the British bourgeoisie, must be destroyed. And what conclusion does the revisionist Mr Woddis reach? That the next 'Labour' Government must democratise the army - *"this chief instrument of the state power"* of the bourgeoisie. Only those who suffer from the incurable malady of *'*parliamentary cretinism*, which holds those infected by it fast in an imaginary world and robs them of all sense, all memory, all understanding of the rude external world"* (K. Marx, *Eighteenth Brumaire of Louis Bonaparte*) can come to such a conclusion as does Mr Woddis. Only senseless and stupid yokels who have lost all touch with *"Her Majesty, the Logic"* (Lenin) can argue in the way you do, Messrs the revisionists!

What jokers you are in even allowing yourselves to think that the *"monopolies"* will sit back while your most favourite mistress, the next *"Labour Government committed to Left policies"*, carries out a programme of *"democratising"* the army! In such a situation, would not *"the monopolies feel it necessary for the defence of their profits and their system"* to want the army *" to perform a ... role in keeping down the British people"* and disposing of at one stroke the parliamentary buffoons, the 'left' 'Labour' and other sham socialist MPs, and your 'Left Labour Government' in a manner similar to the one by which the Chilean Fascist Junta disposed of the Popular Unity Government? There is not the slightest doubt that they would. The revisionists, in characteristic petty-bourgeois fashion, may want to run away and hide from stern reality, but this won't make reality disappear. As the well-known Chinese saying puts it: *"the tree may prefer the calm, but the wind will not subside."*

It must be said, however, that the bourgeoisie certainly does not suffer from the affliction of *"constitutionalism"* and *"democratism"*. Nor does the army. They are ever-prepared and leave nobody in doubt as to their intentions. Recently Mr Barber, the Chancellor of the Exchequer, made a television broadcast in which he warned that people should know what happened in those countries where parliamentary democracy [i.e. the rule of the bourgeoisie] was flouted. He did not spell out the answer, which, however, is self-evident. The answer is that if the bourgeoisie is not allowed to rule "peacefully" by practising deception through parliament, than it will have no alternative left for itself but to institute a naked fascist dictatorship. Premier Heath had this to say in his speech to the United Nations in October 1970:

"In the 1970s civil war, not war between the nations, will be the main danger we face."

And what the army thinks of its role becomes crystal clear from the following statement of Brigadier Frank Kitson:

"If a genuine and serious grievance arose such as might result from a significant drop in the standard of living, all those who now dissipate their protest over a wide variety of causes might concentrate their efforts and produce a situation beyond the power of the police to handle. Should this happen, the army would be required to restore the position rapidly."

The gentlemen of the bourgeoisie are revealing their intentions with praiseworthy candour; and, for this they deserve our hearty thanks, for by their candour they are dispelling all illusions so carefully nurtured and fostered by our petty-bourgeois democrats - the revisionists and Trotskyites.

The attitude of the revisionists can only be explained by their complete betrayal and renunciation of Marxism. They renounced the Marxist proposition that the task of the proletarian revolution is to smash the bourgeois state machine. Instead, they have set themselves the task of *"laying hold of the ready-made state machinery, and wielding it for"* their *"own purposes"*. Here, for example, is what their programme, British Road to Socialism, says on the matter under discussion:

'*The leading positions in the Ministries and departments, the armed forces and the police, the nationalised industries and other authorities must therefore be filled by men and women loyal to socialism ... this ensures that the socialist policies determined on by Parliament are fully implemented."*

Who but the most ordinary lackeys of the bourgeoisie could reduce the question of the bringing about of socialism, of the tasks of proletarian revolution, to the level of getting a few Ministerial and departmental posts, as does the above quotation from the *British Road to Socialism*!

From the above renunciation of Marxism flow all the sins of revisionism.

The opportunists have completely *"forgotten"* the teachings of Marxism on the inevitability of violent revolution to smash the state of the bourgeoisie. It is considered a sign of bad taste in modern revisionist circles to talk or even to think about the significance of the following *"veritable panegyric on violent revolution"* sung by Engels:

"... That force, however, plays another role in history, a revolutionary role; that, in the words of Marx, it is the midwife of every old society which is pregnant with the new, that it is the instrument by the aid of which the social movement forces its way through and shatters the dead, fossilised political forms – of this there is not a word in Herr Dühring. It is only with sighs and groans that he admits the possibility that force will perhaps be necessary for the overthrow of the economic system of exploitation – unfortunately, because all use of force, forsooth, demoralises the person who uses it. And this in spite of the immense moral and spiritual impetus which has resulted from every victorious revolution! And this in Germany, where a violent collision – which indeed may be forced on the people – would at least have the advantage of wiping out the servility which has permeated the national consciousness as a result of the humiliation of the Thirty Years' War. And this parson's mode of thought – lifeless, insipid and impotent – claims to impose itself on the most revolutionary party which history has known!" (Engels: *Anti-Duhring*)

And, as Lenin put it:

"The necessity of systematically imbuing the masses with this *and precisely this view of violent revolution lies at the root of all the teachings of Marx and Engels."* (*State and Revolution*)

It is our proletarian duty to expose the betrayal by the opportunists of the teachings of Marx. We must continue to bring to the knowledge of the masses of proletarians that *"the supersession of the bourgeois state by the proletarian state is impossible without a violent revolution. The abolition of the proletarian state, i.e., of the state in general, is impossible except through the process of 'withering away'"* (Lenin, *State and Revolution*).

The idea of violent revolution plays no part in the opportunists' daily propaganda and agitation, which is mainly geared to oiling the bourgeois electoral machine in the interests of the bourgeois 'Labour' Party, i.e., in the interests of Imperialism.

3. It creates the illusion that the 'Labour' Party is the vehicle of Socialism; that the next 'Labour' Government will not *"compromise with big business"*; that it will be *"committed to left policies which will put the burdens of the crisis on the rich"*; that it will *"stand up to big capitalist monopolies"*; that it will shift *"the balance of wealth and power in favour of the people"* **and so on and so forth.**

What is the basis for the above hallucinations? It can only be that the revisionist gentry have lost touch with reality. What is the basis for asserting that the 'Labour' Party is different (in terms of the class whose interest it serves) from what it used to be, that it will behave in a way which is different from the one in which it has done hitherto? There clearly is no such basis. Look at the record of the 'Labour' Party and of all the past 'Labour' Governments and you will find that it is a record of service to imperialism, of class collaboration and of anti-communism. Here is, in brief, the record of past 'Labour' Governments.

LABOUR GOVERNMENT OF 1923: It was the first 'Labour' Government. This Government was concerned not to bring socialism but reassure the ruling class that it had nothing to fear from a 'Labour' Government; that the 'Labour' Government was just as much in favour of protecting the *"national interest"* (i.e., the interests of the imperialist bourgeoisie) as any other Government. Here are a few statements of the 'Labour' leaders during the period of the first 'Labour' Government:-

"He was sure that the King would be generous to him and understand the very difficult position he was in vis-à-vis his own extremists." (R. MacDonald).

"We must show the country [i.e., the ruling bourgeoisie], *we are not under the domination of the wild men."* (Snowden).

Sidney Webb launched vicious attacks on strikes saying that *"those little bands of wrecking communists are undoubtedly at work".*

LABOUR GOVERNMENT OF 1929: When this Government took office, the unemployment figure in the country was just over a million. The main 'achievement' of this 'socialist' Government was to have helped the figure of those unemployed to reach 2,700,000.

Eventually MacDonald, the 'socialist', ended up by forming a 'National

Government' with the Tories.

LABOUR GOVERNMENT OF 1945: A week after this Government took office it used troops to break a strike that had been going on in the London docks for 10 weeks. Some three months later it used more than 20,000 troops to break a national docks strike. In 1951 it used Order 1305 — a wartime law prohibiting strikes — to prosecute seven trade unionists. The 'socialism' of this Government is said to be responsible for the 'welfare state'. The facts, however, are that no Government — 'Labour' or Tory — could have done otherwise in the world situation just after the Second World War. Imperialism, in particular British Imperialism, had been seriously weakened as a result of the war and the working class was in a relatively stronger position to press its demands. Only this can explain the following statement made at that time by Mr Quintin Hogg (now Lord Hailsham, Chancellor in the present Tory Government):

"If you do not give the people reform they are going to give you social revolution"

Only this can explain the fact that in a number of European countries, notably Germany, which was ruled by the right-wing Christian Democrats, the same sort of welfare reforms were put into effect which in Britain are trumpeted forth as the fruits of socialism.[1]

As regards foreign policy, the 'Labour' Party pursued an even more reactionary and rabidly anti-Communist path than the one followed by the Tories. Defining his attitude towards Bevin, the 'Labour' Foreign Minister in the Attlee 'Labour' Government, the Conservative Sir Anthony Eden had this to say:

"In Parliament I usually followed him [Bevin] in debate and I would have publicly agreed with him more if I had not been anxious to embarrass him less."

The same 'Socialist' Government of Attlee was responsible for taking the French, who had been thrown out by the national liberation forces, back to Vietnam and thus starting a bloody conflict which has still not been concluded[2]. This Government was also responsible for suppressing with savage brutality

---

1 As to how this welfare state was achieved by passing the burdens of reconstruction on to the colonial peoples, the reader is already aware of it.

2 This was written in 1974.

the liberation war of the Malayan people. This Government also sent troops, on the orders of US imperialism, to wage a war of aggression and extermination against the heroic Korean people.

LABOUR GOVERNMENT OF 1964: This was supposed to be a 'left'-wing 'Labour' Government which was to have tackled monopoly capitalism and opened the way to socialism. What did it do? Its main 'achievements' were: it put up prescription charges; it increased the price of school meals and dental charges went up; it stopped free school milk for over 11s; it increased the application of the means-test; it introduced a statutory 'incomes policy' (i.e., a wage freeze); it defeated the seamen's strike; and Harold Wilson the 'left'-winger personally launched an attack on the communists, whom he called *"politically motivated"* — a phrase which has ever since become the daily currency of Fleet Street imperialist journalism; it introduced 'In Place of Strife', which was in no way different from the Tory Industrial Relations Act. Mr Wilson by way of an attack on wages said that *"one man's wage increase is another man's price increase"* — a phrase which only the other day the Tory Chancellor of the Exchequer used with great relish in a television programme. According to Mr Wilson then wages were the cause of inflation. How, then, can he now assert in the present election campaign that they are not? Obviously, the 'Labour' Party 'Socialists' are no different from the Tories. They both, like all bourgeois politicians, act according to the honoured and dishonest custom of bourgeois politics, namely, say one thing while in office and quite another out of office, and say one thing but do another. This is the essence of bourgeois politics and the hypocrisy attendant upon it.

In foreign policy the Wilson Government was just as, if not more, reactionary than the Tory Government. Who, for example, does not know of the "full support" given by this 'socialist' Government to the fascist atrocities and piratical acts committed by US imperialism in its war of aggression against the Vietnamese and other Indochinese peoples. Not a murmur was raised by these 'socialist' hyenas against the butchery of the Indochinese people by the US imperialist war machine. And yet, Mr Wilson's 'conscience' was so pricked that when the Soviet revisionists expelled a fascist writer, Alexander Solzhenitsyn, from the Soviet Union, he was moved to send a telegram of protest to the Soviet Embassy. The same Wilson and his 'socialist' colleagues sided with the Israeli fascists in the last Arab-Israeli war.

Thus it can be seen that the 'Labour' Governments have been no different from the Tory or Liberal Governments. They are all in the service of Imperialism. It is not surprising, in view of what has been stated above, that the Tories, by way of justification of their policies, always say: *"we are only doing what you did when you were in office."*

If the record of 'Labour' is, as has been shown above, a disgraceful betrayal of socialism, the record of the TUC is not very comforting either. During the General Strike of 1926 the TUC declared:

"The General Council does not challenge one rule, law or custom of the Constitution."

And there has not been the slightest shift from this position of the TUC. Vic Feathers and Len Murrays of our day are the worthy successors of the TUC traitors (to the working class) of 1926.

The revisionists say that the next 'Labour' Government will be different from previous Governments. But even the revisionists dare not deny that the previous 'Labour' Governments have served Imperialism. Here, for example, it is the admission that even the revisionists are forced to make on this score:

"A new Labour Government is the only alternative in Government terms to a Tory Government.

"But a Labour Government similar to the Wilson Governments of 1964-66 and 1966-70 will solve nothing.

"The Labour Governments antagonised millions of working people ... because they put the interests of big business before the interests of working people, attempted to introduce anti-trade union legislation, lined up with American policy [butchery would be a better expression] *in Vietnam and elsewhere, refused to seriously challenge the racists* [the truth would be, they actually gave every encouragement to the racists by their conduct over immigration legislation and Rhodesia] *at home and abroad and dropped any pretence of taking Britain in a Socialist direction* [this really is a crime for it makes it impossible for the revisionists to play the role of the tail end of social democracy by pretending that the 'Labour' Party will bring Socialism - HB].

"This approach of the Wilson Governments of the late 60s was the same as other post-war Labour Governments [and what about the pre-war ones? It means presumably that at least the pre-war 'Labour' Governments were taking Britain in a Socialist direction! - HB] *under Attlee.*

"It is basically a Tory-type approach — tackle Britain's crisis along traditional lines and oppose any proposals that would start making inroads into the power, profits, and privileges of the rich and giant monopolies." (Morning

Star, Saturday Feb 16, 1974, '*Vote Communist for a new type of government*' — '*Labour, Yes — but with a difference*' by Gordon McLennan).

In view of this, how is it possible for anyone, other than a servile lackey — and a most ordinary one at that — of imperialism, to argue that the next 'Labour' Government will be socialist when the previous ones have served imperialism? On the contrary, all the indications are that the most important function of the next 'Labour' government will be to pursue a vigorous policy of class collaboration and class harmony. Mr Wilson says that the Heath Government is *"God's gift to militants"*, which means that Mr Wilson's target, like that of Mr Heath, are the militants, except that Mr Wilson will go about it in a way which is more successful, which is less likely to stoke up class confrontation and class conflagration, which is more likely to promote class conciliation, than Mr Heath's way of doing things. Also, the 'Labour' Party, with its connections with trade-union bureaucracy and with its 'socialist' phraseology is more likely to be successful, hence dangerous, than the Tories. In other words, what we have here is difference in style, not a difference in policy, purpose or aim.

What the next 'Labour' Government will be like is shown by the behaviour of the 'Labour' Party in opposition since 1970. On every single important issue that concerned the working class of this country, the 'Labour' Party has supported the Tory Government and opposed the working class. On the wage freeze introduced by the Tory Government, here is what Mr Wilson, the 'Socialist', had to say:

"If the Government get their law we take the view that the law should be honoured even if we regard it as unfair. Certainly we would not lend our support to any who seek by illegal or other means to destroy it."

Exactly similar advice was given by 'Labour' to the Clay Cross Councillors who refused to implement the Housing Finance Act (the notorious 'Fair Rents Act, which put up the rents astronomically), to the working class on the question of the Industrial Relations Act, and to the London dockers, who were being prosecuted under this Act. Indeed, the shadow spokesman of 'Labour', Reg Prentice[1], condemned the five London dockers (who had been jailed under the Industrial Relations Act and then freed by the strike of the dockers) for

---

1 He was later to leave the Labour Party and join the Conservatives

"seeking self-advertisement" and martyrdom. The 'Labour' opposition has done nothing to free the Shrewsbury building workers jailed for picketing.

All this too, the revisionists are forced to admit. In the same article that we quoted above, Gordon McLennan, national organiser of the CPGB and parliamentary candidate for St Pancras North, writes:

"Watching the performance of Wilson and other right-wing labour leaders [Now Wilson is right-wing; he was a 'left'-winger in opposition, which only goes to show that on joining a 'Labour' Government the other 'left'-wingers of this world will just as inevitably be metamorphosed into right-wingers - HB] *in the course of this election campaign doesn't inspire confidence that this will happen* [i.e. that the next 'Labour' Government will act differently] *if they determine the policy and actions of the right government.* [sic]

"Wilson seems to be engaging in a contest with Heath as to who is best at being tough with the Communists."

Facts are stubborn things. They have forced even the ostriches of our movement, i.e., the revisionists, to recognise them as facts. In typical ostrich fashion, however, the revisionists refuse to draw the correct conclusion from these facts; instead they bury their heads in the sand and continue to cling to the desperately-held hope that the next 'Labour' Government will mark a break with the previous ones. They argue that the next 'Labour' Government will be different for two reasons. Firstly, because the 'left' in the 'Labour' Party is very much stronger now than in the past. These 'Left' 'Labour' MPs are represented by the Tribune group, which claims, however, that it has no differences of "principle" with the rights. This is how the 'Tribune' puts the matter:

"There are differences between the policy of this paper and the views which Mr Wilson puts forward. ***But they are of emphasis rather than of principle.****"* [My emphasis - HB].

In other words, there are no differences of principle between the rights and the 'lefts' in the 'Labour' Party, and, if there are no such differences of principle, how, one may ask, can anyone expect a 'left' 'Labour' Government to usher in the Golden Age of Socialism when the previous 'Labour' Governments have not done so? The answer is that one cannot, and those who do expect Socialism from the next 'Labour' (be it 'Left') Government are deluding themselves and duping the masses.

And, secondly, the revisionists say, because the next Parliament is likely to have Communist MPs, who will exercise pressure along with 'Left' 'Labour'

MPs on the right-wing Government of Wilson, Callaghan, Jenkins, Prentice and co. So you are urged to vote Communist, for:

"Every Communist vote is a vote for a new type of Labour Government, one which will stand up to big business and fight for what the working people want and deserve.

"We are going to need such a government in the days ahead. We are more likely to get it if there are Communist MPs in Parliament." (Gordon McLennan in the *Morning Star* of Feb 16, 1974).

It is very likely that there will be one 'Communist' MP in the next Parliament, namely, Jimmy Reid, of the revisionist CPGB. There you have a ready-made formula for, and a gateway to, Socialism: A right-wing 'Labour' Government headed by Wilson + Jimmy Reid = The Dictatorship of the Proletariat. It makes one wonder if people like Lenin were fools to organise, through such hardship and sacrifice of struggle, for the socialist revolution when they could have easily sent, according to the above formula, a couple of Bolshevik Deputies to the Duma to back up the Mensheviks. Such is the disgraceful level to which socialist revolution has been reduced by these miserable 'socialists' of the CPGB.

But we know how the next 'Labour' government (if there is to be one) is likely to respond to the pressure of 'Communist' MPs (i.e. Jimmy Reid, if he is 'lucky' enough to get in). The way it is likely to respond to such pressure is shown by the recent controversy surrounding certain statements made by the miners' leader, Mick McGahey of the CPGB. Here is what McGahey said in connection with the possible use of troops by the Government to deal with the miners' strike:

"If troops were called in I would speak to t&Â

%t see them as a reactionary mass, there are many working class lads in the armed forces and even some miners' sons."

Though Mr McGahey would not ask the troops to mutiny, he " ... *would let them know the facts of the dispute. We would do this by distributing leaflets and information to them, but that would only be done after they were called in."*

When asked to clarify the meaning of his above statement, Mr McGahey had this to say, according to the *'Evening Standard'* of Jan 29, 1974:

"I would not ask any troops to disobey orders. Far from it - I would not ask them to accept responsibility for the miners' struggle ... This is not conspir-

acy. *This is not mutiny. This is only allowing other people to understand the purpose for which they are employed.*"

As can be seen, Mr McGahey's statement is pretty weak, and the subsequent 'clarification' by him of this statement renders it useless.

But what was the reaction of the 'Labour' Party to McGahey's weak statement rendered useless by subsequent 'clarification'?

The official 'Labour' Party made its position clear through a statement issued by J Callaghan and Ron Hayward, the Chairman and Secretary of the 'Labour' Party respectively. This statement reads, in part:

"We utterly repudiate any attempt by Communists or others to use the miners as a political battering ram to bring about a general strike or to call on troops to disobey lawful orders in the event of a strike. This is silly and dangerous nonsense."

Harold Wilson introduced a motion in the House of 'Commons' bitterly attacking McGahey. Nearly a hundred 'Labour' MPs signed this motion.

In view of the foregoing, would the revisionists still persist in their senseless hope of achieving socialism through the next *"Labour Government committed to left policies"*? All the indications are that they will. There are none so deaf as those who will not hear, as the saying puts it. Let them do so and face the consequences of it in the not too distant future.

For our part, we say that if the coming General Election does return (and this is not very likely) a 'Labour' Government, such a Government will have only one function, namely, "to serve as a cloak to cover the nakedness of imperialism" (Stalin, Collected Works, Vol. 6, p.293). Such is the essence of social-democracy. And the British 'Labour' Party is no exception to it. Quite the contrary.

We shall also remark that the revisionists have given up, except in name, the fight for socialism; they do not fight against imperialism and they do not fight against bourgeois parliamentarism. On the contrary, they embellish bourgeois parliamentarism and imperialism. This embellishment is clear not only in view of what has been already stated, but also in view of the following remarks taken from the various issues of the *Morning Star*, newspaper of the CPGB.

We have already quoted the *Morning Star* of Feb 2, 1974, which carried the following embellishment of bourgeois Parliamentarism:

"What's wrong with Parliament is that we are not in it."

Mr Gollan returned to this subject on 18 February while speaking at an election meeting in support of Dr Alistair Wilson, Communist candidate for Aberdare. In this speech Mr Gollan urged people to *"elect Communist MPs"* because to do so *"would transform Parliament from a place where shadow-boxing takes place to an arena for a fight for the needs of the working class"* (reported in Morning Star, Tuesday Feb 19, 1974).

According to Marxism-Leninism, the essence of bourgeois parliamentarism is *"To decide once every few years which member of the ruling class is to repress and crush the people through Parliament"* (Lenin.)

According to revisionism, however, bourgeois parliament can be *"transformed"* into *"an arena for a fight for the needs of the working class"*!

Such utter vulgarisations of Marxism-Leninism can only repel the workers who are in the least capable of thinking and being revolutionary.

Here is an example of how the CPGB revisionists embellish chauvinism and imperialism and how they betray proletarian internationalism.

The same notorious issue (on second thoughts, each issue is more notorious than the preceding) of the *Morning Star*, that is, of Saturday Feb 2, 1974, also carries an article, *'End the Red-Baiting - Attack the Tories'* by Joan Maynard. At one place this article reads:

"Workers are to be controlled while the ruling class enjoys unlimited freedom to exploit the workers. The multi-nationals and <u>oil-sheikhs</u> do as they wish. The only restriction is on the workers."

And further down, Joan Maynard continues:

"All the facts indicate that the Tories want a showdown with the workers. How different their attitude to the oil sheikhs. All conciliation is there."

Some miserable 'socialists' may call the above utterances of Maynard an expression of solidarity with the struggle of the miners. Revolutionary Marxist-Leninists - the only genuine socialists - will, however, regard them as the rallying call of a social imperialist to set the proletariat of Britain upon the oppressed and super-exploited people of the Arab lands.

We know that Joan Maynard is a member of the National Executive of the Labour Party, and she is, in all likelihood, not a member of the CPGB. But that the newspaper of this 'Communist' Party should print such blatantly chauvinistic and imperialistic jingoism as the one contained in Maynard's article only goes to show that the newspaper and the Party of this newspaper are in agreement with it, which in turn only goes to show the utter degeneration which this so-called Communist Party has suffered.

Instead of fighting against imperialism, the CPGB moans about the foolishness of the Tories, whose policies, it is claimed by the CPGB, ruined the British Empire and British Imperialism, and gave birth to the balance of payments deficit and other disasters. In the *Morning Star* of Jan 16, 1974, in an article *'Miners - will the Tories never learn'*, Robin Page Arnot had this to say on the General Strike of 1926:

"The miners did not give in. The struggle went on and on. Nearly a million miners resisted for over seven months. The British economy was ruined. The British Empire, or rather British Imperialism, suffered a self-inflicted blow from which it did not easily recover - if it did recover.

"The final result was that there was no victory. **Everybody lost.** *The miners were defeated, but at such cost that generations of Tory ministers swore that never again would they risk a confrontation with the miners.*[1]*"* (My emphasis - HB).

If British Imperialism suffered a blow as a consequence of the General Strike of 1926, in particular the miners' struggle, then one cannot be a revolutionary and still come to the conclusion that *'EVERYBODY LOST"*. If British Imperialism lost then the British proletariat must have gained. But Mr Robin Page Arnot has reached the conclusion that he has because, consciously or unconsciously - it matters little - he has come to identify the interests of the British proletariat with those of British Imperialism. Once that is done, the conclusion is self-evident: *"Don't ruin British Imperialism"* for that would be *"Everyone's loss"*! That is the logic of the Arnots of this world and of the CPGB, which, incidentally, also furnishes a clue as to why they so fervently desire the return of a 'Labour' government. Such a government, since, as shown above, it cannot bring socialism, can presumably only be required to safeguard British Imperialism and to prevent the Tories from further *"ruining"* it and thus causing loss to *"everybody"*. Mr Arnot, you have let the cat out of the bag with most praiseworthy zeal!

The *Morning Star* of Friday Feb 8, 1974, threatens the Tories in the following blood-curdling manner:

---

1   What a sad and miserable contrast the present-day Robin Page Arnot is to the revolutionary that he was in the 1920s and 1930s. In terms of degeneration, revisionism has claimed its toll.

"But the Tories are not going to be allowed to fight the election on their chosen ground despite rush tactics based on desperate attempts to avoid retribution for [guess what?] *the balance of payments deficit and other disasters of Tory rule being exposed for the simplest Tory voter to see." ('Dirty Work - 20 days to sack the Tories' by Peter Zinkin).*

Thus it is abundantly clear that the revisionists of the CPGB do not fight against imperialism and against bourgeois parliamentarism.

They have substituted the fight against the Tories for the fight against Imperialism, and in so doing they are betraying the working class.

We shall now leave the revisionists to rest in peace, so to speak, and turn to their twin brother, namely, Trotskyism.

III

Trotskyites and the slogan:

'A GENERAL ELECTION TO KICK OUT THE TORIES AND TO ELECT A LABOUR GOVERNMENT COMMITTED TO LEFT POLICIES'

As stated above, this slogan is just as much the slogan of the various Trotskyist organisations as it is of the revisionist CPGB. The only difference is that whereas the revisionists put forward this slogan openly, the Trotskyites put it forward disguisedly - covering it under the camouflage of 'revolutionary' and 'left' phrases. Stalin once remarked:

"Capitulation in practice as the content, 'Left' phrases and 'revolutionary' adventurist postures, as the form disguising and advertising the defeatist content - such is the essence of Trotskyism."

Even those who have only superficially observed the content and form of Trotskyism in practice will need no convincing about the great truth contained in the above remark of Comrade Stalin. Trotskyism outbids everybody in 'revolutionary' and 'left' phrasemongering; in practice, however, it is even more of an ally of social democracy and of imperialism than revisionism. The different Trotskyist organisations in this country form no exception; they mouth 'revolutionary' phrases, which make them seemingly better than the revisionists in the eyes of people who are not very experienced in matters of politics, but in practice these organisations fight shoulder to shoulder with the revisionists in order to strengthen social democracy, which is one of the biggest props of imperialism and which *"serves as a screen for the nakedness of imperialism".* Let us now deal specifically with the position of the three main Trotskyite organisations - Workers' Revolutionary Party (WRP - formerly the Socialist Labour League), the International Socialists and the International Marxist Group - in regard to the slogan calling for the election of a 'Labour' Government.

The Position of the Workers' Revolutionary Party

The WRP issued its election manifesto on Feb 11, 1974. At various places in it we read the following charming things about the 'Labour' Party and the TUC leaders:

"... *The Labour Party leaders have already disowned the miners and they have produced a manifesto which **does not contain a single socialist measure** to protect the working class against rising prices and onrushing unemployment.*" [My emphasis - HB]

"... *Scanlon, Jones, Basnett, Chapple, Jackson and Greene have allowed Phases One, Two and Three to be imposed on their members. **Not a shot have they fired** in defence of the right of trade unions to conduct free wage negotiations nor in the defence of the standard of living of their members, totalling some 5 million.*" [My emphasis - HB]

"*The Labour Party leaders have no policy to meet the crisis. They have ignored every single rank-and-file demand to nationalise the monopolies. Instead, they are **planning another round of collaboration** with them just as they did from 1964 to 1970.*" [My emphasis - HB]

"*Wilson, Callaghan and Crosland have all made clear that their only electoral undertaking to the working class is 'years of austerity' - the very thing that is being demanded by that well known socialist the Governor of the Bank of England!*"

Having listed the above formidable reasons as to why the working class should not vote Labour, the WRP in characteristic Trotskyist fashion departs from simple logic - let alone revolutionary dialectics - and ends up by advising the working class to vote Labour in the very next sentence which follows the above-quoted paragraph ending with the words "*... Bank of England*". Let the WRP manifesto speak for itself:

"*We call on all Labour Party members and trade unionists to vote Labour in constituencies where the Workers' Revolutionary Party is not standing. We call on the electors to return a Labour Government ...*"

Why should the electors return a 'Labour' Government? Here is the answer given by the WRP manifesto:

"*In the struggle to implement the socialist policies we have outlined, they* [the 'Labour' Government] *will be exposed and must be driven out.*"

In other words, according to the WRP, the sole reason for returning a government of those *"who have disowned the miners"*, whose manifesto does not contain *"a single socialist measure"*, who plan *"another round of collaboration"* with the monopolies, and who promise the working class nothing other than *"years of austerity"*, is to *"expose"* and *"drive out"* such a government. The question, however, is this: Is such an argument valid in the conditions of and in the year 1974? No, such an argument is invalid and without foundation today. The masses of people have very little faith in the 'Labour' Party and are refusing to vote Labour. Today the 'Labour' Party is thoroughly discredited in the eyes of the working millions, who are refusing to vote (at the last General Election 11 million abstained). And it is only the radical wing of social-democracy - revisionism or Trotskyism - which is now engaged in an attempt at bringing the disillusioned masses back into the vice of social-democracy. The bourgeoisie are very concerned, to put it mildly, over the increasing abstentions at the successive General Elections. They are going all out to get a big turn-out. Hence, the endless election programmes and Party political broadcasts on Radio and Television. The bourgeoisie are equally concerned about too-humiliating a defeat for the 'Labour' Party, which is, and has been for so long, the safety-valve of British Imperialism. This is how the *Daily Telegraph* of a few weeks ago put the matter:

> "What could it conceivably profit Mr Heath and his Party if - with their majority increased, labour in ruins and Mr Wilson a political ghost - militant trade unionists could still bludgeon the community into surrender! The voice of the ballot box would have counted for little. The extra recruits to the Tory back benches would be joining a paper army. The Conservative Party would come to wish that it had been spared such a victory, and Mr Heath might soon join Mr Wilson in the shadows."

There is a lot of good bourgeois common sense contained in the above paragraph.

In these circumstances, when the masses of people are deserting the 'Labour' Party in disgust, and when the imperialist bourgeoisie itself does not want to see the 'Labour' Party suffer a crushing defeat (for without the 'Labour' Party leadership of the working class the bourgeoisie would find it very difficult, if not impossible, to remain in power for long) - in these circumstances, for people calling themselves 'Marxists' to advocate the support by the masses of the 'Labour' Party means to desert the camp of Socialism for the camp of imperialism, it means to actively join the bourgeoisie in the latter's attempts at the continued subjection of the working class.

REVISIONISTS' & TROTSKYITES' BETRAYAL OF MARXIAN TEACHING ON THE STATE

Attempts are made by the Trotskyites (and also by revisionists) to justify their embellishment of social democracy by making a reference to the remarks Comrade Lenin made in 1920, in which he expressed the view that Labour victory against the Liberals and the Tories would be helpful to the cause of Communism in Britain because such a victory, he argued, would have the effect of exposing the leaders of the 'Labour' Party (MacDonald, Snowden, Henderson), who were regarded as 'socialists' by the masses of British people, for what they were, namely, traitors to the working class. It is funny to watch the tragi-comical spectacle of this gentry - the Trotskyites and revisionists - who hate every single one of Comrade Lenin's revolutionary teachings, turning to Lenin to get some help for their bankrupt theories and to prevent them from being shipwrecked. One must not forget that every time the revolutionary Marxists quote Lenin (and quote him in the proper context, unlike the Trotskyists and revisionists who mostly quote him out of context), these same opportunists say: *"Lenin is not God! The way you quote him is as though he had laid down a tablet!"*, and so on and so forth. Facts, however, prove that it is the opportunists who fail, or refuse, to understand the profound essence of Comrade Lenin's revolutionary teachings; it is they - the opportunists - who are trying to use Lenin's quotations to cover up their support for social-democracy and imperialism.

To return to Lenin's remarks about the victory of the 'Labour' Party being helpful to communism. What the opportunists refuse to see is that Comrade Lenin's remarks were conditioned by the fact that at that time *"the majority of the workers of Great Britain still follow*[ed] *the lead of the British Kerenskys or Sheidemanns* [i.e., MacDonalds and Snowdens and Hendersons - HB] *and"* had *"not yet had the experience of a government composed of these people ..."* (*'Left-Wing' Communism, an Infantile Disorder*).

Can anybody now honestly say that the *"majority of the workers"* in Britain still follow the lead of the present-day *"British Kerenskys"* - the Wilsons, Callaghans, Jenkins, Prentices, Castles, Foots, etc.? Even the Trotskyites do not maintain this. Is there anybody in existence who is really so far removed from reality as to maintain that the workers *"have not yet had the experience of a government composed of these people* [i.e. the British Kerenskys]*"*? Not even the Trotskyites, in our opinion, are so far removed from reality as to maintain this. In absence of the two important qualifications which conditioned, and could not but condition, Comrade Lenin's above remarks, what precisely is the purpose of quoting Comrade Lenin? The purpose can only be to discredit Lenin and to cover the bankruptcy of those who quote him out of context; the purpose can only be to cover, to conceal, the migration of the opportunists to the camp of imperialism behind a quotation from Comrade Lenin. In brief, the purpose can only be to use the letter of Leninism in the opportunists' fight against the spirit of Leninism.

In order to show the reader the hollowness of the 'revolutionary' phrasemongering of the WRP and its utter inability to understand Leninism, let us refer to an article by Vanessa Redgrave, a member of the WRP and its parliamentary candidate for Newham North East, which appeared in the *'Guardian'* of Tuesday 19 Feb, 1974. According to this article, Miss Redgrave told the *'Guardian'* that in Britain we were in the midst of a **revolutionary** crisis and that capitalism would not last in Britain for more than two years. Every member of the WRP believes that. Miss Redgrave is not alone in maintaining so. If we are in the midst of a revolutionary crisis - and Miss Redgrave and her 'Party' maintain that we are - what the hell, we may ask, are Miss Redgrave and the WRP taking part in parliamentary elections for? If we are in the midst of a revolutionary crisis, should not Miss Redgrave and her 'Party' be organising the revolutionary uprising rather than play-acting in the East End or West End? One thing or the other! Either we are in a revolutionary situation, in which case Miss Redgrave and her 'Party' are not doing anything about organising the proletariat for the imminent overthrow of British Imperialism, and are, therefore, not to be taken seriously. Or we are not in a revolutionary situation; in which case Miss Redgrave and her 'Party' are indulging in hollow and meaningless 'Left' phrasemongering designed to cover their desertion to social-democracy and their betrayal of the interests of the working class.

We are certainly not in a revolutionary situation as yet. And when such a situation does arrive, neither Miss Redgrave nor her 'Party' will be able to recognise it, nor would they lead it. They will then completely merge with social-democracy and fight the 'Stalinist bureaucrats', i.e., revolutionary Marxist-Leninists, who will most certainly one day lead successfully the British proletariat in overthrowing the rule of British Imperialism.

Whether or not British Imperialism has more than two years of life left to it, it is more or less certain, judging from all past experience and the turnover of the membership of various Trotskyite organisations, Miss Redgrave won't last two full years in the WRP. She has been promised an instant revolution by the WRP in typical Trotskyist fashion; and, when this instant revolution fails to materialise, Miss Redgrave will just as instantly disappear from the scene, so to speak, to once again become a *"romantic Tory"*, to whom the name of Churchill sounds marvellous, and who likes Kipling and dislikes the *"smell of socialism"*. Miss Redgrave and her 'Party' should know that it is one thing to set a date for the transformation of a rotten Socialist Labour League into an equally rotten Workers' Revolutionary Party, but quite another to fix a date for the demise of British Imperialism. The former requires but a resolution, the latter requires painstaking, persistent, persevering and principled work over a long period of time - something that the likes of the petty-bourgeois Redgraves and the equally petty-bourgeois WRPs of this world are incapable of.

The Position of the International Socialists

The International Socialists (IS) recognise in words that socialism cannot come through Parliament, that it is necessary to smash the bourgeois state machine, that such a *"powerful weapon"* as the bourgeois army *"cannot be wished away through the ballot box. It has to be broken from the grasp of the ruling class"* ('Socialist Worker', 9 Feb, 1974) 'Why Soldiers put the boot in'). IS have produced a pamphlet under the title *"Can Socialism Come Through Parliament?"*, in which they make, among others, the following statements about Parliament, the 'Labour' Party and the elections:

"Today the functions of Parliament" are to act *"as a safety valve over certain issues, it helps ensure an orderly change in personnel every few years - from Labour to Tory and back again."* (pp.5-6).

Parliament is *"today ... a side-show"* (p.6, my emphasis - HB).

"Parliamentary democracy is a sham anyway".

In the elections *"there is usually no choice anyway"*.

"Voting gives us no control over the MPs or their golden pledges. Who voted for Labour in 1964 for more unemployment, a wage freeze, higher prescription charges and attacks on unions? Once elected we can do nothing ... until five years later when there will be a further choice between Tweedledum and Tweedledee." (p.8, my emphasis - HB)

The pamphlet contains a long, and correct for a change, denunciation of the 'Labour' Party, the past 'Labour' Governments, and of the TUC. Having recited the *"miserable"* record of the 'Labour' Party, the pamphlet goes on to say:

*"Despite this miserable history **some socialists still say** that we should give the Labour Party another chance."* (p.16, my emphasis - HB).

Then follow three pages of denunciation of those socialists, in particular the CPGB, who hold the view that the 'Labour' Party should be given another chance and that the 'Labour' Party can be *"transformed into an instrument of socialism"*. The pamphlet states:

*"... No longer do the workers look towards Parliament for massive change. And if they don't do this, then **what is the point** of actively working in the Labour Party?"* (p.17).

According to IS, the 'Left' cannot capture control of the 'Labour' Party except *"at a time of massive struggles when it is irrelevant."* (p.19).

"To have faith in a Labour Party controlled even by socialists at a time of a national General Strike would be a calamity. **If we can lead a successful General Strike who NEEDS a Parliamentary majority?***"* (p.18, IS's emphasis).

In denunciation of the CPGB's preoccupation with Parliament, the IS say:-

*"**Parliament is no longer where decisions are made. It is fundamentally a talking shop. Real power lies with the monopolies and on the shop floor. But if that is the case then why bother with Parliament?**"* (p.22, IS's emphasis).

Having written the above-quoted statements, the IS took fright, and started backtracking, for the pamphlet goes on to say:

"This is not to say we would boycott elections completely ... . Such elections can be a useful soapbox". (p.30).

"In future elections the International Socialists' attitude will depend on our own strength and the situation. In 1970, for example, we argued that the workers should vote for Labour - not because it was socialist but because large numbers of workers had illusions that it would bring social change. By putting them to the test on unemployment, inflation, trade-union laws and welfare cuts we could more easily show their shortcomings." (p.31, my emphasis - HB).

One has to be an incurable idiot and a philistine to entertain the illusion that in 1970 the 'Labour' Party and the 'Labour' Government needed to be exposed in the eyes of the workers. It is downright falsehood intended to cover the reactionary spinelessness of those like the IS to say that in 1970 *"large numbers of workers had illusions that it* [a 'Labour' Government] *would bring about large social change."* The 1970 election proved that *"large numbers of workers"* had no such illusion - 11 million did not even bother to go to the polling booths. The only people who suffered in 1970, or who suffer today from this *"illusion"*, are the IS and suchlike radical social-democrats. 'Labour' by 1970 had already been *"put to the test on unemployment ..."* etc. and its *"shortcomings"*, or what we would call its reactionary anti-working class nature, had already been exposed. The above statement of IS is even contradicted by the rest of the contents of their own pamphlet which is under discussion. The pamphlet says, for example, that *"in the last 25 years the links between the Labour Party and the working class have got thinner and thinner. Working class votes still go to Labour **but active support does not** ..."* (p.18, my emphasis - HB).

This was further confirmed by Mr John Palmer of the IS Committee, for example, who addressed a meeting held on 21 Feb, 1974, in Seymour Hall, London, to drum up support for the 'Labour' Party. At this meeting Mr Palmer said that nobody wanted to vote Labour, that the Labour Party were not making much of an effort to get people to vote for it (Labour), and that they (meaning IS) were having to work very hard to persuade people to vote Labour. We believe this to be true. To repeat, today the 'Labour' Party is thoroughly discredited in the eyes of the working millions, who are refusing to vote (at the last General Election 11 million abstained). And, it is only the radical wing of social-democracy - revisionism and Trotskyism - which is now engaged in an attempt at bringing the disillusioned masses back into the vice of social-democracy, and which is engaged in prettifying social-democracy.

And what kind of *"soapbox"* is Parliament going to be for IS? Here is the answer given by the IS:

*"... It may be that in the future we would put up IS candidates at Parliamentary elections. If we do, we shall do so **not**[*] with the aim of winning a Parliamentary majority **but with the intention of highlighting a particular issue or dispute**[**] - and getting a wider audience for our case."* (p.31 - * IS's emphasis, ** -my emphasis - HB).

Hitherto revolutionary Socialists - Marxist-Leninists - have always regarded the aim of revolutionaries participating in the *"pig-sty"* of bourgeois parliaments to be the exposure of bourgeois parliamentarism. Now, however, there have appeared 'socialists' of the IS-type who regard the aim of such participation to be *"highlighting a particular issue or dispute"* - the aim is no longer exposure of bourgeois parliamentarism. What a disgrace these sham socialists are to Marxism!

People who in a 33 page pamphlet have fulminated on 29 and three quarter pages against the 'Labour' Party, against the CPGB, against Parliamentarism, against the elections, etc., and then towards the end of the 30th page begin to make out a case in favour of the 'Labour' Party, in favour of participation in the elections, and in favour of bourgeois Parliamentarism, reveal more to us the truly hollow, empty and phrasemongering nature of their own politics than they enlighten the working class. The IS, like the rest of the opportunist gentry - the various other Trotskyist organisations and the revisionists - have proved to us that they are one of the biggest 'left' and 'revolutionary' phrasemongering hypocrites, who are *"virtuosos in the art of prostituting Marxism"* (Lenin: *The Collapse of the Second International*), and of deceiving the masses, who wrote the first 29 3/4 pages of their pamphlet in order to deceive and to *"gull the rural Simple Simons"*, and who wrote the last quarter of page 30 and the first half of page 31 *"to gladden the hearts"* of the bourgeoisie. Such is the essence of IS.

Thus it was very clear to every competent and experienced Marxist-Leninist even when this pamphlet came out (which was not very long ago - it came out after September 1973 in any case) which way the IS would go. It was very clear to us that IS, like the rest of the opportunist fraternity, would, in the event of an election, become one of the biggest and most enthusiastic supporters of turning the masses into electoral fodder for the social-democratic electoral machine. And so it has. As the saying goes: coming events cast their shadow before.

IS Slogan: *'Vote Labour, Step up the fight'*. Why should the working class vote Labour?

The IS attempt to give an answer to this question in an article in the *'Socialist Worker'* of 16 Feb, 1974, under the title *'Vote Labour, Step up the Fight'*. We reproduce below a few paragraphs from this article, which is a characteristic piece of meaningless, contradictory, inconsistent and illogical Trotskyist mumbo jumbo; it is a typical example of how the Trotskyists always attempt to cover their inevitable capitulation to the bourgeoisie behind a barrage of 'left' phrases and 'revolutionary' slogans. Here are some of the gems from the IS article in support of 'Labour':

"No worker should have any doubt about what is at stake in the election. The Tories are campaigning for a new majority with which to hammer at trade-union organisation and working-class living standards. The working class has to respond with a massive anti-Tory vote. And that means a Labour vote.

"If the Tories are successful, they will have achieved a major gain for

their class - *the 7 per cent of the population who own 84 per cent of the wealth"*. A Tory *"electoral victory would signify that many workers were blaming their own organisations for the crisis. It would make the miners feel isolated from other sections of the workers. It would give encouragement to every non-unionist, every scab and every racialist. And to this extent it would weaken the ability of all workers to resist cuts in living standards, anti-union laws and attacks on picketing.*

"By contrast, a massive Labour vote will represent a rebuttal of the Tories' attack. It would mean that the vast majority of workers had come out in support of the miners and in defence of the unions.

"But the need for a massive Labour vote should not be confused with having illusions about how a Labour government would behave. All the present Tory attacks were pioneered by the Labour government of 1964-70. A LABOUR GOVERNMENT ELECTED IN TWO WEEKS' TIME WOULD BE FORCED TO BEHAVE VERY MUCH IN THE SAME WAY AS THE TORIES.

"The reason is that the present Tory attacks on living conditions and union organisation are the ONLY way in which governments which accept capitalism can deal with the economic crisis. LABOUR IS AS MUCH COMMITTED TO KEEPING CAPITALISM INTACT AS THE TORIES. IT WILL BE FORCED TO TAKE THE SAME SORT OF MEASURES TO TRY TO DEAL WITH CAPITALISM'S PROBLEMS.

"But one thing will hinder the Labour politicians in the efforts to copy the Tories' methods - a massive Labour vote. For such a vote will mean rejection of the argument that workers are to blame for the crisis. It will make much more difficult any attempts by a Labour government to shift the blame on to workers' organisations.

"For these reasons we insist: Support the miners. Defend the unions. Kick out the Tories. Vote Labour. Step up the fight." [My emphasis - HB]

Lurking behind the arguments in the above-quoted paragraph, we can see the opportunists who are *"completely saturated with philistinism"*, and who, at bottom, not only do not believe in revolution, in the creative power of revolution, but live *"in mortal dread of it"*. The essence of these arguments is this: let us elect a Labour Government, for otherwise the Tories will get in again. The IS refuse to explain (because they are incapable of explaining) as to why a Tory "electoral victory would signify that many workers are blaming their organisations for the crisis". There is no reason to believe that a Tory victory would have this effect. A Tory victory would have only one meaning in the present situation, namely, it would mean a defeat for the 'Labour' Party. The 'Labour' Party's defeat would not mean that the workers love the Tories; it would only mean that the workers don't much love 'Labour' either. And in sending out this message clearly and loudly (by mass abstentions) the 'backward' workers would have shown a greater degree of political consciousness than the 'advanced Marxists' of the IS and other reformist organisations.

A 'Labour' Government, we are told, within two weeks of getting elected *"would be forced to behave very much in the same way as the Tories"*, whom we must keep out because, presumably, we want Tory policies from a 'Labour' Government and not from a Tory Government. We are told *"Labour is as much committed to keeping capitalism intact as the Tories. It will be forced to take the same sort of measures to try to deal with capitalism's problems"*, but we must organise *"a massive Labour vote"* because, argue the IS, *"a massive Labour vote" "will make much more difficult any attempts by a Labour government to shift the blame on to the workers' organisations."* Is there any sense in all this jibberish? For those who are endowed with ordinary human thinking, there is no sense whatever in all this. If the Tories win, it means the workers are *"blaming their own organisations for the crisis"*, it means a mandate for the Tories to attack the working class; if, however, Labour wins, then even though Labour will take the *"same sort of measures"* and *"behave very much in the same way as do the Tories"*, we are told, it will mean a victory for the people - especially if Labour wins with a *"massive vote"* for such a *"massive vote"* would prevent the 'Labour Government from blaming the workers' organisations for the crisis! Would not a massive Labour vote be taken as a sign of endorsement of Labour policies? We are sure it would.

In any case, you yourselves tell us, gentlemen of the IS, that *"a Labour Government elected in two weeks' time would be forced to behave very much in the same way as the Tories"*. And this is true. No Labour Government can bring socialism because no Labour Government is prepared to hurt capitalism; because socialism can only be established by smashing the bourgeois state machine and the 'Labour' Party does not stand for that sort of 'nonsense'; because the 'Labour' Party works within the bounds of capitalism. More than that. Even if the 'Labour' Party sincerely wanted to bring Socialism they could not because the ruling class won't let them. The 1964 Wilson Government was forced by the workings of the capitalist system to 'forget' its election promises, to deflate the economy, and to economise on social services in order to prevent the further deterioration of the balance of payments deficit by stopping the flight of money from this country to the overseas money markets. Here is how Harold

Wilson describes in his autobiography his encounter with the Governor of the Bank of England, Lord Cromer, who visited Wilson in Downing Street on 24 Nov, 1964:-

"I said that we had now reached a situation where a newly-elected government with a mandate from the people was being told, not so much by the Governor of the Bank of England but by international speculators, that the policies on which we had fought the election could not be implemented; that the government would be forced into the adoption of Tory politics to which it was fundamentally opposed. The Governor confirmed that that was, in fact, the case.

"I asked him if this meant that it was impossible for any government, whatever its party label, whatever its manifesto on which it has fought an election, to continue, unless it immediately reverted to full-scale Tory policies.

"He had to admit that that was what his argument meant, because of the sheer compulsion of the economic dictation of those who exercised decisive economic power."

No need to say, Harold Wilson submitted to the sound advice of Lord Cromer to forget about the silly little things in Labour's Manifesto. Had he not done so, money would not have been alone in fleeing the country; it would have been fleeing in the pleasant company of the Wilsons, Callaghans, Jenkins, Castles, etc. of this world.

So, there could be no Socialism, for, to quote that well-known 'socialist' Wilson once again:

"You cannot go cap in hand to the central bankers as the Tories have been forced to do [and as Wilson was forced to do within barely a month and a half after uttering these words -HB] *and maintain your freedom of action, whether on policies maintaining full employment here in Britain or even on social policies. The Central Bankers will before long be demanding* [and they did - HB] *that Britain puts her house in order and their idea of an orderly house usually means vicious inroads into the welfare state* [like those that took place during Wilson's Premiership - HB], *and a one-sided pay pause* [Wilson's statutory incomes policy - HB]. *The Government will then launch into savage cuts. The brunt will fall again on wages, on salaries, on the ordinary family struggling to make ends meet."*

How very true. Harold Wilson made the above remarks in a speech on 3 October, 1964 (less than two weeks before the 1964 General Election); and he proved the truth of his remark on 24 November, 1964 (see the above-quoted remarks from his autobiography).

Socialism can only be brought by smashing the bourgeois state machine and establishing the dictatorship of the proletariat.

In view of what has just been stated above, we ask the IS gentry: why should the working class worry whether the Tories or the 'Labour' Party wins? Why should they be forced to choose between, to borrow your own apt expression, *"Tweedledum and Tweedledec"*? Why should they *"bother with Parliament"* when you have been telling them all along that Parliament is a *"side-show"*? Why should they follow the advice of some miserable 'socialists' and vote 'Labour' despite the *"miserable history"* of 'Labour' all about which they have learnt from your pamphlet: *'Can Socialism come through Parliament?'* ? Why should the working class believe you now when you say that the Tories are attacking democratic rights when, only a few weeks ago, you yourselves in your pamphlet argued against the CPGB in the following language: *"And neither is it true that the monopolies are attacking 'the concept of democracy'. On the contrary, great efforts go into persuading us that Parliament does work and that voting is worthwhile"* (p.21 *'Can Socialism come through Parliament'*, IS's emphasis).

Yes! *"Great efforts"* are indeed being gone into persuading us that *"... voting is worthwhile"* and not just by the monopolies, but also by such 'Socialist' lackeys of the monopolies as the IS and various other petty-bourgeois vultures of the working-class movement.

So, it turns out that what IS had written in its pamphlet only a few weeks ago was a mere polemical sally motivated by reasons of jealousy. What they had stated were the rantings and ravings of the opportunist, and hypocritical, petty bourgeoisie, rather than the serious battle cry of proletarian revolutionaries. Workers who are in the least capable of thinking will learn to treat the hypocritical rantings of the IS for what they are, namely the whining of the cowardly philistines who fear revolution,and who have no intention of preparing for it.

Then the article *'Vote Labour, Step up the Fight'*, in typical philistine manner, begins to come out with sighs and groans about Labour not fighting the election on clear class lines:

"If Labour took up the Tory challenge and fought this election on clear class lines they would win easily."

The petty-bourgeois is an incurable utopian. He tries desperately to cling to the hope of getting from life what life cannot give. The IS are a petty-bourgeois organisation. We have seen how they denounced the 'Labour' Party for its *"shortcomings"* - for its attacks on the working class - and yet, in characteristically petty-bourgeois manner, they expect this selfsame 'Labour' Party to *"fight this election on clear class lines"*! And they expect this from a party about whom only six lines further down in this very article they write:

"The problem for Labour is that it is impossible for them to really attack the Tory record. When they were in office many of their policies were identical to the Tories'. If they were returned now, many of these same policies would be re-implemented."

"The problem for" IS is how to find the best and the most appropriate 'revolutionary' phrases to cloak the rotten bourgeois content of their politics, to cloak their subservience to social-democracy and to imperialism. This is obviously a great *"problem"* for them, for people are beginning to realise that the IS and their like serve no other purpose than to act as a screen to cover the nakedness of social-democracy and of imperialism.

The rest of their article is devoted to further moans and complaints that the Labour election campaign has no life in it, how it should be conducted, and if Labour and the TUC leadership won't take up this challenge then the socialists should do so.

"Their refusal to wage such a campaign multiplies the responsibility for socialists to fight this class election on a class programme.

"We have to insist on a Labour vote as the first line of defence against the government offensive."

And, as was to be expected, towards the end the article contains the following fraudulent proviso:

"No amount of tampering with the system can change this. Only a complete revolutionary transformation of society can do so, with the taking of economic power away from the ruling class and the organisation of production for need and not for profit."

It is the very first paragraph (quoted above) of this article, rather than the last-quoted fraudulent remark, which reveals the real nature of the politics of the IS. The first paragraph (in conjunction with the rest of the article) shows that the IS are not a socialist organisation but an organisation of anti-Tories, and they try their best, like all other opportunist anti-Tories masquerading as

Socialists, to pass their anti-Toryism off as Socialism. But that won't do. Anti-Toryism is not and cannot be synonymous with Socialism.

We believe that this article is going to earn for the members of the IS the sad notoriety of being people with *"brain*[s] *all the vitality of which had fled to the tongue"* (Marx *'Civil War in France'*).

To the 'reasons' (dealt with above) given by the IS in the above article, they have added three more reasons as to why the working class should vote Labour. At their meeting in Seymour Hall (see above) the IS speakers listed these reasons as follows:-

(1) That the Labour Party has been branded as an *"extremist"* by the Tories, therefore it is our duty, say the IS, to defend this 'extremist' Labour Party.

(2) That the Labour victory would be a 'huge morale booster' for the working class.

(3) That, although the Labour Government won't solve all problems, it will make some differences; that it will repeal the Industrial Relations Act, freeze rents, which will constitute real gains.

As to the first point, it is the kind of banality which can only repel workers who are in the least politically conscious. According to this 'logic', we should be defending Enoch Powell, because the Tories call him too extremist (Anthony Barber, Chancellor of the Exchequer, called Mr Powell *"a fanatic"* at the last Conservative Party Conference).

In making the second point, IS say that the Labour Government would be forced back to the same politics as the Tories. But they add that *"if a Labour Government is in, the working class will be more willing to defend its standards"*. One would have thought, on the basis of concrete historical experience, that the working class usually puts up with far more attacks on it from a 'Labour' Government than from a Conservative government.

Lastly, the third point. IS themselves say that Labour would act just the same as the Tories. How then can one say that the working class will stand to gain from a Labour victory?

IS are saying *"Vote Labour, No illusions"*. But, in the light of the foregoing, it is clear that the IS, along with the other opportunist organisations, are engaged in creating a lot of illusions about the 'Labour' Party by saying the next 'Labour' Government will bring about some real gains to the working class; just at a time when we need to express with the utmost revolutionary ruthlessness the rotten nature of social democracy which acts as a prop for imperialism, what we get, not unexpectedly mind you, from the petty-bourgeois IS and suchlike opportunist organisations, is precisely the opposite, namely, reactionary spinelessness.

The Position of the IMG (International Marxist Group)

The IMG line is the same as that of its sister opportunist organisations - IS, WRP and the CPGB. The IMG also wants the working class to vote Labour in this election. Here is what they have to say on this score:-

"The International Marxist Group is in favour of people voting Labour. A victory for the Tories would be a defeat for the working class, while a victory for Labour would encourage the fighting spirit and self-confidence of the workers' movement. For this reason the outcome of the election will affect not only Parliament but also the far more important struggle outside. "But no confidence whatsoever can be placed in the Labour traitors. We say: vote Labour. But rely on your own struggles ..." ('*Red Weekly*' of 8 Feb 1974).

The same theme is repeated by the '*Red Weekly*' of 15 Feb 1974, which says:

"We call for a vote for Labour ... because a victory for Labour would increase the combativity of the workers".

This argument is in the same vein as the IS one which talks about the Labour victory acting as a *"morale-booster"* for the working class. None of these opportunists explain why a Labour victory would act as a morale-booster for the working class - especially when the 'Labour' Party is thoroughly discredited in the eyes of the working class. The working class had plenty of morale-boosters - and real ones - in the last three years.

The working class got a real, and not a phoney, boost to its morale when the miners a couple of winters ago forced by their action the government to concede the Wilberforce award; the working class got a real, not a phoney, boost to its morale when the London dockers by their actions forced the ruling class to free the 5 dockers from Pentonville; the working class will get another real boost to its morale from the success of the present struggle of the miners. The working class does not need a phoney boost to its morale by the return of yet another Government of 'Labour' traitors.

What the sham socialists of the IMG and IS are doing is confusing their own petty-bourgeois needs for the needs of the working class; it is the sham socialists and the petty-bourgeois philistines who are in need of a phoney morale-booster, not the working class. The working class has had enough of

'Labour' traitors and is therefore refusing to vote. The task of the revolutionaries is to turn the disillusionment of the masses with the 'Labour' Party (which is a form of unconscious socialist striving) into a conscious revolutionary revolt against monopoly capitalism and for socialism; it is not our task to push the masses back into the captivity of social-democracy. But the IMG and other opportunist 'Marxists' are engaged in feverishly helping social-democracy to captivate the masses of proletarians.

Thus, it emerges from the foregoing that the policy of the Trotskyists is just as opportunist as that of the revisionists. Though the Trotskyists from time-to-time pay lip service to the need to smash the bourgeois state, their practice shows that they are one of the biggest supporters of social-democracy. It is not accidental that neither the revisionists nor the Trotskyites ever mention the need to fight for the establishment of the "*dictatorship of the proletariat*". They have all kinds of vague expressions, but they shun this expression like the devil shuns holy water.

Lenin says:

"*... Those who recognise only the class struggle are not yet Marxists; they may be found to be still within the boundaries of bourgeois thinking and bourgeois politics. To confine Marxism to the doctrine of the class struggle means curtailing Marxism, distorting it, reducing it to something which is acceptable to the bourgeoisie. Only he is a Marxist who extends the recognition of the class struggle to the recognition of the dictatorship of the proletariat. This is what constitutes the most profound difference between the Marxist and the ordinary petty (as well as big) bourgeois. This is the touchstone on which real understanding and recognition of Marxism is to be tested ...* " (State and Revolution)

It is perfectly clear that the Trotskyists and revisionists are "*still within the boundaries of bourgeois thinking and bourgeois politics*", that they are not Marxists, but ordinary petty (not big) bourgeois. They are spreading opportunism in the working-class movement, and it is the job of true revolutionaries to fight against their opportunism for "*the fight against imperialism is a sham and a humbug unless it is inseparably bound up with the fight against opportunism*" (Lenin, '*Imperialism, the Highest Stage of Capitalism*').

It is equally clear that, despite the verbal fights in which the Trotskyists engage from time to time against the CPGB, there is not a single respect in which they are any different from or better than the CPGB revisionists, whom the Trotskyists, by way of slander against Comrade Stalin, call Stalinists.

The only difference is that of form. The CPGB are open capitulators; the Trotskyists on the other hand, are disguised capitulators. Just as the Bukharinites and Trotskyites joined in a counter-revolutionary bloc in the USSR to oppose the revolutionary line of the CPSU(B) headed by Comrade Stalin, so the revisionists of the CPGB and the Trotskyists in Britain invariably join forces and form a bloc to defeat revolutionary politics. Anyone who is at all acquainted with the working class movement, the students' movement, the women's liberation movement, and the Indo-China Solidarity Movement is bound to know this. The Trotskyists as well as the revisionists attack Comrade Stalin; they both refuse to recognise the dictatorship of the proletariat; they both attack those countries in which there is the dictatorship of the proletariat; they both embellish social-democracy and imperialism. We know already how the CPGB plans to make the next Labour government (if Labour wins the election) keep to its promise to carry out a *"left policy"*. It says :

"Every communist vote is a vote for a new type of Labour government, one which will stand up to big business ..."

"We are going to need such a government .... we are much more likely to get it if there are communist MPs in Parliament."

This is the position of what the Trotskyists would call the 'Stalinist' CPGB. What, then, we may enquire, is the position of the anti-Stalinist IMG? We find that the position of the anti-Stalinist IMG Trotskyists is every bit as 'Stalinist' as that of the CPGB. Here is what the IMG says on the question under discussion:

"But a vote for revolutionary candidates will be the clearest call of all for escalating the struggle against the scabbing of parliamentarians. The epitome of such a scab is Reg Prentice, whom John Ross [IMG candidate] *will be fighting in Newham."*

Just as the revisionist formula boils down to: A Right-wing Labour Government + Jimmy Reid = the Dictatorship of the Proletariat, so the Trotskyist IMG formula comes down to: A Right-wing Labour Government + John Ross (or Tariq Ali) = the Dictatorship of the Proletariat.

The WRP has no differences with the 'Stalinist' CPGB except over the question whether there should be a Labour Government committed to *"socialist policies"* or committed to *"left policies"*.

All this goes to show that the CPGB is not Stalinist. To be a Stalinist means to be a revolutionary Marxist-Leninist; it means to fight for the Dictatorship of the Proletariat and to defend it. If the CPGB were Stalinist, it would be impossible for it to have a policy which was roughly the same as that of the Trotskyists; it would be impossible for them to co-operate with each other the way they actually do. No, the CPGB are not a 'Stalinist' Party. They are a rotten revisionist Party. And, that being the case, similarity between their policy and the policy of the Trotskyists, and co-operation between them, is not only possible but inevitable. Both of them - the open (revisionist) and disguised (Trotskyist) opportunists are the agents of the bourgeoisie in the proletarian movement. The kind of 'socialism' they are fighting for is clear from the above. What 'Socialism' means to Trotskyists, for example, is clear from the wholehearted support they have always rendered to the counter-revolutionary CIA-led Hungarian uprising of 1956. The inspirers of that counter-revolutionary uprising were the CIA, Cardinal Mintzenty and the Roman Catholic Church, and the reactionary former landlords and bourgeois classes of Hungary. No doubt some workers took part in it; that, however, could not turn it into a revolutionary uprising any more than the participation by some workers in the Kronstadt rebellion against the Bolshevik regime turned the latter rebellion into a revolutionary uprising.

The Trotskyists and revisionist fraternity are not socialists. They represent a *"heap of petty bourgeois refuse"* which has been collected over many decades. Our task is to work hard to expose and to remove these opportunist 'socialist' leaders, for *"the proletariat cannot perform its epoch-making emancipatory mission unless it removes these* [philistine] *leaders from its path, unless it sweeps them out of its way ... "* (Lenin, 'Greetings to the Hungarian Workers').

To sum up. It is clear that the slogan: *'A General Election to kick out the Tories and to elect a Labour Government committed to Left policies'* is a slogan adopted by the revisionists as well as by the Trotskyists. It is equally clear that this slogan of the revisionist, Trotskyist gang is an opportunist slogan, for it substitutes the fight against the Tories for the fight against Imperialism, and, therefore, constitutes a betrayal of the working class. No amount of rhetoric can hide this truth!

First published by the Association of Communist Workers,
24th February, 1974.

Part Three

The Coal Strike of 1984 - 85

"British capital attacked the miners ... primarily because the miners have always been, and still remain, the advanced detachment of the British proletariat. It was the strategy of British capital to curb this advanced detachment, to lower their wages and lengthen their working day, in order then, having settled accounts with this main detachment, to make the other detachments of the working class also toe the line."

J.V.Stalin apropos the 1926 British General Strike

"The Scargill affair depended on a coincidence of purpose between an exotic array of interests, foremost among which were the Thatcher administration and the Labour leadership"

S.Milne ('The Enemy Within')

LALKAR July 1983

Tories seeking confrontation with the miners

Arthur Scargill, President of the National Union of Mineworkers, has for some time been warning Britain's coal miners that the National Coal Board (NCB) was planning to close 70 pits, which it regards as being uneconomic, with the loss of 70,000 jobs. The coal miners' leader's warnings were characterised as alarmist talk by the press, the NCB and the government alike.

The election over, the Monopolies Commission has published its recommendations which call for the closure of precisely the 70 pits and entailing a job loss of precisely the 70,000 that Mr Scargill had been at pains to drive home. This is not only tragic for the workers in the coal industry facing the executioner's axe, but is also the height of lunacy in economic terms, for, as Scargill has pointed out, the closure of these uneconomic pits will cost the taxpayer £4.3 billion, whereas keeping them open will cost only £2 billion! In other words, it will be far more uneconomic to close the uneconomic pits. This example is typical of the madhouse economics of capitalism.

The NCB would doubtless wish to pass all these losses on to the shoulders of the remaining workers in the coal industry. Encouraged by the Conservative election victory, the NCB, under its next Chairman Ian MacGregor, is expected to take a tough stance on the miners' pay negotiations. Britain's miners will be expected to take a cut in their living standards, with a proposed basic wage increase of little more than half the rate of inflation. The low pay offer, the appointment of that butcher Ian MacGregor as the Chairman of the NCB, an acceleration of pit closures and with coal stocks expected to reach 60 million tonnes by this December (being the equivalent of 6 months' supply for domestic use), all the signs are that the Tories and the NCB are preparing to challenge the mineworkers and to inflict a decisive defeat on them. Writing in the Business Section of the *Observer* of 19 June, 1983, Mr Robert Taylor, its Labour Editor, says:

> "In the aftermath of their election landslide, the Conservatives seem to be in the mood to confront the miners with the grim economic facts of life, and risk a showdown."

If this happens the mineworkers will have to stand up and fight, or accept increasingly a reversion to conditions and pay norms decidedly of the pre-2nd world war era. What is at stake is not just the future of the coal industry and of the workers in it, important though they are, but the very conditions of existence of the entire working class. Miners are still the most advanced detachment of the British working class, and the Tories may yet live to learn that in taking on the mineworkers they had bitten off more than they could chew.

LALKAR April 1984

Government and NCB declare class war on miners

The overwhelming majority of Britain's miners have been out on strike for just over three weeks, and 140 out of the country's 170 coal pits are closed. The significance of this dispute may be gauged from the remarks made by the *Sunday Times*, one of the most representative spokesmen of British imperialism. In its leader column of 18 March, which was ostensibly devoted to welcoming Chancellor Nigel Lawson's budget the previous Tuesday, the *Sunday Times* compared Mr Arthur Scargill, the President of the National Union of Mineworkers (NUM), to General Galtieri, the erstwhile Argentinian fascist dictator, and went on to say that welcome and important though Lawson's budget was for improvement of the chronically depressed British economy, even more important for its success was the defeat of the NUM. His remark is hardly to be surprised at, for ever since the working class appeared on the historical stage as a separate class, with its distinct entity and its distinct political programme for safeguarding and advancing its own economic and political interests, the cry of the bourgeois all over the world has been that the enemy at home (the proletariat) is more dangerous than the enemy abroad. It was so at the time of the Paris Commune, when the French bourgeoisie was happy to commit treason against the French nation by surrendering to the Prussian invaders in return for the latter's support in suppressing the Commune, and it has been so since then.

From the leading article of the *Sunday Times*, and from the remarks of other official and unofficial bourgeois spokesmen, it is clear that the bourgeoisie have, through their attack on the NUM and their declared determination to defeat the coal strike, declared a class war against the entire British working class, not just the miners. In the light of this it is strange to hear complaints from British imperialist media that Arthur Scargill, in an interview with the London Correspondent of the Soviet paper *Trud* (Labour), had spoken of the miners' strike as a class war. These bourgeois gentlemen are jokers, for they think that they have the sole prerogative of waging a class war, that they can wage a class war against the working class, but the latter must not declare, let alone wage in earnest, a class war against the bourgeoisie. As a matter of fact,

Scargill never used the expression 'class war'. This is what he said:

"The workers see and know that businessmen, stockbrokers, and the big press proprietors easily spend more on a bottle of wine than an old age pensioner gets to live on for a week. Figuratively speaking, this is the barrel of social gunpowder which has been exploded by miners' anger."

From the standpoint of the working class, the sad thing is not that Mr Scargill spoke, albeit implicitly, of the conditions leading to social explosions and class wars, but that working-class leaders these days studiously avoid all such references.

Why the coal strike?

In many ways the present strike has been forced on the NUM by the National Coal Board (NCB) and the government, who want to defeat the miners at any cost, for at the moment only the miners stand in the way of the government and the whole of the employing class in achieving complete victory and in depressing still further the living standards of the British working class.

This strike must be seen against the background of economic depression, which, with its 3.25 million unemployed and the consequent emasculation of the economist TUC leadership, has produced, temporarily at least, a state of demoralisation in the working class. The impotence of the TUC leadership has been shown again and again through its failure to mobilise the working class against unemployment, against anti-working class and anti-union legislation, against the lowering of living standards, against war-mongering and even against union busting at the Cheltenham GCHQ. Thus only the miners, with their long and proud tradition of determined struggle and class solidarity stand in the way.

British monopoly capitalism, in order to be successful in the game of international competition for markets, has had to bring down the cost of production, has had to shed jobs, restructure industry and increase the productivity of labour. In other words, it has to cheapen the cost of labour power or depress wages and thus the living standards of working people. The stakes are extremely high, and the bourgeoisie is not going to give up this struggle easily, and therefore the present coal strike can by no means be regarded as a mere skirmish of the type that is a never-ending characteristic of the capitalist mode of production.

The miners are a hard nut to crack, and the government and the NCB know this. So they have been making the maximum of preparations to provoke the miners into strike action at a time that the government and the NCB think are most favourable for them to inflict a mortal blow against the NUM. Knowing that the winter was coming to a close, that coal stocks stood at a record 24 million tons, the NCB made a derisory offer of a wage increase of 5. 2%, telling the NUM to take it or leave it. The NUM responded by an overtime ban which, contrary to the claims of the NCB, resulted in 20 weeks in a loss of output to the order of 9. 5 million tonnes and 4. 4 million tonnes of sales. The net financial loss to the NCB was £135 million. It was in conditions like these that Ian MacGregor, Chairman of the NCB, gave notice that 4 million tonnes will be cut from capacity bringing it down to 97.4 million tonnes, with the loss of around 20, 000 jobs. This is on top of the 20, 000 that the NCB made redundant in the financial year 1983-4 through trickery, inducement and bribery, which sadly so many workers shortsightedly fell for.

The strategy of the NCB and of the entire bourgeoisie was to isolate the miners in militant areas, for example Yorkshire, South Wales and Kent, from those in the so-called moderate areas, such as Notts, and to isolate the NUM from the rest of the organised labour movement, and combine all this with a barrage of propaganda, police intimidation and more bribery to miners to agree to further redundancies, and force the NUM to hold a national strike ballot with the hope that such a ballot will fail to get the necessary 55% support.

But to the great disappointment of the NCB, the NUM have so far avoided falling into this trap and have instead adopted the very intelligent and perfectly legitimate tactic of calling on the regions to go on strike against the pit closures. Striking miners have picketed pits which had not done so and the reaction of the bourgeois state to this perfectly lawful activity has been to turn large areas of the country into a para-military state. The police action against the miners has been almost unbelievable in its ferocity and magnitude. Not only has there been massive and brutal force used by the police on the picket lines, but also people have been harassed hundreds of miles away from the scene of picketing just on the suspicion of being miners on their way to picket lines. Mr Mick McGahey, the Vice President of the NUM, has quite correctly remarked that the *"NCB's use of force, fear and intimidation to try to secure pit closures was the beginning of a totalitarian state in our country."*

In fact the police tactics were so outrageous that when that despicable and revolting bourgeois flunkey, Home Secretary Leon Brittan, tried to justify the police action in the name of 'the right to work' (sick joke, coming as it does from a member of the government which has presided over a record increase in unemployment). Even the *Guardian*, which like the rest of the bourgeois media, would dearly like to see the NUM defeated, could restrain itself no more and wrote in its leading article on 3 April 1984 in the following terms:

"*For with every day that passes in this dispute, evidence is accumulating of police activity that may or may not be legal but in any event should be considered quite outrageous in a democratic society. The original controversy over the miners stopped at the Dartford tunnel, and whether the police warned them of possible trouble or threatened them with arrest, has faded into the shadow in view of what has been claimed and reported since then.*

"*For there can be no doubt that the police are threatening the miners with arrest if they cross the county boundaries into Nottinghamshire. ... The county has been virtually sealed off. Journalists are having to produce their press passes simply in order to proceed down the roads. A clergyman in a car was stopped from crossing the border, and the police apparently told him that his dog-collar might be a disguise. Four miners from Doncaster who were turned away from the Clipstone pit say they were arrested while having a drink and a game of darts in a Nottinghamshire pub, and were held in police cells for three hours before being released without being charged.*

"*The lack of charges in such cases is important because it demonstrates that no offence has been committed.*

"*But there is evidence of an even worse assault on basic liberties. At Mansfield police station, miners say they were questioned by officers - thought to be special branch - on how they had voted at the general election, how they would choose between Communist and Conservative parties, who they had voted for as president of the NUM, which newspapers they read. What had any of this to do with the police? Who, in fact were these officers and to whom were they accountable? ... Is all this information being stored on police computers along with the car numbers of miners who have committed no offence at all? The Home Secretary has said that freedom is vulnerable to those who collaborate to deny the citizen his basic human rights to work, to vote and to go about his lawful business. But Mr Brittan's government has not exactly helped millions with their basic right to work; is about to abolish municipal elections; and sanctions police interference with lawful travel around the country. Must we conclude he was talking about himself?*"

But with this sole and honourable exception the rest of the media have either maintained a shameful silence over police brutality and intimidation or, worse still, zealously applauded the police action. And these Fleet Street prostitutes wish to be taken seriously when they pose as the defenders and upholders of the democratic liberties of the Polish working class!

If the tactics of police brutality have been counter-productive, equally unsuccessful have been the bourgeois attempts to isolate the NUM from other unions. For as we go to press, the National Union of Seamen, ASLEF, the train drivers' union, and the T&GWU have promised to support the NUM by refusing to move coal and by respecting picket lines[1]. In view of such solidarity from other unions, it is all the sadder, therefore, that the Notts miners have overturned the recommendations of their area executive council that picket lines must be respected. It is much to be hoped that the Notts miners will soon be able to realise that the miners on strike are as much fighting for the miners of Nottinghamshire as for miners in other areas. Nay, more than that, they are fighting for the entire working class. If the miners lose this fight every worker in the country would live to regret the day.

As long ago as June 1926, Joseph Stalin remarked, apropos the 1926 British General Strike:

"British capital attacked the miners not only because the mining industry is badly equipped technically and is in need of 'rationalisation', but primarily because the miners have always been, and still remain, the advanced detachment of the British proletariat. It was the strategy of British capital to curb this advanced detachment, to lower their wages and lengthen their working day, in order then, having settled accounts with this main detachment, to make the other detachments of the working class also toe the line."

Every word in the remarks quoted immediately above is not only true but has a topical ring about it. At the time of the General Strike of 1926, the miners, who were in the front line, were defeated thanks to the venality, cowardice and spinelessness of the TUC leadership. They have now re-emerged, after a period between the 1950s and early 1970s when the mining industry was run down in the face of cheap oil, with the resultant reduction in the workforce from 500, 000 to 252, 000, to show that they are still the proud bearers of the British working-class standard. It is not surprising, with their history of unity and staunch fighting tradition, that it should be the miners who now take on the brunt of the government's and employers' assault.

---

1   Sadly, this was not to last long (note to present edition)

Learning from the defeat of 1926, the British working class should render the utmost of support to their brethren in the NUM and help them win. The miners can and will win provided they mobilise their members, strengthen their ties with workers in other industries and unions, are able to expose those leaders in the NUM and the TUC who are either venal, or cowardly, or simply spineless, and, provided that they are able to turn the struggle into a political struggle - and this in the final analysis must involve challenging the authority of the government and raising the question of power.

LALKAR May 1984

May Day Resolution - Support the Miners

As the working class of Britain approaches this year's May Day, the coal-miners' strike enters its eighth week. When this strike started in the first week of March, the National Coal Board (NCB), various Government spokesmen and the bourgeois press had confidently and arrogantly predicted its swift collapse. The NCB and the Government had expected the large coal stocks, the presence of some venal and spineless right-wingers within the NUM, the defiance by large numbers of miners in Nottinghamshire of the strike call, the unwillingness of the treacherous leadership of the TUC to come to the aid of the NUM, and police intimidation and brutality on the picket lines, to cause the strike to crumble. With this in mind the Government, the NCB and the ever compliant bourgeois press worked tirelessly to sow divisions within the NUM, among the miners and in the wider trade union movement. For this reason, they played on the single theme of a national ballot, hoping that the miners' ballot would not produce the necessary 55% required at the time for a national stoppage.

Tables turned

But the tables were turned on the NCB and the Government at the NUM Executive meeting in Sheffield on 12th April. More than 2,500 striking miners surrounded the union headquarters demanding a continuation of the strike. Arthur Scargill, the NUM President, and his deputy Mick McGahey, both of whom are supposedly out of touch with the rank and file, got a heroes' welcome, while right-wing fainthearts such as Ray Chadburn, Trevor Bell and Jack Jones were booed and roughed up, by the thousands lobbying the executive. In the face of such spirited militancy and determination, the Chadburns and Bells of the NUM simply crumbled. The executive decided not to call for a ballot. Instead it decided to call a Special Delegate Conference to which it resolved to recommend a revision of the Union Rule 44, requiring 55% for a national strike and lowering it to 50%.

The delegate conference, which took place the following Thursday, April

19, endorsed both these decisions.

Following the decisions of the NUM executive and in the face of the determination on the part of the strikers themselves, although *The Sun, The Mail* and the rest of the popular (i.e. gutter) press are still mindlessly proclaiming that the strike is about to collapse, the serious and more intelligent sections of the imperialist press have changed their tune and are no longer displaying the confidence and arrogance characteristic of them only a month or so ago. "The phoney war is over. The rea, struggle, the most profound and serious labour challenge to have faced the Thatche*r government, has begun*", so wrote the *Financial Times.* As we go to press, the latest *Sunday Times* (29. 4. 84) declares in its leading article that "The time has come for a peace settlement in the coal strike ... the angry rhetoric of Mr. Scargill *and the nonsense and bluffness of ... Ian MacGregor give the impression of total war for high stakes; but more experienced negotiators on both sides of the industry may be in the mood to find common ground that can avoid an agonising conflict through the summer."* Concludes the *Sunday Times: "Nobody wants to see the miners destroyed in a senseless conflict, which is why the demands for a quick end to the dispute are building up behind the scenes.*

"Olive branches should not be denounced as signs of appeasement or surrender. It is not in the nation's interest that we should have a decimated and bankrupt coal industry".[1]

Anyone reading the above lines would find it difficult to imagine that only 6 weeks ago the same *Sunday Times,* comparing Arthur Scargill to the fascist Argentine dictator Galtieri, declared: *"The defeat of Mr. Scargill's miners will do more for the economic prospects of Britain than any chancellor could in one budget."*

And further: *"It was always possible that the economic regeneration of Britain could not be achieved without a return match between the government and the miners, this time the government winning, thereby proving that the unions had been decisively tamed."*

Now, however, the same sages of the *Sunday Times,* so keen on a return match with the miners only six weeks ago, caution against *"some government*

---

[1] Yet, in its class hatred of the miners, this is precisely the result that the bourgeoisie succeeded in achieving (note to the present edition)

ministers who yearn for a showdown with the miners as belated revenge for their humiliation 10 years ago."

Such then is the extent of the success of the miners' militant stance and determination, which find their corresponding reflection in the serious bourgeois press.

Miners can win

Thus there is every indication that the miners can win, provided they close their ranks, maintain picketing of those areas where some men are still mistakenly defying the strike call and crossing picket lines helped by a massive police presence, stop coal being moved to power stations and steelworks and strengthen links with ordinary workers in the labour movement at large.

The NUM are facing their most crucial test in the coming week. Mr Scargill told a rally in Cardiff of 15, 000 South Wales miners on Saturday 28 April that if the Nottinghamshire members joined the strike the union could win in a *"matter of weeks"*! The NUM President went on: *"It is not good enough for you merely to be on strike. Faced with a neo-fascist state in Nottinghamshire I want to see every miner on the picket line.*

"I ask you to make this national demonstration the biggest ever seen in Great Britain. Those same police who are arguing they're only giving the workers the right to go into work will kick lumps out of you in exactly the same way that they are kicking lumps out of our lads at the moment."

Mr Scargill went on: *"If the police say we can't go in then we'll walk in. If it means that by going to our own demonstration or going to our own picket lines to talk to our members or any other trade unionist we've got to be arrested, then so be it."*

Then he launched a withering attack on the ineffectiveness of the Government's labour laws. He said: *"We have already scored tremendous victories. They've got three pieces of legislation called anti-trade union laws through parliament and they haven't dared to introduce them as far as the miners' union is concenied."*

The government are preparing to face the pickets with *a "thick blue line"* and the police have been given powers to halt buses, coaches and cars travelling from any part of the country with pickets. Everyone in the labour movement, every conscious and thinking worker, must render all possible support to the NUM. The present coal strike is no ordinary labour dispute of the type that occurs hourly and daily under the conditions of capitalism; it is no mere strike over pay. It is a strike not only for the future of the coal industry and of whole mining communities, but also for the future of the British working class. It started as and has become the longest strike in history against unemployment. It is a strike FOR THE RIGHT TO WORK. Therefore, in the final analysis, it is a strike, albeit instinctively, against the capitalist mode of production; for the latter by its very nature is incapable of guaranteeing this right.

The defeat of the NUM would have very grave consequences for all sections of the working class. The *Observer* of 8 April, 1984, quite correctly stated that *"The defeat of the miners would also remove the last formidable bastion to the government's wider strategy of unblocking the labour market in the course of economic freedom"*, i.e., depressing of the working class living standards still further through even more unemployment. Let every worker realise that the miners are what stands today between the total autocracy of British capital and the total submission and humiliation of the British working class. A working class that ceases to struggle becomes indistinguishable from savages and must sooner or later find itself thrown by Capital into the depths of savagery and degradation. It is precisely to forestall such a possibility becoming an actuality, and in the interests of working-class progress and social advance, that every worker must make a May Day pledge to support the miners through to victory.

LALKAR July1984

111 DAYS OF THE COAL STRIKE

Today, Saturday 30 June, the miners' strike enters its 111th day. So far there have been more than 3,000 arrests, hundreds of reported injuries and two deaths. Every striking miner has lost over £2,000 in lost wages and families are going through real hardship. According to the NUM President Mr Scargill, the NCB is losing £150 million a week (£90 million in lost production and £60 million in running expenses), though the bourgeois economists reckon this loss to be only £30 million a week. The damage to the rest of the economy is untold. Already it is the longest and most bitter pit strike since 1926, and there is still no end in sight; in fact all the signs are that the strike will last into the winter. The time has therefore come for us to look at the origins of this strike, its causes, its effects, both social and economic, so far and the way it is likely to end up.

Strike imposed by Government and NCB.

From the start of this strike it has been clear that the government wanted a coal strike in order to defeat the coal miners. For without defeating the coalminers, the most advanced detachment of the British working class, the government and the bourgeoisie cannot defeat the British working class, cannot successfully depress their living standards and conditions which in turn is a necessary prerequisite for enhancing and strengthening the competitiveness of British monopoly capitalism by lowering the cost of production per unit. The Tories had a particular reason of their own. The Tory government of Edward Heath was literally booted out of office as a direct consequence of the miners' victorious strike in 1974. So, they have ever since wanted to wreak vengeance on the NUM. These sentiments were admirably expressed by the *Sunday Times* editorial of 18 March in which this Tory leader writer could hardly restrain his enthusiasm at the prospect of a return match with the miners resulting in a government victory.

The present strike was sparked off by the unexpected, sudden and provocative announcement on 1 March by the NCB of its intention to close Cortonwood Colliery in Yorkshire. Only a short time ago the NCB had given the assurance that it would not close Cortonwood for at least another 5 years.

The 820 workforce, stunned by the announcement, decided almost unanimously, at a meeting on Sunday 4 March in Brampton Parish Hall, to strike. Within a couple of days, Yorkshire area leaders called all 54,000 members out on strike and the Scottish area followed suit.

In a further act of provocation, Ian MacGregor, NCB Chairman, used a scheduled consultative meeting with the leaders of the three mining unions to announce that the Cortonwood decision was part of a plan (the existence of which plan it had hitherto denied) to close 20 pits and lose 20,000 jobs over the next 12 months. In the circumstances, MacGregor's statement was nothing short of explosive and was meant to be so. He was evidently being urged to be insolent and provocative by a government that desperately wanted a coal strike for which it had been making the necessary preparations for at least 3 years, if not longer.

Prolonged and detailed preparations by the government.

The Tory government's preparations began in earnest in 1981 when Margaret Thatcher was forced to retreat by the threat of a strike against plans to close 21 pits over 12 months. These plans were shelved for the time being at least, and the NCB's borrowing powers increased to £4.3 billion. While retreating, the government immediately started making preparations for a confrontation with the NUM by taking the following steps: (a) coal stocks were built up despite the high storage costs, with the result that these stocks stood as high as 30 million tonnes at power stations alone at the start of the present strike, compared with only 11.9 million tonnes in 1974; (b) the appointment of Ian MacGregor, the "Yankee butcher", as the miners aptly describe him, to be the chairman of the NCB and that of Peter Walker as Energy Secretary were clear, if unstated, declarations of the government's intention; (c) despite higher oil and construction costs, the building of oilfired power stations such as the 2,640 megawatt giant at the Isle of Grain, was completed; existing oil-fired stations were replaced by cheaper coalburning ones, but the oil stations were kept ready for use; (d) the so-called National Reporting Centre (NRC) at Scotland Yard which coordinates deployment of police in emergencies, was streamlined in the wake of the 1981 inner city explosions; (e) redundancy payments to miners were increased in an attempt to bribe them into accepting the pit closures without much fuss or resistance. Having made these prolonged and detailed preparations, the government, seeing that the previously instituted NUM overtime ban was biting hard and wishing to avoid a fight with the miners in the unfavourable winter conditions, when the need for energy is at its height, announced its pit closure plans, hoping that the miners would not choose to fight when the odds were stacked so heavily against them. The response of the miners came as nothing short of a surprise to the NCB and the government.

NUM accept the challenge.

Faced with the pit closure plan of the NCB, the miners had to either accept this plan on their knees, or they had to stand up and fight and oppose the closure of their industry. The overwhelming majority of the miners chose to stand up and fight. 80% of them have been on strike for 111 days. Despite scabbing by many thousand Nottinghamshire men and the lack of support from the steel men, despite police brutality, intimidation and harassment on the picket line and elsewhere, despite a campaign of lies and vilification directed by the bourgeois media against the miners, in particular against their President, despite the destitution and the hardship faced by mining families, the determination of the strikers to continue with the strike and win is unshakable.

The dauntless spirit and the unbreakable solidarity that prevails among the mining communities may be gauged from the following two examples, representative of tens of thousands of others that go unreported. The *Sunday Times* of 17 June reported that *"an elderly miner's widow went to see Mr Scargill recently. She had saved £100 for a holiday but felt that she could not take it while the miners were on strike and wanted him to have it for strike funds. Mr Scargill, so the story goes, broke down and wept."* The second example concerns Mrs Fitzpatrick, wife of a miner and mother of two more, and the family living on £48 per week that she gets as a cleaner at the NCB offices at Brampton. In the midst of this grim poverty she is reported to have said: *"We have got our backs to the wall. That wall will break before we move."* People with such nobility of spirit and possessed of such self-sacrificing heroism are difficult to defeat.

Government weapons: starvation, police brutality and propaganda.

The government's three weapons - starvation, police brutality and lying propaganda against the NUM have failed to produce thus far the results desired by it. That the mining families are facing real hardship, of that there is no doubt. The government is attempting to starve the miners back to work, but the attempt has failed dismally. The miners get no strike pay, yet £15 is deducted from the families' supplementary benefit as though the miners were in receipt of strike pay. The frenzied hatred of the bourgeois state for working people is best judged by the treatment of the Johnson family. Mr Johnson is a coal miner on strike, with a wife, a 3-year old daughter and a baby on the way. The family was existing on £30 a week supplementary benefit and £6.50 a week child benefit. When Mrs Johnson started getting her £25 maternity grant, the family found they were worse off than before they got £25 plus £4.62. If it had happened elsewhere, the 'civilised' gentlemen of Fleet Street would have effortlessly fulminated against such medieval barbarism.

Police Brutality

Siege 83, code name for the anti-NUM operation, is being masterminded by the NRC, under the direction of Mr David Hall, Chief Constable of Humberside. Housed in Room 1309, the NRC comprises a web of communications linking the 43 local forces in England and Wales. It is from here that the brute force used by the police on the picket line is being planned and directed. The NRC is in fact a "national operational centre", as Mr John Alderson, a former Chief Constable of Cornwall and Devon correctly stated.

The miners on the picket line have faced thousands of police officers on horse back and the riot-trained Police Support Units (PSUs) with their long shields and visored helmets, not to speak of the truncheons which they use freely to earn their £800 a week. It is now admitted even by some Fleet Street journalists that the police on the picket line are not only making their own law but even breaking the normal rules that are supposed to govern their conduct. Recently, when a miner, upon being stopped by a police officer, demanded to know what law gave the officer the right to stop him going home after a mass picket at Orgreave, the officer pointed at his blue uniform and said "This law". Miners have been photographed against their will, though there is no law giving the police such a right. Criminal law recognises the right to picket peacefully, yet the police refuse to allow more than 6 pickets at any site! The mere questioning of such police tactics results in arrest. The compliant magistrates release these arrested miners only on condition that they stay away from property belonging to the NCB and electricity and steel plants although these men have committed no crimes. The police brutality at Orgreave and elsewhere, the cavalry charges against peaceful pickets, the massive use of the police as a direct government agency for the suppression of an industrial dispute, have revealed the real face of our lovable, and peaceloving Bobbies, namely, the iron fist behind the velvet glove of the bourgeois state. No longer can the pretence be maintained that the police are simply an impartial law enforcement agency desperately trying to preserve 'law and order'. All the same these tactics have thus far failed to subdue the fighting spirit of the miners.

Failure of calumnious propaganda

Fleet street and government propaganda too have failed. In fact, trade unionists in the media have struck back, forcing their employers to print the real truth about the NUM strike rather than the miserable lies daily spewed out by the Fleet Street harpies. This is a most welcome development, which working people are bound increasingly to use in the future.

Strike costs

Although the NCB and the government continue to put a brave face on developments, the damaging effects of the strike and its effectiveness have begun to percolate through. Even according to the most respectable bourgeois statistics, the strike is costing 'about £70 million a week', which means that it has so far cost at least £1,120 million, which is nearly the equivalent of the cost of the Falklands war. According to Mr Gavin Davies, chief economist at stockbrokers Simon and Coates, the weekly costs to the Treasury include a £2530 million net loss incurred by the NCB, a £1725 million loss borne by the CEGB, £10 million lost in tax revenues from the striking miners, £3 million lost by British Rail and £500,000 extra paid out in social security to strikers' families. Mr Davies also calculated that the index of all industrial production for April will be 33.5% below what it would otherwise have been and could be 44.5% down if the strike continues and becomes more solid. And none of these figures take into account any knock-on effects of the strike which are bound to become more and more prominent with the continuation of the strike.

Mr Davies concludes by saying that *"in a six-to-nine month strike, direct effects alone would be easily enough to wipe out the whole of the expected 3% growth in the industrial output as a whole"*.

Dr Paul Neild, chief economist at brokers Phillips and Drew, while agreeing with Mr Davies' assumptions on fall in industrial production, goes on to forecast that the monthly balance of trade figures could show an adverse movement of £150 million because of the sharp increase in oil imports and the drop in oil exports as oilfired stations take over from the coal-fired ones.

Political Strike

But despite these huge losses, the NCB and the government are prepared to see the strike carry on. This is because from the very beginning the government have regarded this as a political strike. The miners have always haunted the Tories, especially the present Thatcher administration. To exorcise the miners has therefore been the most ardent desire of this most reactionary post-war government in Britain. That is why the Thatcher government provoked the NUM in an attempt to inflict a devastating defeat on it, and through it on the rest of the working class. If the Thatcher government finds itself locked in a political challenge to its authority, and ultimately its survival, it has no one to blame save its own provocations. The government supporters in Fleet Street too share the blame. Not only the real gutter press (popular press if you please) but also the more serious papers, such as the *Sunday Times*, the *Daily Telegraph*, the *Times* and the *Financial Times*, have all egged the government on and advised it not to agree to a compromise settlement.

The *Telegraph*, a kind of right wing *Socialist Worker*, is even against negotiations between the NCB and the NUM. In a leading article entitled *Not a Time to Wobble*, it poured forth on 25 May thus:

"But negotiations often develop a momentum of their own in major national strikes. Once the public's hopes of a settlement have been raised, a string of concessions begins to seem preferable to a breakdown."

Concludes the *Telegraph:* " ... *a continued strike is preferable to any settlement other than a clear victory for the government and the Coal Board ... The foreign exchange markets see this dispute as a test of the dominance of trade union power in Britain. A government victory would stimulate greatly increased confidence and investment ... similarly, the young militant miners who have grown experienced in the tactics of violent intimidation would be tempted by anything short of a clear defeat to try again when the coal stocks were lower and winter coming on...*"

In other words, the government's objective in this strike is not simply to win acceptance for its pit closure plan, but to castrate the trade union movement and to render it incapable of the least resistance to the ceaseless and daily encroachments of King Capital.

The *Sunday Times* too, in its leading article of 20 May 1984, under the title *Scargill's Strike*, gleefully stated that for the Cabinet Wets who "held prominent positions in the Heath Cabinet during the last miners' strike in 1974 when Mr Scargill rubbed their noses in the dirt ... this is a revenge match and they do not intend to lose a second time. As for Mr Ian MacGregor, *the Coal Board chief, he sees himself in a highstakes poker game ... There are no draws in poker, only big winners and losers.*"

The *Sunday Times* concludes with exactly the same type of frenzied anti-union and rabidly anti-working class plea as did the *Telegraph*. Let the *Sunday*

Times speak for itself:

"*The miners' strike is a watershed in British politics. It offers the chance to end a disastrous era which gave the unions a veto over government policy and allowed them to bring down administrations, Labour and Tory, which crossed their paths. To put these days behind us will be healthy for the democratic future of Britain, never mind its economy, which also stands to benefit from a less obstructionist union movement. When the stakes are that high, losing cannot be contemplated. But neither can fudge, compromise or easy ways out.*"

Tasks of the working-class movement

Precisely because the NCB, the government and the entire bourgeois class are pursuing, through and in the coal strike, the aim of liquidating the trade-union movement, the working class for its part must see to it that the NUM emerge victorious from this battle, for the NUM are fighting in the front line for every working-class man, woman and child - yes, child - in this country. Their fight against pit closures is a fight against unemployment and for the future of our children and grandchildren. If the NUM lose, then no one's job will be safe. Even if the NUM win, which is very likely, the working class of this country face a most difficult period ahead. But with the NUM defeated, which we sincerely hope will not take place, the working class would find itself utterly defenceless. In order to defeat the NUM, the government are sparing no effort. They have even directly intervened in pay negotiations between the British Railways Board and the Railmen's union and have instructed the rail chief, Bob Reid, to agree to a higher pay award without productivity strings attached to it, in an attempt to buy off the railmen and thus prevent them from giving support to the miners (see the *Daily Mirror* of 6 June). The railmen for their part ought to understand and appreciate the effective solidarity they received from the miners in getting a better pay settlement and they ought to pay this debt of gratitude to the miners by refusing to move coke and iron ore to steel plants and power stations. In fact, be it said to their honour, they already are doing so. It is a pity that the steelmen have so far failed in their bounden duty to back the miners. All other unions and trade unionists up and down the country must step up their efforts in support of the miners. The government and the ruling class are hoping to recoup a hundred times over their losses during the strike by depressing working class wages, which will be the inevitable and swift result of an NUM defeat. The working class on its part must help the NUM to victory and thus ensure that the above depressing prediction never passes from the realm of possibility into that of actuality.

Miners certain to win.

All the signs point to a victory for the NUM. The 80% who have been on strike for nearly 4 months are rock solid in their determination to continue till victory and the drift back to work that the NCB and the government had hoped for has not materialised. Wives of the striking miners, far from being a drag on the strikers, have been playing an increasing part in the dispute. They have been raising funds and providing meals. Now more are appearing on the picket line.

Miners support groups have been formed and are working tirelessly all over the country. Coal stocks are dwindling and the CEGB and the energy department, their protestations to the contrary and apparent outward calm notwithstanding, are planning swingeing power cuts. The costs of the strike are mounting. The police operation alone has cost £70 million so far. The government provoked the present strike in order to break the power of the NUM, but at the end of the strike it will find this union more powerful and more united than ever before. Even the *Times* of 21 June 1984 made the following rare admission: *" ... the strike has revitalised interest in the union at branch level, turning it into a welfare state in miniature. Deprived of most social security benefits, the strikers turn to their union for food and sustenance. They get it. And for many of them it is the £2 a day picketing allowance.*

"Many simply stay at home, but in their thousands, particularly the young miners, they have been challenging the civil law to go secondary picketing. Their first-hand experience on the picket lines and on the strike committees is regarded by the left as more influential than a thousand NUM summer schools or seminars on the theory of trade union practice.

"Ironically, the dispute that some politicians hoped would break the power of the NUM has actually created new cadres for the future."

We end this article with the following words of Arthur Scargill: *"I appeal to every person in this land: Back us to the hilt and roll back the tide of dole queue misery, insecurity, poverty and fear"*. And further *"Let the Coal Board take note: Our young miners have not been fooled by your propaganda. They have gone through hardship and incredible acts of heroism because of one central fact:*

"They know that the dole queue spells a LIFETIME OF HARDSHIP".

LALKAR August 1984

Resolutely support the Miners - Fight the Enemy Within

Fight to Finish

As we go to press, the miners' strike enters its 21st week, with not the slightest sign of an end in sight. All the signs are that this strike will not be ended by a face-saving formula of the type that ends most industrial disputes, but only by the surrender of one side or the other.

For both sides it is a life and death question. The miners on their part are fighting for their very existence and that of their children and grandchildren - they are fighting against unemployment, the misery of the dole queue and for the right to work.

The government, on the other hand, has from its inception invested this strike, which it provoked having made lengthy, careful and detailed preparations, with a political importance of such dimensions that its defeat would not only threaten the government plans for depressing working-class living standards by castrating the trade union and labour movement, but also put a question mark against the very survival of the Thatcher government.

Preference of non-intervention

For a long time, Margaret Thatcher and her administration maintained the hypocritical pretence that the strike had nothing to do with the government, that it was simply an industrial dispute between the National Coal Board and the National Union of Mineworkers. So the government 'refused' nominally to intervene, while being invited to do so by that useless opportunist windbag, Kinnock, the leader of the Labour opposition, and the rest of his imbecile front bench.

On the contrary, it reserved its real and effective intervention from day one of the strike - and even earlier, for, to repeat, the government had prepared for this strike over a number of years - for such behind-the-scenes activities aimed at breaking this strike as police intimidation and violence on the picket line[1], telling the NCB and British Steel not to use government legislation against the NUM; manipulating public sector pay negotiations of workers in British Rail and the Gas and Electricity industries; denying social security benefits to the miners' families; and last, but not least, encouraging the port employers, whom it had encouraged earlier to work for scrapping the dock labour scheme to settle with the dockers and thus end the disastrous - that is, for the government - dock strike.

Dock Strike

It turned out, however, that all this behind-the-scenes intervention came to nought, that all the police brutality unleashed by the government, all the calumnious propaganda unleashed by the Fleet Street press barons on the miners melted away in the face of the grim determination of the miners.

Far from breaking the NUM strike, it encouraged another important group of workers, the dockers, to take strike action to defend their jobs. The national dock stoppage started on 10th July after the British Steel Corporation had used non-registered labour at Inningham on Humberside to unload blacked iron ore for the beleaguered Scunthorpe Steelworks. In response to this provocative action (which came in the aftermath of a consistent campaign by the port employers demanding from the government an end to the 36-year old Dock Labour scheme, whereby the dockers enjoy security of employment and the union has some say in the size of the whole force), the National Docks Committee of the T&GWU called for a national stoppage. The dockers to a man responded to the call, and within hours all the country's major ports, and with them all imports and exports, were brought to a sudden grinding halt.

Shock waves in the City

This decision, along with a third collapse in the peace process in the miners' dispute, sent shock waves through the City. The action of these two "crack divisions" of the labour movement, as one newspaper put it, proved too much. The pound fell dramatically (below $1.30 for the first time ever, which in turn forced higher interest rates), billions of pounds have been wiped off share values and, to use the picturesque language of *The Miner*, the NUM journal of 14

---

2   As to the real extent of Government intervention, much more has come to light since then, which we now know thanks to Seamus Milne's book 'The Enemy Within'.

July, *"The squeals of businessmen are getting louder by the day."*. Thus the government finds itself in an industrial siege of its own creation, and financial mayhem grows by the day. The 2% higher interest rates have already pushed up the mortgage lending rate by two and a half percent. The electricity generated by oil is costing more than £20 million extra every week and is bound to result in higher electricity prices. All this cannot but affect the inflation rate, and thus drive a coach and horses through the government's entire economic strategy.

Government and Fleet Street Rattled

This state of affairs rattled the government and its friends in Fleet Street. Almost for the first time, the *Sunday Times* started criticising the Thatcher government.. The opening line of its editorial on 15 July said: *"The Thatcher government has been consistently shooting itself in the foot for some time now"*. Continued the *Sunday Times*, using a World War 2 analogy:

"But last week, for the first time since the miners' strike began 18 weeks ago, Arthur Scargill drew blood. The dockers opened up their second front and the City and the international financial markets took fright. Result: the public is being hurt not by the power cuts that everybody feared but by higher mortgage rates and dearer money all round. The pound slipped below $1.30 for the first time ever, creating pressures for higher interest rates which no government wedded to monetary controls as the heart of its anti-inflation strategy could ignore.

"All this happens at a time when the government's grip on affairs looks more unsure than ever, prompting much talk of crisis and much nonsense about Tory back-bench coups."

Realising that the miners on strike were more united than ever before in their determination to win, that public sympathy for the NUM, far from declining, was, at long last, beginning to grow, and fearing a government sell-out, the *Sunday Times* goes on to warn:

"Mr Scargill is greatly cheered, the public wearies for a settlement and the government's predilection for botching everything from Liverpools to the GLC encourages belief that it may also be on the brink of sanctioning a sellout in the pits. If Mrs Thatcher wants to experience a real run on the pound, then she should go right ahead."

It goes on to express doubts as to whether Mrs Thatcher is fully aware of the grave situation, accusing her of becoming ; *"increasingly isolated from savvy political advice*" and *depending "too much on a few figures in Downing Street whose judgment on political matters has been generally appalling".* In what amounts to a chilling threat, the *Sunday Times* issues the following warning:' *'Well, let her be in no doubt: if the miners' strike is settled on any terms which allow Mr Scargill plausibly to claim that he has had his way, then the past 18 weeks will have been a waste of time ... Mrs Thatcher, in such an event, might as well ask the pantechnicon to pull up outside the Downing Street back door."*

The *Sunday Times* concludes by advising the government to drop its pretence of non-intervention and go on to the offensive. *"It is time for the government to come out of the closet and go on the offensive ... It needs to come out from behind Mr Ian MacGregor and deal directly with the strike, indicating that, as the battle escalates, the government is going to conduct the strategy itself. There is a difference between intervening with beer and sandwiches in Downing Street and intervention to spell out the strength of the government's case and the increasingly political challenge of Mr Scargill. The pretence that it is all a matter for the Coal Board and the union is a nonsense when it is the future of the government which is at stake."*

On Monday 16 July, *The Times*, owned by the same 'democrats' as the *Sunday Times*, to wit, the press baron and billionaire, Rupert Murdoch, followed *the Sunday Times* by demanding that the government make preparations for a State of Emergency. On Tuesday it accused the ministers of a *"wobbly nerve in a political establishment that does not like a punch-up and which feels that the British public will not forgive its leaders for distracting it from a quiet life"* and advised it to go on the offensive to meet the *"challenge from the trade unions and the hard Left."*

The enemy within

Faced with these demands from such representative and authoritative spokesmen of British monopoly capitalism as the *Sunday Times* and *The Times*, Her Majesty's ministers, from the Prime Minister downward, could hardly be expected to resist, for British monopoly capital has a way of letting it be known who rules. In the fashion of the Pavlovian dogs, one after the other the ministers complied, with a volley of abuse directed against the NUM and its President Arthur Scargill. And on Thursday 19 July, the Iron Lady herself bowed to these demands. Speaking before the 1922 Committee of Conservative backbenchers, she described the miners as *"the enemy within,"* and Arthur Scargill, their President, as a greater threat to democracy than the former Argentine fascist dictator, General Galtieri. That the Thatcher government aimed at castrating the entire trade union and labour movement, not just the miners, she made clear to the Tory backbenchers by saying that once the miners' strike is over *"we have to take on the militants in other unions"*.

Welcome candour

Thus the cat is out of the bag, and, with the above pronouncements of our 'free' press and the government, even the least thinking and least intelligent among the working class can clearly perceive the aims of the government and the bourgeoisie. These aims are nothing short of attempts at securing the complete and total submission of the British working class to the needs, interests and dictates of British monopoly capital. The working class for its part must take up the gauntlet and intensify a thousand-fold its struggle against the "enemy within" - the bourgeoisie and the Thatcher government. Our enemies are not abroad, they are within these isles. And if the bourgeoisie, through its flunkey Prime Minister and other ministers, through its press and media, have concentrated the minds of working people on this, the most fundamental question, with admirable candour, we ought to thank this gentry from the bottom of our hearts. Only 'Liberal' imperialist spokesmen, such as the *Observer* can feel embarrassed by Thatcher's pronouncements. Fearing the consequences of such candour the *Observer* of 22 July, in its editorial entitled *An unhelpful equation*, squeaked and bemoaned in the following tones: *"Mrs Thatcher appeared to declare war on the miners last Thursday night* [only last Thursday night?] ... *in so doing she heightened the stakes wantonly in what is turning out to be the bitterest industrial conflict for over half a century.*

"To describe the striking miners as the enemy within, and to evoke the Falklands spirit in order to crush them", it is said, *"is unworthy of any Prime-Minister who wishes to govern this country in the interest of all the people. Such dangerous stridency matches the revolutionary rhetoric of Mr Arthur Scargill himself ... Mrs Thatcher's words will merely harden attitudes on the striking coalfields. They will delight Mr Scargill and his red guards, who believe in class struggle to the finish."*

Whether the *Observer*'s description of Mr Scargill or of his so-called Red Guards is correct or not, that is not the issue. What is correct is that, as feared by the *Observer*, Mrs Thatcher's words would, far from crushing the miners, only serve to strengthen their resolve to win. The *Observer*, therefore, wants the government to maintain the pretence that it governs in the name of ALL the people, to *"drop the hyperbole and speak the language of peace"*, for, *"the* longer this strike continues the graver the dangers are to the social [i.e., bourgeois] *fabric of our society, to the rule of law and to the art of compromise that has always ensured in the past that Britain avoided the total triumph of one side over another in an industrial conflict".* With an air of sad helplessness the *Observer* adds: *"Nowadays the ways of conciliation are despised by the Prime Minister as signs of weakness, a view shared by Mr Scargill."* It must be said, in this instance, our teachers by negative example are the avowed and strident imperialist spokesmen not the liberal imperialists who pull the wool over the eyes of working people by such dangerous nonsense as the government governing on behalf of ALL the people. The truth is that 'our' government governs in the interests of a tiny handful, in the interests of the magnates of industry and the kings of finance capital, who own all our 'free' press and who regard the working class as at best a necessary evil (for if there is no working class, there is no capitalism) and at worst an enemy within. If that truth has oozed out, in the heat generated by the miners' strike, that is a gain more important than many wage rises.

Let us fight the enemy within

Let the working class learn this lesson well and fight with greater determination than ever before against "the enemy within". Let every worker rally round the NUM and the miners on strike. In the coming days the NUM will need this support, for as this issue goes into print, we have just heard that the High Court has imposed a fine of £50,000 on the Welsh NUM for defiance of its injunction not to interfere with coal supplies to Port Talbot Steelworks by a private haulage firm. It is not the first time that the judiciary have acted so blatantly and despicably. Two weeks ago, it made an order prohibiting the NUM from discussing rule changes at its extraordinary conference in Sheffield on Wednesday 11 July - an order which the NUM have treated with the contempt it deserved by going ahead with the necessary rule changes. The NUM has been given until Wednesday 1 August to pay the fine or face sequestration of its funds. We have just heard that the South Wales miners' executive have decided, in accordance with NUM and TUC policy, not to pay the fine. In any case, one thing is certain - the miners can neither be starved, nor bullied, nor sequestrated into submission. In the words of Mr Scargill: *"As long as the government says it can hold out, we can hold out a week longer".* He continued, in a speech to many thousand miners, their wives and families, in South Wales on Friday (27th July) night: *"Has it not yet percolated to the minds of the Establishment that they cannot sequestrate the minds and wills of ordinary people who are fighting for the defence of their jobs in mining communities?"*

Let all working people work tirelessly for a miners' victory. And if that victory has the incidental effect of obliging Mrs Thatcher to ask the pantechnicon to pull up outside the Downing Street back door, that sadly cannot be helped and is none of our concern. We should be concerned to keep the miners and other sections of the working class in their jobs rather than one individual, no matter how highly she thinks of herself. The support for the strike continues to be solid; the miners' wives are doing a magnificent job of organising communal kitchens and doing picket duty; the mining families have gone through the pain barrier; the coal stocks are dwindling and the winter is approaching; swingeing power cuts are approaching; support for the miners is growing. In other words, there is everything for the miners to play for. In view of the above, the *'Miner'* of 14th July was not indulging in any unwarranted optimism when it declared that *"the NUM is heading for the greatest industrial victory in the post-war history of Great Britain."* The miners are bound to be victorious and deserve this victory every bit.

LALKAR September 1984

TUC Conference must support the NUM Dockers Open Second Front

Next Monday (Sept 3rd) as the TUC Annual Conference opens in Brighton, the miners' strike would very nearly be six months old. When the strike started at the beginning of March of this year, the Coal Board (NCB), the Government and the bourgeois media had cockily predicted its swift collapse. The miners, 80% of whom have been on strike and who show no signs of caving in, through their perseverance, determination and incredible acts of heroism, have wiped the grin off the smug faces of their enemies. In their fight against pit closures and redundancies, against the destruction of their communities, against the misery of the dole queue, the miners have been waging a battle which is as heroic as it is selfless and noble - for the fight for the right to work and the emancipation of the working class from the misery and degradation of unemployment is not the private affair of the NUM, but the common cause of the entire labour and trade union movement. It is precisely for this reason the TUC Conference must decide to give its total support to the NUM.

Deeds not Rhetoric

This total support must not be limited to ritual declarations of support for the miners. The NUM have specifically demanded the following three forms of support:

FIRST, that the TUC accept the NUM's demand for 10p a week levy on all trade union members to net in approximately three-quarters of a million pounds a week to help with the strike.

SECONDLY, that the TUC make a decision that picket lines be respected, with all trade unionists instructed not to cross picket lines.

THIRDLY, that trade unionists refuse to use materials handled by scab labour in an effort to break the NUM strike.

Support or Betrayal

These are perfectly simple, clear and legitimate demands, which must meet with the enthusiastic support of the delegates at the Conference. The TUC Conference, starting next Monday, is the most historic for many decades, and its decisions will have a far-reaching effect for many, many years to come. This is how Mr Scargill, the NUM President (in a speech on Saturday, 25th August, at a rally of thousands of miners and their supporters at Dalkeith, near Edinburgh), succinctly put the matter:

"I believe that the trade union movement was established in order that we could support each other in our hour of need. In a week's time the TUC has an opportunity to either support the miners' union in its historic struggle to maintain an industry, our pits and our communities, as well as carrying out TUC policy; or it can turn away: and in doing so it would be stained for all time with what would be described as an act of betrayal."

Already there are signs that the Conference will witness a split between the platform and the floor, with the labour aristocrats - the Murrays, the Chapples, the Duffys and suchlike labour lieutenants of capitalism - scabbing on the miners, and the rank and file delegates swinging their support on the side of the NUM. The TUC leadership, which only yesterday deserted the NGA in the latter's dispute with the notorious Mr Shah&, have, in return for 'supporting' the NUM, demanded control in the running of the strike. Support indeed! The NUM, realising that 'support' under such conditions would be no less than the kiss of Judas, have steered clear of such a course. The delegates at the Conference must show their strength and in doing so either compel the platform to agree to support the NUM, or inflict a crushing defeat on it.

National Dock Strike

The T&GWU (the transport union) Executive's policy is to support the miners and that means stopping coal and ore carriers berthing at Hunterston and other ports. On Wednesday, 22nd August, British Steel ordered the bulk carrier *Ostier* to dock and unload (using scab labour in the process) its cargo at Hunterston terminal on the Clyde in a direct and deliberate challenge to the TGWU, which had stated in advance that the berthing and unloading of the carrier, carrying 93,000 tons of imported coal for the Ravenscraig Steel Works, would lead to industrial action. In response to this provocation by British Steel, it is hardly to be surprised at that the TGWU ordered, on Friday, 24th August, an immediate national dock strike, indicating that lorry drivers may be called out later to present an effective challenge to the British Steel Corporation.

The Second Front

The dock strike, which has been correctly described by the bourgeois press as the second front, is a most welcome development. From 10 September the railwaymen will be going ahead with their planned work-to-rule. The dockers' and railwaymen's actions in support of the NUM and in defence of working people have terribly upset bourgeois spokesmen and evoked from them a chorus of denunciations The 'liberal' *Observer* sees in these actions "*further alarming evidence of the willingness of some union leaders to use industrial muscle to achieve blatant political ends*" and "*use of coercion to bring the Government to its knees and victory for the miners*" (26-8-84). The *Sunday Times* characterises the dock strike as typifying "*all that is worst about the British trade union movement*" and as an attempt by "*left-wing elite of union professionals ... to hijack its members into bringing Britain's trade with the world to a juddering halt*" (26-8-84).

Mr David Steel, the Liberal leader, known as the "nice man" of British bourgeois politics, fulminates thus: "*the issue now has nothing to do with dockers' jobs. It is about the power of militant trade union leaders in one industry ... literally blackmailing the country*".

The Transport Minister, the hapless Nicholas Ridley, has described it as the "craziest" ever dreamed up. "*It is a political strike engineered to support the crumbling miners' dispute*", he adds. Well, Mr Ridley should recognise a political strike when he sees one, after he has been preparing for exactly such a political confrontation since 1978 ...

The above random bouquet of abuse hurled at the dockers and the NUM is a sure guarantee that these groups of workers are on the right track, that they are acting in defence of the real and legitimate interests of the working class, for, to put it in the inimitable and immortal words of the great 19th century Russian poet, Nekrasov,

"*I hear the voice of approbation*

Not in the dulcet sounds of praise

But in the roar of irritation."

Picketing and Violence

The response to the stoppage ordered by the TGWU has been mixed, and all the indications are that the action will be 75% effective, that there will be dockers, particularly at Felixstowe and Dover, who are likely to defy the Union's strike call. It is equally clear that the striking dockers are bound to picket these places and that the pickets will face the full might of the riot police and the propaganda barrage from our 'free' press and its penny-a-liner hacks who pride themselves on "*the freedom of totally un-representative speech*", to use the terminology (pregnant with a meaning far richer than that intended by its author) of Mr C.C.O'Brien (*Observer*, 12-8-84).

Her Majesty's Ministers and the media, so adept at construing police violence on the picket lines as intimidation and coercion by the pickets, are bound to intensify their shrill pronouncements against the picketing miners and dockers. The Labour leadership will, as hitherto, mindlessly repeat these calumnious lies and condemn violence on the part of the strikers. Mr Kinnock, the Labour leader and his deputy, Roy Hattersley, are engaged in the shameful task of out-Torying the Tories. But workers everywhere must stand firm and defend the right to picket freely without police intimidation, harassment, violence and cavalry charges. Mr Scargill was quite right, when, speaking at the NUM wives' rally in London on 11-8-84, attended by more than 20,000, he put the blame for picket line violence on the police, declaring, amid loud applause, "*I take a class stand. I am not prepared to condemn pickets whose only crime is to fight for the right to work*". This is a standpoint which must permeate every thinking worker. No amount of dreadful and blood-curdling condemnations emanating from the mouths of the lucratively rewarded and highly-placed lap dogs of the ruling class will frighten the working class into abandoning its collective approach, for organisation is one of the most important instruments of the advancement of the working class. Without an organisation the working class is nothing. The bourgeoisie would like the workers to fight singly, as individuals, but the workers know from experience that they can only win collectively, and more importantly, as a class.

Incredible Heroism and the Professorial understanding of it

The striking miners have, by their determination to win, their steadfastness in the midst of hardship, courage in the face of danger, and, above all, by their display of collective comradeship, surprised friend and foe alike. That the bourgeois mind, trained in and used to debating in the stuffy studies of the intelligentsia, is incapable of understanding the extent to which the working class, given the right historical and political circumstances, is capable of performing legendary deeds and acts of selfless heroism, is shown by an article, in the *Sunday Times* of 12th August by a certain Professor Musgrove, under the title of *Lost Kingdom of the Mining Men*. Our worthy professor, unable to grasp the issues at stake, unable to understand why the miners are prepared to endure such hardship for a strike that enters its 25th week, 'explains' it in terms of the migration of the more intelligent from the striking areas to others not on strike, and in terms of the North-South divide and working-class youth culture. The miners are on strike because they are thick, come from the North and are in the vice-like grip of *"working-class youth culture which is aggressive, defiant, anarchic"*. Thus Herr Professor: *"In the past 30 years two social processes have siphoned off men of initiative and ability; educational selection has left a residue of D and E stream secondary modern and comprehensive school pupils for pit work - there has been a massive haemorrhage of talent from mining communities; and earlier pit closure programmes have set up eddies of selective migration which have drained away the most enterprising men from the more northerly fields."*

And further: *"We did not solve the educational problem by raising the school-leaving age to 15, still less to 16. Five years in the E-stream of a comprehensive school is an excellent training in sheer bloody-mindedness if not actual subversion. For both teachers and pupils, degradation and desperation may alternate, at best, with 'having a laugh'.*

"This is not education; it is a species of trench warfare, it is anticipatory socialisation for the mass picket line."

What conclusions can a sensible person draw from the above premises, assuming these to be correct? Surely, that our education system and the streaming within it are defective and discriminate against the vast majority of working class children and that pit closures must be halted at all costs lest there should be an even greater drain of the intelligent and talented among the miners to other areas, leaving behind a 'mindless' heap who are only fit for the picket line. The Professor, being unable to think through to the logical conclusions of his own, if wrong, premises, or being frightened by these conclusions, simply side-stepped the whole issue and launched into the affray with the following mindless tirade, born out of his utter failure to understand the economic and political issues connected with the NUM strike: *"It is the diluted human residues that remain, especially in Yorkshire and Durham, that have been most effectively manipulated and mobilised by the tactics of the NUM. They have been bounced into a strike without a ballot and have learned to repeat slogans ('No pit closures on economic grounds' 'Cowards hide behind ballots') whose horrendous implications they do not begin to grasp."*

So educational selection and migration have left behind a load of thickies, *"diluted human residues"* if it pleases our obtuse professor. What then is the solution? Let the Professor regale the reader with the following abuse:

"The programme on which the NUM is fighting is industrial and social

Luddism of an extreme kind: not only would obsolescent technology be preserved for ever, but obsolescent pit villages, too."

Migration drains away the talented and the intelligentsia so let us have more of the same by way of a solution! Well, thanks for the 'explanation', as well as the 'solution', worthy Professor! We feel much enlightened by your penetrating analysis! Gentlemen such as these, with nothing but total chaos and confusion in their heads, are paid handsome salaries to confuse and befuddle the minds of our youth in our colleges and universities. No wonder then that working-class children, whom educational selection has siphoned off to universities and other institutions of higher education, where they are preyed upon for years by the likes of our Professor in the name of education - which is the despair of the teacher and the taught alike - are unlikely to have the clarity of mind and singleness of purpose to stand on the picket line.

Obsolete System

It is not worth bothering the reader with the rest of the Professor's 'analysis'. He starts from incorrect premises and ends up by drawing even more erroneous conclusions. He is incapable of understanding that if the NUM appear to be fighting on a conservative programme, which would preserve obsolescent technology forever, then it is only a reflection of the fact that they are fighting within the constraints of a system of production which has been historically obsolete for nearly a hundred years, to wit, capitalism. The real "*industrial and social Luddism of an extreme kind*" is indulged in by those who spare no effort in artificially propping up capitalism, which produces anarchic competition, unemployment, lower depths of utter destitution, savagery, degeneration, little wars and world wars.

But, perhaps we have misunderstood our dear Professor. Perhaps he is criticising the NUM for not fighting for the abolition and overthrow of this obsolete system. If so, the Professor ought to express himself a bit more lucidly so that his advice could penetrate the skulls of the "*diluted human residues*" manning our picket lines and industrial enterprises.

In the light of our Professor's analysis, we cannot help recalling the following remark of Karl Marx apropos John Stuart Mill:

> "*On the level plain simple mounds look like hills; and the imbecile flatness of the present bourgeoisie is to be measured by the altitude of its great intellects*" (*Capital* Vol 1, Ch XVI)

If anything, the imbecile flatness of the bourgeoisie today is even more striking if the altitude of its great intellects is any guide. The class conscious proletariat will increasingly treat with well-deserved contempt the utter nonsense emanating from our professorial gentry and other sections of bourgeois opinion makers and hirelings of imperialism. The NUM strikers will have no difficulty in ignoring with disdain the reactionary outpourings of our Professor and others like him who are paid and pressed into the service of an obsolete system.

NUM victory inevitable

The Government, the NCB and the media have tried every trick to break the miners' strike. Large amounts of bribes, and massive police protection, have been given to a few scabs, who have been portrayed as the "bravest" men in Britain. Cabinet Ministers, newspaper editors and TV journalists have produced a crescendo of abuse aimed at the NUM. The judiciary has shamelessly joined in this battle to beat the NUM. Cavalry charges have been organised by the police against the pickets. In short, everything has been done to intimidate, isolate and defeat the strike. But the strikers, the real heroes, have braved such odds almost single-handedly. Now, the dockers have joined them. Let all other sections of the working class rally round the NUM. Let the TUC Conference next week declare its whole-hearted, unreserved and unstinting support for the NUM. Let the guiding slogan of the working-class movement today be:

VICTORY TO THE MINERS!

LALKAR October 1984

Miners poised for a historic victory - Signs of disintegration and panic in the bourgeois camp

As the October issue of *Lalkar* goes to press, the coal strike is in its thirtieth week, with not the slightest prospect in sight of its settlement in the coming few weeks. The parties to the dispute - the NUM, the NCB **and**, yes **and**, the Government - are still as far apart, if not further apart, now as they were at the beginning of the dispute on 12th March. This became patently obvious during the latest series of talks, arranged in the week of the TUC Conference, held between the NUM and the NCB from Sunday 9th Sept. to Friday 14th Sept. The talks broke down because of the NCB's continuing intransigence and insistence that uneconomic pits must close. The NUM could hardly be expected to compromise on this issue, over which 80% of the membership have been on strike and during which they have suffered so much deprivation and hardship, death (5 dead so far) and suffering, cavalry charges and baton attacks, denial of supplementary benefits and death grants and, last but not least, been subjected to a ceaseless barrage of abuse, malicious lies and calumnious propaganda and a campaign of systematic misrepresentation by Fleet Street and the rest of the media.

Fight to the Finish

In the light of the failure of the latest talks, it is more than ever clear that there will be no negotiated outcome of this dispute in the traditional sense of this expression, that any negotiations which result in an agreement between the two sides would do no more than give legal expression to, and record, the victory of one side and the defeat of the other. It is literally a fight to the finish now. This being the case it is the bounden duty of every class conscious worker to spare no effort in support of the miners, to give unreserved and unstinting support to the NUM and rally round the latter, for all the reasons that have repeatedly been given in these columns over the past seven months.

Elemental Force

The NUM strike has swept all before it and it has become the touchstone for distinguishing between friends and foes of the working-class movement. The impact of this strike, like that of an irresistible force, is felt in every conference hall and meeting place; the conduct of the Government and Cabinet proceedings is dominated by this, the most important event of the decade. The NUM strike has mobilised not just the miners but the working class of this country in a manner that no other event has done for nearly half a century. Even those in the labour movement who do not wish to support the NUM have little choice but to make professions of support for the strike, such is the elemental force unleashed by the resistance of the miners and their dauntless courage in pursuit of their jobs, the right to work, and the fight for saving their pits and communities.

NUM gain strength

As the strike has progressed, the NUM have gained increasing strength, while the Government and the NCB have lost considerable ground. Despite all the tricks, the misrepresentation and lying propaganda, police violence and cavalry charges, the attempts to starve the miners back to work, the police convoys to transport scabs to work, the NCB and the Government's much-trumpeted and expected return to work has not materialised. The support for the strike is as solid today as when the dispute started. And even a *Daily Express* opinion poll says that if a strike ballot was to be held today, more than 2/3rds of the membership would vote in favour of strike action. This might have surprised the Fleet Street barons, whose lies against the NUM might have convinced them that the majority of the NUM membership was against the strike. To us it is no surprise, for 80% of the membership, by staying on strike for seven months in the face of incredible hardship, have given an eloquent answer to the ballot cretins of all shades and persuasions

Labour Movement rallies round NUM

The attempts of the NCB and the Government to isolate the NUM from the rest of the labour movement have failed too, just as ignominiously as their attempts to intimidate and starve the miners back to work. Last month's TUC Conference at Brighton resolved to give "total support" to the NUM; it resolved to stop the movement, and use, of blacked coal or substituted toil. Negotiations are presently taking place between the NUM and the other unions concerned on implementing TUC policy. Notwithstanding the treachery of the EEPTU and the power engineering union's leadership, the show of support for the miners is expected to be considerable, and all trade union rank and file must do everything to ensure that the policy agreed at Brighton is carried out in letter and spirit.

Even the Labour Party leadership, which has hitherto given no more than verbal, token and lukewarm support to the NUM, has been forced to support at its Conference (presently being held in Blackpool), the NUM resolution on the coal dispute in its entirety and without any amendment. ... Mr Arthur Scargill, the NUM President, has come to symbolise the heroism in struggle, and the determination, of the working class to resist the onslaughts of capitalism, their refusal to be pushed around. And, as such, he has been given a hero's welcome both at Brighton and in Blackpool.

Disintegration and Panic in the Bourgeois Camp

If the NUM stock has risen to new heights, that of the NCB and the Government has been depressed to new depths. We read, even in *The Times*, no friends of the NUM, of serious splits in the Cabinet over the conduct of the coal strike. Former Cabinet Ministers, and high-ranking Conservatives, of the stature of Mr Francis Pym and Sir Ian Gilmour, while making ritual denunciations of Mr Scargill and the NUM, have criticised the Government not having the "human touch" and for rising unemployment. Even an as incurably reactionary and rabidly anti-working class journalist as Mr Peregrine Worsthorne of the *Sunday Telegraph* has begun to propagate against a Thatcher victory, for he perceives, and correctly so, that it would send the wrong signals to the Government and make the presently intolerable unemployment situation even worse (see Mr Worsthorne's article in the *Sunday Telegraph* of 23rd Sept.). What used to be called the "Tory Party at prayer", to wit, the clergy, have begun openly to criticise the Government. The Bishop of Durham, the Right Rev. David Jenkins, caused an uproar in Government circles when, during his enthronement sermon, he gave the call that the miners must not be defeated, and followed it up by making public his reply to the Energy Secretary, Peter Walker's, letter which the latter had written, out of acute embarrassment, and by way of criticism of the Bishop and in an endeavour to shut him up. Parts of this letter are nothing short of a damning indictment of the Government, considering the source from which this letter emanates. Here are a couple of extracts from the Bishop's letter:

"Unfortunately, the Government to which you belong does not seem to care for the steadily increasing number of people who are unemployed, and are otherwise marginalized in society, and does not seem to care that it does not seem to care. (You probably saw Mr Pym's gently cautious words on the

subject in 'The Times' of September the 19th in an article headed 'Miners: Now for the Human Touch').

"On all the statistical tables known to me it seems a simple matter of fact that government's fiscal measures consistently improve the lot of (to use titles from one such table) 'senior managers' and 'company directors' while causing losses to 'jobless man with family' and 'semi-skilled worker'.

"This seems a gratuitous refusal to care and a rather insulting determination to make sure the already under-privileged bear an even greater share of the cost of our undoubted economic difficulties, and of our undoubtedly required greater economic realism. It is also difficult to believe that the Government does care for all the members of our society when cuts are repeatedly made on those services which are of particular value to the poor, but money can always be found for military adventures in the Falklands pretending to be still a great power in defence matters or keeping up the police forces. I do not say that we can do without either defence or police expenditure, but the emphasis does seem to be persistently on non-caring and aggressive directions."

On top of the factors listed above, the position of the NUM is becoming almost impregnable because of the following:

Winter: The winter is fast approaching. In the words of the *Miner* (NUM weekly): "*September draws on, the nights draw in, the temperature drops and the coalburning rises. No amount of Government propaganda or smooth ministerial tongues can disguise the fact that time is now on our side*".

Costs: The costs of the strike are reaching astronomical proportions. As we go to press, the strike has already cost more than £3,300 millions, and its weekly cost is conservatively put at £105 million.

NACODS Strike Ballot: The pit deputies' union, NACODS (National Association of Colliery Overmen, Deputies and Shotfirers), refusing to be pushed around any further, refusing to put up any longer with the NCB bully tactics, have already voted overwhelmingly in favour of strike action. The pit deputies were outraged when the NCB, in a characteristically autocratic warning, told them that if the NACODS men didn't agree to go into work in armoured vans or with police escorts if necessary, their pay will be stopped. An infuriated Mr Ken Sampey, the President of NACODS, reacted to this threat thus: "*We have run far enough and we will run no further. We are all sick and fed up with MacGregor's attitude ...*"

Mr Sampey's sentiments were fully endorsed at a one-day delegate conference of the 16,000 strong union which voted unanimously in favour of a strike ballot. The Executive of the Union, equally unanimously, "strongly recommended" a strike vote against the NCB's new guidelines (issued on 15th August) and in protest at the failure in implementing new conciliation procedures AND AGAINST CAPACITY CUTBACKS. The result of the ballot, thus held, was announced on 28th September and, to repeat, it was overwhelmingly in favour of strike action.

Since then, the NCB, in a desperate effort to prevent pit deputies, without whose supervision all mines will shut, from going on strike, have withdrawn the guidelines. This belated action of the NCB will not do much to save its skin, for not only has the issue widened this time to include capacity cutbacks, but also, with the withdrawal of the new guidelines, the deputies have no incentive for crossing the NUM picket lines as they won't be losing any pay if they don't. Either way the NCB finds itself in the position of a man dying of thirst, but possessed with a cup of poisoned drink. If he does not drink he dies, if he drinks he dies all the same.

The NCB and the Government are heading for a crash. They have prepared for and provoked the present Coal Strike, they have invested it with great political importance, with great fanfare and much blowing of trumpets. Much encouraged by the "*apologetic, shambling knee-bending defeatism*", to borrow the apt terminology of the *Miner* of 21st September, of the TUC at its Blackpool Conference in 1983, their appetite whetted by the victories in the *Stockport Messenger* and the GCHQ affairs, the Government decided to attack the NUM as a prelude to subduing, subjugating and castrating the entire labour and trade-union movement in the interests of British monopoly capitalism. But, alas for the Government, the adventure has misfired and the gamble has failed. The sheer determination, the incredible heroism, and the prodigious perseverance in struggle, of the NUM has stemmed the defeatist tide and turned the despair and retreat on a Napoleonic scale of the trade-union movement into its opposite, so that the working-class movement has begun to walk tall, hold its head high and attained the realisation that bowing one's head and retreating in the face of attack is the surest recipe for further disasters and retreats; it has begun to understand the truth contained in the following words of Mick McGahey, uttered before a cheering TUC Conference in Brighton:

"*If you stop running, they can't chase you* ". The NUM has taught the working-class movement of Britain to stop running, and it is on the verge of teaching the Government and the entire bourgeoisie to stop chasing. The NUM, and with it the working class of this country, are poised for an historic victory, just as the Government are heading for an historic defeat. The victory of the NUM is inevitable, as is the defeat of the Government.

LALKAR October 1984

The NUM strike & the Renegade Jimmy Reid

Breath-taking apostasy

One of the well-known aphorisms of the working-class movement is that those who stand on the slippery slope of opportunism soon roll down to the bottom. The latest, though unfortunately not the last, example of the undoubted truth contained in it is furnished by the breath-taking apostasy of Mr Jimmy Reid. Not so long ago, Mr Reid was a prominent member of the Communist Party of Great Britain (CPGB) and led the Upper Clyde Shipyard workers' sit-in during the days of the Heath government. He then, almost overnight and without as much as prior hint of differences with it, resigned from the CPGB and joined the Labour Party, whose Parliamentary candidate he was at the last election. In a short space of time Jimmy Reid, who only a few years ago was regarded by Fleet Street and the rest of the media as an ogre, has been tamed into the kind of flunkey much admired by the bourgeoisie and held out by the latter as an example to be followed by the working-class movement. So complete has been the bourgeois taming of Mr Reid, so speedy has been his metamorphosis from being a communist of a sort to an ordinary bourgeois philistine of the worst kind, that it is impossible to distinguish his utterances on the present coal strike from the mad ravings of such guardians of our 'free' press as the *Sun*, the *Daily Mail* and the *Daily Express*. The only difference is that whereas very few working people believe all the malicious lies put out by the hired hacks of the barons of Fleet Street, they are much more likely to swallow hook, line and sinker the filth propagated by a man with the past credentials of Jimmy Reid, with his long association with the working-class movement, just as during the thirties the lies spread against the Soviet Union and Stalin by Trotsky and other renegades were much more easily accepted by workers in the West than those spread by the imperialist press. It is precisely for this reason that the imperialist press provided generous space to Trotsky to vent his reactionary spleen against the successful building of socialism in the USSR under the leadership of the CPSU headed by J.V. Stalin. Renegades are, after all, one of the best propaganda weapons of hostile classes. Thus it is that the *Observer* of Sunday 16 September allotted its centre page to our 'own' renegade, Mr Reid, to strike blows against the working class, in the name of the working class, and in the real interests of the bourgeoisie.

Precisely because Mr Reid has a working class past, a record of service, some of it very proud, in the working class movement, many workers may, notwithstanding his recent complete desertion from the working-class to the bourgeois camp, be inclined to put some faith in his words. It is therefore necessary to nail down his lies and to refute Mr Reid point by point.

NUM strike - a "disaster" for the Labour Movement.

The first, and from his and the Labour Party's point of view the most important, point that he makes is that the NUM strike is bound to hurt the British Labour movement. Mr Reid repeats this refrain over and over again. No matter how the present strike ends, according to him *"the main casualty will undoubtedly be the democratic Left"*, i.e., bourgeois and petty-bourgeois Left, *"in British politics. It will also undermine the electoral fight-back of Labour, and could even mean a further decline of the party's mass base among the working class."* And further: *"Above all, I would argue, it* [the strike] *has been a disaster for the British Labour Movement which, at the end of the day, will have to pick up the bill and pay the price."*

Reading the remarks quoted immediately above, one cannot avoid the temptation of predicting that Mr Reid is already preparing the ground for leaving the Labour Party and going over to the SDP or the Conservatives, or whichever party happens to be in fashion and popular in bourgeois electoral terms. But that is by the by. Let us deal with the substance of his remarks. First of all, it is simply not true that the NUM strike has hurt the Labour Party's electoral fortunes. At the last general election the Labour Party suffered the most humiliating and disastrous electoral defeat for nearly 50 years, and even Mr Reid's not inconsiderable talent for misrepresentation and standing facts on their head, not even his total inability to understand social phenomena, can be stretched to blame that defeat on the NUM strike - if for no other reason than that there was no coal strike at that time. How does Mr Reid explain that defeat? He does not. He simply passes over it in silence. There are many causes for it, which *Lalkar* discussed and analysed in great detail at the time[1] and

---

1   See LALKAR of July 1983.

which it would be an unjustifiable digression from the subject under discussion to go into in this article. This much, however, is certain: that one of the chief, if not the chief, causes of Labour's defeat was its imperialist chauvinism during the Falklands/Malvinas war, its desire to out-Thatcher Mrs Thatcher and to be even more jingoist than the Tories. Swift retribution in the form of the most disastrous electoral defeat was meted out to Labour for its shameful stance during the Falklands crisis, for working people roused on a platform of imperialist chauvinism were bound to cast their votes in favour of the genuine representatives of this sordid merchandise, i.e., the Tories.

Secondly, since the coal strike started, the Labour Party's ratings in the opinion polls have remained pretty well neck and neck with the Tories, thus registering a great improvement in comparison with its performance at the last general election.

Thirdly, the working class in this country has begun to learn that it cannot entrust its fate to any of the bourgeois Parties, the Labour Party included, that it has to be self-reliant and struggle for the preservation of its hard-won rights and for their enhancement. It has learnt that the advent of a Labour government, far from bringing to earth the proverbial Kingdom of Heaven for working people, only means the continuation of bourgeois rule and exploitation with a different style and honeyed 'socialist' phrases. If workers were to follow Mr Reid's advice, they would make themselves utterly useless for, according to this advice, they should not struggle when Labour is out of office because that would prejudice its "electoral fight back", and they should not fight when Labour is in office because that would prejudice its chances of staying in office. Mr Reid's advice is a perfect recipe for the total emasculation of the working class - it expects of the working class that it should subordinate its class interests to the electoral interests of an opportunist bourgeois party, which never has represented, and never will, the interests of the British working class. Instinctively the working class recognises such advice to be defective and objectively treats it with the contempt it deserves. The British labour movement is far greater than, and its interests far above, the Labour Party - something which the likes of Mr Reid and other petty-bourgeois philistines, "*the democratic Left in British politics*" if it pleases Mr Reid, fail to understand.

Far from being a "disaster for the British Labour movement", the NUM strike has been the best thing that has happened to it in the last 10 years. The labour movement was first emasculated by the Wilson-Callaghan Labour governments and the class collaboration between the TUC bosses and the Labour cabinets. That was followed by four-and-a-half years of Thatcherism, which laid waste one sector after another of British industry. During the five years of Mrs Thatcher's premiership, the number of unemployed has trebled to 3.25 million, not taking into account nearly a million who do not find themselves in the unemployment statistics because of various fraudulent devices such as the so-called training schemes. During the same time there has been a loss of £40,000 million worth of output and an outflow of investment capital of £40,000 million, and the investment stock has gone down by £30,000 million. Thatcherism has ruled supreme, the Labour Party rendered impotent and the TUC at its 1983 Conference resolved to accept this 'new realism' and capitulate. It was against this atmosphere of defeatism and hopelessness that the NUM strike started nearly seven months ago, and its progress has lifted a demoralised working class and brought hope in place of hopelessness, and light in place of darkness. And if various renegades like Mr Reid bemoan the 'disasters' allegedly brought by this strike to the labour movement, then this is more a sign of the renegacy and degeneration of this petty-bourgeois gentry than a measure of the misfortunes of the British labour movement. The Reids of this world are a reflection and a product of the bourgeois influence in the working-class movement and they act as megaphones and conduits for transmitting that influence as well as defeatism and capitulation preached by the bourgeoisie to the working class.

Lastly, it is not all that unlikely that the victory for the NUM might produce the removal of Mrs Thatcher and a total disarray in the Conservative Party, leading in the course of time to Labour's victory, just as the NUM strike of 1974 led to the defeat of the Heath government and the election victory of the Labour Party. Labour will get the benefits of rising militancy on the part of the working class, for unfortunately there is at the present time no party in existence with the ability to command support among working people and at the same time to represent the interests of the working class.

Who is to blame for the strike?

Having made the assertion, refuted above, that the NUM strike had been a disaster for the "British labour movement" our renegade, Mr Reid, launches into a tirade against Arthur Scargill the NUM President. This tirade is in the best (i.e., the worst) traditions of the gutter press. In an effort to explain the origins of the present strike and the tactics of the NUM during the course of it, Mr Reid says:

"Scargill had been desperate for a fight ever since winning the NUM

Presidency.

"Twice before he had urged strike action only to be rejected by the membership in national ballots".

Having thus blamed Scargill for the present strike, he reduces his entire 'explanation' to the following sordid personal attack on the NUM President:

"This is part of the problem. As someone who has known Arthur for nearly 30 years, I understand how bitter he must have felt at what he was bound to consider a personal rebuff.

"He tends to perceive the universe from the standpoint of the sun. His nature seems to demand that he must be the centre of attraction around which everything must revolve".

And Mr Reid adds disarmingly *"it doesn't make for objective thinking'*. It certainly does not, Mr Reid, for great events cannot be explained away in terms of personal characteristics of this or that individual. It is really like explaining the two imperialist world wars in terms of Kaiser Wilhelm and Adolf Hitler and saying that Anglo-American-French imperialism would not have come to blows with German imperialism had it not been for the existence of Kaiser Wilhelm or Hitler as the case may be. There were far deeper economic causes that had been preparing for decades almost unnoticed till they broke out in cataclysmic fashion into the two world wars. It really is like asserting that if Richard the Lionheart had been born in the 19th century, there would have been no capitalism. We have had too much 'explanation' of great historical events and phenomena of this nature; our schools still continue to teach 'history' in this nauseating fashion. It is time that a stop was put to this nauseating nonsense which explains nothing. That Mr Reid, who once professed to be a Marxist and who, therefore, must have acquired a knowledge of at least the rudiments of historical materialism, should offer the sort of 'explanation' of the coal strike that he has is once again a proof of his apostasy rather than an explanation of the origins or the continuation of the coal strike. Mr Reid's tirade against Scargill will only serve to produce heat but not enlightenment. Even assuming that Mr Scargill were motivated by personal 'egotism' and 'political adventurism', as Mr Reid alleges, why should the NUM Executive, including Mick McGahey and, more importantly, the 120,000 strikers, follow Mr Scargill in the satisfaction of the latter's egotism? Surely they don't *"perceive the universe from the standpoint of the sun"?*

Be that as it may, let us look at the accusation that Scargill had been desperate for a fight. Mr Reid himself annihilates this assertion by remarking earlier: *"Let us get one thing clear - Mrs Thatcher wanted a showdown with the NUM"*... (and there is no need to attribute this to Mrs Thatcher's personal attributes). That is correct: the entire bourgeois press has given extensive coverage to the Tory Party and the Tory government's preparations, stretching back to 1979, aimed at defeating the NUM as a means of emasculating the entire trade-union movement. We have ourselves reported on this matter in detail in previous issues, in particular in the July issue of *Lalkar*. Even bourgeois journalism, provided it is of the serious type, does not dare to deny that the Thatcher government wanted a showdown with the NUM, prepared for such a showdown and provoked it on March 6 by announcing the closure of Cortonwood. It was the rank and file who decided almost unanimously to go on strike and other areas followed. The NUM leadership was left with the choice of either making the stoppage official or refusing to legitimise it. To its credit, it made it official.

If twice before the membership had rejected the Executive's call for strike action, events have only gone on to demonstrate how shortsighted the membership had been in rejecting, on the basis of short-term allurements in the form of bonus payments and overtime earnings, that call. By their two rejections, they only strengthened their enemies whom they were forced to fight at a time chosen by these self-same enemies.

The question is: should the miners have accepted the challenge presented to them by the NCB and the government who had, to repeat, made every conceivable preparation in the form of coal stocks, building oil-fired power stations, streamlining the police through the so-called National Reporting Centre at Scotland Yard, dividing the miners through bonus schemes and large redundancy payments and suchlike bribery, etc.? Mr Reid, repeating like a parrot a formula learnt by rote, answers in the negative thus:

"As a trade union activist over many years I have a rather simple attitude in these matters. If the boss wants you to fight at a particular time and place, then my inclination is to refuse the invitation. If possible, you pick a time and circumstances which favour you and not the employer."

Very simple, not to say a simpleton's attitude! It is undoubtedly true that one should avoid a fight at a time and on a terrain of one's enemy's choice. But it is truer still that in certain situations and circumstances one either fights at a time of one's enemy's choosing or one must capitulate and go down on one's knees. If Cortonwood and other collieries had been allowed to close with the loss of 20,000 jobs on the grounds that the time was not auspicious, that would have been the worst capitulation, even if dressed up as a tactical retreat. After the completion and implementation of the NCB programme of closures, it would hardly have been possible for the NUM to persuade the miners to strike in the interests of those who had already left the industry with redundancy payments just because it was winter time and the coal stocks were low. Social life is like nature. It is far too varied, rich and complex to be fitted into the straitjacket of formulas learnt by rote by the likes of Mr Reid.

Ballot

Having made the erroneous assertion - an assertion contradicted by Mr Reid himself - our worthy philistine moves on to criticise the NUM for not holding a ballot before the strike action. This is a familiar refrain of Fleet Street and Her Majesty's government, which, not surprisingly, Mr Reid is playing to packed bourgeois audiences. Nothing that the NUM has done contradicts its rule book; nothing in the actions of the NUM constitutes a denial of the constitutional or democratic rights of the membership. There were two ways the present strike could have been initiated - through a national ballot or through area decisions. The NUM simply chose the latter method.

Mr Reid and others like him are mistaken if they believe that a national ballot in favour of strike action would have produced greater unity among the miners. Nottinghamshire has a very long history of scabbing; it even tried to form bosses' unions during' the 1920s and the word Spencerism originated there. These are facts with which Mr Reid is very well acquainted. And yet he goes on to utter the following lie:

"Until this year I had never seen or heard of miners picketing miners. It was unnecessary. A vote for strike action was honoured by all".

Even after a ballot in favour of strike action it was all too unlikely that the Notts area would come out. What, it may be asked, was to be gained from holding a ballot in these circumstances? None other than incurring extra expenditure, giving the NCB, the government and Fleet Street extra time to put out malicious and calumnious propaganda aimed at influencing the miners against strike action, and, last but not least, dampening the zeal of the membership, seething with rage at the NCB's announcement for the closure of the Cortonwood colliery, who wanted immediate action. The hope of the bourgeoisie and of its flunkeys, Mr Reid included, was that the ballot would produce a result favourable to the NCB and government. But, unfortunately for the NCB and the government, the NUM never gave its enemies the chance to find that out. To the bourgeoisie and to its petty-bourgeois hangers-on, formal democracy counts for more than does real democracy. The moment working people step outside of the formal limits prescribed for them by their masters, when they come on to the political stage independently and truly begin to exercise democracy of the masses - proletarian democracy - this frightens the bourgeoisie and its ideologues out of their wits. With their minds stultified by decades of bourgeois phrasemongering, they cry wolf about the violation of democracy. The fact is that the striking miners have dragged democracy out of the stuffy studies of the intelligentsia and dragged it into the streets and made it a common concern of the working class of this country. The fact that more than 75% of the miners, by staying away from work for more than 6 months, by suffering the most incredible of hardships during this strike, by braving police violence on the picket line, by defying attempts to starve them back to work, have given the most eloquent proof of their commitment to the present strike - all this does not count for a thing with the hired lackeys of the bourgeoisie and various philistines à la Reid who mindlessly repeat themselves *ad nauseam*, chanting *"the ballot box is not an expendable luxury"*. That the miners overwhelmingly support the present strike against pit closures and for the right to work has at long last been recognised by the TUC who, at its Conference at Brighton in the first week of September, resolved to give *"total support"* to the NUM. But, notwithstanding the above recognition and resolution, the scabs of the labour movement have already declared their determination to defy the TUC resolution. Frank Chapple and his successor Eric Hammond have openly stated that they would not support the NUM even if a thousand such resolutions were passed. And these are the gentlemen who shout most about the miners having been deprived of the ballot, and yet ignore a ballot of the entire labour movement.

Coercion and violence

Not being able to comprehend the unyielding stubbornness and incredible heroism shown by the miners during the present strike, Mr Reid ascribes it to the alleged coercion practised by the flying pickets: Thus Mr Reid:

"The responsibility of leadership was to convince miners of the need to take action and to express this conviction through the ballot box. Instead, they chose to spread the strike by flying pickets within the coal industry. Picketing as a means of coercion became a substitute for winning minds. Moral ascendancy, crucial to winning allies for the cause of workers was jettisoned right from the start. The hate, intolerance and consequential violence all stemmed

from the same contagious source - the decision to deny the miners their right to a vote as laid down in the union's constitution".

The whole point is that the leadership did not have to convince the miners to go on strike, for it was the miners themselves who, outraged by the NCB's pit closure announcement, decided to strike in area after area. The NUM could either give official recognition to these actions, or hiding behind ballot cretinism, scab on the membership. It decided to back the membership.

As to violence on the picket line, we shall deal with it in a separate article in the next issue, where we shall demonstrate that it is the striking miners who are the real victims of violence, hate and intolerance. Facts blow sky high Mr Reid's fictitious fabrications and bourgeois pacifism, which he preaches to the workers in the name of 'moral ascendancy'.

Ballot box

Mr Reid's sermon on the indispensability of the ballot box and on what stands in the way of the "*advance of socialist ideas in Britain and Western Europe*" is full of such a mixture of confusion of ideas and a total inability to understand the class basis of socialism and the nature of the state, that it would take a very long separate article to disentangle this confusion. So we shall for the present resist the strong temptation to comment on his remarks in this regard.

Will the NUM emerge bleeding?

Towards the end Mr Reid makes the assertion that:

"*The miners' union will come out of this strike bleeding, torn apart and demoralised by a surfeit of rhetoric unrelated to reality. The likelihood is that the union will be finished as an effective fighting force for the rest of this century.*"

Even the ordinary bourgeois journalists do not dare to utter such a blatant untruth. The fact is that the NUM has never been stronger. Nay, more than that. The present strike has not merely strengthened the NUM, it has even breathed some life into the rest of the trade union movement, which hitherto lay prostrate before the apparently unstoppable reactionary current of Thatcherism. Even the *Times*, which cannot be suspected of being a friend of the NUM, said on 21 June, 1984:

"*Ironically, the dispute that some politicians hoped would break the power of the NUM has actually created new cadres for the future*".

Only the renegacy of Mr Reid, the fact that he has become an incurable reactionary and stuffed his head with philistine catch-phrases about democracy in general and the 'indispensability' of the ballot box in particular, and his desire to win acceptance in bourgeois circles, prevents him from seeing what even the ordinary hired hacks still manage to see. Hence his terribly clever, not to say terribly stupid, and snooty remarks about Stalinism.

In most of his article, abuse and invective, normally perfectly legitimate in a polemical work, simply serve as a substitute for reasoned argument. Whenever he is at a loss for an argument, a tirade against Scargill always sees him through. Hence his references to Mr Scargill as the 'sun', 'egotistic', 'adventurist', and finally as the 'Ayatollah'. He ends his article by exhorting everyone in the labour movement to rally round in defence of democracy and "democratic socialism" (i.e., bourgeois socialism) against the "*Ayatollahs who are out to destroy the labour movement*": Mr Reid's article is bound to get him the applause of the bourgeoisie. It is equally bound to get him recognition in working-class circles as not only a renegade but also *"a genius in the way of bourgeois stupidity"*, as old V.I. Lenin would have put it.

LALKAR October 1984

Contempt of court proceedings against the NUM

Today, the 1st of October, as this issue goes to press, the news has come through that five leaders of the NUM face committal proceedings and possible imprisonment for alleged contempt of court. Mr Scargill was served with a writ on the floor of the Labour Party Conference in Blackpool by an official of the High Court, who got into the Conference hall with the help of a *Daily Express* photographer. The five officials singled out in a series of writs are: Mr Scargill, Mr Mick McGahey (NUM Vice President), Mr Peter Heathfield (General Secretary of the Union), Mr Jack Taylor (President of the Yorkshire miners) and Mr Gordon Butler (General Secretary of the Derbyshire miners).

The five were given 48 hours to appear in court and explain their conduct. The contempt proceedings arise from the judgment given by Judge Nicholls of the High Court that the miners' strike in Yorkshire is unlawful, and that no disciplinary action should be taken against men who cross the picket lines. This judgment was yet another example of the blatant interference by the judiciary in industrial relations. Mr Scargill, therefore, quite correctly declared his intention to ignore the court's ruling. His defiance was broadcast first on Channel 4 News on Friday evening a few hours after Judge Nicholls gave his ruling, and was repeated on Sunday after a meeting of the miners' delegation to the Labour Party Conference in Blackpool.

Judge Nicholls' judgment was given in a case brought by the two notorious scabs and traitors from Yorkshire, Robert Taylor and Ken Foulstone, both from Manton Colliery, whose heavy legal costs and travelling expenses, staying in five-star hotels, are being paid by undisclosed businessmen, in these proceedings against the NUM. It is understood that the same shameless pair initiated committal proceedings against the NUM officials.

The High Court notice to Mr Scargill alleges that he is in contempt of court for defying court orders that: (a) He should not threaten disciplinary proceedings against the miners who cross picket lines; and (b) He should not continue to declare the strike in Yorkshire as official in defiance of the court ruling.

Mr Scargill and his union have decided to treat with well-deserved utter contempt this contempt of court ruling The five officials have declared that they will not appear on Thursday to 'purge' their alleged contempt. Mr Scargill has declared:

"I want to make it clear that if the offence I have committed is contempt, I plead guilty. Because the only crime I have committed is to fight for my class and my members".

His stand has been unanimously endorsed by the NUM 24-man national executive, which has restated its intention to continue making the strike in Yorkshire official and the union's longstanding refusal to comply with Court orders issued during the 30-week dispute.

This determined and rocklike stand of the union puts the judiciary and the Government in a fix. For, although the writ outlines the possible penalties facing Mr Scargill and his colleagues, including fines, sequestration of union funds and imprisonment in Pentonville, it is unlikely that the NUM five will end up in prison, for sending them to prison will nor settle the dispute. Not just the miners, but the entire labour movement is bound to react sharply to such an event and all too likely to make sure that the NUM five are freed, carried shoulder high by thousands of workers, just as in 1972, the five dockers committed to prison for contempt by the National Industrial Relations Court (then headed by Sir John Donaldson, now Master of the Rolls), were freed and carried by thousands of jubilant workers. Even Lord Denning, who cannot be suspected of even a shred of sympathy with any working man, and who was involved in the Appeal Court in freeing the Pentonville Five, recently wrote in his book, *The Closing Chapter*: "Never again could an industrial court hope to enforce orders by committing persons to prison".

Such then is the experience of someone closely involved in the 1972 dockers' case. The latest judgments of the High Court in the miners' case only go to show that the judiciary have learnt nothing from the past 150 years of the history of industrial relations in this country, or from the experience of 1972. In their zeal to help the bourgeoisie, the judges are pronouncing judgments which will serve no other purpose than to bring the judiciary into contempt. And this contempt is bound to be the only outcome of the present contempt proceedings in the High Court.

LALKAR October 1984

Mr Steel's humbug on democracy

The Liberal Party has provided a neat illustration of the hypocrisy of the bourgeois attitude to democracy. We hear a lot of cant about democracy from the representatives of the bourgeoisie, and in recent months they have been baying in unison that the National Union of Mineworkers is "undemocratic". It MUST, according to them, hold a national ballot for without one the miners' strike is "undemocratic". They ignore the sound, working-class democracy that is operating in the NUM (see *The Miners Strike and the Renegade Jimmy Reid* starting on page 232 of this book).

The Liberal Party leader, Mr Steel, has been as sanctimoniously vociferous on this issue as the rest, but it is interesting to see what happens when democracy comes home to roost. It came home to roost at the Liberal Party Conference, when, despite strong opposition from Mr Steel, the Assembly voted for the unilateral abandonment of Cruise missiles. Here was a democratic ballot for Mr Steel. His response was to say that he will use his power as leader to keep this decision out of the Party manifesto, just as he rejected an Assembly vote opposing the deployment of Cruise missiles in 1981. He even went as far as saying that resolutions of the Liberal Party Assembly do not have the status of holy writ !

So, according to Mr Steel, the NUM must have a ballot, but he can ignore ballots in his own Party Conference! This should come as no surprise to us, for the bourgeoisie has always been prepared to abandon democracy when it suited its own class interests. Neither should it surprise us that bourgeois representatives try to distort the fact that the NUM has taken hold of working-class democracy and is USING it in its class interests.

LALKAR November 1984

NUM Strike - a fight to the finish

As this issue goes to press, the coal strike enters its 35th week. The last round of peace talks between the NUM and the NCB collapsed after 10 hours on Wednesday night (October 31st), with no date fixed for any further negotiations. The failure of the talks comes as no surprise, for the NUM, though nominally facing the NCB across the table, were actually dealing with a third party not present at the negotiations, but whose hand guided the NCB, to wit, the Government. And the Government has, right from the start of the coal strike, declared that it regards the NUM as the enemy within, and its President, Mr Scargill, as nothing less than a Galtieri, the former Argentinian military dictator.

On the eve of the latest talks, Nigel Lawson, the Chancellor of the Exchequer, had blatantly declared that the Government was prepared to spend any amount of money to defeat the NUM. He even admitted, for the first time, the high costs of the strike, adding that this year his public sector borrowing targets, the present Government's holy of holies, would overshoot by £1.5 billion, and that the expected growth rate of 3% in the economy will now only be 2.25% - all due to the coal stoppage. Peter Walker, the Energy Secretary, for his part, has made it clear that the NUM should not, and would not be offered a better deal than that offered to, and accepted by NACODS.

Since NACODS called off strike action on the basis of an agreement in which the NCB have made only cosmetic concessions in the form of a new procedure for looking at pit closures, the NUM, after 8 months on strike, could hardly be expected to make a sudden reversal, for, as Arthur Scargill said, it is hardly a consolation to a person already condemned to death that he will be tried under a new procedure. The NUM position remains, as it has been all along, that of no pit closures, except on grounds of exhaustion and safety. The NCB, not only refuses to withdraw its pit closure programme and guarantee the future of the 5 threatened pits, but actually has a much larger hit list, under which it proposes to close 70 pits with the loss of 70, 000 jobs, as revealed in a secret NCB document, made public by the NUM President only the other day.

There is thus an unbridgeable gap between the NUM and the NCB. After the failure of the last round of talks in the middle of September, we wrote in our Oct. issue: "... *it is more than ever clear that there will be no negotiated outcome of this dispute ... that any negotiations which result in an agreement between the two sides would do no more than give legal expression to, and record, the victory of one side and the defeat of the other. It is literally a fight to the finish now*". These words have been borne out by the progress of events and are even more true today.

This being the case, every attempt must be made by every class conscious worker, by all trade unionists, by all those who claim to support the NUM, to spare no effort in rendering unstinting and unreserved support to the NUM in the latter's fight for the right to work, for saving jobs and communities. Even with NACODS calling off strike action, the NUM can, and shall, win.

Winter and Coal Stocks

Winter is already on us. The coal stocks at power stations now stand at 14 million tonnes. At this time last year, power stations in England and Wales were burning 1.6 million tonnes of coal a week, rising steadily to 1.8 million tonnes a week in mid-December and staying at or above that level for about 3 months. Even with the present level of oil burnt, and if the winter is as mild as last year - which no one can guarantee - with only half last year's consumption needed to balance the system, the power stations will be completely exhausted of their stocks in 17 weeks. Even at this reduced level of consumption, stocks will be down to 7 million tonnes at the end of January, and under 4 million at the end of February. Power cuts will become inevitable by the middle of February, which means that the government's claim of being able to last through to the Spring without power cuts is hollow and meaningless bluster.

When coal stocks come down to somewhere between 8 and 4 million tonnes, the government will have either to order power cuts or to take the drastic step of moving the 20 million tonnes of coal stockpiled at NCB pitheads, mostly in strike-bound areas. But that carries the danger, almost certain to be realised, of picketing at the mines and a blacking of fuel by the rail transport workers.

Power Workers

There is also the probability that the power workers will turn the screw on power supplies this winter. If, or rather when, that happens, a settlement on the NUM's terms will have to be conceded. To that end, the main unions - with the electricians and power engineers abstaining - have sent round guidelines for the embargo of deliveries of oil and coal. According to the *Financial Times* of 17

October, *"if the call is even half heeded, they believe, there could be power cuts by Christmas."* The most important thing for the NUM and the rest of the working-class movement now is to see to it that the 20 million tonnes of coal stockpiled at pitheads is not allowed to be moved; and if moved through a massive police and scabbing operation, or through the use of troops, that these supplies are blacked.

Government and NCB demoralised

Another factor making for a NUM victory is that the morale of the NCB and the government has slumped with the progress of the strike, just as the morale of the NUM and the striking miners has reached a new high. Open and unfettered warfare prevails in the NCB. One week the NCB appoint Mr Michael Eaton as a new 'Mr Fixit', the following week the NCB Chairman relieves him of his duties; one day Mr MacGregor puts his industrial relations director into cold Storage, another day he sends the head of the Board's public relations, Mr Geoffrey Kirk, on leave . Even the *Daily Mail* asks the question: *"Is MacGregor turning into Mr Magoo?"* Mrs Thatcher has begun to distance herself from Ian MacGregor, and the entire bourgeois press has begun to suggest that he has lost his marbles and ought therefore to be rewarded with the joys of retirement - after all he has earned them!

The government's own unpopularity increases by the day. Even the *Times*, that unfailing friend of the Thatcher administration, has begun to write articles critical of the government's economic and social direction (see the *Times* editorial *Hand-To-Mouth Leadership* of October 9). The Archbishop of Canterbury, the spiritual head of the British ruling class, slammed at the dangerous effect of Thatcherism on the social fabric of a system so dear to the Archbishop, has questioned the objectives of the government's economic policy: *"if the human consequences of such aims mean unemployment on an unprecedented scale, poverty, bureaucracy, despair about the future of some communities, inequitable sharing of the sacrifice called for"*. The unemployment figures, rising daily, and the attendant misery, are bound not only to add to the unpopularity of the Thatcher government, but also to help explain the NUM fight for jobs and for the right to work. More and more workers are seeing the sense behind the NUM struggle, namely, that it is the first major, and longest, strike against unemployment and for the right to work.

The bourgeois media have panicked to such an extent that it is not uncommon for them to refer to the NUM strike - wrongly in our view - as an insurrection.

Mrs Thatcher, in her speech to the Conservative Party Conference, referred to the *"emergence of an organised revolutionary minority who are prepared to exploit industrial disputes but whose real aim was the breakdown of law and order and the destruction of democratic parliamentary government"*. If the miners' strike scares Mrs Thatcher into making such panic-stricken statements, one wonders what a real revolutionary insurrection would compel this iron lady to bring forth!

Courts Discredited

The attempts of the courts to silence the NUM have, far from silencing the Union and its President, only served to discredit the courts and reveal them in their real colours as the judicial arm of the bourgeoisie, eager as ever to launch into the fray in an attempt to suppress all working-class resistance to the rule of King Capital. Arthur Scargill and the NUM defied the court order declaring the strike in Yorkshire and Derbyshire to be illegal, and were in turn fined for contempt of court. Arthur Scargill refused to pay the fine and some anonymous benefactor (for all we know it was the NCB) paid it and got the courts off the hook. The NUM funds have been sequestered for its refusal to pay the £200,000 fine imposed on it. The Union has responded by saying that it will operate from the street if necessary.

The TUC and Labour leadership fail to sell out the NUM

All attempts by the TUC and the Labour front bench to sell the miners down the river have met with total failure, and the NUM strike has increasingly shown the Labour leadership to be a tedious irrelevance to the struggles of the working class of this country. Matters have reached such a pass that the *Sunday Times* of 7 October was forced to make the following observation apropos the Labour Party in the wake of the latter's Conference, which came to be dominated by the coal dispute: "A once great party of state now finds itself stranded on the shores of extremism where it will take an extraordinary Spring tide of common sense and devotion to Labour's long-term interests to float off again ... Mr Kinnock's *newly minted authority has been devalued at its very first test. Unless he can assert himself ... he faces the same fate as Kerensky at the hands of those who plot revolution ...*"

By way of warning to bourgeois circles against underestimating Arthur Scargill, the *Financial Times'* makes the following assessment of the achievements of the NUM and of Mr Scargill:

"*He has followed a logic of conflict unerringly and unshakeably: he has *fought a class war and has shamed the middle-of-the-roaders and the big talkers in the TUC into helping him practise what they so lightly preached, to the point where only those who have explicitly thrown out Marxist ideals - like the electricians - can counterpose him. He is the left-wing meeting hall's word made flesh long after anyone thought that possible - and he and his union will now try to work their way through the body politic".*

Support for the NUM grows

Last, but not least, national and international support for the NUM has built up on an unprecedented scale. Miners' support groups exist, and are functioning very efficiently, in every locality; food and money contributions are pouring in; political meetings and rallies are being held in all parts of the country to which miners' representatives are invited almost without fail. The whole working-class movement has been set in motion in support of the NUM by the sheer determination, dauntless courage and heroic effort shown by the NUM strikers in pursuit of their right to work, to save pits and jobs. Internationally too there has been an admirable show of moral and material support for the NUM.

In the light of the foregoing, it may be concluded with certainty that the NUM are bound to be victorious - no matter how long it takes.

LALKAR November 1984

Whose Libyan connection?

Honesty in politics is the result of strength, hypocrisy the result of weakness. Nothing demonstrates the truth contained in the above adage more than the howls and the outcry emanating from all sections and sectors of bourgeois opinion, from all bourgeois political parties, the Labour Party included, in connection with what our 'free' press gloatingly and maliciously describe as the NUM's Libyan connection. This storm in a teacup arose from the visit, at the end of the third week of October, by the Chief Executive of the NUM, Mr Roger Windsor, to Libya, at the invitation of the Libyan trade unions. Contrary to what the Fleet Street barons have put out, there was nothing secret or out of the ordinary about this visit, which was of a routine nature to explain the NUM's case to fellow trade unionists in Libya. During his visit, Mr Windsor met Col. Gaddaffi, the Libyan leader[1]. This meeting was shown on Libyan TV, and Mr Windsor's visit was given wide coverage in the Libyan press. And yet, reading the reports in the Fleet Street press, one gets the impression of a cloak and dagger affair, which bears no resemblance to the actual visit made by Mr Windsor.

Fleet Street has condemned the visit as yet another example of Arthur Scargill's undemocratic proclivities. Energy Secretary Peter Walker has, with ill-disguised glee, made the sanctimonious statement that a person is judged by the company he keeps, implying that Mr Scargill should be judged in the context of the nature and quality of the official leadership of all those countries to which the NUM sends delegations at the invitation of trade unions of those countries. He went on to denounce the NUM for *"negotiating with people who have provided funds for terrorist activities throughout Europe."* Not wishing to lag behind in this bourgeois game of condemning the best in British trade un-

---

1 We know now from Mr Milne's book, 'The Enemy Within', that Windsor was planted in the NUM by the intelligence agencies of Britain and that he insisted, at the latter's prompting, in embracing Col. Gadaffi in front of television cameras for the sole purpose of handing a propaganda weapon to the bourgeoisie in their attack on the NUM. None of this, however, is any way distracts from this article (note to present edition).

ionism, Norman Willis, the TUC General Secretary, has condemned the visit in sweeping terms. Neil Kinnock, the Labour leader, ever ready to oblige the Tories and ever willing to dance to the baton of the Fleet Street barons, has weighed in with the following statement: "*The Gadaffi regime is vile ... any offers from them would be an insult to everything the British Labour movement stands for.*"

The above high-sounding phrases remind us of the devil in Turgenev, whose motto was to condemn most of all those evils that he himself possessed. In the present instance, the media, Her Majesty's government as well as Her Majesty's most loyal, not to say craven, opposition, and some venal trade unionists, taking their cue from the devil in an effort to hide their own guilt, have indulged in an orgy of orchestrated abuse against the NUM with the purpose basically of breaking the NUM 8-month old strike. The above gentry have tried every trick - from the question of a ballot to that of violence on the picket lines - but they have failed. Now they are busily working the 'Libyan affair' in the hope that if they throw enough muck about, some of it might stick on the NUM. But this attempt will fail just as assuredly as have all previous attempts, for the working people are much more mature today and have far greater access to facts than they did in the 1920s when the appearance in 'our' press of a fake letter, allegedly from Zinoviev in the USSR, was sufficient to give the Tories a resounding victory in a general election.

What are the facts? The facts are that the ruling class of this country has the cosiest of relations with the nastiest of regimes, which include Botha's South Africa, Pinochet's Chile, Israel of Begin, Shamir and Sharon, King Fahd's Saudi Arabia, Reagan's America, to name but a few. Compared with the murderous activities of these regimes, both within and outside their national frontiers, the activities of Col. Gadaffi take on the appearance of those of a small-time crook. The US administration has murdered hundreds of thousands of people in wars abroad (Korea, Vietnam and Latin America) and through CIA operations (Chile). Israel only yesterday did to death more than 2,000 Palestinians in the Sabra and Chatila refugee camps in Lebanon, to say nothing of its Nazi-like policies within the whole of Palestine. Botha's regime, through its barbaric system of apartheid, daily oppresses, tortures and murders the black people of South Africa in their hundreds and degrades three-fourths of the country's population by condemning it to an existence unfit for human beings. All this has not prevented British imperialism from reaping huge profits through investments in, and trade with, these countries. All this has not prevented the governments of this country, Labour and Tory alike, from maintaining extremely friendly and diplomatic relations with these nasty regimes. Be that as it may, we shall confine ourselves to the facts concerning Libya and the Libyan connection of bourgeois Britain.

The Ministers in Mrs Thatcher's government have been falling over each other for three years in urging British businessmen to negotiate with the Libyan government. In October, 1981, a senior Libyan Minister, Omar Muntassir, visited Britain on a trade mission, and saw senior officials of the British Steel Corporation, including Ian MacGregor, then BSC Chairman and now the head of the NCB. Muntassir also had a friendly round of talks with Douglas Hurd, who was at that time Minister of State in the Department of Trade and is now Northern Ireland Secretary.

In December, 1981, Lord Trefgarne, a Foreign Office Minister said: *"It is possible to point to constructive dialogue with the Libyan government which bodes well for the future"*. In February, 1982, a trade delegation, including highly-placed men from John Laings, Wimpeys and GEC, under the leadership of the government-financed Committee for Middle East Trade (COMET), left for Libya. In March, 1982, Britain refused to follow the Reagan administration's total boycott of Libya. On the contrary, COMET came up with a 5-year plan for businessmen interested in doing business with Libya. In October 1982, Gerard Vaughan, a junior minister then at the Department of Trade, had this to say in a letter to a Labour back-bencher: *"Far from discouraging British firms from entering the Libyan market, we have responded positively to Libyan overtures for UK involvement in her development plan"*.

Also in October, 1982, the Libyan Embassy in Britain held a lavish party in the Intercontinental, London, to celebrate the anniversary of the Gaddaffi regime. And if you think - your imagination having been worked on by Fleet Street - that it was Arthur Scargill who was sipping cocktails with everyone else present, you would be wrong. For it was none other than Mr Douglas Hurd, now defending us from 'Irish terrorists'. In February 1983, Kenneth Clarke, a junior Health Minister, went to Libya to negotiate contracts for training Libyan medical students and for opening a hospital. British business did much better in Libya in 1983 than in 1982, notwithstanding regular complaints about Libyan terrorism. Even after the siege of the Libyan People's Bureau, resulting in the death of WPC Yvonne Fletcher, 60% of all the consultancies in Libya are still in the hands of British firms, including British Rail and British Telecom. British Airways are still training Libyan engineers and, according to the official list in the British embassy in Tripoli, there are 98 British firms presently trading in Libya. £300 million left Libya this year and found its way into the coffers of these companies! So much then for the hypocritical fulminations of Tory ministers such as Peter Walker and their Fleet Street patrons.

As to Labour's Neil Kinnock and his characterisation of the Gadaffi government as a *"vile regime"*, here is one single fact that proves the hollow, empty and hypocritical essence of his remark: We wonder if we could take Mr Kinnock's memory back to September, 1977, when the Libyan Embassy, on express instructions of the leader of this *"vile regime"*, Col. Gaddaffi, threw an exquisitely grand party in London's Grosvenor Hotel, attended by 1,250 guests, all of whom toasted this *"vile regime"* in Chateau La Tour and Louis Roederer crystal. The Tories were doubtless present in great numbers at this jamboree, which cost a quarter of a million pounds. But take note Mr Kinnock: also present were three Labour Cabinet Ministers, - Roy Mason, Albert Booth and David Ennals.

In the light of the above facts, one cannot but marvel at the audacity of these gentlemen who, with virginal naïveté and an air of injured innocence, raise such a lot of fuss about the NUM's contacts with Libyan trade unionists. It is to the credit of the NUM and its President Arthur Scargill that they have refused to knuckle under to the vicious propaganda directed against them. And it is to the credit of the Libyan people and their leader Col. Gaddaffi that they should show internationalist solidarity with the British miners.

LALKAR December 1984

Time for labour movement to redeem its IOUs
NCB's back-to-work abysmal failure

As November draws to a close and December sets in, the miners' dispute completes its ninth month and enters the tenth with not the slightest chance of a settlement in the offing. The miners have just weathered the latest of the NCB-Government offensives against them, namely the *'back to work'* campaign. This campaign failed just as abysmally as the previous campaigns to lure or intimidate the miners, notwithstanding the fact that this latest offensive was well-prepared and co-ordinated between the government, the NCB and the police on the one hand, and all the instruments of bourgeois propaganda, from Fleet Street to the television channels, on the other hand. The NCB used every manner of bribery in order to turn strikers into scabs. The police used all their, by now notorious, bully-boy tactics to get scabs through the picket lines without giving a single opportunity to the pickets to talk to those returning to 'work'. The Coal Board cooked the books, exaggerated the number of strikers who had fallen for the NCB-police carrot-and-stick tactics. The faithful media, representing the interests of money bags, Kings of finance and magnates of industry, obligingly presented the trickle back to work as a flood, with a view to scoring a psychological victory against the strikers and persuading them that in the face of this 'stampede' to work, all resistance was as foolish as it was futile. Her Majesty's Ministers spoke of the miners voting with their feet - the same Ministers who stubbornly refuse to recognise that three fourths of the miners still continue to vote with their feet by being on strike.

It must be said to the honour of the 140,000 (out of a total of 180,000 miners) that, in the face of such heavy odds, confronting such formidable foes, they emerged not only with their honour and principles intact and unsullied but also triumphant. Their victory is all the more significant as it was achieved at a time of the year when Christmas is just knocking at the door. Normally this time is associated with festivities, feasting, eating, drinking, exchange of presents, and particularly presents for the children. For the miners who have been on strike, for their families and especially their children, Christmas 1984 will bring merely the continuation of the last nine months of hunger, malnutrition deprivation and misery. The government and the NCB know that, and it has been their calculation, in typical bourgeois humanitarian style, to starve the miners back to work. In the circumstances the miners on strike faced a cruel dilemma: crawl back to work and lose everything that they fought for during the last nine months, and into the bargain carry forever the stigma of a scab; or stay on strike and suffer further deprivation and bring it upon their families, in particular the children. It is understandable that in the face of such a terrible choice, some strikers could no longer bear the strain and decided to become scabs. But 98% of the strikers stood firm and have emerged from this trial much strengthened and resolved to carry their fight through to victory.

To the gigantic, not to say costly, police protection of the scabs and the massive propaganda unleashed by the ruling class press and broadcasting services, the NCB added, by way of a bribe, the Christmas pay packet of £1,400 for all those strikers who returned to work before 19 November, this date being later extended for another week when the results hoped for by the NCB and the government failed to materialise. (It must be remembered that a substantial part of this £1,400 belongs to the miners anyway, for the Christmas 'bonus' includes holiday pay which the miners have earned and which will be theirs when they go back to work eventually after a settlement). In the face of the NCB tactics, Mr Scargill, the NUM President, at a rally on 11 November at Newcastle upon Tyne hammered out a clear warning to miners crossing picket lines. He told an audience of more than 2,000 in the City Hall that in 10 years' time they would be able to look back *"In a way that those who have crawled through our picket lines will never do.*

"You have suffered hardship and deprivation, but colleagues, you will not always be poor. But to the end of time they will be scabs", he said to thunderous applause.

"You will be able to look back and say with pride that in 1984 you took part in a struggle not only to save your pits and your jobs and your communities and your culture, but in the process, you retained your dignity as human beings.

"You are the finest example of trade-unionism in the world."

Even if we take the NCB figures, which are laundered and therefore suspect, no more than 2-3% of the strikers have returned to 'work'. This is admitted to even by the most respectable *"hired coolies of the pen of imperialism"*, to use Lenin's apt and vivid terminology. For instance, writing in the

'*Observer*' of 18 November, Mr Steve Vines, the labour editor of that newspaper, in an article entitled '*The beginning of the end*' in which he gloatingly predicts the "*virtual certainty of defeat*" for the miners and pronounces funeral rites on the NUM - in this same article, Mr Vines makes the following useful admission: "*Even today the much-publicised drift back to work is relatively confined...*". That this admission is grudging is only to be expected, for this single sentence demolishes the thrust of his article, namely, that the miners face the "*virtual certainty of defeat*". And further when Mr Vines adds the following few lines appearing in quotation marks, he achieves even for him the not too difficult task of totally annihilating his own proposition.

"*The running of the strike itself however, is much more diffuse, by-passing to a large extent even the union's regional structure. Individual pit branches have set up elaborate arrangements for picketing, soup kitchens, collections, aid advice and campaigning and have acquired a momentum of their own. Miners' wives have come into their own. Debbie Alan from the Yorkshire Women's Support Group, ironically acknowledges Mrs Thatcher's contribution to their new-found self-confidence and political activism - 'She has released energies in women that will never be suppressed again,' she said.*"

Mr Vines, it must be admitted is the master of self-annihilatory rigmarole. This, however, in no way detracts from his admission that the "*much-publicised drift back to work is relatively confined*" and that the NUM strike is far from crumbling.

Mr Vines is by no means the only one to make the above observations. Historian Dai Smith, of the University of Cardiff, writing in the '*Listener*' of 15 November makes similar points. In his article: '*The Longest Strike*', in which he compares the 1926 coal dispute with the present, he observes that the strike "*remains relatively solid*", that if Mr Scargill "*were to be removed tomorrow, the strike would not cave in. No more than Cook in 1926 is Arthur Scargill the brains of this struggle, but he is its gut feeling. Its strength lies, as in 1926, not in the prospect of victory or defeat but in the belief that for mining communities, even more than for their pits, there is no alternative to this resistance*".

Dai Smith goes on to observe that "*It may be an overstatement to assert that 'an alternative welfare system' has now sprung up, but a skeletal structure is discernible*" and that "*all over South Wales kids drop pocket money in collection boxes and strut around plastered in yellow 'Coal Not Dole' stickers. 1926 has a more direct echo too. Pigeons and rabbits are shot, and Welsh hills* are not only good grazing for sheep, there're good for bold rustlers with 2.2 guns."

On the changed attitude towards the police, Mr Smith continued:

"In 1926, the police in South Wales were seen as an army of occupation. It took decades to reconcile police and miners after that. What has been happening on picket lines has rekindled the same kind of bitterness: 'If I'd seen four or five boys giving a copper a kicking in our place I'd 've helped him. Not now. I've no respect for them. My kids call 'em scabs. It's awful but it's true. First thing she done was to give 'em massive pay rises. You can see why now'."

Dai Smith makes the following last observation:

"This strike has now lasted longer than the agony of 1926. That is already for these men and women a sort of victory. There are some things now on which, no matter what happens, they cannot be beaten. Those things are their individual courage, their communal values, their creative initiatives."

And he concludes his article by citing the words of Peter Evans, the former chairman of Deep Duffryn:

"Victory to me is a return to what we wanted in 1981, a reversal of the idea of South Wales as a peripheral area, marginal to the rest of the industry. We want more than investment. We want commitment. We had investment in Deep Duffryn but no commitment. She's ripped the mask off. It's her class or ours. Them and Us. In 1926 it was the employers, now it's the State. And we understand that".

People who show such forbearance in the face of hardship, such ingenuity in adversity, such calm in the face of provocation, such valour and heroism in the face of danger, and such persistence and perseverance in the course of struggle are far from beaten. Nay, such people shall never be beaten.

And if Mr Vines and his fellow hacks, putting their trust in their own articles, for writing which they are handsomely rewarded, believe otherwise their shock will be all the greater when the miners' victory comes.

Time for the labour movement to redeem its IOUs

If the NUM have put up such a magnificent fight, the same cannot be said of the rest of the labour movement. Neither the TUC nor the Labour Party leadership have lifted a finger in support of the NUM. On the contrary, this despicable gentry have done their damnedest best (or rather worst) to stab the miners in the back. At crucial moments during the progress of this dispute these labour lieutenants of capitalism have intervened in order to cause the NUM to capitulate.

Violence

At a time when the police were beating the hell out of the NUM pickets and staging cavalry charges against them, Neil Kinnock the 'Labour' leader, came up with a statement condemning the miners for picket-line violence, thus helping the government, the NCB and the police by blaming the NUM for police violence. His speech at the TUC Conference at Brighton led to such revulsion on the part of the ordinary delegates, not to mention millions of workers outside, that he was obliged to 'modify' his remarks at the Labour Party Conference the following month at Blackpool. In the latter Conference he equated the resistance of the pickets to the police violence itself and went on to condemn both the *"violence of the battering ram carriers"* (i.e. the pickets) and *"the violence of cavalry charges"* (the police). This same hoary tale of picket violence was revived by Norman Willis, the General Secretary of the TUC, when he recently spoke at a miners' rally in South Wales, apparently in 'support' of the miners. He condemned picket violence for which he received a kiss of death from Mrs Thatcher in the form of an appreciation of the *"great courage"* shown by this *"distinguished trade unionist"*. And this Mr Willis was surprised when the miners greeted his remarks with such contempt that they refused to listen to his nauseating insipid sermon on non-violence and dangled a hangman's noose over his head.

Let us, however, look at the facts and see who really has been the victim of violence. The figures, and pictures in the newspapers and on television screens, speak for themselves. Here are the figures:

* Two deaths on the picket lines.

* Five miners put on life-support machines

* Three miners with fractured skulls.

* Ten miners with broken ribs.

* Over 2,500 cases of miners with cracked ribs, broken arms and torn shoulder muscles caused by being dragged handcuffed across the ground.

In all 4,000 miners have been injured.

The Home Office claim that 750 policemen have been injured during the strike, a figure which doubtless includes over 700 cases of mild cuts and bruises.

In the face of these facts, one would have thought that any person with a sense of fairness and justice, let alone a sense of loyalty to the working class, would have unequivocally and unhesitatingly made an outright condemnation of police violence. But alas, it is not only Mrs Thatcher and her fellow Tories, ever loyal to British imperialist capitalism, but also the Labour and TUC leadership, with one voice and in unison, who condemn the miners for picket-line violence. The working class has a right to ask this revolting gentry: on whose side are you, gentlemen?

The police violence on the picket line has been fully backed and reinforced by a massive judicial assault, which has torn the mask of impartiality from the face of the courts and exposed them to be one of the chief instruments of bourgeois oppression and subjugation of the working class - as the judicial arm of the bourgeois state for forcibly holding down the working class in the interests of the capitalist class. Here are some figures which furnish eloquent proof of the despicable role played by the judiciary.

By the end of October, police chiefs had made more than one million deployments of policemen during the strike. At any given time up to 8,000 policemen have been used. 7,428 arrests have been made and 8,020 charges have been brought against the miners. Of the 2,524 cases so far dealt with, 2,034 have resulted in convictions. 43 miners have been imprisoned, 6 sent to detention centres, 9 detained in police custody, 2 in youth custody and 25 given suspended sentences. 1,051 miners have been given punitive fines of more than £50. The appeal of nine Yorkshire miners against blanket bail conditions in Nottinghamshire has been dismissed by a High Court judge. 94.5% of those charged within Notts. are on conditional bail. On 10 October, the High Court fined Arthur Scargill £1,000 and the NUM £200,000 for contempt of court. Scargill's fine, as we reported in the last issue, has been paid off by an 'anonymous donor' and the NUM has refused to pay. So on the 25th October, the High Court ordered Union funds to be sequestrated. Price Waterhouse, accountants acting as sequestrators for the court, have so far managed to lay their hands on £8,174 only.

North Derbyshire scabs, with the full support of the 'Freedom Association', a fascistic outfit speaking for the entire bourgeois class, and the press, are now seeking to prevent their area union spending any money on the strike. The 'National Working Miners Committee' is considering action against members of the NUM Executive Committee individually for the £200,000. South Wales scabs are seeking an injunction to get the strike in South Wales declared unofficial. In view of the judgement of Judge Nicholls, declaring the strike in Yorkshire unofficial, it is not difficult to guess the likely outcome of this case.

New all embracing criminal charges, such as 'besetting', last used in the 1926 General Strike, have been dug up by the police. All that the police have to prove is that the accused was part of a picket line near the place of work of a working miner with the intention of compelling him to stay away from work. People collecting food and money for the miners have been arrested on all kinds of trumped up charges, including begging. Only a few days ago, a 'Santa Claus' collecting gifts for children of striking miners was arrested. Surely it is time for such guardians of morality as Thatcher, Owen, Steel and Kinnock, not to mention the flunky press and media, to say that *"this has gone too far"*, and that *"this has gone beyond the bounds of decency"*. Instead of condemnation of the actions of the police and the class war declared on the NUM and the rest of the working class by the judiciary, we get from the leadership of the TUC and the Labour Party sickening sermons on legality and obeying the law. Just at a time when the courts have launched a frontal attack on the NUM, just as we hear that a certain judge, Mervyn-Jones, has removed Mr Scargill and other officers of the union from the trusteeship of the NUM funds on the alleged ground that these officials are not fit to be trustees and that the union funds are not safe in their hands (the real reason is that by appointing their own trustees the courts want to get the union funds home from abroad and thus jeopardise these funds), these sermons of the Labour leadership are nothing short of a cruel mockery. When the Labour leadership, in the face of this judicial assault, described above, continues mindlessly to preach to the NUM obedience and legality, we have once again the right to ask: on whose side are you, gentlemen?

The Libyan affair

Another example of the TUC and the Labour Party's attempts to sabotage the miners' struggle was the so-called Libyan affair (for details see article in Lalkar, reproduced on page 250 in this book). At the end of October, the NCB was a shambles. MacGregor was being criticised in the bourgeois press for his handling of the strike; the *'Daily Mail'* even went to the length of comparing him with the cartoon character Mr Magoo, and the more serious press called for his removal, with the presentation of a peerage. But the *'Sunday Times'* story about the visit of the Chief Executive of the NUM to Libya came and served to divert attention from what was described by the British Association of Colliery Management as incompetence at the highest level in the NCB. Neil Kinnock and Norman Willis, without even the courtesy of a consultation with the NUM, launched into the fray against the NUM.

"By any measure of political, civil, trade union or human rights, the Gaddafi regime is vile. Any offers from them ... would be an insult to everything the British trade-union movement stands for. If such offers are ever made, then of course they must and will be rejected", said Mr Kinnock

"I have expressed to Mr Scargill my condemnation of the meeting with Col. Gaddafi. This has created the impression that the NUM is prepared to consort with a government which is heavily implicated in terrorist campaigns outside its own borders" said Mr Willis.

Both these gentlemen have little difficulty about maintaining a diplomatic silence about the murders committed by British imperialism in many places, including in the Six Counties.

Both these gentlemen maintain a deafening silence over the connections of British imperialism with the allegedly 'vile' regime of Col. Gaddafi and the fact that last year Britain got £300 million out of this Libyan connection, that is, £300 million more than the NUM got from Libya. Kinnock has gone to the length, disgraceful even by his own standards, of refusing to speak at the 5 major rallies organised by the NUM to rally support for the dispute, on the flimsy excuse that his *"diary is full"*. And yet, having done nothing to support the NUM in this dispute, having on the contrary done everything to sabotage its struggle, Kinnock and Willis want to determine the course of this strike and the way it is run.

TUC - "All possible support short of actual support"

These are the words with which a reactionary like John Craven, writing in the *'Daily Telegraph'* of Wednesday 21 November, aptly summed up the position of the TUC. It is three months since at its Brighton Conference in the first week of September, the TUC resolved to give *"full support"* to the NUM. As expected, that resolution has remained on paper and the TUC, far from helping the NUM, has actually done everything to undermine their fight to save pits, jobs and mining communities. During October the TUC tried to get control over the dispute with a view to imposing an unprincipled compromise on the NUM. It went to the length of negotiating, at the offices of the government conciliation body ACAS, with the pit deputies' union NACODS and the NCB, while the NUM and Scargill were left waiting outside. The TUC put pressure on the pit deputies, if they needed such pressure, to settle their dispute - an act surely calculated to isolate and undermine the NUM and to strengthen the position of the NCB and the government.

On 30 October Jack Eccles, this year's Chairman of the TUC and Assistant General Secretary of GMBATU, who also happens to be one of a team of 'wise men' appointed by the TUC to monitor the miners' dispute, speaking on BBC radio, attributed the continuation of the coal strike to *"the rigidity of our colleagues in the NUM"*. He went on to imply that the NUM were causing job losses in industry by continuing the strike. The other members of this committee are David Basnett, General Secretary of GMBATU and Mr Ray Buckton, leader of the train drivers. This leaves poor old Mr Buckton in a minority of one. What can be expected by way of help for the NUM from a body of 'wise men', two of whose members, belonging to the same union, blame the NUM for the continuation of the dispute? The conduct of the TUC reminds one of the Italian proverb which runs like this: *'God save me from my friends, my enemies I can take care of myself'*. The NUM needs greater protection against such 'friends' from the TUC than it does against its open and avowed enemies.

Instead of removing Mr Eccles from this committee for his blatant anti-NUM statement, this is all that Mr N Willis in characteristic opportunist style could say: *"Mr Eccles is speaking for himself in this matter. He is not speaking for the TUC. I do not share his views"*. The matter should be formulated differently: has Mr Eccles or anyone else, being a member of a TUC committee allegedly set up to help the NUM, the right to *"speak for himself"* and not for the official policy of the TUC? No doubt when Mr Willis attacks the NUM his fellow opportunists on the TUC have no difficulty in excusing him by declaring that Mr Willis *"speaks for himself"*. And so the cosy opportunist clique carry on with their work of sabotaging working-class struggles in the service of British monopoly capitalism.

When the government and the NCB have turned their backs on any honourable settlement with the NUM, when they have repeatedly sabotaged every peace effort and scuttled negotiations, the TUC and Labour leadership, instead of making every effort in support of the NUM, continue to say they *"are convinced that this dispute can be settled by negotiations"* provided there is *'will and determination on both sides to try to find a way through"*. Since it is known to even the most gullible and unintelligent that there is no *'will and determination"* on the other side - i.e., that of the NCB and government - to *"try to find a way"* through negotiation, is it not time for the TUC-Labour leadership to honour their promises of *"full support"* for the NUM - is it not time, in the words of Mr Peter Heathfield, the General Secretary of the NUM, for them to redeem their IOUs?

In the coming weeks, as indicated in the last issue, owing to the fast dwindling of coal stocks, the government will either have to resort to power cuts or move coal from the pit heads to the power stations. Friends of the NUM, every class conscious worker, every trade unionist, must play his part in seeing to it that this coal is not allowed to be moved, and if moved, it will be blacked by the power workers. Every worker must see to it that the call given by Mr Scargill in his Newcastle upon Tyne City Hall speech, in which he asked *"ordinary rank-and-file trade unionists to take industrial action in support of this union* [the NUM]", is positively answered. In addition, efforts must be increased a hundred-fold to render financial support to the miners in the difficult time ahead.

The coal industry is worth saving. It produces coal worth £3.5 billion every year and it buys from the rest of British industry goods worth £1 billion a year. It represents the energy future of this country Even more important, the NUM is worth fighting for. Through the survival and victory of the NUM lies the bright road of survival and victory for the rest of the organised labour movement. For, and this can never be overemphasised, today the NUM alone stands between the total victory of finance capitalism in Britain and the complete emasculation of the trade union and labour movement for a long time to come.

LALKAR February 1985

Hammer blows of the miners' strike hit home: pound collapses

Fight to the finish.

As the February issue of *Lalkar* goes into print the coal strike, nearing the completion of 11 months and due to enter the 12th month on March 6, shows not the slightest sign of ending. We have repeatedly stated that this strike cannot be settled by negotiation in the ordinary way that most strikes are settled under the conditions of capitalism; that whereas on the side of the NCB and the government it is aimed at beating and destroying the NUM as a prelude to beating and destroying the entire organised labour and trade-union movement, on the NUM's side it is aimed at preserving jobs present and future, and whole communities and defending the rights of the entire labour movement against the vicious onslaught of British imperialism launched against it through the present Tory administration of Margaret Thatcher; that, in the final analysis, the NUM's fight for the right to work is a fight against capitalism, for capitalism, with its ever-recurring crisis of overproduction and increasing pauperisation of the proletariat, can never guarantee this right, except during periods of temporary boom, which of late have been characterised by their absence; that any negotiations which settle this strike will do no more than record the victory of one side and the defeat of the other.

Collapse of talks about talks.

It therefore comes to us as no surprise that the latest attempts at talks about talks has collapsed even before it started, for neither side is in a position to concede anything to the other. On Tuesday 29 January, this collapse became inevitable as the NCB, egged on by the government, demanded the acceptance in writing by the NUM that 'uneconomic' pits will have to close as a pre-condition for starting new talks. On Tuesday night the NUM told the NCB in a letter that it was prepared to talk, without preconditions, on new initiatives proposed by Mr Peter Heathfield - the NUM General Secretary - in his talks with Mr Merrik Spanton, board member for personnel. The following evening (30th), the NCB asked for details in writing of initiatives and the NUM countered the same night by proposing an agenda which would include the withdrawal of the NCB plans to cut 4 million tonnes of so-called uneconomic capacity and shut 5 named pits. The NUM letter went on to say that the colliery closures should be considered only in line with the Plan for Coal. It also demanded an amnesty for 500/600 sacked miners. The NCB refused to budge on these reasonable and legitimate demands, which have been the core of the 11-month old coal strike. The 26-man NUM Executive Committee unanimously re-affirmed its opposition to the Board's demand for a prior commitment to cuts in 'uneconomic' capacity.

So outrageous was this demand by the Board that even Mr Peter McNestry, the NACODS general secretary, was forced to say that the NCB's insistence on it would vitiate the agreement reached between his union and the NCB *"if one of the parties - be it NACODS or NUM - had to accept ... closure of uneconomic pits"*.

Government victim of its own propaganda.

It is clear that the government and the NCB, in rejecting negotiations and adopting a bellicose and insolent posture, have become the victims of their own massive campaign of disinformation and deliberate lies. They have been lying for 11 months on every single question that has any bearing - close or remote - on this strike and asserting that the strike is crumbling. Is it, then, to be surprised at that they should take their own lies, as well as the lies of their billionaire friends in Fleet Street and the rest of the media, as a guide to policy decisions? Living in this world of make-believe, they have rejected negotiations with the NUM in the evident belief that the drift back to work will surge and that the NUM Executive should, to use the language of the *Financial Times*, *"be left to sweat it out while the reality - as the Board sees it - that the strike is ending is driven home"*. That this is a cruel self-deception can be seen from the following points, all of which show that the miners are actually winning and that the government's conduct, far from beating the miners, can only cause the utter ruin of its economic strategy, already in tatters.

140,000 on strike

First and foremost, notwithstanding the lying assertions of the government, the NCB and the bourgeois media to the contrary, the truth is that 140,000 NUM members out of a total workforce of 196,000 are still on strike following the Board's multi-million pound post-Xmas propaganda failure and show little sign of returning to work.

£5 billion cost

Secondly, the costs of the strike have soared to beyond the £5 billion mark, i.e. £100 for every man, woman and child in Britain. The electricity industry alone has lost £1.3 billion in extra costs. The cost of extra oil to burn in power stations has risen from £200 million a month in July to £364 million in January. Coal exports have fallen by £23 million a month, and the overall cost to the balance of payments in January was £347 million.

The collapse of the Pound.

Thirdly, the above two factors, though hidden from the public through what the *Miner* of January 17 justly describes as *"perhaps the most massive news blackout ever mounted in peace-time Britain"* and the suppression of information and distortion to a degree which would have made the Nazi propagandists blush - with the sole aim of sapping and lowering the morale of the striking miners - have nevertheless cut through the propaganda fog and have had the desired effect on the decisions of the ruthlessly calculating gentry from the world of international finance capital. The dramatic, even catastrophic, fall of the pound is a real and sober comment - a comment that speaks volumes - on the part of this gentry on the state of the British economy and the effects of the coal strike on it. By this single act of causing the pound's collapse, the international financiers have sent a very loud, if unspoken, message that they have no confidence in the British economy, and in particular in the Thatcher government's strategy.

The government, with pretended virgin innocence, declares that the pound's fall is unrelated to the coal strike. It asserts that the fall of the pound is due to a strong dollar, cut in North Sea oil prices, panicky reaction of the market, in other words, due to any factor except the real one. The truth, however, is that it is the coal strike that is mainly responsible for frustrating the government's economic strategy and the consequent evaporation of international finance confidence and the collapse of the pound. A strong dollar does not explain the fact that the pound has also plummeted in value against other major international currencies by 13% since the start of the strike (its fall against the dollar being 20%). Equally, the cut in the price of oil does not explain the pound's fall, for oil is priced in dollars and therefore a strong dollar means more oil revenue for Britain.

The government has lied about the real reason for the pound's fall, to wit, the coal strike, because such an admission would be a morale booster for the strikers and a devastating blow to its own propaganda and disinformation campaign. Hence its iron curtain on truth and attempts to insulate ordinary people against the bacillus of truth. But facts are facts and no iron curtain can stand in the way of the inexorable, relentless and sober march of mistress Reality. More and more people, even in high places, are beginning to speak the truth.

Former Prime Minister Edward Heath, speaking on Radio 4's *Today* programme on January 15, admitted that the major reason for the pound's fall was the coal strike: "*People abroad*", he said, "are worried about a prolonged miners' strike *which is very damaging*". The ever-widening political divisions within even the Tory party are further reflection of this worry.

The *Financial Times*, that barometer of British finance capital, made the following candid admission it its editorial of Monday January 14: "*Not least, the strike has been damaging to the British economy ... the year 1984 would have been calmer economically* [you bet !!] *if the strike had not taken place. Residual problems will remain even when it is over ... The effects of the strike must be reverberating throughout the economy in lots of ways that have yet to be reported*" ('Challenging Mr Scargill').

Government's economic strategy in ruin.

Fourthly, as a result of the above, the government is under increasing pressure of every type from every direction. It has been forced to sanction a steep rise in interest rates, and as a result the Stock Exchange went on to record the sharpest fall in prices ever seen. By 2 p.m. on Monday 28 January, the Financial Times index had lost 44.1 points. Later it recovered somewhat but still left a net fall of 24. 9 on the day. Through the temporary re-introduction of Minimum Lending Rate - MLR - it has made what for it is the most painful U-turn, which is tantamount to an admission on its part that the whole of its monetarist strategy of letting market forces find their own solutions is now in tatters. Small wonder then that foreign confidence in the government's ability to manage the economy is disappearing as currency speculators and kings of finance flee the country by planeloads with sackfuls of money.

The pound's fall will add approximately £300 million a month to the balance of payments deficit alone. The continued low value of the pound, making imports far more expensive - and necessitating high interest rates to prevent the pound from sliding still further, are bound to give an upward twist to the rate of inflation. When the Thatcher administration came to office in 1979, inflation stood at just over 9%. To bring it down by 4 percentage points, unemployment had to reach 4 million. But if the present economic trends continue, by the time of the next general election we might end up with both 9% inflation and 4 million unemployed. Meanwhile Chancellor Lawson, that rabid reactionary poodle of the City, would have to shelve his plans to cut taxes in the next budget, when he had hoped to give a small gift of between £1-1.5 billion to his friends in the monopoly capitalist fraternity - a fact which is hardly likely to amuse them or endear him to them.

Fifthly, even some very respectable professional people, who cannot be suspected of even a modicum of sympathy for the striking miners, have begun to question the economic justifications for the NCB's pit closure programme. In the January issue of the journal *Accountancy*, hardly an organ of the Bolshevik Party, four eminent professors and lecturers in the field of accountancy from the Manchester Business School, Sheffield and Manchester Universities and UMIST (University of Manchester Institute of Science and Technology) give a shattering blow, albeit in very restrained and professional terminology, to the NCB's economic arguments. As it is not possible for us in the present article to summarise the arguments of these four distinguished professionals we advise everyone to read their article in *Accountancy*. In it they reach the conclusion, on the basis of the NCB's own statistics, as well as those of the Monopolies and Mergers Commission, that:

"Careful scrutiny of NCB accounts produces the conclusion that they fail to form an adequate basis for informed management decisions, since they are almost bound to be misleading in any attempts to identify the changes in expected future cash flows consequent upon particular pit closures. While we are not in a position to identify whether these documents are used for pit closure decisions, the information contained in them IS used in public justification for such decisions.

"The standard accounting statement for pits - the F23 - is, as far as can be ascertained, used as a blueprint for making budgets, projections of pit profit and loss in the future and, more importantly, to justify decision-making, at least in public debate. Its decision-making rationale cannot therefore be ignored, yet for this purpose, as will be shown, the F23 is fundamentally flawed".

More and more people are beginning to see through the NCB's and the government's phony economic justifications, they are beginning to realise that more than anything else what is at stake in this strike is the government's political motivation to smash the NUM and thereafter the entire organised labour and trade-union movement. The NCB's latest insolent rejection of talks with the NUM will only serve to enlighten ordinary workers still further and strengthen their resolve to help the striking miners. The unanimous re-affirmation by the Executive Committee of the NUM of its opposition to the board's insolent demands is a reflection of this realisation and anger felt by many working people at the tactics of the Board.

Sixthly, although Fleet Street newspapers and radio and TV stations are deleting all references to power reductions and cuts with the aim of depriving the miners of major morale-boosting news of this kind, CEGB officials have admitted that some power stations in the South-East, notably Littlebrook in Kent, and Calshot in Hampshire, are being "*run to destruction*" and notices in government offices are urging power economies right down "*to minimising use of kettles*". Cuts in power supply have been reported as far afield as Stafford, Stockport, Nottinghamshire, Essex, North and East London, Welwyn Garden City and North Kent. The oil burnt in the South East is 40 times the pre-strike level; no coal is moving; and in Yorkshire the electricity board has been reduced to using the sweepings of reduced coal dumps accumulated in preparation for the strike.

Miners bound to win.

In the light of the foregoing, the picture that emerges is diametrically the opposite of that painted by the government, the NCB and the bourgeois media. While the government is under increasing pressure - economic and political - and its difficulties increase by the hour, the NUM and the striking miners stand proudly unbowed, ready to make every sacrifice in defence of the right to work; while the government is in the process of being deserted by its friends from the money bags fraternity, the NUM gain daily increasing support nationally and internationally; while time is against the Thatcher government, it is running in favour of the NUM. Time will teach a bitter lesson to those Jeremiahs of doom ranging from the bourgeois press to the false friends from the Labour Party-TUC leadership who had begun to pronounce the final rites on the NUM and had begun to chortle about getting rid of the NUM militants and even Scargill. The NUM is bound to win, despite the treacherous leadership of the Willis-Kinnock clique. With this sure knowledge let every class-conscious worker, let every trade unionist, let every progressive and every genuine socialist, let every decent man, woman and child commit himself or herself to working tirelessly for a magnificent victory of the NUM and the working class and an ignominious defeat for the arrogant, heartless, cruel representatives of British billionaires, to wit, the Thatcher government.

The miners have withstood physical and mental violence, they have weathered the onslaughts of psychological warfare, they have resisted the temptation of bribery, they have successfully overcome the torments of hunger, they have stood firm in the face of calumnious lies, malicious libel and vile propaganda of hatred. They are the true heroes of the working class and worthy successors of the Tolpuddle martyrs and countless other glorious sons of the British and international proletariat.

The NUM cause is as noble as it is just. It shall be victorious.

MOBILISE:
(1) For the TUC's Day of Action for the Miners on February 11.
(2) For the National Demonstration in support of the Miners of February 24.

LALKAR March 1985

NUM calls off the coal strike on a defiant note

As we were going to press, the news arrived that the NUM Delegate Conference, meeting at the TUC Headquarters in London on Sunday 3rd March had voted, by the narrowest of majorities (98 to 91), to call off the strike and to arrange for an organised return to work on Tuesday 5th March, a year almost to the day after the strike began. In the circumstances. we had to consign to the dustbin the article on the coal strike that would otherwise have appeared on the front page on the anniversary of this, the most heroic of the great industrial battles in the annals of the history of the British proletariat.

This is how Mr Scargill announced the back-to-work decision from the steps of the TUC Headquarters to waiting miners:

"Following the decision of today's Conference taken by the very narrowest of margins, there will be an organised and disciplined return to work on Tuesday".

Understandably the announcement was greeted by cries of "Judas" and "Traitor, you have sold us out". Mr Scargill, who had been in favour of the continuation of the strike, replied: *"I can only come out here and reflect the decision of the Conference, which was taken democratically".*

Mr Scargill, defiant and dignified even in the midst of such difficult circumstances, refusing to concede that the NUM had been defeated, went on to say: *"This dispute will go on until we stop pit closures, stop job losses and win the right to return to work for all those dismissed".*

Dismissing suggestions that he might consider quitting as NUM President, Mr Scargill said: *"I feel terrific. My only immediate plans are to get some fish and chips - if that is all right with the Queen".*

Went on the NUM President: *"Not only has the Coal Board's threat to close five pits been withdrawn but the proposed closures for the last year have not been implemented".* This was the plan announced on March 6th last year, to cut coal capacity by 4 million tonnes with the closure of 20 pits and the loss of 20,000 mining jobs in 12 months.

At a press conference inside, Mr Scargill blamed the end of the strike on the failure "*with a few exceptions*" of other unions to back the miners. The major reason for the return to work, said the NUM President, was "that the trade union movement *in Britain, with a few notable exceptions have left this union isolated.*

"They have not carried out TUC *Congress decisions, to their eternal shame.*

"*We faced not an employer, but a Government aided and abetted by the judiciary, the police and you people in the media. At the end of this time our people have suffered tremendous hardship*".

Added Mr Scargill: "*We will continue to fight pit closures and job losses - and make no mistake, don't underestimate this union's ability to fight pit closures and job losses.*

"*This union will continue to fight, and if that means we have to consider taking action again, then we shall do so*".

Earlier, addressing the miners waiting outside the TUC Headquarters, Mr Scargill said: "*I want to thank you from the bottom of my heart for the magnificent support you have given*",

Thus came to an end this most bitterly fought dispute. For an analysis of the coal strike, the reasons for its outbreak and for its failure to achieve the aims it surely was so capable of, its gains and lessons, see the front-page article entitled The British Coal Strike, 1984-85[1].

---

1   The next article produced in the present book.

LALKAR March 1985

The British Coal Strike 1984-5

As reported elsewhere in this issue, the NUM has called off the coal strike and decided to arrange an organised and dignified return to work without signing any agreement with the Coal Board on pit closures or on the question of amnesty for the 718 miners vindictively sacked by the NCB during the strike on all kinds of trumped up charges. While calling off the strike, the NUM has promised to continue the struggle. Only time will tell how this struggle develops but for the moment one may be pardoned for saying that the dispute has gone underground. The time has, therefore, come to review the whole course of this, the most historic of the industrial battles ever fought by the British proletariat, to look at the causes that precipitated it, the reasons for its failure to achieve the kind of magnificent and historic victory that it was surely capable of scoring, as well as the lessons and gains of this strike.

Reasons for the strike

From its very inception we have consistently maintained that the coal strike was forced on the NUM by the NCB and the government with the aim, openly expressed, of defeating the miners at any cost, for only the miners stood in the way of the government and the entire bourgeoisie in achieving complete victory and in depressing still further the condition of the British working class.

We insisted throughout that the strike had to be seen in the context of the worst economic depression since the 1930s, which with its officially admitted (much more as a matter of fact) 3.25 million unemployed and the consequent emasculation of the thoroughly economist and utterly rotten leadership of the TUC, had produced, albeit temporarily, a state of demoralisation in the working class. Such was the impotence of the TUC that not only had it consistently failed to mobilise the working class against unemployment and the government's anti-working class and anti-trade union legislation, but also against union bashing at the Cheltenham GCHQ, the government's intelligence gathering centre. This left only the miners, with their long and legendary tradition of determined struggle and class solidarity, in the way of the government.

We have continued to stress that British monopoly capitalism, in order to be successful in the game of international competition for markets, is obliged to bring down the cost of production, shed jobs, restructure industry and increase the productivity of labour. In other words, it is obliged to cheapen the cost of labour power or depress wages and, consequently, the standard of living of the British working class. Thus it was clear from the outset that the stakes were extremely high and the bourgeoisie was not going to give up the struggle easily, and that, therefore, the coal strike could by no means be regarded merely as one of the skirmishes of the ordinary type, which are the never-ending characteristic of the capitalist mode of production.

The above facts were recognised by all the representative spokesmen, by all officialdom, by the governmental and other agencies. Chancellor Lawson considered and said so in Parliament, that all the money spent on defeating the NUM was a good investment for this "nation", i.e., for British monopoly capitalism. Mrs Thatcher compared the NUM President, Mr Scargill, to the erstwhile dictator of Argentina, to wit, the fascist General Galtieri and characterised the miners as "the enemy within", who had to be defeated. The entire bourgeois media - Fleet Street, radio and TV networks with one voice said the same thing.

Now that the strike is over, *"the government will draw two main lessons: first, that it can press ahead with the closure of uneconomic pits ..., and second the balance of industrial power has been shifted, so that further changes can be introduced to remove rigidities in the labour market* [i.e., break down the resistance of the working class]" So writes Mr Peter Riddall, Political Editor of the *Financial Times* on March 4th, the morrow after the ending of the strike, adding *"... if the miners, the traditional vanguard of the labour movement, fail, who else can succeed? "*

The above then were the reasons for this momentous and historic strike. And the miners had but little option other than to accept the challenge so insolently thrown at them by the Conservatives.

Heroic struggle of the NUM

It must be said at the beginning that in no way can the leadership of the NUM, in particular its three chief functionaries - Mr Scargill, his Vice President Mr McGahey and the General Secretary Mr Peter Heathfield - be blamed for the failure of the strike. The NUM leadership gave a superb account of itself and, against such heavy odds and faced by such hostility on the part of the bourgeois press and other media of disinformation, distortion and lies, moved heaven and earth to mobilise the membership, the overwhelming majority of whom literally performed miracles. The leadership of the NUM and the strikers suffered for a whole year a most scurrilous campaign of distortion, hatred and calumnious propaganda directed against them; they braved for a whole year police brutality on the picket line and a most oppressive denial of civil liberties on and off picket duty; they bore with fortitude the pangs of hunger and starvation imposed by a cruel government which even denied them and their families their social security entitlements; they stood firm in the face of the most vicious judicial onslaught on the working people of this country since the General Strike of 1926. For all the failures of this strike, the NUM leadership and the striking miners emerge as the real heroes and real victors of this struggle, for they have shown by their example of self-sacrificing heroism, commitment to principle, their adherence to the interests of their class - the working class - their perseverance in struggle, what working people are capable of achieving once they make up their mind to stand up and fight. *Lalkar* and the Indian Workers' Association (GB) salute the NUM leadership and the striking miners for the latter's singular contribution to development of the class struggle of the British working class. Their example shall continue to serve for a long time both as a source of inspiration and hope to the working people of this country and elsewhere.

The treacherous role of the TUC/Labour Party

If the NUM leadership are not to blame for this failure, who then is to blame? The blame lies fairly and squarely at the doorstep of the leadership of the TUC and the so-called Labour Party. From the first day of the strike the role of this pusillanimous, impotent, castrated and, above all, treacherous, leadership has been to work overtime to defeat the NUM. At best it dissociated itself from the strike, and at worst, especially at crucial junctures, it openly joined the NCB, the government and the media in denouncing the strikers. Because of the groundswell of rank and file, if unorganised, support for the NUM, the TUC and the Labour leadership had to pay lip service to supporting the NUM and pass Congress/Conference motions promising *"full support"* for the miners, but actually doing nothing to mobilise industrial action in support of the NUM. Nay, more than that, frustrating any attempts to do so. The members of the TUC Liaison Committee, set up to monitor and help the NUM, actually publicly blamed the NUM for the continuation of the strike. While the police were literally bleeding the miners on picket duty to death and launching cavalry charges on them wielding batons, Messrs Willis, Kinnock and Hattersley denounced the miners for violence! Hattersley, far from denouncing the Tory party and its chieftains for organising picket violence through the police, for turning picket lines into battle grounds for hunting down workers on strike, actually went to the shameful length of greeting Mr John Wakeham, the Conservative Chief Whip, on the latter's return from hospital after the Brighton bombing to the House of Commons as a *"triumph of democracy over terrorism"*! Instead of defending the right of the NUM to accept financial and other help from workers and trade unions all over the world, Messrs Willis and Kinnock sang the so-called 'Libyan Connection' song in a thousand refrains. Even after the calling off of the strike, when the question of amnesty for 718 miners sacked by the NCB has become so important, and when the NCB and the government have so insolently rejected the very idea of such an amnesty, this windbag Kinnock, this opportunist and anti-working class leader of the opportunist, rotten and anti-working class 'Labour' Party, has, as required by his masters, the British bourgeoisie, come out against any amnesty for those who *"committed serious crimes of violence"*. These are the kind of leaders of the working class who, to use the apt terminology of Joseph Stalin, *"are dazzled by the glamour of capitalism, who are overwhelmed by the might of capital and who dream of 'getting on in the world' and associating with 'men of substance'"* They have nothing in common with the mass of the workers, whom they do not understand, do not represent, and on whom they have turned their backs, becoming ever more closely identified with the bourgeoisie in their manner of life and station. Engels correctly called such leaders bourgeoisified leaders of the working class.

At a time when the bourgeoisie had mobilised all its authority, from the Queen to the shabbiest police constable, when it had invoked the authority of the judiciary and the police, when it had unleashed through Fleet Street, the BBC, ITV and the various radio stations, a systematic campaign of lies, distortion, disinformation and suppression of truth, the TUC/Labour leadership not only left the miners isolated and undefended, but even joined their enemies in the latter's campaign of vilification of the NUM. If the TUC/Labour leadership had put one-tenth of the effort into mobilising support for the miners that it put into its repeated and treacherous attempts at *"getting a negotiated settlement"*, the NUM would have been victorious. This coterie, rotten to the core, is even more frightened than the bourgeoisie itself of a working class victory, for the positions, the manner of life and the mode of existence of this clique of bourgeoisified leaders are inextricably intertwined with the very life and existence of imperialism.

Lessons

The foremost lesson that the British proletariat must learn from this heroic coal strike is to get rid of these opportunist and bourgeoisified leaders and replace them with the real leaders of the working class, leaders who not only come from the ranks of the working class but also truly represent the real interests of that class.

Party of the proletariat

Secondly, the British proletariat must learn to recognise the Labour Party for the opportunist outfit that it really is, which exists for the bourgeois corruption of the working class in the interests of the bourgeoisie and the upper stratum of the working class - the labour aristocracy; the British proletariat must recognise the truth that the Labour Party is a deadly agent of the bourgeoisie in the ranks of the working class. It must, therefore, replace that party with its own party of the proletariat which, while being indissolubly connected with the working class, will act as its vanguard, defending the true interests of the proletariat through thick and thin. Had such a party, with prestige and connections among British workers, existed, the course, and the end product, of this strike would have been different. For such a party would have ensured that workers at power stations and elsewhere came to the support of the miners, that the miners were not left alone to slog it out. The creation of such a vanguard party of the proletariat, a revolutionary, a truly Communist party, is one of the most urgent tasks facing the British working class, who for the moment have no one to turn to except any of the hundred varieties of the various equally opportunist downright reactionary and counter-revolutionary Trotskyist groupings or the revisionist CPGB at present busily tearing itself apart on the issue of whether it should be more broad or less, whether it should unite with the likes of Benn or the leadership of the SDP/Liberal Alliance in broad coalition against the Tories.

The bourgeois essence of the state

Thirdly, the course and the outcome of the coal strike cannot but convince the British working class that Parliament, the courts, the police, the Queen and other attributes of bourgeois rule are nothing but a shield of the capitalist class against the proletariat. The strike has torn the mask of a fetish and inviolable shrine from parliament, the judiciary and the police alike. The workers from now on cannot but look upon the police as uniformed and paid thugs of the bourgeoisie rather than, as was hitherto all too common, as protectors of our lives and civil liberties. They cannot but look upon the judges as the most prejudiced, biased and anti-working class poodles of monopoly capitalism rather than as impartial arbiters of disputes; they cannot but look upon parliament as an instrument of bourgeois rule, rather than as a representative institution of the working masses. The workers are bound to realise that they too need to create their own institutions as a weapon against the bourgeoisie. The learning of these lessons will, we think, be one of the most important achievements of the British working class.

Fourthly, the British working class cannot but convince itself from the experience of the strike that without political power, without removing the power of capital, it cannot solve its problems. Therefore in their difficult struggle against organised capital, the basic question is that of power, and until it is settled, it is impossible to solve either the crisis in the coal industry or the crisis in the rest of British industry. For capitalism has no solution other than unemployment, misery, degradation and war.

The bourgeoisie has its own solutions - solutions which suit its class interests. The working class, too, must have its own solutions - solutions which accord with its class interests. Turning logic and facts on their head, but in strict adherence to its class interests and the logic of class struggle, the *Daily Mail* in its editorial of 4 March, pours forth thus:

"The cost has been grisly. Billions of pounds that could have been spent on bringing hope to the unemployed have had to be invested in fighting the strike. The pound has been hit, economic recovery retarded; the scope for tax cuts in the coming Budget severely limited. But the price of allowing Arthur Scargill to claim victory would have been so profoundly grievous as to transcend all the hardship and expense of the past twelve months. The half-brick would have been worth more than the ballot box. Contempt for the law would have been seen to pay a sinister dividend. Class war would have yielded a brutal return.

"The ballot box will not be mocked."

The fact of the matter is that the money spent on defeating the coal strike would not have been spent on bringing hope to the unemployed any more than money spent during the Falklands War would have been spent on bringing hope to the unemployed. One of the reasons that the British bourgeoisie and its political committee, namely, the government, fought the coal strike with a zeal and a determination worthy of a better cause was that the NUM had dared to raise their voice and struggle against unemployment. The ruling class has been willing and able to spend more money in order to have unchallenged power to make working people redundant than was needed to keep the pits open. Nor can it be otherwise in the conditions of capitalism for the latter is inseparable from the crises of overproduction and the consequent misery inflicted thereby on countless millions at home and abroad. So, in essence, both the sides were fighting as it were a class war, the bourgeoisie to maintain the unchallenged sway of capitalist conditions and mode of production and the NUM for the right to work which cannot be guaranteed under the conditions of capitalism except for comparatively small and exceptional periods. The only difference was that the British ruling class was fully conscious and clear about the issues at stake, whereas the same cannot be said for the working class side of this equation, in particular of the TUC/Labour leadership, who shudder at the mere thought of transcending the bounds of bourgeois legality, let alone bourgeois rule, who throughout the strike preached respect for legality to the coal strikers while the other side and its machinery and forces of law enforcement made and broke laws with abandon. Thus, contempt for the law has been seen to "*pay a sinister dividend*" and class war has "*yielded a brutal return*" for the bourgeoisie.

The British working class cannot but be convinced by this experience not to shun class war, but wage it with the vigour, determination and ruthlessness with which it has been waged against it by the bourgeoisie. Let the bourgeoisie be our teacher in the school of class war.

Fifthly, the British working class cannot but realise now that the miners are the advanced detachment of the British working class and that theirs is an example that the working class must follow in its struggle. Just at a time when the entire bourgeoisie are demanding the head of Mr Scargill, working people everywhere, in particular in the NUM, must rally round their leadership, they must understand that the chorus of abuse hurled by the ruling class and their lickspittles in the trade-union and labour movement is only indicative of the admiration, if full of hatred, of the bourgeoisie for the NUM leadership's brilliant leadership of the strike. For, in the immortal words of the great Russian poet, Nekrasov,

> "*I hear the voice of approbation,
> Not in the dulcet sounds of praise,
> But in the roar of irritation*".

The bourgeoisie are abusing the NUM leadership because the latter have hit hard and hurt the former. This is praise indeed for the NUM. Now that the strike is over, the truth about the costs of the strike, which stand close to £7 billion, is suddenly beginning to ooze out even from the whores of Fleet Street and the rest of the media (see 'Facts and Figures' at end of this article).

The workers should place the blame where it belongs - at the door of the TUC-Labour leadership. The working class cannot be defeated except by itself. The NUM have not been defeated by the Tories, they have been betrayed and left isolated by the Labour Party and the TUC, who have refused to carry out the resolutions of the TUC Congress and done everything possible to frustrate and sabotage the NUM struggle. The Murrays, the Chapples, the Basnetts, the Willises, the Kinnocks and suchlike scum have, true to form, proved to be the true labour lieutenants of British imperialism. The *Daily Mail* correctly addressed the Prime Minister thus: "Margaret Thatcher *should not forget that it was trade unionists themselves who played a decisive role in worsting Scargill.*" Sure they did.

Then there is the role of the Notts miners, who from day one of the strike acted as scabs and even went to the despicable length of having their own union's funds sequestrated. The names of Foulstone, Butcher and such other despicable creatures will be a matter for eternal derision in working-class circles. Those who have crossed the NUM picket lines, be they miners or lorry drivers, will live to regret it, for shortly it will be their turn to be picked on. By not helping the miners, they have only been strengthening their enemies against themselves.

Sixthly, in sustaining the strike, a memorable role has been played by working class women, in particular by miners' wives and girlfriends. During the course of the strike they, through hard work, adversity and ingenuity, created an alternative welfare system and a collectivist attitude which even the bourgeois journalists admit and fear, will not be easily displaced. If this strike made Scargill, Heathfield and McGahey into working class heroes, it no less made heroines of Betty Heathfield, Ann Scargill and countless other working class brave women. The mobilisation of women, their equal participation in struggle, their equality, are indispensable to the advance of the working class. And it is one of the great achievements of this strike that it brought to the fore the working women of this country, not at the behest and in defence of the interests of the bourgeoisie, as was the case during the two world wars, but at the behest and in defence of the interests of the proletariat. The working class of this country cannot but be convinced by the experience of this strike of the need to fight for the equality of women, not in the bourgeois feminist fashion, but in the true spirit of scientific socialism.

Let the most eloquent tribute of International Working Women's Day this year be for the heroism displayed by the women from the mining communities during the strike, and let tribute be paid to them every year hence as it is to other important heroines of the working class movement.

Seventhly, during the course of the strike the black proletarians of Britain have played an outstanding role, a role that has won the recognition and admiration of the NUM and other best sections of the labour movement, in supporting this strike. It has brought the two closer. It has endowed a feeling of fellowship and engendered comradely sentiments between them, for the strikers came to realise that what mattered in the arena of class struggle was less one's skin colour but more one's class position. If this point was not driven home by the Grunwick and Stockport Messenger struggles, it certainly is the merit of the present strike to have done so. The strike also brought home the truth about police brutality and victimisation of black workers. The police behaviour at picket lines brought to the British workers what the black, Irish and other oppressed minorities have had to face for decades. The British working class cannot but convince itself, in the light of this strike, that black workers are their friends and comrades in struggle, who in turn must be supported in their struggle against racialism, discrimination and racialist and fascist violence.

Finally, a most dirty and vicious role was played during the strike by the bourgeois media. The working class cannot but be convinced of the need now to distrust every word in this media and to create its alternative sources of information and propaganda. It must also use its power in the printing industry to stop the publication of anti-working class filth in the bourgeois press. One of the merits, and gains, of the NUM strike has been the successful attempts on a number of occasions by print workers to force the owners either to forgo the publication of some scurrilous article aimed against the NUM, or to secure the right of reply for the NUM. This is a lesson, and an achievement, that the working class cannot but desire to build on.

The above, then, are the chief lessons and gains of the NUM strike, which everyone in the working-class movement must tirelessly work to learn, gain from and build on in the impending and future struggles of the working class in its march towards its social emancipation. But the most important lesson the working class must learn is to value the role of the necessity for waging an uncompromising and ruthless class struggle against the rule of capital. In this context it must develop a spirit of uncompromising intolerance towards all bourgeois agents in the working class and must systematically expel and boot them out. Unless it does that, it will no more see victory than it will see its own ears.

LALKAR March 1985   **Facts and Figures**

The longest major strike in British history was triggered on March 1 1984 when the National Coal Board announced it wanted to close Cortonwood Colliery, Yorkshire. Five days later the Yorkshire NUM called an indefinite strike.

* Most reliable estimates put the cost of the strike at between £2bn. and £3bn. Increased use of oil cost the electricity industry £1.2bn. The coal industry's losses have increased by about £1bn.

* 61 coal faces have been lost as a result of lack of maintenance or water damage.

* The number on strike hit a peak of 150,000 in the early days (out of a possible 195,000 NUM members). Last week 96,000 (52 per cent) were at work. Miners have lost an average of £9,000 each.

* Three men died as a direct result of the strike, at least two suicides appear to be connected with it.

* Coal stocks, 23m. tonnes 1st March, are now about 12.5m tonnes. Imports increased from 5.2m tonnes in 1983 to 10m tonnes last year.

* Stockbrokers Phillips & Drew estimate that the balance of trade figures were hit to the tune of £2.5 bn; GNP over the past 12 months would have grown by 3.4 per cent, did grow 2.3 per cent; industrial production would have grown by 3.5 was 0.5; wage rises would have grown by 7.7 per cent, did grow by 6.8 per cent.

* 9,778 arrests were made during the dispute: 7,785 people have been charged and 149 custodial sentences imposed.

These figures are taken from the *Financial Times* of 4 March and, as far as the costs of the strike are concerned, represent a gross under-estimation. The actual costs of the strike are close to £7 billion, spoken of by the NUM President, Mr Scargill. Also, these figures are silent on the effect of the strike on the international value of sterling. They are equally silent on the continuing cost to taxpayers of around £250 million a year in extra debt servicing, which is the equivalent of 1% on corporation tax, or a rise of 1% on all income tax allowances and thresholds. But surely, if slowly, the truth, so long hidden from the public, will ooze out.

LALKAR August/September 1985

Scabs out to form a bosses' union

The course of the year-long historic coal strike and the conduct of the scabs from the Notts coalfields during the strike, clearly indicated that the Notts scab leaders were out to form a break-away union, which would be in the pocket of the National Coal Board (NCB) and the Thatcher administration. During the strike, the Notts area not only refused to join the strike, but was also instrumental in taking every legal and extra-legal action in an effort to smash the NUM as the finest and most advanced detachment of the British working class. Now, four months after the end of the strike, the Notts scabs have declared that they are forming a break-away union. Although in view of the behaviour of the Notts area, the split was almost inevitable, the occasion for the split was the decision by the NUM Conference to dismiss Roy Link and David Prendergast, the Notts area scab leaders, and the adoption of rule changes giving the NUM Executive Committee greater powers over individual areas. The decision of the scab leaders to form a bosses' union, of the type set up in 1926 by the Labour MP George Spencer, has been endorsed by the Notts delegates by a majority of 228 to 20.

This split has come about, not because of the tactics of the Scargill leadership before, during and after the strike, as is being presented by the entire bourgeois media, the shameless Labour Party leadership and the Euro-Communists of the Communist Party of Great Britain (CPGB), but because of a consistent and determined attempt by the Notts scabs (supported by the NCB, the Government and the entire bourgeois class) to destroy the NUM. Nor will this split necessarily weaken the NUM, as is being maintained by the detractors of Scargill. For what on earth is the point of having scabs in the Union who merely use their membership of it to destroy the Union from within and who, far from giving any strength to the Union, only undermine and sap its foundations? There are those who have maintained that concessions should have been made to the scabs in order to avoid a split and to preserve unity. Such people fail to realise, however, that "*one can go to pieces through unity*" to use Engels' apt expression. Unity with the scabs can only be a recipe for self-destruction.

In the present circumstances, when the entire working-class movement is experiencing divisions, splits of the kind taking place in the NUM are inevitable and can only lead to the freeing of the trade unions from the stranglehold of the opportunist scabs who are like millstones round the neck of militant and fighting trade unionism. And it is the need of the hour to strengthen the fighting ability of the NUM, now that the NCB, yet again confirming everything that Scargill has ever said on this score, is poised to produce a new 'Plan for Coal' with the aim of cutting capacity by 30 million tonnes over the coming four years by closing what the NCB calls 'uneconomic' pits. The result could be the loss of 50 pits and 50,000 jobs in addition to the 25,000 already lost. Most of these job losses will have to be borne by South Wales, Scotland, Kent and the North East. The Coal Industry Bill gives the industry two years to make a profit as prelude to its privatisation, which, since the ending of the coal strike is discussed more and more openly and daringly in the editorial columns of the serious bourgeois press, though during the strike there was all-pervading deadly hush and deafening silence on this question.

The NCB and the Government will have their way unless the NUM can resist these closures. Scargill knows this fact more than anybody else. That is why, at the NUM Conference, he called for industrial action over the issue of wages as well as closures. But such is the apostasy of the Labour leadership that Kinnock, in the run-up to the Brecon and Radnor by-election, characterised Scargill's call as a 'fantasy'. And when Tony Benn, supported by a mere 37 Labour MPs, introduced in Parliament an Amnesty Bill pardoning convicted miners, not wishing to lag behind the Tory Home Secretary, Brittan, who characterised the Bill as enshrining "*the morality of the terrorist and the revolutionary*", Kinnock too launched a virulent attack on it:

"*This Bill cannot be taken seriously by anyone. I cannot even imagine that it was drafted with any serious purpose*". Kinnock and his acolytes in the Labour Party and the TUC shun the question of convicted miners as a thief shuns the place where he has committed a crime. They want to forget all about it since, in their perception, the issue is an electoral liability and stands in the way of Mr Kinnock getting the tenancy of 10 Downing Street by Labour being returned to office. It was with people like Kinnock and his supporters in the trade-union movement, including in the NUM, in mind that Arthur Scargill said:

"We are involved in a class war *and any attempt to deny that flies in the face of reality. Confronted by our enemies' mobilisation, we are entitled, indeed obliged, to call upon our class for massive support"*. And again it was with the same critics from the whining fraternity in mind, that Scargill, at the recent Yorkshire Miners' Gala, drove some important lessons of the strike home. Denying that the miners had been defeated, Mr Scargill went on to say:

"*Let no one talk to me about defeat in the course of the miners' strike.*

"*Those who talk about defeat don't understand the nature of class war.*"

He said that in 1973 the people of Viet Nam had suffered a setback, yet only two years later they stormed Saigon, adding that in Cuba the setback of 1956 had become the victory of 1959. "These weren't defeats, these were steps on the way to victory and that's what the miners' strike of 1984-85 *was*," said Scargill.

Summarising the lessons of the strike, the NUM leader said that the greatest victory was "*the struggle itself. People became conscious, began to understand for the first time in their lives that there is something wrong with a world which spends billions on death and the arms race, while it can't provide the money to save kids from starving in Ethiopia*".

Notwithstanding the attempts of Kinnock, Willis and their supporters in the NUM to attack and isolate Scargill, a large number of miners have bitter and fresh memories of Kinnock's treachery during the coal strike. That is why at the Durham Miners' Gala on 13th July, he was heckled and many miners staged a walkout as he began speaking. Only a determined struggle against revolting opportunists in the NUM who, with the desire of covering up for Kinnock, attack Scargill, can ensure the emergence of a healthy and vigorous NUM. Only such a resolute struggle can ensure that the breakaway scab outfit of Messrs Link and Prendergast gets the support of no more than half of the Notts miners when they hold the ballot on this issue in the coming months.

Lalkar August/September 1990

Hands off Arthur Scargill and Peter Heathfield

A scurrilous and vindictive assault has been launched against Arthur Scargill, the President of the National Union of Mineworkers, and Peter Heathfield its General Secretary. Scargill and Heathfield had succeeded in putting considerable amounts of union funds beyond the reach of sequestrators who had been appointed at the height of the miners' strike to seize the union's assets with a view to crippling the strike. In this way, by preserving union funds for the purposes for which they were intended, Scargill and Heathfield succeeded in 'cheating' the bourgeoisie of its 'legitimate' prey. Determined that these devices should not be used by other unions to protect their funds, nor by the NUM ever again, a great hue and cry has been raised in the bourgeois press about Scargill and Heathfield 'abusing' union funds.

The assault has been carefully planned and is designed to advance simultaneously on various fronts:

1. **The legal front:** to keep assets out of the hands of sequestrators it is necessary to ensure that these funds cannot be identified as belonging to the union. The NUM has been panicked into bringing court actions to establish that funds held by the International Miners' Organisation (IMO) do in fact "belong" to the NUM, even though not held in their name. For the NUM to bring such an action is the crassest stupidity, which we can only assume was prompted by sheer funk on the part of other National Executive members of the NUM, afraid that they would be held personally responsible for "cheating" the bourgeoisie if they did not endorse the action. If it succeeds it will mean that if at any future date the NUM tries to take militant strike action and sequestrators are again appointed to seize its funds, then the funds held on their behalf by the IMO will also be seized.

2. **Undermining workers' trust of each other and of their leadership:** All devices that seek to avoid some kind of penalty or liability by disclaiming ownership of property or funds while nevertheless taking benefit from them depend on being able to entrust this property or these funds to a third party who -

while being the legal owner - can absolutely be trusted to use the assets only for the purpose for which they are intended. Arthur Scargill and Peter Heathfield have always, quite rightly - and much to the fury of the bourgeois class - enjoyed the reputation of being sea-green incorruptibles. By attempting to besmirch this reputation, what the bourgeoisie is actually trying to do is to prevent workers trusting each other, or their leaders, enough to permit them to set up such devices. By forcing working-class leaders to account to the workers for every penny that has gone through their hands, means, in the current conditions of attack on the ability of the working class to organise to promote its own interests, accounting to the bourgeoisie. If workers are not prepared to trust Arthur Scargill and Peter Heathfield there is nobody that they could trust. Hence they could never hide union assets from sequestrators appointed by the bourgeoisie.

3. Terror tactics: The bourgeoisie are out to destroy Arthur Scargill personally. The purpose of this is to let the working class know who is boss and what they can expect if they show any defiance in the face of the capitalist attacks on their livelihoods. By making an example of Arthur Scargill, who most personifies all the characteristics needed for effective union leadership, the bourgeoisie hopes to frighten off those who might otherwise follow in his footsteps. As can be seen, these terror tactics have already reduced most of the NUM executive to a quivering mass of jelly. It is to be hoped that mineworkers as a whole will prove to be made of sterner stuff and perhaps be able to convince their 'leadership' of the need to show stamina and guts. That this is something the bourgeoisie, at least, understands is demonstrated by the *Guardian* of 12 July 1990, where Keith Harper, in an article entitled *Putting Arthur to the Sword* writes:

"*Norman Willis, David Blunkett and the combined political and industrial might of Labour's establishment are doing their best to unseat him* [Scargill], *but his survival remains in the hands of the membership. His own area, Yorkshire, holds the key. Numerically, it is more than a third of the NUM's size. ... To be sure of unseating him, his numerous critics within the union would have to rely on Yorkshire acting the Brutus to Mr Scargill's Caesar.*"

Judging by Arthur Scargill's reception at the Durham Miners' Gala last week, there is every hope that the masses of ordinary mineworkers are still willing to stand and fight with him and for him till the death if necessary, as even the *Guardian* acknowledges when it writes: "*Incredibly, Mr Scargill is still the union, broken and beaten though it is. His executive colleagues mur-*

mur but they do not strike out, and the Conference in Durham has not raised one finger in anger against him." The reason Arthur Scargill is supported by ordinary miners is that they are not yet as broken or as beaten as the *Guardian* thinks they ought to be, and they defend Arthur Scargill because they know that in doing so they are fighting not for Arthur Scargill as an individual, or for Peter Heathfield as an individual, but for themselves as workers, for their right to organise to resist the onslaught of capital, for their right to fight back, for their right to have leaders who are fighters too.

Again the *Guardian* article referred to above is remarkably frank on the issue:

"Coal is aching for a period of industrial stability, and the likely arrival of a new chairman to replace Lord Haslam next January would allow it and the miners to start with a clean sheet.

"Lord Haslam's successor would be assured of a better start with a new NUM leader than with an old class warrior like Mr Scargill, who is still itching to lead his tattered troops over the trenches on issues like privatisation and pay ...

"The departure of Mr Scargill would certainly lead to an easier relationship between British Coal and its workforce ... "

When and if all the working class can muster is leaders of the Norman Willis and David Blunkett ilk, then the *Guardian* truly will be able to say that the unions are *"broken and beaten"*, for nobody could accuse these congenital capitulators of itching to lead troops over the trenches, but that time is not yet here. What sort of working class leaders are they that would write to Arthur Scargill, as did Norman Willis, demanding reassurance that the NUM had received no money from Libya? Who but the imperialist bourgeoisie has any quarrel with Libya that is sufficiently serious to warrant not accepting money from Libyan workers? The British imperialist bourgeoisie that DOES have a major quarrel with the Libyan government nevertheless continues to maintain trade worth several hundred million pounds a year with Libya, but British workers are supposed to boycott any cash that any Libyan hand has touched! It is self evident that all Norman Willis is interested in is collaborating with the British bourgeoisie to cripple militant unionism. Norman Willis tries to prevent the NUM accepting funds, and the courts confiscate such funds as it has accumulated. Such are the 'working-class' leaders that the British bourgeoisie thinks the working class should have. Further comment is unnecessary.

Another reason for Norman Willis and others of his ilk to join in the hue and cry against Arthur Scargill is to ensure they sabotage his chances of securing nomination as Labour Party candidate for the Barnsley constituency at the next general election. This is why the Labour and TUC leadership are united, through a combination of innuendo and silence, in participating in the vile bourgeois conspiracy to malign Arthur Scargill, a man who is easily the best trade unionist since the second world war and who, in terms of his strength of character, courage, honesty and intellectual ability stands head and shoulders above the despicable Norman Willises and Windbag Kinnocks of this world. Not content with their role in sabotaging the 1984 miners' strike, they now wish to press their advantage home by hounding out the very man whose resolute leadership made possible the continuation of that very important battle on behalf of the British working class.

If the working class is unable to force the bourgeoisie to back down, this will put the last nail in the coffin of militant unionism in this country. Unions have already been largely tamed by the bourgeoisie forcing all kinds of legislation on them that saps their vitality. If the moves against Arthur Scargill and Peter Heathfield succeed in depriving the unions of principled, courageous and intelligent leadership, what then will be left?

The IWA(GB) pledges itself to do its utmost to defend Arthur Scargill and Peter Heathfield and urges all its members to do everything they can at their places of work and elsewhere to mobilise workers to understand what is at stake here and do whatever is necessary to ensure that the bourgeoisie is forced to back off.

LALKAR October/November 1992

ONLY MASS MOBILISATION CAN WIN VICTORY

Fight Shoulder to Shoulder with the Miners

On Wednesday 21 October London was host to the largest demonstration in more than 20 years. The announcement of the government's pit closure programme, under which 31 pits are to be closed with the loss of 30,000 jobs in the mining industry alone, was the occasion for the pent-up energy of the working class to burst forth with a force that surprised friend and foe alike. Outraged by the callousness with which the government wielded its butcher's knife, the total disregard and contempt in which it held the working people, the rabid class hatred it displayed towards the miners, well over 100,000 people (the organisers' claim of 200,000 is nearer the mark than the police figure of 50,000 and the bourgeois media's derisory 30,000) literally laid siege to the capital to demonstrate their anger at the government and, more importantly, their determination to fight tooth and nail the pit closures in particular and unemployment generally. Miners, their families, friends and supporters from all trades and professions, from all industries and from every part of the country, were there to send the message to the House of Commons, due to hold a crucial debate on the coal industry, that enough is enough, that the working class will brook no further bullying, that it will stand up and fight. The *Evening Standard* of 21 October, in its first edition, bore the headline *"Miners take over London"*. In a later edition the same day its banner headline read: *"Cheers as the Miners March - Biggest Demo on Streets of London Since Poll Tax Riots"*. To get a picture of the scene and atmosphere surrounding this mammoth gathering, here are a few excerpts from the *Evening Standard's* report:

"Miners, their families and supporters brought the West End grinding to a halt as they marched the capital's streets in a desperate effort to save Britain's coal industry from devastation.

"London was a city under good-natured siege. Cheering and applauding locals thronged the street to watch the marching hordes, whose singing and

chanting masked anger and frustration.

"The miners, their ranks swollen by left-wing groups from all over London, were then [i.e., after a mass rally in Hyde Park] taking their protest to Parliament - adding further passion to tonight's crucial Commons debate on the coal industry."

The march was led by Arthur Scargill, the NUM President, who was flanked by Bill Morris, General Secretary of the T&G, and Labour MPs Tony Benn and Dennis Skinner. Roads were closed off along the route of the demonstration through Kensington, a rich shopping and fashionable area, and major traffic jams built up throughout the West End and far beyond. So huge was the demonstration that *"tailbacks threatened to reach beyond Oxford Street on one side and as far as Hammersmith on the other" (Evening Standard)*.

Such was the anger aroused by the industrial vandalism of the government that sympathy for the miners spilled beyond the working class. Cheering and indications of support for the demonstrators came from some most unexpected quarters. Says the *Evening Standard*:

"Well-heeled shoppers and office workers lined the Kensington streets in a show of solidarity. Knots of trade unionists gathered outside pubs shouting, cheering and waving in this quintessentially Tory heartland.

"Some antique shops and expensive restaurants posted banners of support in their windows, and London buses full of passengers clapped and cheered as they slowly drove past the procession ... "

"The predominant colour, of course, was red with a profusion of trades union banners and political posters. It seemed like every second marcher carried a banner which read: 'Sack Major not the Miners'".

The rally

On reaching Hyde Park, the rally was addressed by prominent trade unionists, representing transport, rail and other unions, as well as some Labour MPs and churchmen. But the star of the rally was the miners' leader Arthur Scargill who, in an impassioned and ruthlessly logical speech, subjected the government's economic policy to devastating analysis, which exposed the hollowness of the government's assertions that the economic case for pit closures was unanswerable. As we do not possess a verbatim report of Mr Scargill's speech, we are summarising, in our own language, some of the important points he made to the cheering crowd at this rally, amid repeated applause.

Mr Scargill made the important economic argument that coal-produced electricity was the cheapest; that electricity produced by gas-burning power stations was 30% dearer than that produced by coal-powered stations, whereas that produced by nuclear power stations was 350% more expensive. Nuclear power stations, he said, received a subsidy of £1.3 billion a year. If that subsidy was given to coal, every one of the pits in the land would be profitable. The Germans give a huge subsidy to support their coal industry. British coal, he argued, was the most efficiently produced, and cheapest, in Europe. These sums and calculations, he added sarcastically, could be understood even by journalists working for the *Sun* newspaper. Of course, the coal imported from Colombia and South Africa was cheaper than British coal. To loud applause he added that British miners do not want to compete with coal produced in the conditions of child slavery prevalent in the Colombian mines nor with that produced by the super-exploited black workers in South Africa who are the victims of *apartheid*.

He called on the government to institute an independent review not only of the coal industry, but embracing all aspects of energy policy, including nuclear subsidies and the structure of electricity privatisation. Above all, he demanded that not a single pit be closed pending the outcome of such a review. Failing this, his Union, with the support of workers in other unions, would continue to step up the campaign. In ringing tones, he declared his men were not mere statistics - they were people with families and feelings, who could not at will be thrown on the scrap heap. *"Our people are not bleeps on a computer screen. They are human beings and they have got a right to work in the industry to which they have invested and devoted their lives."*

He thanked everyone who had come to the demonstration in support of the miners, especially the women who were representing those miners who had been unable to attend because of threats from British Coal that they would lose their redundancy money if they associated themselves with any protest or strike action.

He went on to damn the government for spending upwards of £10 billion on defending the pound, which went straight into the pockets of speculators - both British and foreign - and for its willingness to pay £1.2 billion in redundancy payments in order to put 30,000 miners out of work. If all this money had been invested in the mines, there would have been no need to close a single pit.

"For the first time in years," said Mr Scargill, *"working men and women*

have expressed their outrage and indignation at a government completely devoid of compassion and understanding"; adding that the labour movement had this week crossed the Rubicon in its fight against pit closures.

Alluding to the breakaway Union of Democratic Miners, whose scab labour contributed greatly to the defeat of the 1984-5 coal strike, Mr Scargill said that some people thought the time had come for reconciliation. He went on to say that his position was, and is, that every miner should return to the NUM. He ended his speech with the words: *"it is a pleasure to be the President of the Union,"* receiving a very long ovation.

All in all, it was a day spiritually most uplifting, a day which brought hope, through struggle, to millions of working people, hitherto groping in hopeless darkness.

Government U-turn?

The outrage felt by the working class throughout the country, and the mass mobilisation for the 21 October demonstration, had the effect of concentrating the government's mind wonderfully. In the Commons debate the same evening, the President of the Board of Trade, Michael Heseltine, who had only 48 hours earlier insisted that the economic case for pit closures was *"unanswerable"* and that the government would not change its mind, was obliged to announce a moratorium on the closure of 21 out of the 31 pits on his original hit list; that the case for closures would be scrutinised separately for all pits; that there would be a review of the coal industry; that the impact of legislation introduced by the government which affected the markets for coal and electricity-generation industries would be covered by the review of UK energy policy, as would be the subsidies for the nuclear industry; that the review by his department would be wide-ranging and would consider evidence from all interested parties, including the trade unions; that the inquiry would be *"without restrictions"* and have *"no pre-ordained outcome;"* and that he would be producing a White Paper on the coal crisis embracing most of the contentious aspects of energy policy.

Scepticism

With these assurances, and what looked like a U-turn, the government scraped through the division lobby with a majority of 13 (320 to 307). In the end only 6 Tory MPs voted against the government and another 5 abstained.

Working people are rightly sceptical of government intentions and they fear that the government is engaged in a manoeuvre to buy time in order to be able to implement its programme of pit closures when things have quietened down. Arthur Scargill, speaking at the rally in Central Hall, Westminster, later that day, warned that the government's manoeuvring over pit closures was a *"body swerve"*, not a U-turn, and he called for an even larger demonstration on Sunday 27 October to help bring about a complete reversal of government policy.

John Martin, a 30-year old miner from Hatfield Main, to be mothballed in May, spoke contemptuously of Heseltine: *"All he's done is bought his backbenchers to get through today's vote. He's done so many U-turns he's going round in circles."*

What adds weight to this suspicion and scepticism is, first, that Heseltine has refused to include in his review what he terms as the 10 most 'uneconomical' pits. Second, that the firm of consultants to be hired by him are none other than Boyds, an international mining consultancy firm who are also to act as the government's key coal advisers on the privatisation of the coal industry. Every attempt must be made to get an independent review body to prevent a rigged review which would only rubber stamp the government's pit closure programme.

Describing the government as a *"bunch of rascals,"* Paddy Ashdown, the Liberal Democrat leader, had this to say in the House of Commons debate:

"Our job is to make sure this is a real review on a level playing field. We will move heaven and earth to make sure that happens and to ensure they don't rig the review and kill off the coal industry slowly.

"We must make sure this bunch of rascals are made to live up to their promises."

Accusing the government off rigging the market to kill of the coal industry quickly, he added:

"We must not allow them to kill off coal slowly.

"They have rigged the market to help their friends and to pursue their obsessions with huge subsidies for other energy resources while giving coal nothing.

"This industry has been betrayed. Our long-term energy resource was in danger of just being thrown away."

The only way to make this *"bunch of rascals live up to their promises"* is to keep the pressure on and to step up the mass mobilisation against pit closures. No complacency must be allowed to dull the vigilance of the working class. As Dennis Skinner, Secretary of the miners' parliamentary group, correctly remarked at the rally in Central Hall:

"History has a quaint way of turning full circle. We're on the crest of a wave and we mustn't let this moment pass. We're not going to win this battle in Parliament. We didn't get rid of the poll tax in Parliament. We got rid of it on the streets."

Let us all mobilise for Sunday's rally and for the struggle to follow.

LALKAR October/November 1992

SUPPORT THE MINERS

Fight this Deliberate Industrial Vandalism

In the afternoon of the unlucky Tuesday 13th, British Coal announced the country's biggest industrial cutbacks, bringing Britain's once proud coal industry to its knees by a programme of pit closures. According to this announcement, 31 collieries are to be closed with the resultant loss of 30,000 jobs, representing three-quarters of the workforce.

Six of the pits on the hit list were due for closure as early as Friday 17th October, another 19 will disappear by Christmas, with the rest to be closed within five months, leaving behind a trail of devastation, destroying towns and villages which for generations have had no means of livelihood other than coal. These closures will sound the death knell for deep mining in Lancashire, North Staffordshire, North Wales and North Derbyshire. As to Warwickshire, South Staffordshire, the North East, South Wales and Scotland - these will simply be reduced to one pit each.

Industrial Vandalism

At the end of the historic and heroic miners' strike of 1984-85, there were 169 pits with a workforce of 170,000. By next spring, the number of pits will be reduced to just 19 and the workforce to 18,000. But even their survival, according to British Coal, depends on new contracts, yet to be struck, with electricity generators, National Power and PowerGen, the main customers of British Coal.

The electricity generators were obliged to buy British coal for three years after privatisation of electricity in 1990. With this obligation due to expire next March, they can buy cheap imported coal or switch over to gas-fired electricity generators. According to THEIR assertion, British Coal, at £47 per ton, is £11 dearer than imported coal. They are thus expected to reduce their orders of British coal from the present 65 million tonnes to 40 million tonnes next year, and 30 million tonnes for each of the following four years - and what is more at greatly reduced prices.

Quite correctly, Mr Arthur Scargill, the President of the National Union of Mineworkers (NUM), denounced the decision as *"the most savage, brutal act of vandalism in modern times"* and urged the miners to take every possible action to fight the closures. The miners, he said, *"have a choice: either to lie down and let this happen, or stand up and fight back"* against this *"deliberate political act of industrial vandalism perpetrated against an already decimated industrial landscape"*.

For once, even the rabidly reactionary Tory tabloids agreed with Mr Scargill. Universal condemnation greeted the announcement of pit closures. The following headlines in the Wednesday (14th October) press are self-explanatory: *"Thrown on the Slag Heap"* (Daily Mirror); *"Massacre of the Miners"* (Daily Express); *"The Great Mine Disaster"* (Daily Mail); *"Villages of the Damned"* (Daily Star). Today, another of the tabloids, carried a picture of a sacked miner and asked Prime Minister John Major, the heart-rending question: *"What will he* [the sacked miner] *do now Mr Major?"* Likewise, The Sun showed a sacked miner on its front page with the caption *"Devastated miner after yesterday's axe"*.

The banner headlines in the serious press conveyed the same pain and outrage felt in the mining communities at the butchery involved in 31 pit closures.

At Calverton Colliery, near Nottingham, managers had barely finished congratulating the 752 workforce for digging 40,500 tonnes of coal in one week, when they had to face them again to break the news of pit closure. One miner remarked: *"It is the final irony. We worked hard to set the record and this is our reward"*.

Since 1985, productivity in the coal industry has trebled, while in the past six years alone it has doubled. Last year British Coal made a profit of £170 million. Referring to the decision of the electricity generating duopoly (represented by National Power and Powergen) to switch over to gas and imported coal, Neil Clarke, chairman of British Coal, said: *"The bear-squeeze on the demand for coal has been scant reward for efforts which have seen productivity rise more than double in six years"*.

Need to Lower Costs

In order to understand the present programme of pit closures, which have brought about a near decimation of the coal industry, it is important to grasp that this is part and parcel of British capital's endeavour - which began at the dawn of this century - to reduce costs of production in British industry at the expense of the British working class. With the development of world capitalism and the emergence of Germany, France, the United States and, to a certain extent, Japan, as Britain's competitors in the world market, Britain's former monopoly position was seriously undermined.

The First World War, and the crisis following it, only served to deal a further decisive blow to Britain's monopoly position. In its struggle for survival and the cut-throat competition for markets, British capital had to cut costs and secure a cheapening of commodities, which could only be done by passing the burdens thereof on to the British working class. This struggle for the markets led then, as it does now, to restricted production, the creation of a vast army of the unemployed and the threat of unemployment.

Why Attack the Miners?

That British miners have always been the main target of the blows struck by British capital is no accident. Speaking of the British General Strike of 1926, Joseph Stalin made this penetrating observation:

"British capital attacked the miners not only because the mining industry is badly equipped technically and is in need of 'rationalisation', but primarily because the miners have always been, and still remain, the advanced detachment of the British proletariat. It was the strategy of British capital to curb this advanced detachment, to lower their wages and lengthen their working day, in order then, having settled accounts with this main detachment, to make the other detachments of the working class also toe the line. Hence the heroism with which the British miners are conducting their strike. ..." (J.V.Stalin, CW Vol 8, p.167)

This is a tactic that British capital has followed ever since, particularly since the Seventies of this century, which witnessed the coal strikes of 1972 and 1974 - the last one resulting in the defeat of the Conservative Government of Mr Edward Heath. Ever since then the Tories have vowed to smash the NUM and, if necessary, decimate the coal industry. Ever since then, they have planned methodically to achieve this end. Thanks to the spinelessness and downright treachery of the leadership of the TUC and the Labour Party, the Tories succeeded in defeating the heroic Coal Strike of 1984-85, just as they had done during the 1926 Strike. Having settled accounts with the miners in 1984-85 strike, the Tories - the most bitter enemies of the working class - went on to settle accounts with other detachments of the working class. Consequent upon the defeat of 1984-85 Coal Strike, the British proletariat has been prostrate in the face of successive blows delivered by British monopoly capital.

Scargill Proven Correct

During that heroic Coal Strike, the miners' leader, Arthur Scargill (be it said in parenthesis, that he is one of the very, very few British labour leaders and trade unionists worthy of respect and trust), said that the Tories wanted to destroy the NUM, close down most of the pits, dismember and privatise the coal industry. Nonsense, said the Tories, accusing Mr Scargill of being a paranoid and a scare-monger. Now, less than a decade later, everything he said - and more - has been proven correct. The workforce of 170,000 at the end of the Coal Strike, has already, even before the latest announcement of pit closures, been reduced to the derisory figure of 48,000, and the number of pits cut from 169 to 50 (a loss of 119 pits) in the corresponding period in a steady stream of job cuts and *"rationalisation"*. If Scargill has been proved wrong, it is only to the extent that even he was not able to correctly predict the savage blood-letting and butchery that the Tories had in store in their continuing vendetta against the miners. The *Evening Standard* of Tuesday, 13th October, just hours after the announcement of the pit closures, was obliged to make this admission:

"Whatever you think of Arthur Scargill, he has been consistently right about the fate of the British mining industry. More than 10 years ago the President of the National Union of Mineworkers confidently predicted the dismemberment of British Coal if it was to be sold off to the private sector.

"Today his worst fears have proved all too true as British Coal braces itself against the closure of at least half its pits and the loss of more than 20,000 jobs".

Continues the *Evening Standard*: *"Yet the scale of the redundancy programme involves far more drastic cuts than even Scargill predicted. In effect, the Government is shutting more than half of Britain's deep mining capacity and condemning tens of thousands of workers in some of the most depressed regions to never working again"* (The black hole for British Coal, by Patrick Donovan, in *Evening Standard*, Tuesday, 13 October).

These pit closures are being hurried through because the Conservative Government is in such a rush to privatise the coal industry. The same article, cited immediately above, says: *"In other circumstances the Government could have buffered itself against the political fall-out by the continued subsidy of uneconomic mines. But it has been forced to brazen out mass closures because of its commitment to starting the sale of the mining industry within the current*

Parliament".

And this, notwithstanding the fact that Britain will be left with a rump of an industry which was once one of the country's biggest employers and the Treasury will certainly end up paying far more in closure costs than it can ever hope to recover through its privatisation.

Why the Run-Down?

Everyone admits that the run-down of British Coal stems from the privatisation of electricity three years ago. What few bourgeois commentators - barring the odd one in an unguarded moment - admit is that this privatisation of electricity was no mere accident. This privatisation, and the run-down of British Coal, was methodically prepared by the Conservative Government; the chief aim of this privatisation being to smash trade union militancy, in particular the militancy of British miners, who have for so long been the most advanced detachment of the British proletariat, much to the chagrin of the British ruling class. Lord Lawson of Blaby, who, as Nigel Lawson, served as Energy Minister for some time, discloses in his memoirs that he was determined that the government would never again be beaten by trade-union militancy.

And that old Thatcherite weed, who was Energy Secretary during the long miners' strike in 1984-85, Lord Parkinson, with admirable candour, which must be terribly embarrassing to his more hypocritical colleagues who, while delighted at the devastation and decimation of the coal industry, feign to shed crocodile tears over its demise, had this to say during a Radio Four interview:

"Don't forget, in this great surge of sympathy, that the mineworkers' union did bring down a government and did actually abuse their economic power on innumerable occasions".

Cecil Parkinson, who had pledged to privatise the coal industry, added: *"Try to have a sense of perspective".*

Everyone knows that the decision to run down the coal industry and rely on gas and imported coal is as costly as it is dangerous, that it is bound adversely to affect Britain's balance of payments and exchange rate alike, that there is always the danger lurking round the corner that gas supplies may run out, at the present rate of extraction, sooner than expected and that imported supplies of gas and coal may not always materialise. And yet the Government are ready to take the plunge into this abyss - a plunge which is neither justified on economic grounds nor on those of a proper national energy strategy. Apart from the fact that in the currently rigged structure of the market, in which the power generators and the twelve Regional Electricity Companies (RECs) operate, a lot of the Government's friends will make huge profits in the short term, the chief factor motivating the Government's decision to deal a fatal blow to the coal industry is the class question. The bourgeoisie cannot tolerate those sections of the organised working class whom it perceives to be a threat to its rule. The miners, for so long the advanced detachment of the British working class, have deservedly earned the hatred of the British capitalist class, which will not easily forgive them for bringing down the Heath Government. It is for this reason that the Conservatives, and not they alone, have been waging a relentless class war against the miners.

In its 14th October editorial, that sober representative of British finance capital, the *Financial Times*, commenting upon the pit closures announced by British Coal the previous day, says:

"Coming at the nadir of recession, the loss of 30,000 more jobs is a grave matter. It is proper to ask who is to blame for this state of affairs and whether any other course is available" ('Coal takes the unkindest cut')

By way of an answer to the question thus formulated, it goes on to provide the following candid answer:

"The accusing finger points most obviously at the National Union of Mineworkers and its leader, Mr Arthur Scargill. It was he who proclaimed a mission to defend the coal industry but whose reckless and misguided actions ensured that miners became a symbol of political extremism and their industry a byword for instability and unreliability. The Thatcher government vowed to destroy Mr Scargill's power ... and succeeded in doing so during the 1984-85 miners' strike" (ibid).

Continues the *Financial Times*:

"Since the strike, Mr Scargill has continued his menaces, but ever more hollowly as the industry has crumbled around him. But his ghost has served as a pungent reminder that coal had thrown away its biggest asset, that it is indigenous, plentiful and above all secure. Since British coal has powerful natural disadvantages - it pollutes the air more than gas, oil and nuclear power and is 50 per cent more costly than imported coal - this put British Coal in a very vulnerable position.

"The result has been that as soon as coal's customers in the electric power industry achieved, through privatisation, the freedom to diversify away from

coal, they have done so, even in some cases contracting for gas-fired power stations who economics is questionable" (ibid).

In other words, coal is cheaper, but it is cheaper still, from the bourgeois point of view, to get rid of working-class militancy. There you have it. A frank and clear and cynical statement of class reality by a sober and calculating spokesman of the robber barons of British monopoly capitalism. The *Financial Times* is read only by a very small number of people. Its function is to inform the ruling class, unlike the mass circulation tabloids whose job it is to misinform the working-class millions. The *Financial Times* can, therefore, afford to present the truth with far greater frankness and cynicism than the 'popular' dailies.

Having described the destruction of British Coal as *"a triumph of market economics, albeit with painful consequences"*, the *Financial Times* goes on to annihilate this assertion by admitting that privatised British Gas is *"imperfectly exposed to market forces"* - a euphemism for monopoly control of the market, in which last year alone gas prices went up by 30 per cent. And electricity, with its inadequately regulated monopoly of National Power and Powergen, is a candidate for draconian scrutiny by the competition authorities. Then there is the nuclear power industry, still in state hands, heavily subsidised and due for review in 1994. This industry is already pressing for investment in additional power stations, further threatening the coal industry !!

In other words, British Coal has become the victim of privatised giant gas and electricity companies and the subsidised nuclear power industry, which is kept alive at a huge cost to the tax payer for the sole purpose of producing weapons grade enriched uranium. In a nutshell, British Coal has become a victim to British imperialism's need to destroy working-class militancy at home and suppress national liberation and revolutionary struggles abroad. If the *Financial Times* is pleased to characterise this naked class war against coal, in which the latter fights with its hands tied to its back, as *"a triumph of market economics"* that is only because the defence of the selfish interests of a small clique of the Kings of Finance obliges it to make nonsensical, mutually contradictory and self-annihilatory utterances. For what other explanation can there be for someone describing the extinction of the coal industry at the hands of the subsidised nuclear industry and the giant gas and electricity monopolies as a triumph of market economics?

After all this, and having earlier described the economics of gas-fired power stations as *"questionable"*, the *Financial Times*, with an air of triumph, goes on to declare:

"*There is no case for paying British Coal to produce fuel no one wishes to buy, and none for denying to the British economy the benefits of low world energy prices*".

And only one sentence further down, its conscience stricken, the *Financial Times* adds:

"*But as they line up for their redundancy pay, Britain's coal miners will be right to reflect that the harsh wind of market forces has not blown uniformly across British energy policy*".

How true and how strange this triumph of market economics!

After all this, the only thing that this high priest of high finance has to offer the victims of this capitalist butchery is a bit of nauseatingly disgusting charity, and it concludes its editorial with these high-sounding, unctuous, words:

"*It is not possible to judge whether the £1bn the government said yesterday it would make available to help regenerate the economies of shattered mining communities is an adequate sum. As victims of the energy policy errors of the 1980s as well as of their own misjudgments, the miners deserve generosity*".

Yes indeed! Having condemned the mining communities to a permanent place in the dole queue, having shattered the lives of whole communities, having destroyed entire villages and towns, finance capital can afford to be generous.

Are Coal-Fired Power Stations more Expensive?

If the above is the main reason for devastation of British coal, what are the Government's pretended reasons for this industrial vandalism? We are told that coal-fired power stations are more expensive than gas-fired, and the Government claims that electricity bills, as a result of pit closures, will be 3 per cent lower than would otherwise have been the case, with obvious benefits for industrial competitiveness. This claim, however, is disputed by the most authoritative of sources. Prof. Nigel Lucas of Imperial College, a well-known authority in the field of energy, and many others have put forth convincing evidence to show that coal-fired power stations produce the cheapest electricity. Even the House of Commons Energy Select Committee in its Report of February 1992 characterised the Government's pit closure programme and the replacement of coal-fired power stations by those running on gas as *"doubtful economics"*. Neil Clarke, Chairman of British Coal, warned that the switch from coal-fired to gas power stations, resulting in pit closures, would push up their production costs by 16 per cent and millions of home-owners now face the prospect of soaring electricity bills.

Gas has become the preferred fuel for the new Combined Cycle Gas Turbine (CCGT) power stations despite growing evidence that many will produce electricity at prices higher than coal stations now facing closure. Privatisation of electricity has set, as it always was meant to, the terms of coal's demise. The 12 RECs have, with boundless enthusiasm, become shareholders in, and customers of, new CCGT stations planned for the mid-1990s by way of escaping the duopoly exercised by the two power generators - National Power and Powergen. This is so notwithstanding the evidence suggesting that CCGTs will produce power at 2.8p a unit as against 2.2p a unit for coal-fired power stations whose costs have already been written off.

Last year witnessed a 30 per cent hike in gas prices. The RECs have, nevertheless, signed 15-year gas supply contracts safe in the knowledge that they have guaranteed monopoly markets for the sale of power, even if it is more costly to produce, and can pass the higher costs on to the consumer. And this monopoly operation, deliberately set up under privatisation legislation with the aim of destroying British Coal, is hailed by bourgeois hacks and ideologues as a triumph of market economics. The results of such a device are a foregone conclusion. In a bid to make a quick buck in the conditions of a rigged market, the power generators are switching over from coal to gas, thus delivering a shattering blow to the coal industry as part of the process of *"creative destruction"*, to use an expression coined by the apologists of pit closure programmes, that characterises the operation of capitalism. The next 25 years will bring in a dramatic increase in the use of gas for electricity production and an equally dramatic decrease in the use of coal, whose share in power production is set to decline from 70 per cent in 1990 to 27 per cent in 2020. In the same period the share of gas in the production of electricity is forecast to rise from zero (in 1990) to 57 per cent.

In its editorial column, *The Times* of 14th October, correctly points out that the elimination of British Coal, and its replacement by imports or by exportable gas, *"is not some sad but inevitable product of competitive market forces. It is a direct result of the privatisation of the electricity industry"*. Pointing out that the twin aims of electricity privatisation were the safeguarding of nuclear power and the promotion of competition in electricity generation, *The Times* leader goes on to say:

"Nuclear generation has been protected at a cost to consumers of £1.3 billion a year. As for effective competition, this was introduced only at the margins of the business, with the bizarre effect of raising prices to consumers and to industry and penalising coal.

"New entrants to the generation of electricity, some under the protection of monopoly distribution companies, vied with National Power and PowerGen to build gas-fired plants. When conceived, these provided the cheapest way to expand capacity. The boom will, however, lead to excess capacity, exacerbated by the recession.

"In a truly competitive market, that should bring cheaper electricity at the expense of low returns on investment. PowerGen and National Power are, however, able to resist that by closing coal-fired power stations to keep prices up, while cosy deals by some of the distribution monopolies will leave room for their linked gas stations to run at full tilt at the expense of coal generators. So instead of consumers reaping the benefit of excess capacity and the generators bearing the cost, consumers will get nothing and the coal industry has been set as the victim" (A Black Day for Coal).

So much then for cheap electricity.

Arguing for damage limitation, *The Times* goes on to urge that the Government's *"first action should be to scrap the coal contract negotiations and start again. The contracts have shown up the artificiality of competition. The electricity industry has effectively acted in concert. British Coal should be allowed to use its own countervailing market power, insisting on much longer contracts without any ludicrous clause that will allow generators time to build capacity to import half their coal in order to cut their consumption of British coal later.*

"The power industry's regulatory regime should also be changed to remove its bias against the predictable fixed prices that British Coal can now offer. Imported coal is much cheaper now, just as gas prices were before demand rose, but changes in exchange rates and world energy prices might well alter that sum over the lifetime of power stations. Currently consumers have to bear the risk because most increases in world energy prices can be passed on to them. If the regulator were to prohibit such passing on, generators would have to take the risk of fluctuations in exchange rates. That would make domestic coal, whose price in pounds will remain stable, more attractive.

"Distributors were allowed to become involved in generation to increase competition for the two big generators, but their entry, perversely, is stifling the working of the market by protecting some of the new gas-fired power stations. Distributors should be banned from owning stakes in generators".

Thus it is clear that the pit closures are not the result of market forces, for, as *The Guardian* put it, *"the energy market is a Byzantine stitch-up"*.

Towards the end of its editorial, *The Times* goes on to suggest that the Government should challenge the massive subsidies to German coal recently approved by the European Commission. Surely, it would be more sensible to press for the elimination of all subsidies by Britain to her nuclear industry, which presently stand at £1.3 bn a year, and the application of those sums to British Coal, thus reducing the cost by £17 for each of the 73m tonnes of coal mined and making every pit profitable. As *The Daily Telegraph* in its City Comment rightly observed: *"Coal has been invited to pay its way, but in a climate that ensured that it cannot. Effectively, half the coal industry is now being sacrificed to the great nuclear experiment, which forces fossil fuel burners to pay a levy to Nuclear Electric".*

This single act would have the effect of saving the coal industry, rescuing the 30,000 miners now threatened with redundancy and a future of perpetual unemployment, saving another 90,000 jobs in dependent industries whose future is tied to that of coal, and contributing towards a healthier trade balance and a favourable exchange rate. And if in the process it deals a death blow to the nuclear industry that is only to be welcomed, and is not a day too early.

Support the Miners

To conclude, what should be the response of the British proletariat to this class war on the miners? There can, ideally, be only one response, namely, a class war by the proletariat against the bourgeoisie. The crisis in the coal industry in particular, and the current world-wide slump in the capitalist world in general, bluntly raise the question once again of socialising the instruments and means of production not only in the coal industry, but also in every other. The British working class has to gain the understanding that without winning power, without establishing socialism, it is impossible to solve either the crisis in the coal industry or the crisis in the entire British industry.

At the present, however, the British proletariat is leaderless and, therefore, in total disarray, thanks to the treachery of social democracy (including the Trotksyite variety) and the bankruptcy of revisionism. There is no revolutionary Marxist-Leninist party of the proletariat, with the necessary prestige and connections in the working class, capable of resolutely and fearlessly defending the interests of the working class. Had such a party existed, the Heseltines of this world might have thought long and hard before announcing pit closures. Had such a party existed, the working class might already have been on the war path against the bourgeoisie.

As it is, it is left to the Bishop of Sheffield, Rt Rev David Lunn, to call for a *"national uprising"* against pit closures.

In the present circumstances, while making every effort to forge a truly proletarian revolutionary party, the advanced elements and class conscious workers must give every support to the NUM in the latter's struggle against the dismemberment of the coal industry.

We in the Indian Workers' Association (GB) promise to give unstinting support to the NUM and the mining communities in their arduous struggle, just as we did during the 1984-85 heroic coal strike. Everyone and everything for the miners - this is the slogan that must permeate all working-class organisations and guide our activities in the weeks and months to come.

LALKAR October/November 1992

As we go to press

The British Cabinet has decided that 10 of the 31 pits on the hit list will be axed immediately and that a proper review procedure will be followed with respect to the rest. This is no more than a stay of execution by way of a sop to public outrage, even among the Government's own supporters. The so-called Tory rebels are not against closures. They simply want a staggered timetable for these closures so as to avoid the whole affair exploding in the Govern-

Part Four

Social Democracy and Other Economic Struggles

"The atmosphere currently being generated by statements in the national press of 'we intend to have single keying even if it means doing away with the NGA' is most unhelpful in assisting the national leadership of the trades union to play a positive role, and is creating a 'seige mentality' in some quarters of our membership".

Tony Dubbins, the then General-Secretary elect of the NGA

"The German workers have two important advantages over those of the rest of Europe. First, they belong to the most theoretical people of Europe; and they have retained that sense of theory which the so-called 'educated' classes of Germany have almost completely lost. Without German philosophy, which preceded it, particularly that of Hegel, German scientific socialism - the only scientific socialism that has ever existed - would never have come into being. Without a sense of theory among the workers, this scientific socialism would never have entered their flesh and blood as much as is the case. What an immeasureable advantage this is may be seen ... from the indifference towards all theory which is one of the main reasons why the English working-class movement crawls along so slowly in spite of the splendid organisation of the individual unions ..."

Engels (Preface to the Peasant War in Germany)

Part Four

Social Democracy
and
Other Economic Struggles

LALKAR June 1981

The People's March for Jobs

On May 1st, two columns of workers, one from Merseyside and one from Yorkshire, set out to march to London. They met at Northampton, and others from North Wales joined them. The marchers carried a bright green banner with the inscription 'The People's March for Jobs' and behind the banner were just over 500 men and women wearing green jackets. All the marchers were sponsored, mostly by trade unions, but also by ethnic groups, youth clubs, churches and others. Men and women, young and old, black and white, able bodied as well as the disabled - even the blind - were represented in the march. Skinheads from Bolton, punks from Manchester, the mother and her unemployed son from Whaley Bridge, also marched the 280 miles traversed by the People's March.

Background to the March

The March was organised by the North West, West Midlands and South-East Regional Councils of the TUC against a background of mounting unemployment. The whole of the capitalist world is in the grip of a most serious economic crisis, the worst since the end of the second world war. In the USA and Western Europe alone (not to mention other capitalist countries), the number of unemployed is over 25 million. Even according to official statistics, 2.6 million are out of work in Britain. Actually, of course, the figure is much closer to 3.5 million for hundreds of thousands don't bother to sign on. Included among the latter are, for instance, women not entitled to unemployment benefits (and two out of three women are not entitled to these benefits) as well as disgruntled blacks and others. The unemployment among blacks is even worse than among whites. In this regard the government's figure of 12% for unemployment among blacks is an underestimation which can only be treated with suspicion. If 10% of the total workforce is unemployed nationally, the picture is even more depressing in some regions where the unemployed represent a quarter, or even more, of the workforce. Add to these figures a quarter of a million people who are on short time, some working no more than one or two days a week. A further quarter of a million are in temporary jobs through various government schemes. To get a true picture, imagine (and this is true) that since December 1980, jobs have been disappearing at the rate of 100,000 a month; every month 170 companies go into liquidation. And the prospects for the future are, if anything, even more grim and depressing. The real misery caused by unemployment can never be revealed by the unemployment statistics; it can only be gleaned from the increase in suicides, broken marriages, broken homes, stress and mental illness, from alcoholism, degradation, demoralisation and brutalization of the population; and from an increase in crime as well as the growth of racism and fascism. In these circumstances, there was growing pressure from ordinary workers that something be done about it. So the regional councils' response was to organise this march.

The achievements

The main achievement of the marchers has been their success in drawing attention to the plight of the unemployed in a way that no amount of statistical material could have done. The marchers wherever they went have been welcomed by tens of thousands of workers who lined the pavements to cheer them on and to express their solidarity with them. Rallies were held in all the places visited by the marchers, and the effect has, by and large, been to bring dignity to their struggle and strengthen their resolve, and that of the entire working class, in the fight against unemployment. The marchers made everyone think about the question of unemployment and the message that emerged, albeit instinctively and implicitly, was that unemployment was a man-made act and not a natural phenomenon.

The second achievement of the marchers was their contribution to the cause of the unity of the working class. Men and women, young and old, black and white, etc., all marched in complete harmony with the utmost discipline, with the slogan 'Workers united can never be defeated'. This is an experience that must be enlarged and applied throughout the length and breadth of the country. The March ended in London on Sunday 31 May, with a march from Hyde Park to Trafalgar Square, where a Rally, which attracted over 150,000 workers, was held.

Limitations

The chief limitation of the March was the narrow political outlook imposed by its TUC organisers and their supporters on the March, which was hemmed in by the bourgeois blinkers of social democracy. Notwithstanding the claim made by the regional councils in their 'People's March: Official Souvenir' that *"the People's March is not party political,"* and that *"No organisation has been allowed to take advantage of the March to promote itself"*, the March was throughout sought to be used to campaign for victory for the Labour Party at the next general election and to bring nearer, if possible, the date of that election. In other words, it was throughout sought to be used as an antiTory and pro-Labour vehicle. We in the IWA(GB) hate the Tories no less than anyone else does in the labour movement. However, we do not think that a change from one bourgeois government to another bourgeois government, from Tory to Labour or vice versa, offers any solution to the problem of unemployment. Our unshakeable view is that unemployment is a necessary concomitant of capitalism, not that of Toryism, and that those who wish to put an end to unemployment must in all earnestness work to destroy capitalism and replace it by socialism, under which production is carried on for the satisfaction of the constantly rising material and cultural requirements of the working class and not for the extraction of the maximum profits by a handful of monopoly capitalists.

In the same souvenir issue referred to above, we find the following statement: *"But the People's March has not been about determining whose economic doctrine is the most correct."* And what a pity and a shame that it was not. If capitalist economic doctrines have failed to put an end to unemployment under Tory and Labour governments (unemployment has been on the increase since 1967), should the working class not jettison its faith in these doctrines and turn to socialist economic science and a socialist system of society, which alone can solve the problem under consideration? The March should not have been a mere *"exercise in common humanity"* but should have been more than that: an exercise and an important step in rousing the anger of the working class against capitalism, an important step in preparing it in the fight against the whole system of capitalism.

Our stance

The IWA(GB) position was put forward by our General Secretary, Cde Avtar Jouhl, at the Rally in Trafalgar Square. Whereas the other speakers tried to perpetuate illusions of the working class by simply calling for a return of a Labour government, Cde Jouhl was one of only two speakers (the other being Arthur Scargill of the Yorkshire miners) who held capitalism rather than the Tories responsible for unemployment, be its level high or low. And Avtar alone boldly called for the fight to establish a socialist Britain in which the Marxist-Leninist economic programme would be put into effect for ending forever unemployment and as the basis for the everlasting prosperity of the working class of this country. This idea and this alone must permeate every section of the working class.

LALKAR December 1982

TUC Betrayal of Hospital Workers

Amid much trumpeting and breast beating the TUC leadership promised massive support for the health workers' pay claim. In the event they orchestrated a damp squib. Now, left to their own devices, the nurses and 'ancillary' hospital workers have a very hard task on their hands. It is doubtful if they will be able to gain much more than the cunningly thought out deal that the government is now offering.

Such a deal would be a defeat in several ways. Firstly, it represents a wage cut in real terms for this group of already appallingly poorly-paid workers. Secondly, it is designed to divide the hospital workers in future wage battles. Thirdly, for all to see, the TUC has been shown to fail to 'put its money where its mouth is'.

With touching modesty, Mr Albert Spanswick, chairman of the TUC health services committee, which was set up to coordinate the 'action', said on 9 November:

"We have made immense progress, it has been worth 7 months of dispute."

What is the reality of this *"immense progress"?* This 'progress' is contained in the following events, spanning 7 months.

The government's first response to the health workers' claim for a 12% rise was a paltry 6.4% for the nurses and 4% for the 'ancillaries', accompanied by much emphasis that there was no more money available. This 'offer' was rejected by the TUC-affiliated unions representing nurses and other hospital workers (NUPE, COHSE, TGWU, NALGO) and the professional associations of nurses (Royal College of Nursing - RCN) midwives and health visitors, which although not affiliated to the TUC take part in pay negotiations.

By September Mr Fowler had upped the offer to 7.5% for nurses, 6.5% for ambulance crews and pharmacists and 6% for 'ancillaries', but had linked it to a 4% rise next year.

This offer too was rejected, not only by the members (including a large number of nurses and nursing auxiliaries) of the TUC affiliated unions, but also by the membership of the RCN against the advice of their negotiators. Mr Spanswick himself dismissed the offer and various permutations that amounted to the same total sum as a *"deliberate tactic designed to take the steam out of next week's demonstration"*, i.e., the TUC day of action on 22 September 1982).

What then happened to provoke Mr Spanswick's victorious statement on 9 November? Mr Fowler had announced a new offer in Parliament that day, a whole 0.5% added to next year's 4%! He also promised a pay review body to report on nurses' pay in 1984. This is progress indeed, but it is progress in the government's strategy of being hard while at the same time trying to prise the nurses away from the other hospital workers with the old formula of 'divide and rule'. The government's hope is that the new offer will achieve this where the previous one failed, for it gives the leadership of the RCN another chance to persuade its members to accept and by instituting a pay review body for nurses would effectively separate them from other hospital workers in future pay battles. Mr Fowler had the insolence to add that the government reserved the right to ignore the findings of the pay review body!

It would now be easy to dismiss Mr Spanswick's *"immense progress worth 7 months of dispute"* as a load of hot air if it did not represent another important change in the circumstances facing the health workers while they consider this latest offer. For it is not in fact a cry of victory, but a statement that as far as the TUC is concerned the fight is over. The 'great campaign' that was to bring 'industrial muscle' into the dispute came and went on 22 September, leaving the health service workers to decide whether to accept or struggle on alone against an intransigent government.

This is not the fault of the health service workers themselves, who have achieved considerable unity of action and shown great determination arising out of the despair of their economic circumstances. They had also judged the mood of their fellow workers and skilfully conducted their campaign so that they kept public sympathy. There was considerable support for the hospital workers in spite of the fact that the strikes were affecting ordinary people. This support was not based solely on sympathy, but on a growing awareness, particularly in the public sector, that the outcome of this struggle would affect other pay negotiations. There is also growing awareness that the state of the health service affects the standard of living of all workers. It is part of the 'social wage' and not only are the health service workers themselves being paid badly and forced to work long hours, but there is the 'promise' of further staff cuts, of further reduction in facilities, of further hospital closures. Indeed, the service offered by the NHS has been so appallingly savaged by financial cuts, that the actions of the health workers seemed like a minor irritation compared to the chronic waiting lists for beds, the hours spent waiting in outpatients' departments, and the ever longer journeys to the nearest hospital that still has a casualty department.

Instead of mobilising and coordinating the ground-swell of support, the TUC leadership did its best to defuse and dissipate it. The mood of the union memberships pressurised their leaders into some brave speeches at the TU Congress as the day of action on 22 September approached. There were statements like 'we will do it much better than we tried to do in 1926' and 'we are going to be out again, and if they don't move we are going to be out again'. But even at the Congress these speeches were belied by the beginning of plans to replace a whole day stoppage by partial stoppages. By the 22nd, the calls from various union leaderships were down to 1 or 2 hours, or even 'decide locally what you want to do,' if anything. But in spite of this lukewarm, to say the least, lead, September 22 was impressive and it was impressive because the union memberships wanted to take action and did take action, in many cases in excess of their leaderships' call.

So the TUC health service committee (chaired by Mr Spanswick) decided that it would be better not to have any more national action but to have regional days of action instead. This was the death knell that dissipated the support and it was not surprising that ground was very quickly lost as leaders refused to lead. All that was left for Mr Spanswick was to mutiny on his knees and 'proclaim victory'!

The fact of the matter is that the TUC leadership **cannot** lead effective action in the present circumstances. It has sold out to the imperialist bourgeoisie and is not prepared to challenge the system of imperialism. Its role is to confine the economic struggles of the working class within the framework of imperialism. At times of economic crisis, that means that the working class must bear the brunt of the burden, for the monopoly capitalist class cannot do so and remain monopoly capitalist. So, failing to challenge imperialism, all that the TUC leadership can do in the circumstances is to play charades, as it has done with its empty 'support' for the health workers' struggle and before that with the People's March for Jobs, the campaign around which has all but been abandoned.

But the very development of capitalism that produces such hardship for the working class also produces the conditions that render capitalism an obsolete system. And the present, imperialist, stage of capitalism is capitalism at its most obsolete. As long ago as 1865 Marx noted the everpresent necessity for the working class to struggle against the deterioration of its living standards. He said: *"By cowardly giving way in their everyday conflict with capital, they [the workers] would certainly disqualify themselves for the initiating of any larger movement."* But, he added: *"At the same time, and quite apart from the general servitude involved in the wages system, the working class ought not to exaggerate to themselves the ultimate working of these everyday struggles. They ought not to forget that they are fighting with effects, but not with the causes of those effects; that they are retarding the downward movement, but not changing its direction; that they are applying palliatives, not curing the malady. They ought, therefore, not to be exclusively absorbed in these unavoidable guerrilla fights incessantly springing up from the never-ceasing encroachments of capital or changes of the market. They ought to understand that, with all the miseries it imposes upon them, the present system simultaneously engenders the material conditions and the social forms necessary for an economical reconstruction of society. Instead of the **conservative** motto, 'A fair day's wage for a fair day's work!' they ought to inscribe on their banner the **revolutionary** watchword, 'Abolition of the wages system'."* (Marx, *Value, Prices and Profit*).

Yes, the urgent task that faces the working class is to challenge the system of imperialism and overthrow it. Only then will it effect its escape from the endless struggle to resist deterioration in its conditions, only then will it achieve its emancipation from exploitation and oppression. And in the process, trades union bureaucrats who serve the interests of imperialism and not the interests of the working class must be thrown onto the rubbish heap where they belong.

LALKAR September 1983

TUC leaders capitulate to Tory government

TUC leaders have embarked on talks with the government for the first time since December, 1981. Meeting at their request with Norman Tebbit, Employment Secretary, marks their capitulation to the Conservative government. The first session on 18 August discussed the Youth Training Scheme (YTS). Further talks are planned on Tebbit's proposals for union legislation - ballots on union leadership, strikes and political funds.

Bellicose posturing by Len Murray and other prominent TUC leaders about fighting proposed legislation and refusing to speak to Norman Tebbit has collapsed. Their approach to, and comments on, the first talks show how far they have sunk.

The TUC went into the talks *"pressing"* for a £1.50 increase in the £25 YTS weekly allowance and a lowering of the £4 threshold for travelling allowance. The £1.50 increase had been favoured by a majority of the Manpower Services Commission (MSC), with the dissent of the employers representatives and the refusal of Mr Tebbit. Saying that he did not expect criticism for entering the talks before the Congress had the chance to discuss relations with the Conservative government, Len Murray added that young people would expect the TUC to represent them on questions such as the YTS allowance. Yet the YTS is being criticised across the country for providing cheap labour without real training or job prospects, depressing wages, undermining existing training and being forced on young people by the threat of loss of supplementary benefit. Do not young people and the working class in general expect to be represented on these important issues? The TUC leaders obviously cannot cope with that, so they tried to tinker about with the allowance.

What is far worse is that they came out saying that they had made progress. This progress consisted of a flat refusal by Norman Tebbit! But wait a minute, the TUC leaders said they had gained a commitment that Mr Tebbit would consult members of the MSC before squashing any of its future decisions. As the MSC is by now quite used to accepting what it does not like (before or after 'consultation') Mr Tebbit's claim that he made no *"concessions"* seems a reasonable one. So where is the progress? Mr Bill Keys, General Secretary of SOGAT said, pompously and meaninglessly: *"By your deeds you will be judged. I had the impression this afternoon that Norman Tebbit was listening."* Clive Jenkins, General Secretary of ASTMS, thought that the session made the prospect of future discussions more hopeful: *"The Secretary of State was sensitive to the criticisms we made this afternoon"*, he said. Mr Tebbit has done enough deeds to be well and truly judged by now, and the fact that he 'listens' to Bill Keys before giving a flat refusal is not much comfort. Nor is Clive Jenkins' assessment of his 'sensitiveness', for Mr Tebbit, sensitive as ever, said after the talks: *"My position has not changed at all. The TUC, before the general election, entertained some hopes of a Labour Government returning and, therefore, thought they had no need to talk to me. The TUC is now taking a realistic attitude about politics - that is, that the Government is here for another four or five years and probably for another four or five years after that."*

That the TUC leaders should come to this sorry pass is no accident, but a logical conclusion of their political position. They continually preach, by word and deed, that the problems of the working class can be solved under the conditions of imperialism. And to make matters worse they actively and violently oppose anything which challenges or threatens the role of the imperialist bourgeoisie, which even suggests that the emancipation of the working class can only be achieved through the overthrow of imperialism and the establishment of socialism. Their bankrupt, reactionary politics renders them useless for even the economic struggle to defend workers' present conditions. It leads them logically to the *"realistic attitude"* in this 'difficult economic climate' of going cap-in-hand to the Government on its own terms to see what crumbs are available.

Mr Bill Keys and his fellow TUC leaders would be well advised to remember that *"by your deeds you will be judged."* There are not many crumbs at the moment, for Mr Tebbit explained to them that if he had agreed to increase the YTS allowance, private sector companies would not have enough money to finance their part of the scheme. this is what the TUC described as a *"businesslike"* and *"civilised"* meeting.

Prospects for future talks are therefore bleak. Len Murray said that they will *"test the ice"* on Mr Tebbit's White Paper proposals for further union legislation. It is more likely that they will sit on the bank and agree with Mr

Tebbit that the ice does look rather thin, much better to skirt gingerly round the edge. The use of strong words like *"action"* is transparent hypocrisy when Len Murray puts them into sentences like:

"What is the alternative, but to get into the action and get something for our members".

This conclusion has been borne out by Len Murray's statements to the *Guardian* on unemployment. He said that he foresaw greater leisure emphasis in the future and the need for agreements on patterns of work and leisure: *"I do not think full employment is desirable or even necessary. I don't see why we should accept full employment axiomatically ... It's a good thing that people should have more time to engage in creative non-employment."* He said that *"in order to preserve living standards there will have to be an agreement about who gets what, and how work is divided."*

This is not the scene in which there is a planned economy, with production for need rather than profit, and where need is being fulfilled by advanced technology, with a good standard of living for all, so that the expansion of creative leisure time becomes the order of the day. No, we are in a situation of capitalist crisis of overproduction, where every effort is made to make the working class bear the brunt of the burden, large scale unemployment being an important part of that. In this context it is a shameless betrayal of the working class for Len Murray to propose talks on the basis he has put forward, and add: *"If we can agree that on present trends unemployment is going to reach 5 or 6 million, we ought also to be able to agree on what should be done and how the problem could be tackled."*

What Len Murray is saying is that imperialism cannot be eliminated, so let's share the misery among the working class; that the bourgeoisie will not pay to reduce the misery, so there should be things like work sharing, with those in work accepting a reduced wage. This juggling about does not get rid of unemployment, and unemployment does not cease to be unemployment by giving it another fancy name - *"creative non-employment"* if you please!

As the *Observer* put it in a leading article on 28 August 1983, even Mrs Thatcher *"must have been surprised at her success last week in making a convert out of the General Secretary of the TUC."*

It is clear that Len Murray and the TUC leadership are prepared, as they always have been, to assist the executive of the state -in the present case the Tory government - in their attempt to subdue the working class, undermine its struggle, and make it subservient to the needs of imperialism. That is the dead end to which economism has reduced the cretins of the TUC. This is really a juncture at which the working class has to decide either to follow Len Murray's economism and thus become completely defenceless in the conditions of a crisis of the present magnitude, or begin to think along new revolutionary lines and seek its social emancipation.

LALKAR December 1983

SUPPORT THE N.G.A.
SMASH THE BOURGEOIS OFFENSIVE AGAINST THE TRADE UNION MOVEMENT

There is an ancient Chinese saying according to which the tree may prefer the calm but the wind will not subside. The pusillanimous leadership - the Murrays and the Duffys - all wish to avoid at all costs a fight with the government, and the class of employers, but the latter will not go away. In the present conditions of depression, the bourgeoisie, and their management committee, to wit, the government, are bent upon pressing their advantage. In doing so, the bourgeoisie and its governmental spokesmen are forcing the trade-union movement to stand up and fight.

After initial hesitation and minor skirmishing, the battle has now been joined in earnest over the NGA (National Graphical Association) case. The NGA was fined £50,000 for its refusal to end secondary picketing of the Stockport Messenger group after the company had won an injunction against the union's action: the NGA has been fighting hard for a closed shop agreement with the company, and for the reinstatement of six sacked NGA members. The NGA was thus faced with a choice between compliance and defiance, capitulation or a fight to the finish. In the end, on Tuesday 22 November, the NGA Executive decided not to pay the fine imposed on it the previous week by the Manchester High Court. On Friday 25 November, a High Court judge ordered the seizure of the estimated £10 million assets of the NGA and imposed a further £100,000 fine for contempt of court. Making this sequestration order, Mr Justice Eastham said this of the NGA:

"The attitude they have maintained is that they are above the law."

He went on: *"The defendant association objects strongly to recent legislation in relation to industrial relations, namely, the Acts of 1980 and 1982. But they have remained on the statute book".*

His Honour forgot to add that what goes on the statute book can also come off it. And what brings it off the statute book is the resolute struggle of the working class against draconian anti-working class legislation, which is designed not only to politically emasculate the working class but also to render its economic struggle, inevitable under the conditions of capitalism, impotent. The working class cannot simply wait for a parliamentary majority of philanthropic and liberal-minded bourgeois, who, out of the sheer kindness of their hearts, out of feelings of pity for working people, repeal such nasty pieces of legislation. Such kind bourgeois do not exist; they have to be conjured, willed to be precise, into existence through the mighty mass movement of the working class. The NGA, in taking the decision that they have taken, have acted in the best traditions of the working-class movement in this country.

As we go to press, news has reached us that the Court of Appeal has confirmed the High Court order for sequestration of union assets. But already, within minutes of the High Court ordering the print union's assets to be seized, staff at the NGA Head office in Bedford began a spectacular evacuation.

They carried typewriters, other office equipment and documents into their cars and drove off to a secret destination. Special security locks were also fitted to doors of the building in Bromham Road. All of this goes to show the ingenuity with which working people can, once they have decided to challenge the might of the powers that be, in a most businesslike fashion and without much fuss, get on with the job of frustrating conspiracies aimed at decimating their organisations and movement.

The decision of Judge Eastham, and its confirmation by the Court of Appeal, is bound to lead to a complete shutdown of Fleet Street newspapers from tonight (25 November). The NGA are asking the TUC to supply financial and industrial support. And, although the TUC leadership is mortally afraid of a showdown with the government, it will have little option, if it wants to remain in the saddle, but to support the print union, for the spectacle of it sitting back and seeing any union fined out of existence would be fraught with the most fearful consequences.

Working people everywhere must support the NGA's just struggle, for, to borrow the language of the *Financial Times*, of Wednesday 23 November, *"a climbdown by the union, or its defeat by the company and the courts, will confirm the emerging trend of bringing in the new law to redress the old balance of power"*. (*'Now for the Real Test'*). The above-quoted perceptive remark of an extremely intelligent organ of the bourgeoisie reveals very clearly the issues at stake. It is not merely a question of defending the NGA. Nay, it is a question of defending the interests of the entire working class. The working class, not

SOCIAL DEMOCRACY and OTHER ECONOMIC STRUGGLES

the NGA, is under attack. The NGA dispute is merely the occasion, the pretext, of this attack. The entire working class must therefore rally round the NGA and make the NGA dispute its own. Then no law, no courts, no government, no power on earth will be able to prevent the NGA from being victorious. The bourgeoisie, faced with such determination on the part of labouring people, will then have little difficulty in finding some generous 'anonymous businessman' or 'official solicitor' who, by paying the fines imposed on the union, will help extricate it (the bourgeoisie) from is its predicament.

LALKAR February 1984

NGA DISPUTE DROWNS IN LEGAL CRETINISM

As we go to press, the NGA, in their dispute with Mr Eddie Shah, have "purged their contempt", agreed to pay the fines imposed on them and to act within the law in the future. Thus, to all intents and purposes, their dispute is as good as lost. Their dispute had become a lost cause already by mid-December when the TUC General Council decided not to back the NGA's 'unlawful' action. The time has come for us to review this and other such disputes, and draw the necessary lessons from the undoubted setbacks they represent for the working class.

The closing months of 1983 witnessed a spate of important industrial actions by the workers. In almost each one of these cases, the response of the employers, as though by a silent and secret understanding between them, was to resort to court injunctions to frustrate these industrial actions. A lethal combination of treachery by the TUC General Council, especially its General Secretary, Len Murray; the narrow craft mentality, with its utter lack of political consciousness and disdain for the interests of the wider working-class movement, of some unions; the bureaucratic desire of the trade-union leadership to save their own skins, and, above all, a cretin's faith in, and respect for, bourgeois law and a desire to conduct struggle only within the narrow bounds of what is permissible under this law - all this was bound to, and in fact did, result in the workers being defeated in each case.

In the cases of Shell against the TGWU, Robert Maxwell against Sogat 82, David Dimbleby against the NUJ, Sandher & Kang against the TGWU and Mercury against the POEU, recourse by the employers to courts and the granting of injunctions by the courts under the Employment Acts of 1980 and 1982, led to severe setbacks for the workers concerned.

However, the most significant case of all, which had assumed the importance of a trial of strength between not just a single employer and a single union but between the entire class of employers backed by its government, an armoury of anti-working class laws, the courts, the Police and, in the last resort, the armed forces, on the one hand; and the entire working class on the other hand, was that between Mr Eddie Shah, the owner of the Stockport Messenger Group, and the NGA. The *Financial Times* was characteristically perceptive and frank when on Wednesday 23 November it wrote concerning the issues at stake in the following terms:

"A climbdown by the union, or its defeat, will confirm the emergent trend of bringing in the new law to redress the old balance of power." ('Now for the Real Test').

But there was no equivalent understanding of the class issues involved on the part of British trade unionism. Writing in the December issue of *Print*, the official journal of the NGA, Mr Tony Dubbins, the General-Secretary elect, could not help asserting, even in the middle of one of the grimmest disputes that his print union has ever been involved in, the narrow sectional and craft response of the NGA to the introduction of new technology. He writes:

"The term 'craftsman' commands a certain status in the industry, and in the eyes of the NGA members sets them aside and apart from other non-craft people."

No wonder then that people who assume an air of such aristocratic superiority are unfit to mobilise working people in defence of their rights, for the main concern of these labour aristocrats is to ensure the exclusive interests of their union rather than the defence of workers' rights. No wonder then that the above-mentioned article of Mr Dubbins finds pride of place in the employers' 1984 Newspaper Publishers' Handbook. Appropriately entitled *Co-operation ... the Key to a Formula for our Future*, it sets out the NGA's continuing collaboration with the management in the question of introduction of new technology in the printing industry at the expense of jobs. The leadership of the NGA have long begged that it be consulted in bringing in the 'single key' computerisation that does away with most of the NGA's traditional typesetting functions. From this article it would appear that the thing that upsets the NGA leadership most is not that the workers are under attack but that the employers are trying to push through the introduction of new technology without even the pretence of consultations with the union leadership. Goes on Mr Dubbins:

The atmosphere currently being generated by statements in the national press of 'we intend to have single keying even if it means doing away with the NGA' is most unhelpful in assisting the national leadership of the trades union to play a positive role, and is creating a 'siege mentality' in some quarters of our membership".

'Siege mentality' is precisely what the working class needs to fight to the bitter end against the class that exploits and oppresses it. It is this 'siege mentality' that brings out what is most noble, self-sacrificing and heroic, in the working class, that the exploiting classes fear like the plague, and shudder even to contemplate. Curiously enough, the trade union leadership are also frightened to death of the growth of precisely such a 'siege mentality', just in case it should become so powerful as to force the leadership to come out of their cosy class-collaborationist niches and, for a change, lead the working class struggles rather than playing their 'positive role' in the service of British monopoly capitalism.

Mr Eddie Shah on the other hand, and from his class viewpoint, throughout displayed an admirable clarity of thought and purpose. He all along refused to reinstate the six sacked NGA workers and consistently refused to accept post-entry closed shop. With this purpose in mind, and knowing full well that in this battle he could not win alone, he enlisted not only the help of the Employment Acts 1980 and 1982, but also of the police, the government, the Institute of Directors - in a word, the class of employers. While Mr Shah and the bourgeois class as a whole were busy putting the boot in, the NGA top leadership, instead of organising to face the employers' onslaught, were busily making pathetic pleas for fair play from the other side:

"Every time we get to the winning post he [Mr Shah] *moves it"* exclaimed a confused, perplexed, exasperated and irate Mr Dubbins at the height of the dispute. Mr Shah and the rest of the employing class should be our teachers: this is how the working class should press its advantage and let the bourgeoisie complain about the workers moving the winning post each time they, the bourgeoisie, reach it.

Mr Joe Wade, the retiring General Secretary of the NGA, did no better. He too expressed his anger and outrage at Mr Shah's bloody-mindedness:

"Every time the NGA declared peace, Mr Shah declared war and all the NGA's efforts to find a peaceful solution have been thwarted by Mr Shah who is evidently determined not only to win the dispute, but to destroy the NGA in the process."

Have you, Mr Wade, the right even to talk of a peaceful solution in the face of fierce attack by the enemy? Having joined battle, has a general the right to make his chief concern the saving of his army rather than defeating the enemy? Each time one goes to war one risks the possibility of losing not only the war but even one's army. And one will never win unless one is determined to fight with utmost ferocity and determination to win, unless one organises to win. Mr Wade's above remark, however, reveals the sad fact that throughout its dispute with Mr Shah, the NGA's chief concern was to save the union, to concentrate on finding a peaceful solution rather than going all out for victory. When the union leadership was working with such zeal, worthy of a better cause, for its own defeat, no one, in particular the NGA, should be surprised when that foregone defeat actually takes place.

But the NGA was forced into a corner, thanks to the stubbornness of Mr Shah, and had to defend its patch. Eddie Shah set up the print shop for his weekly free newspaper in Warrington early in 1983 with the sole purpose of doing away with the customary closed shop agreements in the printing industry. When the NGA members went on strike to enforce a closed shop, Shah sacked eight union members. When the NGA pickets surrounded the Warrington plant, Shah got an injunction. The NGA pickets defied the injunction and the union was fined £50,000 for its refusal to end secondary picketing of the Stockport Messenger Group. The NGA decided on Tuesday 22 November not to pay the fine. On Friday 25 November, a High Court Judge ordered the seizure of the estimated £10 million assets of the NGA and imposed further fines, bringing the total to £675,000.

In these circumstances, the NGA could only continue its fight if it was assured of support from the rest of the trade-union movement in precisely the same fashion as Mr Shah had the solid support of the employers and the government.

The NGA appealed for this help, which the General Council of the TUC was under an obligation to render, as indeed it was obliged to support all the decisions of the April 1982 Wembley conference. The TUC employment policy and organisation committee voted in favour of supporting the NGA but Len Murray, outraged at this decision, immediately came out in defiance of it, without even waiting for the full meeting of the General Council. Of course, he received the well-deserved praise of a grateful bourgeoisie.

The following day Murray was vindicated as the specially-convened meeting of the General Council overturned the decision of the employment committee, which had given its backing to the NGA's 24-hour national print strike due to take place two weeks before Christmas. So the TUC put the knife in only hours before the strike was due to take place. The TUC General Council too won much praise for its statesmanship and judicious handling of the affair, for its part in this act of treachery against the working class of this country.

Although Murray has been much derided and portrayed as a *"pantomime villain"*, as one publication aptly put it, in some of the left press, in fact his actions have, in addition to their betrayal of the working class, brought a welcome relief to a lot of trade-union bureaucrats who had found themselves leading the dispute much to their surprise and against their real wishes simply because of the bloody-mindedness of Eddie Shah rather than because of any commitment to the interests of union members. The atmosphere of class compromise in which such bureaucrats have been nurtured scarcely equipped them to cope with an employer's sudden open rejection of compromise. They were forced into a fight but scarcely knew where to begin to organise their forces.

But no one should be surprised at the above treachery of the General Council. Nor was it sudden: the ground for it has been prepared over a period of two decades.

When the Labour Party came to power in 1964 on a wave of working-class support, it set itself the task of refurbishing British imperialism at the cost of the oppressed nations abroad and the working class at home. The TUC General staff fully collaborated with the Labour government. This collaboration turned into a partnership between the political wing (Labour Party) and the industrial wing (TUC) on a whole host of anti-working class measures culminating in the notorious social contract.

This so infuriated the workers that the Tories, under Mrs Thatcher, won the 1979 general election, on the slogan, among others, of free collective bargaining. Such was the demoralisation in the working-class movement thanks to the activities of the TUC and the Labour Party that the Tory anti-working class Employment legislation of 1980 and 1982 went on the statute book without serious opposition from the working class comparable to that put up against the Heath government's Industrial Relations Act of 1971. Between 1979 and 1983 the policy of the TUC, of the major unions and of the Labour Party has been one of respect for the law and of doing nothing that could hurt Labour's electoral prospects.

In the circumstances such prominent trade unionists as Derek Robinson were handed over to industrial tribunals as sacrificial lambs at the altar of the twin goddesses of the TUC, to wit, the goddess of Law & Order and the goddess of Labour's electoral prospects. All of this did not enhance Labour's electoral chances, for Labour suffered the worst electoral defeat. What this policy did serve to achieve was to demoralise and increasingly render impotent the working-class movement.[1]

At the height of the NGA dispute the General Council and the Labour Party have been concerned to emphasise their respect for the law and their condemnation of violence on the picket line. In these times of apostasy and base betrayal by the 'general staff' of the labour movement, of confusion and utter demoralisation in the ranks of the working class, the following words of Engels ring truer than ever before:

"The German workers have two important advantages over those of the rest of Europe. First, they belong to the most theoretical people of Europe; and they have retained that sense of theory which the so-called 'educated' classes of Germany have almost completely lost. Without German philosophy, which preceded it, particularly that of Hegel, *German scientific socialism - the only scientific socialism that has ever existed - would never have come into being. Without a sense of theory among the workers, this scientific socialism would never have entered their flesh and blood as much as is the case. What an immeasurable advantage this is may be seen ... from the indifference towards all theory which is one of the main reasons why the English working-class movement crawls along so slowly in spite of the splendid organisation of the individual unions ..." (The Preface to the Peasant War in Germany).*

Those who are interested in the victory of the working class must bring this sense of theory and knowledge of scientific socialism to the British working class movement, without which it will continue to crawl along as hitherto. If the present defeats are made the occasion for forging the weapon of scientific socialism and bringing it to the working-class movement, if they are made the occasion for the fight against the rotten trade-union bureaucracy and its legal cretinism, they may yet prove to be blessings in disguise. The working class can never fight for the defence and enhancement of its rights, let alone its social emancipation, within the bounds of bourgeois legality. Especially now in the midst of this protracted economic crisis, which has been seized by the employing class as the occasion for rolling back the frontiers of the rights of the working class and for launching vicious attacks on it, the methods of a bygone

---

1 As to the real reasons for Labour's defeat, namely, the desertion by the privileged sections of the working class to the side of the Conservatives, see Section I of this book (note to present edition).

era, of the prosperous Sixties and early Seventies, will not do. As this crisis develops and deepens still further, the working-class movement must either learn to discard the outmoded and blunt instruments of economism, narrow trade unionism and craft mentality and seize with vigour and determination the sharp and ever-new weapon of scientific socialism, or go down and accept, for the foreseeable future, life on its knees and the unchallenged rule of King Capital and its lackeys in the government.

LALKAR December 1985/January 1986

Liverpool showdown - the collapse of Trotskyite dreams of 'Socialism in one city'

On Friday November 23, the Liverpool Council that had been fighting the government's restrictions on local authority spending finally gave up the fight. In defiance of the government it had increased rates by only 9% while considerably increasing its expenditure on council housing, knowing that if the government did not bail it out, the City would collapse financially. Great sacrifices were made, particularly by individual Councillors, who will almost certainly soon be bankrupted for their defiance, but almost as soon as the fight started for real these sacrifices proved to have been made in vain, as important sections of the struggle's supporters, spurred on by Neil Kinnock, chickened out. Contrary to everything the Council was fighting for - namely sufficient income to run the Council at a proper level - and contrary also to financial common sense, the Council was forced to "capitalise" a major part of its revenue expenditure - in other words, to borrow money from Swiss banks at high rates of interest and subject to loan conditions restrictive of the Council's freedom. The borrowing means that in future years the Council's expenditure on services will be reduced by its need to service the loan, and others that it has contracted (either voluntarily or under pressure) in previous years. This cannot but mean a reduction in services and/or an even greater rate increase. It can be seen therefore, that the people of Liverpool are very much the losers in this defeat of Liverpool Council, which had been fighting virtually single-handedly to maintain the social wage of Liverpool's working class against government onslaught.

The struggle of Liverpool Council has been momentous, and even in defeat it is important to study it, to learn the lessons of the defeat for the working class. In presenting here for the first time in *Lalkar* the facts concerning this struggle we must start with an apology to our readers that we have not turned our attention to this subject sooner. The struggle has been going on now for over two years. It was overshadowed for much of that time by the heroic miners' struggle, but was nevertheless deserving of our attention. We hasten now to put right our past neglect.

Liverpool people support Militant

In essence the struggle was resistance by a local authority to government cuts in public spending insofar as they are aimed at lowering the living standards of the working class. Most local authorities, whether Conservative or Labour controlled, have carried out the government's orders and reduced spending drastically on education, social services, council house repairs, and council house building has virtually come to a standstill. In Liverpool, however, the cuts demanded would cut even deeper than elsewhere. The amenities of Liverpool were already poorer than the average when the government stepped up its pressure on public spending. The people were already resentful. That resentment had already given rise to the Toxteth riots. That resentment also made people sympathetic to the Labour Party left-wingers, the Militant Tendency. However much the bourgeois press tries to 'prove' that the Militant tendency was 'unrepresentative' of the people of Liverpool, that it manipulated its way into power by use of microscopic union branches that were over represented in the District Labour Party, and all the rest of it, it has to be admitted that no number of bureaucratic manoeuvres could have given Militant the ascendancy it had in Liverpool if the people of Liverpool had not been receptive to their call for a no-holds-barred struggle against the government to maintain public services.

Background to the struggle

Liverpool was built on the slave trade. At the end of the 18th century, Liverpool supplied three quarters of British slaving ships. When the slave trade stopped, Liverpool remained a major port for import and export to the Empire. It thrived and basked in the glory of the British Empire. So successful was the port, and so demanding of labour, that Liverpool developed virtually no other industry; its people were not trained for other types of work, never acquired the skills necessary in manufacturing, for instance, had no factory tradition. No city in Britain, therefore, suffered more dramatically from the decline of British imperialism since the end of the first world war than Liverpool. This decline contributed heavily to its port slowly but surely running down, and as it has run down it has brought down the whole of Liverpool. In the early 1930s unemployment in Liverpool was 1.5 times the national average. In the late 1940s it was 2.5 times the national average. Today unemployment is 27%, double the national average.

Between 1971 and 1985, total employment fell by 33%, causing the present unemployment figure to be one of the worst in the country. Furthermore, those who are unemployed stay out of work longer. The figure of those still out of work after a year is 53% (compared with 39% nationally). After a year unemployment benefit ceases and living standards plunge when the family goes on social security. This is the situation of over 14% of Liverpool's work force.

When we look at the situation in Liverpool it is as though we look into a crystal ball predicting the future for the rest of Britain. Liverpool may lead the economic decline, but all the signs are that the rest of Britain is not far behind. This is really the reason why it is important to examine the events in Liverpool Council over the last two years with interest.

Liverpool Council prior to 1982

Rapid economic decline in Liverpool did not in the 1970s lead the Council to try to make good the social disadvantage suffered by its people by means of high public spending. The Council did come to be a relatively major source of what little employment there was, but this was because of the decline of private sector employment, not because of any increase in Council employment. Today 14% of the employed are in fact employed by Liverpool Council. It is no wonder that the people of Liverpool all opposed Council spending cuts that would attack such jobs as remained in Liverpool.

Most working class cities in times of economic decline return Labour councils, the Labour party being traditionally more committed than the other bourgeois parties to Keynesianism. But the Labour Party, for a variety of reasons, did not have a strong hold in Liverpool. One reason was the lack of an industrial working class, in particular the skilled workers. The ideology of workers making good within capitalism, the ideology of the labour aristocracy, created the Labour Party in its own image. The Labour Party did have the support, however, of most of the City's Catholics, which did enable it to capture the Council in the 1950s for the first time. At that time the Labour Council distinguished itself mainly by building tower-blocks, council estates destined to become slums within ten years. As the Labour Party did not have the traditional working class support in Liverpool that kept it in power in many similarly deprived urban areas, its blunders, such as its cheap and nasty council estates, were less readily forgiven. Though Labour was in and out of power in the 1960s, alternating with the Conservatives, in the 1970s, the years when the capitalist crisis began to bite, it was the Liberals who called the tune financially. In fact the Council found itself throughout the 1970s without any party having an overall majority on the Council. However, as the Liberals were the largest party and the Conservatives usually supported them, the Liberals set the Council's budgets for those years. The policies that won favour with the Conservatives were those favourable to the wealthier citizens most likely to support the Conservatives and the Liberals at the polls, at the expense of those who most needed support. This was illustrated by the Liberal policy of giving improvement grants to the owners of cheap houses while putting up Council rents and cutting back repair and renewal of Council housing. Full Conservative support was given to this measure. As a consequence the jerry-built Council houses fell into a really appalling state of repair - a problem inherited by the Labour administration that was returned in 1983. Such repairs as were done in the 1970s were paid for largely from borrowing rather than from revenue, as the Liberal party tried to maintain its popularity by keeping down the rates.

So great was Liberal commitment to low rates that even when a Labour government increased the rate support grant (given to local authorities by central government) in Liverpool by £21 million for the purpose of supporting economically deprived areas, the Liberals used part of the extra grant to CUT rates by 1p in the £. Again Liberals had full support from the Conservatives for these measures.

The rise of Militant influence

Years of this kind of administration left Liverpool, and particularly its working class, in a bad way, so much so that to put matters right needed a great deal more money than would have been spent had expenditure been incurred as and when the need arose. Following the 1979 Council elections, the Labour Party was the majority party in yet another hung Council. However it set itself the task of restoring jobs and services, and to do this proposed for 1980 a 50% rate rise. The alternatives to this were (a) to let the rot continue, or (b) to raise Council rents (the measure most favoured in the previous decade). There was prolonged wrangling over Labour's budget, to such an extent that Labour was only able to force it through because the Conservatives and Liberals could not agree with each other on any alternative proposal: the Conservatives wanted a realistic budget showing money raised from rent increases. The Liberals preferred an unrealistic budget only introducing rent increases at the last moment. By the time the 50% rate rise was forced through there were only 6 weeks left to the next Council elections (in Liverpool one third of the Council is re-elected every two years). The rate rise caused an uproar for nobody had had the benefit of that rate rise all the time that Labour had been the majority party. As a result Labour was trounced in the 1981 election, losing 6 seats.

It was at this point that Militant came into its own. Militant had for some time been putting forward the demand that the cost of restoring the City should be met by central government. They had actually opposed the 50% rate rise, moving an amendment to the Labour budget (much to the joy of Labour's opponents) to the effect that rates should be increased by only 13%, to cover the cost of inflation and new services, that there should be no cuts in jobs or services, but that the Council should unite with the Labour and trade-union movement *"to fight for the money needed from the government"*. Following Labour's election defeat, Militant policy was adopted by the district Labour Party (on which the Militant Tendency was strongly represented). The policy was widely supported outside the Tendency, however. It was supported by Tony Byrne, a non-Militant with considerable influence over other councillors and in the district party. It was supported by council officers Alfred Stocks (Chief Executive) and Michael Reddington (the Treasurer), and it had broad public support.

The latter was proved by the Labour Party's victory in the 1983 Council election which gave it an overall majority - the first time any party had held an overall majority on Liverpool Council for 10 years. The Party had been elected with a mandate to defend jobs and services, and this it set out to do.

Budget Problems

In drawing up its budget, Labour faced a number of problems:

First, substantial rate or rent increases were out.

Second, government policy since 1980 had drastically cut the rate support grants of all local authorities.

Third, the cutting of the rate support grant and the system of imposing penalties on Councils which overspent by cutting the rate support grant still further was arbitrary and happened to affect Liverpool particularly badly. From 1980 the Conservative government set out to reduce public spending by setting 'targets' for the Councils, requiring Councils to reduce their spending by a given percentage below the level of an arbitrarily selected year or forfeit part of its (reduced) rate support grant. The penalties for overspending increased in rate depending on how much was overspent. A Council overspending 1% above its target would have to raise its rates 2p in the £ to make good the deficiency. If it 'overspent' by 6% the rate rise would have to be of the order of 41p in the £. The year chosen as base year for determining Council spending was 1978/79, a year when Liverpool, controlled by the Liberals, had underspent in an irresponsible manner. After various local authorities resisted the choice of 1978/79 as base year, 1981/2 was chosen instead, another year in which Liverpool had suffered a Liberal budget. The result of all this was that compared to 1980/81 expenditure (the year of Liverpool's 50% rate rise), Liverpool's target was 11% lower, as compared to an average of 6% lower for all authorities.

The Council calculated that to balance the books without government aid there were three possibilities:

(a) drastically cutting back local authority services (b) loss of 5,000 Council jobs; or (c) a rate rise of 170%.

The illegal budget

Its mandate from the electorate and the influence of the Militant Tendency and the local authority unions in the district Labour Party precluded the adoption of any of these possibilities, so instead an illegal, deficit budget was proposed. Rates would increase by 9%. The Council would run up a deficit of £160.9 million, and would ultimately run out of cash, bankrupting the city. That is, if government money was not provided.

As soon as the Council announced its illegal budget, it came under pressure from the Labour Party leadership to "obey the law", the perennial excuse for betrayal. Neil Kinnock made speeches commending the 'official Party policy' of councillors staying in office and trying to minimise the effects of cuts (i.e., trying to make cuts more acceptable). He refused to visit the city, and the rapidly rising 'soft' left-winger, David Blunkett, of whom we shall hear more anon, moaned that the 'time was not ripe for law breaking'. This pressure, along with arrogant government statements to the effect that it would never give in, very soon frightened off six Labour councillors who announced that they would not support the deficit budget. When denounced by Militant councillor Derek Hatton, one of the 'rebels' said: *"Labour have taken on the Government and they have lost. I am not going to be intimidated by people I see as extremists"*. He was obviously only prepared to be intimidated by the big battalions.

Anyway, since the Labour Party had a majority of only 3 on the Council, the defection of the 'sensible 6' set every reactionary crowing with delight. The illegal budget prepared by the Labour group was duly presented and duly defeated.

Stalemate

But then what? The 'sensible 6' dared not go so far as to support the alternative budget put forward by the Liberal group (which the Council Treasurer had described as 'doubtfully realistic'), and the Labour group as a whole had no intention of putting through any other budget. Without a budget at all, no rate could be set, no money could be raised from any source, and the City would be bankrupted all the sooner.

People of Liverpool support the illegal budget

No budget had been agreed by May 1984 when the Labour group, defying Labour's national leadership as well as the government, fought yet another Council election. It demanded a clear mandate from the electorate to resort to illegality and bankruptcy if necessary to wring concessions from the government. The Labour Party increased its majority by no less than 7 seats, enough to override the combined efforts of Conservatives, Liberals and 'sensible' Labourites.

At last, the massive popularity of the Labour group's resistance galvanised the Conservative government into action. If an election is a barometer of the political consciousness of the masses, it is one the reactionaries too can read. If ordinary people are prepared to back 'extremists' at the polls, it is a warning sign to the reactionaries that the level of class consciousness is rising, and steps have to be taken quickly to defuse the situation. It must be remembered also that at this time the government was deeply engaged in its struggle to defeat the miners and did not want confrontation on two fronts. Therefore Patrick Jenkin was sent to Liverpool (he was then Conservative Minister for Merseyside) ostensibly to *"look at housing problems as a background to future housing capital allocations"*, the visit having *"no connection with the Council's budget making and rate-fixing process"*. The councillors were made to feel that they had won a great victory when he agreed to meet them! The visit was fixed for the 7th of June, and in the meantime the government, in consultation with local councillors, MPs, etc., set up a 'joint team' of senior civil servants and local authority officials to look into Liverpool's finances, with a view to finding proposals to put before the Minister when he visited on the 7th of June.

Government concessions

The joint report concluded, by way of appeasement, that Liverpool did indeed have grave problems. *"Whitehall Whizz Kids Stumped"*, announced the *Liverpool Echo* when the news was leaked. And when Patrick Jenkin did inspect Liverpool's housing on 7 June, he emerged exclaiming *"I have seen some families living in conditions the like of which I have never seen before. They are very grim"*. He thus opened the way for the government to make concessions to Liverpool as far as was necessary to buy off the confrontation until after the miners' strike was over. The price demanded did not prove excessively great.

The government made the following concessions:

1. The government would allocate £3.1 million of urban programme money to be used to continue support for projects which would otherwise have to be paid for from the rates. Taking overspending penalties into account, this would reduce the deficit by £7.5 million.

2. The government was prepared to add £2.5 million to Liverpool's urban programme allowance, saving £7 million.

3. The government promised help with repayment of loans incurred for the construction of high rise towers which were going to need demolition at some future date, such help to be available to all authorities.

4. The government, finally, would pay £1 million towards certain environmental work.

Total aid amounted to £8.6 million, and reduced grant penalties by £12 million, thus saving £20 million on the Council's budget. But Liverpool had claimed it was short of £160 million!

It follows that in accepting the government's package - which it did - it was the Council which made by far the greatest concessions.

The Council's concessions

This is how the Council 'balanced' its budget:

(a) it 're-opened' the 1983/84 budget which had given rise to a £34.7 million deficit and 'reduced' that deficit to £4.7 million.

(b) it tinkered with the 1984/5 budget in a similar manner.

The balance was made up by increasing the rate rise to 17%.

It is important to appreciate the nature of these 'adjustments'. Debt rescheduling means higher interest charges to pay in future years, as does the 'capitalisation' of housing repairs (i.e., borrowing money to pay for them). Use of the Council's £11 million reserves meant a loss of income on those reserves which could only be made good by a 45% rate increase.

The decoration allowance was snatched away from Council tenants living in substandard housing. The reduction in the figures for salaries and inflation were pure 'creative accounting', i.e., fiction. The original salary figures and the original allowance for inflation were what the Council would have to pay, however much its budget might say otherwise. Real costs were underestimated by about £8 million and the effect of inflation was understated by about £14 million. This deficit would have to be carried forward to the 1985/6 budget.

The concessions made by the government, then, were almost irrelevant in the context of Liverpool's problems. Yet the Labour group hailed them as a great victory. But all they had done was to put off the crisis to the following year, by which time, the government hoped, the miners' struggle would be over and the government could turn its full attention to putting Liverpool Council firmly in its place.

Manoeuvres on the housing budget

Tony Byrne claimed afterwards that he only agreed to compromise with the government because the government had promised that the following year Liverpool would be allowed £130 million for housing, nearly treble its 1984/5 allocation of £46 million. This would indeed have been a significant gain and would have explained acceptance of the compromise. However, when the government announced the funds for local authorities for 1985/6, it actually cut Liverpool's housing funds by almost 20% to £37 million, despite all the crocodile tears it had indulged in about the state of Liverpool's housing. It openly admitted that the reason it was being harsh with Liverpool was that Liverpool was not prepared to spend a higher proportion of its housing budget in assisting private housing.

The government denied any promise to give Liverpool £130 million for housing, or indeed anything at all. The official minutes of the discussions between Patrick Jenkin and the councillors did not, of course, reveal any promise to allocate £130 million to housing, but Byrne was adamant that this promise had been made, and broken.

In the meantime the Council had acted as though the £130 million were in the bag. Contracts had been signed worth £88 million and a further £8 millions-worth were signed after the reduced targets were announced. However, much to the government's disgust, the money to pay was raised by selling the City's mortgages to a French bank, a loophole that the government rushed belatedly to close, but too late to stop Liverpool.

The revenue budget

So once again the real fight over the 1985/6 expenditure was over revenue expenditure. But now the miners' strike was over and the government's concern for Liverpool's problems vanished overnight. The target set by the government for Liverpool was £222 million, but the true cost of maintaining the city's services in 1985/6 was £283 million. To balance the books this time, Liverpool would need a 220% rate increase.

Nevertheless, Liverpool Council was under pressure from its Labour Party 'friends' not to rock the electoral boat. Even the Militant leadership was concerned that none of its people were being selected as Parliamentary candidates and brought pressure on their councillors to behave 'responsibly'. The Council put forward plans for the re-organisation of secondary education (to make it cheaper - fewer teachers) and also confronted the unions of over the refuse service, which by all accounts required improvement. Whether that could be brought about by cuts was another matter. Furthermore they indulged in quite a bit of 'creative accounting' to conceal the true cost of running the city so as not to forfeit as much of its rate support grant. In this way it was able to present its necessary expenditure for 1985/6 as only £265 million. In its effort to do this it had enraged the unions, something that would in due course cost dear.

With its budget then estimated at £265 million, Liverpool joined in the stand of other local authorities against rate capping. It will be recalled that the government imposed maximum amounts that could be raised from the rates on certain high-spending local authorities, which did not, incidentally, include Liverpool. However, a number of local authorities ventured into battle against the government in protest against rate capping. The protest took the form of refusing to set a rate. However the first whiff of the government's gunfire set the local authorities scuttling to set a rate, many 'left-wing' Labourites breathing a sigh of relief that they were outnumbered and outvoted by unashamed right-wingers. Among these was David Blunkett, leader of the Sheffield Council. Liverpool Council, however, along with Lambeth, held out to the last. By the time the action finally collapsed, Liverpool's District Auditor had already served notice that he would be taking proceedings against the council in respect of their failure to set a rate, which proceedings would undoubtedly end in surcharge, disqualification and bankruptcy for the individual councillors.

With nothing to lose, therefore, Liverpool's councillors moved to what it had intended to do all along (which it had tried in vain to persuade the rate-capped local authorities to do in order to close avenues of escape), namely to set a second illegal rate.

Another illegal budget

Once more the Council recalculated its probable deficit, and this time reduced it to £252 million, requiring a 75% rate increase. The council, however, set the rate at a 9% increase only. A district Labour Party meeting on 13 June this year instructed Labour councillors not to make a legal rate. Nobody moved any alternative proposal or amendment, and the resolution was accepted unanimously. Then on the 14th of June the illegal rate was set. It would have taken the defection of only 3 Labour councillors to overturn the illegal rate, but nobody defected.

The illegal rate left the city £117 million short of the money needed for the year. Without the government intervening once more, the money would definitely run out. At this point the whole of Liverpool was behind the Councillors in their defiance. The government, no doubt hopeful of the forces at work in the Labour Party itself, just sat back to wait and see.

The redundancy notices

What happened was that the councillors dreamed up a means of both getting money from the government and keeping the city solvent, but which would do so at the expense of the city's better-paid workers. They announced a plan whereby the Council's workforce would be made redundant. In this way, though the Council would have to pay them redundancy money, it would be less than what would otherwise have been their wages, and all the workers would then have a large claim against the government's redundancy fund. In the case of the Council's lower-paid workers, this would more than make up the loss of wages. The Council would then at the start of the next financial year re-hire everybody. On the face of it, this was quite a clever manoeuvre, but it failed for three reasons:

(a) It was unacceptable to the people of Liverpool as a whole because it put public services in jeopardy; (b) It was unacceptable to better-paid Council workers, who would lose money; and (c) There could be no guarantee that redundant employees would be hired again.

Cuts in education and refuse collection had weakened support for, and trust in, the Council in the unions, and it was in the unions that reaction made its first gains. The teachers in particular were fearful of not being re-appointed as promised. Only the General and Municipal, whose workers stood to benefit financially from the proposal, supported it. Nor would the unions go on strike to help the Council out of its financial difficulties. In this situation the Council made the tactical error of serving the redundancy notices anyway. Although a large minority of workers were prepared to back the Council, either by accepting redundancy or by going on strike, the unanimous support that the Council had so recently enjoyed was gone for good.

Neil Kinnock then pounced to bring the 'soft' left, typified by Michael Meacher and David Blunkett, to heel at the Labour Party Conference in Bournemouth the following month, October. The entire conference was dedicated to attacking the left wing of the party. Arthur Scargill was castigated for his leadership of the miners' struggle and Militant for splitting the party. David Blunkett, in particular, launched an attack on Liverpool Council for daring to put a resolution in support of their actions before the conference. He demanded that in the name of 'party unity' the resolution be withdrawn, and Derek Hatton agreed. Instead David Blunkett persuaded them they should open their books to a committee headed by Maurice Stoneforth, who would come up with 'solutions' to Liverpool's crisis. Militant supporters were totally outwitted by these tactics. One of them, Mulhearn, left the conference believing that Blunkett was on their side.

The committee reports

However, when the committee reported in November, its report contained nothing new. Its terms were almost identical to the previous year's 'joint report'. It claimed there were "painless" ways of solving Liverpool's problems, namely, minimal cuts, a 15% extra rate, and shifting expenditure from the revenue budget to the capital budget, the capital budget being funded for this purpose by loans. In other words 'let's postpone the problem until next year, when it will be worse, but maybe something will turn up'.

It was quite obvious that the report contained no solutions at all. Yet it was greeted with rapture by the Labour Party leadership and by the Blunketts of the world, and so it secured the necessary defections from within the district Labour Party, who promptly ordered its councillors to compromise, at a meeting of 22 November. At this point Tony Byrne produced a deal that he had negotiated with Swiss bankers back in August under which the Council would borrow £25-30 million. Along with another rate increase it would keep the Council afloat to the end of the year. A condition of the loan was the immediate setting of a legal budget. The fight was over.

Tory Minister Kenneth Baker was relieved beyond measure. The Tories had been on the point of appointing commissioners to run Liverpool.

Meanwhile the Labour Party continued its dirty work by fronting the anti-Militant witch hunt. Ian Williams of the Liverpool Labour Party wrote in the *New Statesman* of 29 November: "*... to shield Militant is to defend the 31,000 redundancies and the futile attempt to blackmail an uncaring government by closing the very jobs and services of the slogans* [that appear so prominently in the Militant slogans]. *It is to defend the untruths by which they attempted to con everybody there was no option but civic suicide"*.

So, having sold the Liverpool Council leadership down the river, the Labour Party actually has the gall to blame them for that sale, forgetting that the attempt *"to blackmail an uncaring government"* was rendered futile by the cold feet of the Labour Party. Of course, raising money by way of loan was *"an alternative to civic suicide"* only in the sense that it postponed that suicide for another year, with the Council's income mortgaged to an ever greater extent for the repayment of loans incurred for previous years' expenditure. The alternative to *"civic suicide"* this year is *"civic suicide"* next year or the year after, or a long drawn out and painful death of Liverpool's jobs and services, which *"civic suicide"* was intended to try and prevent. If the attempt to blackmail the Government failed, it is the depths of political bankruptcy to claim that it should never have been made.

Lessons of Liverpool

The first and foremost lesson of Liverpool must be that one cannot fight for the working class effectively within the Labour Party. One often hears that the Labour Party is the 'mass party of the working class' and that to be close to the masses one must join this party. But what happens to revolutionaries who join the Labour Party? They are in a minority and are either forced to bow to the will of the majority, or they ignore the will of the majority and are sooner or later expelled. As the *Labour Activist,* journal of the 'soft' left Labour Co-ordinating Committee rightly put it:

"Kinnock's *speech* [at the Labour Party Conference in Bournemouth attacking the left wing of the party] *marks a watershed ...*

"*The watershed puts two options firmly before the party: either we are going to fight our leadership or we are prepared to build our party. It's a watershed between those who are serious about winning power and those who are not*".

Everything in the Labour Party is geared to electoral victory, and it is axiomatic that electoral victory depends on the Party presenting a 'responsible' alternative, responsible, that is, to the interests of capital.

Note the reverence of the Labour Party leadership for bourgeois legality. Note how at various points concessions were made for the sake of unity. Note how the final blows on the Militants were delivered by supposed left wingers, mesmerised by the dream of electoral gain and "winning power".

It has to be admitted that the Labour Party decimated the Militant would-be revolutionaries far more effectively than the Conservative government could have done. Tory assaults would have made the Militants martyrs to whose call the masses were prepared to rally. But Labour's assault drained all the strength, vitality and support of the Militants, humiliated them and finished them off.

All this proves once again that however hard and arduous it may seem to have to build up a genuine working class party and to break the hold of the sham working class party, the Labour Party, this is the only way forward. While the Labour Party has any influence over mass struggle that struggle is bound to fail.

Any person who becomes a member of the Labour Party, it has to be said, is a traitor to the working class, even though that may be the very last thing that he or she would subjectively want to be. For while the need of the moment is to destroy the Labour Party, its members all spend hours doing everything to build it up. On the one hand they propagandise for the Labour Party, e.g., by canvassing, and on the other hand those members who are genuinely concerned for the interests of the working class effectively perpetuate the myth that these are the Labour Party's concerns as well. In this way they help trap more well-meaning innocents in the Labour Party's spider's web, where in due course they will be turned into counter-revolutionaries "*in the interests of party unity*" to prove that they are "*serious about winning power*".

Furthermore, the task of a revolutionary is to take on the bourgeois state and eventually to overthrow it. The bourgeois state however, is very powerful indeed. Only a working class party with strong links with the working masses

AND THAT IS GUIDED BY THE REVOLUTIONARY THEORY OF MARXISM-LENINISM and maintaining iron discipline over its members can have the strength to lead the struggle to overthrow the bourgeois state, something which by its very nature is alien to, and beyond, Trotskyism. It is obvious that the Labour Party can never fulfil this role. It is but an instrument of the bourgeois state fashioned over decades to serve its every need. If at one time revolutionaries joined it to expose it, they never dreamed of using it for "winning power". Even the time for exposing it is long past. Years of experience have made the nature of the Labour Party obvious to anyone with the slightest inclination to learn, notwithstanding all the efforts of the Militant Tendency and various other Trotskyite renegades to socialism to burnish its tarnished image.

The problem for all Trotskyites is that they represent only petty-bourgeois opposition to the bourgeois state. They are much more appalled by the thought of the dictatorship of the proletariat - working-class state power - than they are even by the injustices they suffer under capitalism. Their efforts, therefore, are geared to trying to force capitalism to become more humane, as if that were possible !

This is how they came to hope that by getting control of Liverpool Council through their membership of the Labour Party they could bring 'socialism in one city' without any need for the dreaded working-class state which they never cease to attack in their speeches and in their publications. They thought that the support of the masses would guarantee them success in the face of the bourgeois counter-attack, but they never stopped acting as agents of the bourgeoisie, and so confused and alienated their supporters.

It is of course to their credit that they fought. They might even have succeeded if other local authorities had united with them, and fought to the bitter end. But the authorities who started the fight were all influenced by the Labour Party, and all chickened out for one reason or another. Without the leadership of a genuine working class party, Liverpool Council was fighting a man-eating tiger with a paper sword. With the Labour Party to 'support' it, it was fighting on quicksand. The councillors could not win.

If there was any place in England for the Trotskyites to put to the test their experiment in 'socialism in one city' it was Liverpool. The experiment failed miserably as it was bound to. This had been guaranteed partly by their tactics and largely by their long-standing, cringing and slavish capitulation to social democracy. These class warriors, these super-revolutionaries, who never tire of denouncing 'socialism in one country' by the Bolshevik Party, nevertheless had pinned their hopes of building socialism in one city - the would-be Soviet Republic of Liverpool - through the instrumentality of the thoroughly corrupt, rotten and bourgeois Labour Party.

This tells us as much about the politics of the Militant Trots as it does about the Labour Party. By thy friends shall ye be known. It is not for nothing that during the imperialist Falklands/Malvinas war, the Militant Trots beat the "drum-roll for war" as luridly as the notorious trench-pacifist Michael Foot. The Labour Party is indeed the only place for such imperialist-minded and chauvinistically-inclined gentry.

The conclusion cannot be avoided that, following in the footsteps of Trotskyism, the working class can never achieve victory. The revolutionary ideology of Marxism-Leninism and its organisational principles alone provide a sure basis for working-class victory.

LALKAR February 1986

Wapping - Unions confronted

Rupert Murdoch has taken advantage of the demoralisation in the trade-union movement, caused by the failure of the miners' strike, to break the resistance of printworkers' unions to the introduction of new technology. He has struck a mortal blow at the unions based on organised craft workers whose skills have become redundant as the result of the development of the new technology. This technology was in fact developed many years ago, and has already been introduced in many countries, but for many years the trade-union movement in this country was able to block its introduction here. They did this not out of infatuation with the old methods, but quite simply to protect the lives and living standards of their members who would otherwise face the dole queue.

The bourgeoisie has decried the unions as diehards standing in the way of progress. But what progress is there for the working class when these machines are introduced?

As Marx pointed out in volume I of *Capital*, *"... The whole system of capitalist production is based on the fact that the workman sells his labour-power as a commodity. Division of labour specialises this labour power, by reducing it to skill in handling a particular tool. So soon as the handing of this tool becomes the work of a machine, then, with the use-value, the exchange value too, of the workman's labour-power vanishes, the workman becomes unsaleable, like paper money thrown out of currency by legal enactment. That portion of the working class, thus by machinery rendered superfluous, i.e,. no longer immediately necessary for the self-expansion of capital, either goes to the wall ... or else floods all the more easily accessible branches of industry, swamps the labour-market, and sinks the price of labour-power below its value."*

Although Marx wrote the above words nearly 100 years ago, really he could be describing the plight of the printworkers today. Their skills no longer have any market value and they are threatened with unemployment in large numbers. The unemployed already constitute 13% of the British workforce, as a result of which demand for the commodity, labour-power, has already dropped well below the supply, with the effect of *"sinking the price of labour power below its value"*. Its value is determined by the value of the means of subsistence of the worker and his family, so that already, on average, the working class living standards have fallen below its historically evolved means of subsistence - the level of subsistence which it has been accustomed to. Thousands of printworkers thrown on to the streets will aggravate the situation for the entire working class.

Yet both the miners' strike and the printworkers' strike has demonstrated a failure of the working class in general to unite to defend its interests, even at a purely trade-union level. The miners obtained resolutions from the TUC, but precious little else. Although workers were generous with financial donations, these were not hurting the capitalist class. The miners needed mass solidarity action, but very little was forthcoming. Likewise, the printworkers looked in vain for solidarity from fellow workers in the electricians' union or the journalists' union. And while the working class is in such appalling disarray as far as defending its class interests is concerned, the ruling class under Thatcher's leadership is more vicious than ever in its attacks on the working class.

It cannot be doubted that Murdoch was encouraged by evidence of working-class disarray and union betrayals to put the boot in as far as the printworkers were concerned. He planned his campaign to smash SOGAT 82 in military style from his bunker in Fortress Wapping, behind double steel gates and a barbed-wire perimeter fence. He secretly imported the new technologies - particularly the direct-input computerised setting (to be done by journalists rather than printworkers) that would render composing-room staff redundant - from US manufacturers ATEX. The machinery was packaged in crates on which the ATEX name was painted over, and ATEX had strict instructions not to inform their own British sales office about the deal, in case the unions got wind of what was in store. Having sneaked in the machinery, Murdoch then did a deal with the EEPTU (notorious for its willingness to reach no-strike deals, and the like) that its members should operate the new machinery, secretly training them in the barbed-wire encampment. From this position of strength Murdoch made a show of 'negotiating' with SOGAT, but he was only interested in negotiating the latter's unconditional surrender and agreement to however many redundancies Murdoch demanded. The union had no choice but to call a strike, whereupon Murdoch dismissed all the strikers. He didn't need any of them anyway. He then shamelessly bribed his journalists by offering them a £2,000 p.a. pay rise and free health service if they came to Wapping, and threatening dismissal if they did not. They came, in defiance of instructions from the NUJ that they should stand by the printworkers and refuse to so. Furthermore, Murdoch is a believer in kicking his enemy while he is down. Although SOGAT was virtually helpless in the face of his onslaught, he threw the weight of Thatcherite labour law at it in connection with its picketing and other industrial action. The Thatcher administration, it will be recalled, started by passing the 1980 Employment Act, which, in the words of the *Observer* of 16.2.86, *"began by clawing back all the legal immunities that Labour had given the unions in 1974. And it sowed the seeds for the collapse of union power as demonstrated by the Wapping dispute. First, it severely curbed secondary industrial action and weakened the closed shops. Then Norman Tebbit's 1982 Employment Act went further and ensured that unions could be sued for organising unlawful industrial action".* Armed, then with these Draconian laws, Murdoch claimed in court that SOGAT, in organising action against various Murdoch companies technically different from the one with which SOGAT was in dispute, was in breach of the law and should be penalised. The court naturally, agreed, following the little-noticed decision in **Dimbleby v. NUJ**, and the legal technicality (originally developed for quite different reasons) that theoretically in law each company is regarded as a separate 'person', totally unrelated to the people who own it. On the basis of such spurious 'reasoning', the court found that SOGAT, in instructing fellow unions not to handle any of Murdoch's newspapers (owned by different Murdoch companies) was guilty of taking secondary action, and fined the union £25,000, which the union refused to pay. As a result its entire assets of £17 million have been seized by sequestrators.

All this has been achieved so quickly that nobody has had much opportunity to come to SOGAT's aid, even supposing that the will to do so is there in the general working-class movement. It is true that in collaboration with the NGA, the transport union and the Union of Communication Workers (whose postmen briefly blacked Murdoch's bingo cards until frightened off by threats of court action and sequestration) have achieved some disruption of distribution of the Murdoch organs. But court action has paralysed the unions, who mostly tend towards a cretinous worship of bourgeois legality at the best of times. Her helplessness in the face of the bourgeois state machine caused Brenda Dean, the General Secretary of SOGAT, to say that there is no point in having a union if it cannot defend its members, and the law will not allow it to do so.

The next step has to be a general commitment by the TUC and its constituent unions to defy the law, making such preparations for the protection of union funds as they can, on the assumption that sequestration will remain a permanent threat to all and any industrial action. Even the *Economist*, which in recent times has been so overtly anti-working class as to be indistinguishable from a Murdoch organ, thinks that the law on secondary action will drive unions to illegality, and ought, therefore, to be changed. In an article entitled *SOGAT's Assets Stripped* in the issue of 15-21 Feb, 1986, the following lines appear:

"*The News International dispute has shown that the law against secondary action is the most crippling of the trade-union reforms, and, unlike others, will never be accepted by the unions. Employers can and ... do divide their companies into numerous smaller ones, so that action affecting anything outside one place of work loses immunity. British unions have the worst of both worlds, as Mr Murdoch's sacking of his strikers has shown, they do not have positive rights (to organise, strike, and so on), and the News International dispute shows how far they have lost many of the compensating advantages of legal immunity...*"

In other words, the *Economist is* worried hat Mrs Thatcher is teaching the working class too much about the class nature of the British state and its laws. If the working class is forced to reject bourgeois law, it is much closer to recognising the need to confront the bourgeois state, and from there it is a relatively short step to recognising the need to overthrow the bourgeois state. The British working class is confronted today more strongly than ever before with the need to follow the advice of Marx:

"*... the general tendency of capitalistic production is not to raise, but to sink the average standard of wages, or to push the v*alue of labour *more or less to* its minimum limit. *Such being the tendency of* things *in this system, is this saying that the working class ought to renounce their resistance against the encroachments of capital, and abandon their attempts at making the best of the occasional chances for their temporary improvement? If they did, they would be degraded to one level mass of broken wretches past salvation. I think I have shown that their struggles for the standard of wages are incidents inseparable from the whole wages system, that in ninety-nine cases out of one hundred their efforts at raising wages are only efforts at maintaining the given value of their labour and that the necessity of debating their price with the capitalist inherent to their condition of having to sell themselves as commodities. By cowardly giving way in their everyday conflict with capital, they would certainly disqualify themselves for the initiating of any larger movement.*

"*At the same time, and quite apart from the general servitude involved in the wages system, the working class ought not to exaggerate to themselves the* ultimate working of these everyday struggles. They ought not to forget that they are fighting with effects, but not with the causes of those effects; that they are retarding the downward movement, but not changing its direction; that they are applying palliatives, not curing the malady. They ought, therefore. not to be exclusively absorbed in these unavoidable guerrilla fights incessantly springing up from the never-ceasing encroachments of capital or changes of the market. They ought to understand that with all the miseries it imposes upon them, the present system simultaneously engenders the material conditions and the social forms necessary for an economic reconstruction of society. Instead of the conservative motto 'A fair day's wages for a fair day's work!' *they ought to inscribe on their banner the revolutionary watchword:* 'Abolition of the wages system!'" (From *Value, Price and Profit*).

LALKAR June 1986

Wapping - Frenzied violence of the bourgeoisie

The sacked printworkers' struggle against the Mafia-connected press mogul, Rupert Murdoch, like the miners' struggle against the NCB and the government during the historic coal strike of 1984-5, has clearly shown the brutality, the violence and the class nature of the bourgeois state. It has demonstrated beyond doubt that the bourgeois state is nothing but an instrument for the suppression of the working class in the interests of the bourgeoisie; and the bourgeois government nothing but the executive committee for managing the affairs of the bourgeoisie. It has also brought home the truth, all too clearly, that the police and the forces of law and order, far from being the 'impartial' servants of the community, the 'keepers of peace' and the 'upholders of the law' that they are represented to be by the bourgeoisie and its paid and unpaid lackeys, are the uniformed thugs and lucratively rewarded storm-troopers of the bourgeoisie against the working class. These uniformed thugs attack, maim and in some cases kill with impunity and complete immunity from the law - indeed they are the Law. If the printworkers of Britain have had to face, as did the miners just over a year ago, cavalry charges, baton attacks, unidentified police in riot gear and the Special Patrol Group - all aimed at intimidating and terrorising the strikers - it does not require much intelligence to imagine the "*lurid frenzy*", to use Engels' apt expression, to which the bourgeoisie would be driven if the slaves of capital were to rise up against the entire system of capitalism.

Let us give the reader a few examples of the 'democratic' nature of our state and our 'peace loving bobbies' when face to face with a few thousand peaceful pickets wanting reinstatement and the recognition of union rights. Although there has been much violence by the police against pickets outside Murdoch's bunker at Wapping ever since the dispute started, the Saturday nights of 3rd, 10th, and 17th May shall go down, after the police carnage at Orgreave during the coal strike, as the worst examples of unprovoked police violence on workers during an industrial dispute in the 20th century in Britain.

On the night of Saturday 3rd May, the police in riot gear and on horseback launched a series of sustained and vicious attacks on pickets over a four-hour period. Every 20 minutes they launched frenzied mounted and riot police assaults on 10,000 peaceful pickets outside the scab News International print works owned by Rupert Murdoch, a close friend and supporter of 'our' 'peace-loving' Prime Minister and the even more 'peace-loving' maniac Reagan, President of the US. At one stage *"riot police emerged showing no numbers and executed a war dance before attacking"*, said Ron Leighton, the NGA-sponsored MP. Added Mr Leighton: *"The purpose of their treatment was to terrorise and intimidate and deter people from going again"*.

The extent to which the police are all-powerful and a Law unto themselves is shown by the fact that Giles Shaw, a Junior Home Office Minister, who met a delegation of angry and outraged printworkers after the infamies of 3rd May, did not even know that unnumbered and unidentified police officers, contrary to the police's own regulations, were being deployed against pickets outside Wapping. He promised that in the future all police must wear their numbers - a promise that has since then been honoured more in its breach than observance. For on 17th May unidentified police were used to kick a printworker unconscious with the full protection of senior officers. The attack on the peaceful pickets came at the Glamis Road end toward 12.30 a.m.

On 10th May the police, on horseback and foot, charged pickets without warning, injuring the workers and local bystanders. Though fewer than the normal number of police (estimated to be 1,747, out of which 150 are riot police and 98 mounted) were visible, large numbers were in reserve, out of sight in the rat-run of back streets straddled by the scab printworks at Wapping. At midnight, when pickets were still successfully blocking Murdoch's lorry convoy, mounted police charged into the pickets at full gallop without as much as a sign of a warning. The riot squad thugs, who had been kept in hiding after their heinous exploits the previous weekend, were brought out to launch the most vicious attack of the night an hour after the lorries had left and when the pickets were outnumbered by 'our' 'gallant' police.

What has been characteristic of police violence against strikers during this dispute, as was so clearly evident during the NUM strike also, was that the police have consistently persisted, after each attack, in hampering ambulance access for the victims of its violence - of the fists behind the gloves, the batons and the horses. That the police are obviously acting under orders to provoke violence and to intimidate and terrorise demonstrators is all too easily confirmed by the fact that they had 12 ambulances at the ready for trouble on the night of Saturday 10th May.

In view of the scenes of unprovoked police violence, heartless brutality and downright thuggery, Tony Benn, MP for Chesterfield, who had been an eye witness on the night of 3rd May, was quite right when he told a 500-strong May Day rally in his constituency:

"*Inside the fortress is the power of capital. Outside are the forces of labour. Inside is the instrument for telling lies. While outside are the people wanting truth* ".

The lies that are manufactured in fortress Wapping find their worthy echoes in fortress Westminster too where bourgeois Members of Parliament, in the service of British monopoly capital and flying in the face of facts, shamelessly condemn "*violence by the pickets*" and praise "*police restraint*". Not only did Mrs Thatcher condemn the pickets and shower praise on the police, but also John Biffen, Leader of the House and allegedly a moderate, waxed eloquent that the police at Wapping had "*been acting under the most severe provocation*". Yes, Mr Biffen, 6000 sacked workers, peacefully gathering to demand their jobs and union rights, can indeed be a "*severe provocation*" to the well-paid uniformed thugs employed by monopoly capital, which is intent on denying the workers even the most elementary of rights - rights won by our forefathers through decades, if not centuries, of struggle and defiance!

This, then, is how the bourgeois representatives of the people represent the bourgeoisie in parliament and misrepresent the working class who vote them into parliament. This is how they represent the workers after a demonstration which ends with 80 pickets being arrested and another 30 put into hospital.

During the dispute at Wapping, a sinister close connection, the existence of which we and the rest of the anti-racist and anti-fascist movement have for a long time insisted on, between the police and the fascists, i.e. between the uniformed racists and racists without uniform, has come into the open daylight. In a Commons debate, Labour's Home Affairs spokesman, Clive Soley, on Thursday 22nd May, called for a thorough review of police tactics at Wapping after evidence that the fascists, acting as *agents provocateurs*, are instigating trouble. He said: "*I know there's a small but definite number of people going to Wapping to stir up trouble*". Mr Soley ought to have added that these fascist *agents provocateurs* were acting hand in glove with the police and on the instructions of the latter. So it is not a case of reviewing police tactics, but of exposing this sinister link between the uniformed thugs and the extreme right, i.e., fascist, representatives of monopoly capital in crisis.

The course of the Wapping dispute has also shed considerable light on the connections between big business and big crime. The *Wapping Post*, published by journalists refusing to cross picket lines and the printworkers, revealed two weeks ago the connection of 'our' most powerful representative of press 'freedom', to wit, Murdoch, and a top US Mafioso, Jimmy 'The Weasel' Frantiano. The latter has revealed a £250,000 deal between union mobsters and Murdoch's picket-busting TNT trucking company. The money was paid for the hiring of Benny 'Eggs' Mangano and Laurence 'Buddy' Garaventi. The money was paid to these gangsters as a "consulting fee" to help TNT ease its way into the tough world of US trucking, where its plunge had been greeted by arson attacks and other forms of sabotage by the Mafia-linked Teamsters Union. "*After the hiring of Benny Eggs and Buddy as consultants, things went more smoothly*" says the *Wapping Post*. The above-mentioned representatives of enlightenment and capitalist freedom, culture and civilisation were personally met by the TNT chief, Sir Peter Abeles and the TNT chief general manager, John Cribb. Sir Peter is a close business partner of long standing of Rupert Murdoch (they jointly control Australia's main domestic airline, Ansett). They both have close connections with Mrs Thatcher, the British Prime Minister, whom they are supposed to have helped over the Westland/Sikorsky affair, for TNT, jointly owned by Sir Peter and R.Murdoch, was the mystery company which bought Westland shares and helped secure the Thatcher-backed victory for Sikorsky. Sir Peter is known to talk frequently about his "*deeply-held free enterprise philosophy*" and his devotion to an "*unregulated business environment*".

Thus it can be seen that arrayed against the printworkers is a united front of big business, the Mafia, the thugs in blue uniforms and riot gear (on horseback as well as on foot), the fascists, the Law Courts, the government and Parliament. To defeat this formidable alliance of the forces of monopoly capitalism; to successfully resist and overcome the violence, intimidation and terror of the forces of 'law and order'; to mount a successful challenge to the government's anti-working-class and anti-trade union Draconian laws and the unquestioning and arrogant enforcement of these laws by our 'impartial' judiciary in the courts of 'justice', who have, over the past two years, revealed with admirable candour the hideousness of their class justice and, incidentally, the poodle-like nature of our judges; to do all this and more, the working class needs a leadership that sadly is characterised by its absence. The present leadership, with some honourable exceptions of people such as Arthur Scargill, is unfit even to defend the already won trade-union rights of the workers, never mind any higher struggles for the total social emancipation of the working class. Nowhere is this truer today than in the case of the leadership of the print union, SOGAT 82, whose General Secretary is Brenda Dean and which comprises 80% of the printworkers. The response of the SOGAT leadership to the cavalry charge of 3rd May outside Wapping was a complete capitulation, for on the following Tuesday, 6th May, its Executive Committee decided to purge their contempt of court by lifting the ban on the wholesale distribution of the Wapping-produced papers by their members. On Thursday 8th May, Mr Justice Hirst, with malicious satisfaction, accepted Ms Dean's *"unqualified apology and expressions of regret"* and set aside the sequestration order imposed under anti-union laws because of SOGAT's refusal to withdraw instructions to members in the wholesale trade to boycott News International's scab papers in solidarity with the 6,000 printworkers sacked by Murdoch. The SOGAT leadership thus finds itself in the dubious position of asking for the support of the labour movement, while at the same time instructing its own members to distribute titles produced with scab labour at Wapping.

It is hardly to be wondered at that this the most humiliating and uncalled for retreat, disgusted the membership. The outraged London print leadership has promised to *"continue mass peaceful demonstrations at Wapping and to extend picketing of TNT depots and wholesalers in the UK"*. The London print leaders have also reaffirmed their position that a settlement with Murdoch's News International must contain the full reinstatement of all the union members sacked by Murdoch and full recognition of the print unions in Wapping on all titles. *"National picketing will continue and will be stepped up. If we have to wear crash helmets when we confront the brutality of the police we will do that too"*, said Mr Bill Freeman, Chairman of the London Group Committee.

With such a pusillanimous leadership as that of SOGAT, the printworkers cannot hope to go into battle and come out victorious. As if the above developments were not enough to severely hamper the path to victory of the sacked printworkers, now the leadership has thrown further spanners into the works by inviting the membership to take part in the feasibility study into News International's offer, which, though represented by Murdoch as a serious effort on his part to settle the dispute amicably, is designed to split the printworkers right down the middle. Under this offer, the sacked printworkers have been offered, as a part of Murdoch's union-bashing scheme, their old printing plant and building at Grays Inn Road and £50 million. Mass meetings of printworkers have rejected their leadership's invitation and have demanded full re-instatement and union recognition as a pre-condition for any settlement. But the leadership, ignoring all this, and the membership's demand for a work-place ballot, went ahead with a postal ballot, the results of which shattered the SOGAT leadership, as the membership rejected the offer by a 2:1 majority. In the light of the foregoing, one wonders whose side the SOGAT leadership are on. One does not have to be a seasoned political observer to conclude that the SOGAT leadership, in close consultation with the treacherous Labour Party and TUC leadership, have decided to give up the sacked printworkers' struggle as a lost cause even before it began, in the interests of the electoral fortunes of the Labour Party. In other words, a most despicable and sordid conspiracy, hatched by the SOGAT leadership and the TUC-Labour clique, is seriously threatening to turn 6,000 sacked printworkers into sacrificial lambs at the altar of Labour's electoral interests and bourgeois electioneering. The printworkers, sacked, as well as others, and the rest of the working class have a duty to expose, oppose and smash this conspiracy to smithereens. They also have a duty to work tirelessly to defeat and remove the present leadership, for with the present leadership the working class will not see victory. This leadership, brought up and reared in the old school, when superprofits from the imperialist table helped to keep the working class more or less content, is totally unfit to represent the unemployed, the under-privileged, the most oppressed and exploited sections of the working class. The world imperialist crisis is causing increasing differentiation within the ranks of the working class. The present trade-union and Labour Party leadership, by and large, is only able to represent the interests of the privileged sections of the working class, apart that is from representing the interests of monopoly capitalism, at which it really excels even the Tories. Hence the need for the most oppressed and exploited to fight on two fronts - against capitalist bosses and against TUC and Labour Party bosses.

Even more than all this. The working class needs a revolutionary Party, a truly communist party, to represent its class interests and to co-ordinate all struggles in the furtherance of these interests and in the struggle for the social emancipation of the working class, i.e., a struggle for not just higher wages, but for the elimination of the wages system itself. At a time when monopoly capital is increasingly making it impossible for the working class to conduct legally even its economic struggle against the daily encroachments of capital, the need for the formation of such a party can never be over-emphasised. Marxist-Leninists must belatedly shoulder this honourable task.

LALKAR May/June 1995

Attempts to terrorise teachers

The government and the bourgeois class which it represents became rather alarmed last month at the signs that school teachers are once again showing signs of militancy and not only that but that parents are backing them. The *Sunday Times* outlined the situation very well in an article on 16 April:

"[T]he government's reforms have unexpectedly driven parents and teachers closer together. By rightly delegating more power to the schools and seeking to cut out the local authorities, the government has made parents and governors ever more conscious of the undoubted problems the leaky roofs, dilapidated classrooms and larger classes. It is ... the latter that has aroused so much parental concern, exacerbated by the threat of cuts and 10,000 teaching redundancies. While parents may have supported, or at least tolerated, earlier reforms, most will not stomach larger classes. Though there is some evidence that bigger classes can be made to work, it defies common sense that standards can be maintained or improved by packing even more children into already crowded classrooms ...

" Enter David Blunkett, the Labour Party Education spokesman, who seemed to undergo a Pauline conversion when Tony Blair decided to send his eldest son to an optout school. Although Mr Blunkett started the year favouring a proposal to impose VAT on school fees (from which he had to beat a hasty retreat), he is now with Mr Blair's encouragement showing all the reforming zeal of a Keith Joseph. Bad schools? Close them. Feeble teachers? Sack them. League tables and testing? Keep them. Free higher education? A graduates' tax, perhaps. More cash? Certainly not, at least not immediately. The Tories moan that he sounds more conservative than they do."

Not surprisingly, when this superconservative David Blunkett came to address the National Union of Teachers to try to convince teachers of the wisdom of the policies his party has adopted in its allout bid to prove its suitability to take over the reins of capitalist government, he met a hostile reception, much to the chagrin of John Bills, the President of the National Union of Teachers and other members of the NUT executive, who had hoped to be able to deliver a 'disciplined' teaching profession to enhance the attraction to the ruling class of allowing the Labour Party to take over the government again at last.

Although the militancy proposed by teachers is modest (one-day strikes at most!) and although the teachers at the conference merely barracked and shouted down Mr Blunkett, who really got away very lightly in view of what he was proposing, one would really imagine from reading the remarks of the press and of the union leadership that Mr Blunkett had been shot dead in cold blood and that the teachers were proposing to run amok with AK47s. John Bills compared protesters to fascists and members of the BNP and said that they should be sacked. Teachers whose faces were televised during the protests were called in by their headmasters and forced, no doubt on the threat of being selected for redundancy, to apologise for "*the effect adverse publicity had brought to their schools*" as a result of their action!

Despite the conference overwhelmingly voting for strike action, the union leadership proceeded to put out a ballot paper to its members accompanied by a union recommendation that teachers should vote against the strike[1]. This recommendation says:

"*The proposed strikes have no positive purpose or attainable objective. They would disrupt education and alienate parents. Those who promoted them saw them as a means for a political attack on the Government. Conference also agreed to support 'all organised opposition to racism and fascism' whether violent or nonviolent.*

"*The attack on David Blunkett, the calls for strikes and more strikes and a willingness to be involved in violent demonstrations are not typical of your union.*"

In other words, the union leaders themselves are joining the bourgeois press and every anti-working class element in our society in trying to terrorise their members into backing off from militant action (even if that militant action is only a 1-day strike) against what even the *Sunday Times* concedes is an impossible situation in the classrooms. Their worry is not that parents will not support the teachers, but that they will.

The teachers' action is backed by parents not because the teachers are 'reasonable' and have not taken strike action up to now, but because the intolerable

---

1 Following the direction of the NUT leadership, teachers duly voted, in the postal ballot, against strike action. They were duly rewarded in August 1995 when, on announcement of better A-level results than had ever previously been known, the entire bourgeois media proclaimed the results were due to 'lowering of standards' rather than teachers' efforts.

workload that has been imposed on teachers and the worsening of their conditions is damaging the quality of education that young people receive in British schools. Parents' interests are being attacked, not just those of the teachers. And things have got so bad that today parents are prepared to be grateful that teachers are prepared to use militancy in the fightback against the cuts. It is spinelessness in the face of education cuts of the kind proposed by the Labour Party that would most damage parent support, not one-day strikes probably not even indefinite strikes.

Part Five

Social Democracy and Imperialist War, Aggression and Occupation

"The whole country's affairs are darkened by the events that have happened. We must all be greatly concerned about them. In my view and the vast majority of those sitting on this side of the House, the central question is this one of conceding political status. That cannot be done without the Government itself giving sure aid to the recruitment of terrorism."

Labour leader **Michael Foot** on the Hunger Strike in Ireland

"The furrowed, white-haired old pacifist was leading nothing less than an opposition drum-roll for war ... it was Labour at its patriotic, flag-waving finest ... "

Daily Telegraph, on **Michael Foot's** performance in the House of Commons on the debate concerning the Falklands war

SOCIAL DEMOCRACY and
IMPERIALIST WAR, AGGRESSION & OCCUPATION

LALKAR June/August/September 1981

Support the National Liberation Struggle of the Irish People

This article was dedicated to the memory of Jagmohan Joshi, General Secretary of the IWA(GB) and an ardent supporter of the cause of Irish liberation, on the second anniversary of his death.

Our salute to the Irish heroes

Since our last issue, not only Bobby Sands, MP for Fermanagh and South Tyrone, but also three other H-Block Hunger Strikers - Francis Hughes, Patrick O'Hara and Raymond McCreash - have died. The truth would be that the above four have been murdered by British imperialism and its representative, the British government. The four were on hunger strike because the British government had intransigently and cruelly denied to them the special category status, to wit, political status, which they had been demanding ever since the last 'Labour' government took it away from them in 1976. Having exhausted all other means of persuading the British occupying power to see reason, the above-named Irish patriots and fighters for Irish national liberation were forced to resort to hunger strike and make the most supreme sacrifice in the cause of Ireland's freedom from 800 years of subjection to English colonialism and imperialism. We in the Indian Workers Association (Great Britain), salute these courageous sons of Ireland. Their heroic struggle against British imperialism, against oppression and for Irish liberation is bound to become not only a part of Ireland's glorious history, but also a part of the history of the oppressed people throughout the world. Time will show that their battle has not been in vain; the whole of Ireland is bound to be united and free.

Heroes' funerals

Treating with much deserved contempt the campaign of lies and vilification launched by British imperialism and its official and unofficial representatives against the hunger strikers, the Irish people gave the dead hunger strikers heroes' funerals. Each of the funerals attracted tens of thousands of mourners. It is estimated that a hundred thousand mourners thronged the funeral of Bobby Sands, MP, in an impressive show of solidarity with the

H-Block hunger strike. And during the day, at Bobby Sands' home in Twinbrook on the outskirts of Belfast, men, women and children streamed in to pay their last respects. Bobby Sands was buried with traditional Republican ceremony. By way of an impressive defiance of British imperialism and the unbending resolve of the Irish people to continue their struggle for national liberation, Bobby Sands' coffin was escorted by seven masked liberation fighters in military uniforms who fired a volley of shots over it, thus asserting Ireland's right to take up arms against British imperialism, on the way to the burial ground. In an emotional funeral oration, Owen Carron, Bobby's election agent, honoured Bobby thus: *"I salute you, Bobby Sands. Yours has been a tough and lonely battle, but you have been victorious."* Referring to the mandate for political status to the Republican prisoners given by the voters of Fermanagh-South Tyrone, and the rejection of this mandate by the British government, Owen Carron went on to say that they could only conclude that *"we must take what they will not give and that there is no way in which freedom can be obtained, and when obtained maintained, except by armed men."*

Equally impressive funerals were given to the other three patriots. Tens of thousands turned out for the funeral in Londonderry of the hunger striker Patsy O'Hara to demonstrate the growing strength of militant Republicanism. The INLA, to which Patsy belonged, put on its biggest show of strength for the funeral, with an unprecedented display of military strength, which was clearly intended not only to honour Patsy, but also to demonstrate the strength, the resilience, the iron will, the virility of the Irish national liberation movement and its determination to fight and defeat British imperialism.

And yet the British government treats these Irish patriots as though they were common criminals. Common criminals indeed! Since when have common criminals had such heroes' funerals given to them?

Impotent rage of vilification

Faced with such overwhelming support for the hunger strikers, the British government could no longer hide its impotent rage and was driven to a campaign of malicious lies, calculated slander and vilification of the hunger strikers in an attempt to belittle their achievements and to discredit their cause. On 5th May [1981], the day Bobby Sands died, Mrs Thatcher, the Prime Minister, in a statement to Parliament, said that to concede the demands of the hunger strikers *"would be a licence to kill innocent men, women and children."* She continued that *"Mr Sands was a convicted criminal. He chose to take his own life. It was a choice his own organisation did not allow to their victims."*

Humphrey Atkins, the Northern Ireland Secretary, followed it up on 7th May and, with heavy irony, asked: *"Is murder any the less murder because the person responsible claims he had a political motive?"*

Mrs Thatcher, during her visit to Northern Ireland on 28 May 1981, returned to the same theme with pseudo-democratic rhetoric of the type learnt by rote by teenage boys and girls belonging to a school debating society. Referring to the hunger strikers' demands, she said: *"The government is not prepared to legitimise their cause by word or deed. And we should be clear what that cause is. It is a dictatorship by force and by fear in Northern Ireland, and in the Republic. These men deny democracy; everywhere they seek power for themselves."*

The above phony arguments of the most official and authoritative representatives of British imperialism have to be answered and we answer them thus:

First, it is not the national liberation fighters who are responsible for the killings of innocent men, women and children in Ireland. British imperialism has no right to be occupying any part of Ireland. England kept subjugated the whole of Ireland for more than 700 years, during which time it very nearly exterminated the Irish race. Only that can explain the fact that there are more Irish outside of Ireland than inside it, that the population of Ireland today is hardly more than it was in the middle of the 19th century. And for the last 60 years British imperialism has been in occupation of a part of Ireland against the will of the Irish - yes, against the will of the Irish people - as a whole and in doing so has not been averse to killing innocent men, women and children. Since the death of Bobby Sands alone, at least three such innocent people have been murdered by the British army of occupation, not to speak of regular killings by the RUC and the fascistic para-military organisations of the so-called loyalists. But if one were to pay attention to the lying utterances of 'responsible' British imperialist functionaries, such things were solely attributable to the IRA. Recently, H Atkins said that sectarian murders by Protestants were *"playing into the hands of the terrorists,"* as if terrorists were by definition all Republicans. And this is said by someone who claims that the British army is in Northern Ireland to keep the peace impartially between the Republicans and non-Republicans. No, the British army of occupation is the chief cause of the misery of the Irish people; and the only way to end that misery is for this army to get out, or be forced out, of Ireland. Once the British guarantee is removed, the 'Loyalists' will see sense, and the stark realities of Ireland will have no difficulty in impressing themselves on every Irishman, regardless of religion. If the Irish were left to themselves, there would be far less bloodshed. Can any sane person argue that 800 years of English rule produced less bloodshed than would otherwise have been the case? Can anyone claim that the British occupation of N Ireland for the last 60 years has been productive of less bloodshed than if there had been no such occupation? It scarcely needs proof that it has not.

Secondly, the hunger strikers have not a choice between life and death, fighting as they are against such a cunning and unscrupulous enemy as British imperialism, which, armed to the teeth, is engaged in an attempt to exterminate the liberation struggle of the Irish. Of course, there would be peace of a kind if the Irish were to accept that their fate was to be subjugated by the British. Quite rightly the Irish refuse to accept such a humiliating peace. British imperialist politicians who wax so eloquent when people subjugated by their rival imperialists fight to throw off their yoke, consider it the height of bad manners that someone should disturb their sleep and peace of mind by fighting against British imperialist domination and exploitation.

Thirdly, the Republican prisoners in the Maze and other concentration camps are not ordinary criminals. Where else, apart from Northern Ireland, in the UK are ordinary criminals tried by special kangaroo courts - and the Diplock Special Courts are nothing if not kangaroo courts - where some bigoted Paisleyite acts as judge and jury and sentences the liberation fighters to long terms in prison on the basis of confessions secured through torture (see Amnesty International's Report and the government's own Bennett Report) and uncorroborated statements of members of the so-called security forces. By singling out the liberation fighters in Ireland for such treatment, British imperialism has implicitly granted a *de facto* political status to them. And what the hunger strikers are demanding is that this *de facto* status should not only be accompanied by a *de jure* recognition of this status but also by all the privileges that are its natural concomitants, namely, those contained in the hunger strikers' demands.

Finally, as to the allegation that the cause of the hunger strikers is the establishment of *"dictatorship by force and fear in N Ireland"*, the truth of the matter is there already does exist such a state in N Ireland without any help from the hunger strikers. British imperialism imposed on N Ireland in 1922 a naked, terroristic - that is a fascist - dictatorship, whose main instruments of policy have been discrimination and oppression of the Republicans (who incidentally happen to be Catholics); this fascist state was able to function by its sole reliance on force and fear. In making this the most absurd of her accusations against the liberation movement, Mrs Thatcher is deliberately falsifying history. The reasons behind this deliberate falsification are not difficult to seek - they are to be sought in the interests of British monopoly capital, whose executive committee, to wit, the British government, Mrs Thatcher has the honour (or dishonour) to head. Engels was not far wrong when he made the following pertinent and penetrating remark:

"*The bourgeoisie turns everything into a commodity, even the writing of history. It is part of their being, of their conditions of existence, to debase all goods. They debase the writing of history. And the best-paid historians are the ones best able to falsify history for the purposes of the bourgeoisie.*" *(History of Ireland).*

The case of the hunger strikers is the liberation of N Ireland and the unification of Ireland free from British imperialist domination and exploitation. For this cause they do not seek any legitimacy from the British government; their cause is already legitimised beyond a shred of doubt by the support of the Irish people, both North and South of the borde. Witness the number of people who voted for Bobby Sands and elected him MP for Fermanagh-South Tyrone in the teeth of opposition from the united forces of British imperialism, the Unionists, the SDLP, Paisleyites, the Church and a host of other such unsavoury organisations. Witness the results of the local government elections in N Ireland on 22 May 1981. Gerry Fitt, for his treachery to the cause of Irish unification, lost his seat on the Belfast City Council which he had held for 23 years. The Irish Republican Socialist Party (the political wing of the INLA) won two out of the three seats it contested on the Belfast Council. The SDLP suffered heavy losses. And, finally, witness the results of the general elections, held on 11th June, in the Republic, which resulted in a much reduced majority for Fianna Fail, the party of the Prime Minister, Charles Haughey, and the victory of the H-Block candidates, Paddy Agnew and the hunger striker Kieran Doherty. Both these constituencies (Lough and Cavan Monaghan, from which Agnew and K Doherty were elected respectively) were Fianna Fail strongholds. This is the price Mr Haughey had to pay for his collaboration with British imperialism. The elections results in the Republic are even more of a blow than was the victory of Bobby Sands in Fermanagh-South Tyrone for British imperialism and its collaborators.

In these, and these facts alone, must be sought the legitimacy of the cause of the hunger strikers - not in the willingness of British imperialism to grant legitimacy to this cause. The cause of Irish liberation is legitimate, for it has the support of the overwhelming majority of the **Irish people as a whole**. This cause is just and shall be victorious. No force on earth can stop that.

Attempts to gag the news media

No propaganda in the world, no ministerial, or prime-ministerial, lies can demolish truth and abolish reality. The facts give lie to the propaganda of the British government. 'Our' government wants us to believe that the hunger strikers are terrorists isolated from the people of Ireland. The truth, however, is that the Irish people rightly regard the hunger strikers as heroes of Irish liberation. 'Our' government wants us to believe that Bobby Sands was an ordinary criminal, but the Irish people elected him to be an MP, and when he died one hundred thousand people thronged to his funeral. So our media - press and TV - which by and large follow the government in describing the Irish liberation fighters as terrorists, in the face of these stubborn facts, had no option but to report these events. And our 'democratic' Prime Minister, sensing as she rightly did that such reporting gave lie to her government's campaign of vilification against the Irish patriots, flew into an impotent rage at the sight of TV pictures of the heroes' funerals given to the hunger strikers by the Irish people. In a crude and ill-disguised attempt to gag the media, Mrs Thatcher, speaking at the Tory Women's conference on 20 May 1981, had this to say:

"Newspapers and television can provoke the very reaction the terrorists seek. It can give the convicted criminals the myth of martyrdom they crave ... "

Even bourgeois journalism - at least the relatively intelligent, decent and democratically inclined section of it - could not tolerate this crude interference by the Prime Minister and her attempts to muzzle all reporting of any disagreeable (to her and her government) events and facts pertaining to Ireland. Sir Ian Trethowan (no great revolutionary), the Director-General of the BBC, was forced to reply to the Prime Minister's criticism of Northern Ireland coverage through the following Shakespearean dialogue, full of irrefutable logic:

*"**Cleopatra:** Thou shalt be whipt with wire, and stew'd in brine, smarting in lingering pickle.*

*"**Messenger:** Gracious Madam, I that do bring the news made not that match."*

All that we have to do is to substitute Mrs Thatcher and the BBC (and *a fortiori* other media) for Cleopatra and the Messenger respectively, and the

British Isles for Ancient Egypt, and we get a picture clear as clear can be. The BBC, through Sir Ian, is telling Mrs Thatcher 'Blame us not, Gracious Madam; we are merely the bearers of ill tidings, not their makers; we are not the creators of the 'Troubles', merely their reporters'.

In reply to the suggestions that the cameras should be 'pulled out' of Northern Ireland, Sir Ian correctly retorts: *"But there was no television at Easter, 1916, nor in the years of the 'Troubles' which followed, let alone in all the earlier periods of violence in Irish history."* (Should the Terrorists be given Air Time, The Times, 4 June 1981).

The conclusion, though implied, is clear enough: if you don't like the violence in Northern Ireland, don't blame the reporters for it, blame the real culprits. And the real culprit is none other than British imperialism whose occupation of a part of Ireland against the wishes, aspirations and interests of the Irish people as a whole is responsible for the 'Troubles' in that unhappy land now as in the past eight centuries of English colonial rule in Ireland. Sir Ian cannot, and does not, make this explicitly clear, nor would we expect him to do so.

Another myth - a myth deliberately propagated by the British government and in particular by the Prime Minister, Mrs Thatcher - that Sir Ian explodes most effectively in the article referred to above - is that the hunger strikers are 'terrorists' who do not command any support among the ordinary citizens of Ireland who want to have nothing to do with these 'men of violence'. *"Criticism of the media,"* says Sir Ian, *"has been particularly sharp over the coverage of the hunger strikers, above all Bobby Sands. One crucial point which many of the critics missed was the significance of the Fermanagh and South Tyrone by-election. Whatever the reasons for Sands being the only Catholic and Republican candidate, electors were free to abstain, or spoil their papers, if they did not wish to support him. Instead over 30,000 of them voted him into Westminster, and so transformed the situation. When last did an elected MP starve himself to death? When last did someone starving himself to death receive a procession of eminent and international emissaries."* (ibid).

When indeed! Thus it is clear that the British government are cracking their heads against the stone walls of mistress reality in blaming the 'Troubles' in Ireland on either the hunger strikers or the media. In short, the British government is bound to lose the propaganda battle as surely as it is bound to defeated in its attempts to stamp out the struggle of the Irish people for national liberation and unification of Ireland.

Labour Party's lackey service to British imperialism

Following in the footsteps of Mrs Thatcher, and trying to outbid her in rendering flunkey service to British imperialism, the leader of the Parliamentary Labour Party, the ever-so-left Mr Michael Foot, with characteristic hypocrisy, uttered the following sanctimonious twaddle:

"The whole country's affairs are darkened by the events that have happened. We must all be greatly concerned about them. In my view and the vast majority of those sitting on this side of the House, the central question is this one of conceding political status. That cannot be done without the Government itself giving sure aid to the recruitment of terrorism.

"If it were conceded it would greatly increase the numbers who were encouraged to join and that in turn would mean a great increase in the numbers of innocent people that would get killed. We believe that the matters in N Ireland and all parts of this country should be settled democratically and not at the point of a gun."

Nothing could reveal more clearly the imperialist prejudices and ossified thinking of a social-imperialist (socialist in words and imperialist in deeds) than the above-quoted remarks of Mr Foot. Like an imperialist chauvinist, not only does Mr Foot regard, as a matter of course, Northern Ireland as part of 'this' country, but he also reveals his trench pacifism when he implies that the only people wanting to settle the Irish question at the point of a gun are the national liberation fighters. Are the British army of occupation in Northern Ireland armed with no more than copies of *Hansard*, containing eloquent, not to say useless and hollow, speeches of the smooth-tongued flunkeys, such as the Foots and Thatchers, of British imperialism? Is it not the British army that has over the centuries tried to settle the issue at the point of a gun? Marx was a thousand times right when he observed in a letter of 29 November 1869 that *"In fact, England never has and never CAN so long as the present relationship lasts* [i.e., that of subjugator and subjugated] *rule Ireland otherwise than by the most abominable reign of terror and the most reprehensible corruption."*

If Mr Foot is really serious about practising democracy, let him put the question of the partition of Ireland to the Irish people in their entirety in an all-Ireland Referendum. We would gladly accept, as indeed would the Irish people, the outcome of such a Referendum. But, has Mr Foot, or any other imperialist politician, the courage to leave this matter to the Irish people as a whole?

It is pure nonsense, of course, for Mr Foot to suggest that the granting of political status would aid recruitment to the ranks of those fighting against British imperialism. What brings such recruitment today is the same cause that has swelled the ranks of Irish freedom fighters over centuries past, namely, the forcible occupation by England of Ireland - the attempts by England to exterminate the Irish people and to assimilate Ireland. The time-honoured practice of English colonialism was to execute the Irish patriots. After the 1916 Easter rebellion, which the British imperialists suppressed most ruthlessly, General Sir John Maxwell declared a state of martial law, arrested 3,500 people, and imprisoned more than half of them in Wales. He then had the leaders of the uprising, including James Connolly and Padraig Pearse, executed. Did that stop the Irish people from fighting with even greater vigour against British imperialism? Did Lloyd George's Black and Tan campaign of terror and mass murder do anything other than to increase the numbers of those who were encouraged to join the fight against British imperialism and for the liberation of Ireland? History affords the irrefutable proof that on each occasion the British colonialists adopted a policy of ruthless repression, of countless arrests and wholesale executions, the Republican movement became more potent as it went underground. So it was in the past and so it is today. If the ruthless repression of the Easter uprising proved only to be a prelude to the establishment of the Republic in the 26 Counties, the present attempts of British imperialism to subdue, with all the military might at its disposal, the Irish national liberation fighters are bound only to be a prelude to the establishment of an independent and united Ireland embracing all its 32 counties. Thus it is clear that the greatest encouragement to the Irish people to join the fight for the liberation of their country is provided by British imperialism. This simple truth, which eludes our 'scholar' and 'historian', to wit, the leader of the Parliamentary Labour Party, Michael Foot, is even known to the reactionary clerical establishment of Ireland, which in no way supports the struggle for the unification of Ireland, which is hostile to the use of arms to achieve that end but which nevertheless realises that the policy of repression pursued by the British government is producing effects completely the opposite of those intended. Listen to the desperate cries of the Roman Catholic primate of all Ireland, Cardinal Thomas O'Fiarich:

> *"In near desperation I appeal to both sides for a compromise ... If the Government continues its rigid stance ... it will ultimately be faced with the wrath of the whole nationalist population. Already, Government policy has provided the IRA with its greatest influx of recruits since Bloody Sunday."* (2 May 1981).

If Mr Foot does not wish to give any encouragement to any Irish person to join the ranks of those who fight against the British occupation of Northern Ireland, let him pursue the only policy that can make his dream come true, namely, work for the withdrawal of the British army of occupation from Northern Ireland so that the Irish people may determine their own affairs without interference from outside parties who have no business to be in Ireland.

The last comment that we must make in regard to the above-quoted remarks of Mr Foot concerns his description of the Irish liberation fighters as terrorists. In doing so, Mr Foot joins a long list of third-rate bourgeois flunkeys who see nothing but terrorism in every war of liberation, in every struggle for national and social emancipation. Ronald Reagan describes the struggle of the Palestinian and El Salvadorean people for national liberation as terrorism, just as his predecessors maligned the struggle for national liberation of the Indo-Chinese people as terrorism. But, then, the US Presidents do not claim to be socialists. Michael Foot, however, not only claims to be a socialist, but left socialist at that! And by describing the present struggle of the Irish people as terrorism, Michael Foot is following in the footsteps of those pedants, who also called themselves socialists, who denounced the Easter uprising of 1916 as a 'putsch'. It is not surprising that Michael Foot's monstrously doctrinaire and pedantic opinion about the liberation fighters in Ireland being terrorists coincides with the opinions of such incurable reactionaries as Ronald Reagan and Margaret Thatcher. Whoever characterises the struggle of the Irish people for the liberation and unification of their country as terrorism is either a hardened reactionary, or a doctrinaire hopelessly incapable of imagining a social revolution as a living thing.

So far we have deliberately concentrated on Michael Foot, for it is he who leads the Labour Party. Let no-one, however, think that Michael Foot is an exceptionally treacherous and malicious individual. He is of his kind; he is a social-democrat who leads a social-democratic party. And social-democracy is nothing if not an agent of the bourgeoisie in the ranks of the working class. Michael Foot has only done what his predecessors in the Labour Party have always done ever since its inception, that is, to betray the working class and serve the interests of British imperialism. For it must never be forgotten that after the Easter uprising when the news reached Westminster that James Connolly, the great Irish socialist and one of the foremost leaders of that uprising, wounded and strapped to a chair, had been executed by a firing squad, Arthur Henderson, the then leader of the Labour Party, led his Parliamentary colleagues in rapturous applause. With the only difference - Henderson did not perpetrate, unlike Michael Foot, the insult of calling the IRA prisoners ordinary criminals. That is the essence of the 'socialist' progress made by the Labour Party in the last 60 years.

During the Second World War a Labour Home Secretary, Herbert Morrison, made sure that the Mosleyites were not only treated as political prisoners but afforded them every comfort. This notwithstanding the fact that they were fascists and open admirers of Hitler and Hitlerite Germany with which Britain was at war. This is how Colin Cross in his book *The Fascists in Britain* describes their extremely comfortable and privileged conditions:

"The leading detainees, including Mosley, were in F wing of Brixton Prison. Their cell doors were unlocked during the daytime and they were allowed freedom of association and the right to purchase their own food from outside.

"During the hot summer of the Battle of Britain they played cricket in the courtyard under the tuition of Gordon-Canning and Ramsay."

After being moved to Holloway Prison, the Mosleyites were not only given a four-roomed flat, but the authorities also allowed them to employ other detainees as domestic servants.

From the foregoing it is clear that in the Labour Party's book of 'socialism' it is better to be a fascist than a fighter for national liberation. For let it be remembered that it was yet again a Labour Home Secretary, Merlyn Rees, who in 1976 deprived the Maze prisoners of the political status (special category status, if you please) which they had had hitherto! There is, therefore, nothing unreasonable in the demands of the hunger strikers that they be treated as political prisoners. And that is what they are: they are fighting for the liberation of their country, they have been tried by political courts (Diplock Courts) and have been locked up for taking up arms against British imperialism's occupation of their country.

Duty of the working class

The working class must not only support the hunger strikers' demands to be considered political prisoners, it must also support the struggle of the Irish people as a whole for self-determination and unification of Ireland. In short, the British working class must demand the withdrawal of the British army from the six counties of Ireland. This demand must be put forward not just in words but backed by deeds. Only such a programme is in the interests of Irish freedom, of accelerating the development of the struggle of the British working class for its own social emancipation because, as Lenin said: *"The British workers could not become free so long as they helped (or even allowed) the keeping of another nation in slavery." (British Liberals and Ireland).*

It is not just a question of the British working class being kind and humane to the Irish people. In supporting the struggle of the Irish people (or any other people for that matter), the British working class would be aiming its blows at all the abominations in Britain. It is in the direct and absolute interests of the British working class to support the struggles for national liberation everywhere, including Ireland. Marx and Engels, the co-founders of scientific socialism, understood this very well and this is how they, with characteristic genius, presented the question of Irish liberation and its inextricable link with the emancipation of the British working class.

In a letter of 20 November 1868, Engels notes that: *"Irish history shows one what a misfortune it is for a nation to have subjugated another nation. All the abominations of the English have their origin in the Irish Pale. I have still to plough through the Cromwellian period, but this much seems certain to me, that things would have taken another turn in England, too, but for the necessity of military rule in Ireland and the creation of a new aristocracy there."*

In other words, the subjugation of the Irish nation was a subjugation of the English proletariat as well; it was a misfortune for the Irish people and the English working class alike.

A year later, on 10 December, 1869, Marx writes that his paper on the Irish question to be read at the Council of the International will be formulated on the following lines:

*" ... Quite apart from all phrases about 'international' and 'humane' justice for Ireland - which are taken for granted in the **international council** - it is in the direct and absolute interest of the English working class to get rid of their present connection with Ireland ... The English working class will **never accomplish anything** until it has got rid of Ireland ... English reaction in England has its roots ... in the subjugation of Ireland."* (Marx's emphasis).

The alternative to the policy of supporting the demand for Irish liberation is for the working class to join the ruling class in Britain in a common front against Ireland and thus forge the chains for its own continued slavery. Marx, therefore, quite correctly insisted that the British working class will never be able to do *"anything decisive here in England until it separates its policy with regard to Ireland in the most definite way from the policy of the ruling classes, until it makes not only common cause with the Irish, but even takes the initia-*

tive in dissolving the Union. And, indeed, this must be done not as a matter of sympathy with Ireland, but as a demand made in the interests of the English proletariat. If not, the English people will remain in the leading-strings of the ruling classes, because it must join with them in a common front against Ireland." (Letter to Kugelmann dated 29 November, 1869).

The 112 years that have elapsed since Marx and Engels made the above remarks, full of genius and penetration, have fully borne out their correctness. It is high time the British working class acted on them, made them an article of its pronunciamento and thus facilitated not only the Irish struggle for national liberation but also the struggle for its own emancipation.

The British workers must stop being duped by the twaddle peddled by the liberal and conservative spokespersons of the bourgeoisie alike to the effect that Britain has none but the most altruistic motives for being in occupation of Northern Ireland. Let the liberal *Guardian* state in its own language its agreement with the conservative Mr Peregrine Worsthorne of the *Sunday Telegraph* in exactly the same fashion as Michael Foot has stated his with Mrs Thatcher:

"*Mr P Worsthorne of the* Sunday Telegraph *is right to point out that Britain's continued attempt to administer Northern Ireland for the benefit of its people is an act of the highest political altruism. There is nothing in it for Britain; nothing at all, but a draw on lives, a hole in the pocket, and a reputation in which the worst regimes of Eastern Europe can take malicious pride.*" (Leading article, 6 May 1981).

It would require a separate article to show what Britain has gained from the subjugation of Ireland throughout the centuries as well as what it gets now. This much is certain though, that the occupation of Northern Ireland by Britain, and the religious bigotry and sectarianism that this occupation fosters, is one of the chief causes of the strength of reaction both in Britain and in Ireland. To strengthen reaction in the British Isles, to impede the development of the social movement for the emancipation of the working class, can hardly be called *"an act of the highest political altruism"* on the part of British imperialism. This reminds us of the well-known remark of Marx and Engels that:

"*Bourgeois socialism attains adequate expression when, and only when, it becomes a mere figure of speech ... It is summed up by the phrase: the bourgeois is a bourgeois - for the benefit of the working class.*" *(The Manifesto of the Communist Party).*

Engels' Prediction

"But if after 700 years of fighting this assimilation [ie., England's attempt at the complete assimilation of Ireland] *has not succeeded; if instead each new wave of invaders flooding Ireland is assimilated by the Irish; if, even today, the Irish are far from being West Britons, as they say, as the Poles are from being West Russians after only 100 years of oppression; if the fighting is not yet over and there is no prospect that it can be ended in any other way than by exterminating the oppressed race - then, all the geographical pretexts in the world are not enough to prove that it is England's destiny to conquer Ireland."* (Engels, *History of Ireland*).

The above remarks of Engels, written over 100 years ago, with suitable modifications resulting from the partition of Ireland in 1921, ring truer today than ever before. If after 800 years of English rule and attempts at the complete assimilation of the whole of Ireland (and, since 1922, the Northern part of it), the Irish are far from being West Britons; if the fighting is not yet over and, there is not prospect that it can be ended in any other way than by exterminating the oppressed Irish nation - then all the geographical, economic, pseudo-constitutional and pseudo-democratic pretexts are not enough to prove that it is England's destiny to rule any part of Ireland. The truth of this statement is more than borne out by the 20th century history of Anglo-Irish relations in general, and the history of the Troubles during the past decade in particular.

Possessed with *"terrific recuperative powers,"* after the most gruesome suppression, after every attempt to exterminate them, the Irish have, after a short respite, emerged stronger than ever before. After the earlier gruesome suppressions and attempts at extermination the Irish rose in rebellion against the English rule during Easter 1916. After the suppression of the Easter uprising, resulting in the execution of the leaders of this uprising - notably that of James Connolly - after Lloyd George's attempts at exterminating them through the terror unleashed by the Black and Tans, the Irish people struck back with unparalleled energy and vigour, forcing the British government and the selfsame Lloyd George to recognise, for the first time, the case for Irish independence. The Irish people were, however, deprived of the fruits of their victory, for which they had fought for 800 years, through the Partition plan under which the Six Counties of Northern Ireland were separated from the rest of the country. These Six Counties have continued to be forcibly occupied by British imperialism against the will and wishes of the Irish people and are the cause of the continuing troubles in Ireland.

Stormont comes crashing down

Having separated these Six Counties from the rest of Ireland, Britain established a puppet government at Stormont. The Stormont government was throughout its 50 years' existence, nothing but a naked terroristic and fascistic dictatorship whose chief function was to discriminate against and oppress and suppress the nationalist elements of the population. But the Irish people, mustering their customary energies, heroism and capacity for sacrifice in the cause of liberating Ireland from English colonial rule, struck back and swept into the dustbin the entire edifice created by British imperialism in the Northern Ireland.

Failure of the British Army to pacify Northern Ireland

For just over a decade British imperialism has instituted a reign of terror in Northern Ireland; it has been engaged in the most gruesome suppression and an attempt at exterminating the heroic fight of the Irish people for national liberation. That this attempt is failing, that the revolutionary war of the Irish people for national liberation is bound to be victorious over British imperialism becomes clearer with each passing day. The march of events reveals that British imperialism can maintain its occupation of Northern Ireland only by exterminating the Irish people, and since it is unable to achieve this extermination, in the final analysis it is unable to maintain this occupation. The Irish people have given ample proof that, in their struggle for national liberation, no sacrifice is too great (in this context, the deaths of the hunger strikers are the latest, though not the only, proof of this iron determination).

Bourgeois spokesmen forced to recognise the truth

This truth is not only the lodestar in the Irish people's struggle for self determination, for Ireland's unity and complete independence from British imperialism, but it has also begun to penetrate the stubborn and thick skulls of the spokesmen for the British bourgeoisie. James Callaghan, the former 'Labour' Prime Minister, has called for an independent state of Northern Ireland. Reportedly there is serious and growing dissent within the British government over the cabinet's policy on Northern Ireland. One minister is reported to have made the remark that : *"It would be better to lead with our chins" (Guardian,* 13 August 1981). The liberal *Guardian* has been forced, not by genuine change of heart but by the sheer impossibility of subjugating Northern Ireland through a military victory over the Republicans, to talk of *"Britain's impossible mission in the North"* of Ireland and of the IRA as a *"national institution whose stated aims, as opposed to methods, are sanctified in the [Irish] Constitution."* The *Guardian* is forced to admit that the success of the Republican struggle in Northern Ireland has been on such a scale as not only to eliminate the SDLP but also seriously to embarrass the Irish government in the Republic. Says the *Guardian*, *"successive statements by the members of the Irish government invite the inference that the new administration is seriously embarrassed by the political gains derived by the IRA from the hunger strikes and does not know where to turn next."* And further: *"the Social Democratic and Labour Party, where the best hope for peaceful constitutional change could be found, has had the ground swept from under it. It dare not fight the by-election next week in Fermanagh and South Tyrone, and has had to leave the Republican Clubs, the heirs to the Official IRA, as the only, and dubious, standard bearer of peaceful nationalism."*

The conservative *Sunday Times*, is no less respectful, if grudging, of the successes and the cause of the IRA; it is no less emphatic in pronouncing the utter defeat of the British government's policy of keeping Northern Ireland in the United Kingdom and calling for the abandonment of that policy. Having stated that the British government has a right to resist the demand of the hunger strikers in the Maze for political status, the *Sunday Times* of 16 August 1981 goes on to say: *"Yet it is vital to make the distinction between method and aim. The methods of the Provisional IRA are hateful, and no humane government ought to countenance them. Its basic aim, on the other hand, is shared by a majority of people on the island of Ireland, and respected by great numbers in the world beyond: a New York Judge's decision that an alleged provisional attempt to kill a British soldier was non-extraditable because political is only the latest indication. That aim is for an end to British rule over those six counties of the island of Ireland where it still survives."* We shall leave aside here the prejudices of the leader writers of the *Sunday Times* which are implicit in the above remarks and according to which the methods and aims of British government policy in Northern Ireland have been 'humane' and 'honourable'. We shall leave aside also the flaws in the *Sunday Times'* argument according to which a judge in New York regarded *"an alleged provisional attempt to kill a British soldier as non-extraditable, because political,"* and at the same time maintain that *"Britain has been right to resist ... a demand for political recognition of men convicted of engaging or assisting in random murder."* We shall also not dilate on the question that what were the national liberation fighters to do if all their most persuasive, authoritative and irrefutable arguments in support of their aim, which, even according to the *Sunday Times*, is *"shared by a majority of the people of the island of Ireland, and respected by great numbers in the world beyond,"* brought them no joy and were rejected by the British government, as indeed they were? It is clear that in the face of such stubborn refusal by the British government to countenance facts, only the 'hateful' methods of the national liberation fighters could prove more persuasive than the most persuasive arguments. That this is so is proven by the belated conversion of the *Sunday Times* to the cause of an Ireland free from British rule and occupation. It is just one example of force, *"hateful methods"* if it pleases the *Sunday Times*, acting as the midwife of a society pregnant with revolution. What is essential and good about the *Sunday Times* remarks quoted above, and which we must welcome with open arms, is that a very respectable, intelligent and authoritative organ of the British ruling classes is literally for the first time forced to recognise the legitimacy of the aim of a united Ireland, to recognise the entire people of the 'island of Ireland', and to pay regard to the opinion of mankind in general which has over a long period of time supported the struggle of the Irish people for national liberation against British colonialism.

The *"hateful methods"* of the Irish patriots have forced the *"sad"* recognition by the *Sunday Times* that *"British policy in Northern Ireland - to try to keep it in the United Kingdom by general consent **has not worked, is not working and will not work** [our emphasis]. Even among those who wish it would work, and know the attempt to have been honourable [!!!] that sad fact is recognised every day. The signs multiply ... the SDLP has again decided not to oppose the terrorist cause in an important by-election; terrorist violence itself persists; and the wretched hunger strike in its support grinds on, defying all predictions of collapse."* (ibid).

Dealing with the threadbare and time-worn argument, repeated *ad nauseam* by all apologists of British occupation of Northern Ireland, that the withdrawal of the British army would provoke a 'bloodbath,' the *Sunday Times* pertinently remarks that *"the luckless British army now provokes by its mere presence part of the bloodletting it came to stop. There is also the possibility that to do nothing now would occasion a fiercer bloodbath later."*

The *Sunday Times'* solution

As far as the solution to the Troubles in Ireland is concerned, the *Sunday Times* is as *"luckless"* in finding it as is the British army in pacifying and subduing Northern Ireland. So, the *Sunday Times* opts for the Callaghan solution, *viz.*, the creation of an independent Northern Ireland. How, one may be pardoned for asking the uncomfortable and rude question, will the so-called majority, i.e., the Unionists, alone in an independent Northern Ireland, be able to subdue the struggle for a united Ireland if this selfsame fraternity has been unable to achieve this nefarious aim with the help of British imperialism and the latter's powerful army, armed with the most sophisticated weapons? But this is a question which will bother only the *Sunday Times* and such other spokespersons of the British bourgeoisie. For our part, we who have always supported the struggle for a united and independent Ireland, free from foreign domination and interference, must rest content with what the *Sunday Times* calls "*a concession to the logic which Britain has reluctantly acknowledged in many other parts of the world, and cannot much longer evade in this most difficult instance,*" to wit, the withdrawal of the British army of occupation from the northern part of the island of Ireland.

The inevitable victory of the Irish struggle for national liberation

And when that happy event occurs, no matter what sadness it brings in the circles of the *Sunday Times* and suchlike spokespersons of the British bourgeoisie, it will spell victory for the Irish people's centuries-old struggle for a united, free and independent Ireland. And that victory against British colonialism and imperialism, in the language of the *Guardian*, "*would be on sale in ballad form all over Ireland* [and beyond] *next morning.*" If the British working class has failed, as it sadly has, to lead the movement for the withdrawal of the British army from Northern Ireland, let it waste no time in adding its own voice to those of the spokespersons of the bourgeoisie who, reading the writing on the wall, are demanding this withdrawal. For the withdrawal of the British army is in the interests not only of the national liberation struggle of the Irish people, but is also directly in the interests of the cause of social emancipation of the British working class itself. If the leading spokespersons of the British ruling classes are being forced to realise that the laws of history are stronger than the laws of artillery, if they are being forced to recognise the sad (for them) truth that the British policy in Ireland is as doomed to failure as the victory of the Irish people's struggle for independence and national unification is inevitable, then let not the British working class lag behind in the cognisance of this truth.

LALKAR April 1982

Hands off the Falklands
Las Malvinas Argentinas

On Friday 2 April, 1982, the Argentine armed forces invaded, and established complete control over, the Falkland Islands, which the Argentines have always laid claim to and which they call Las Islas Malvinas, thus restoring these islands to Argentinean sovereignty. Following this successful Argentinean action, the British government has found itself in the throes of a most severe crisis - of the kind not seen since the days of the Suez crisis more than 25 years ago - and the chief hallmarks of its policy have aptly been described by that great friend of the Tories, the *Daily Telegraph*, as being *"confusion, ambiguity and irresolution"*. The government simply does not know what to do and in which direction to move. It is simply being propelled by the unfolding events into actions and in directions not of its own choosing. This governmental crisis has already produced three ministerial resignations - that of the Foreign Secretary, Lord Carrington, and two of his junior colleagues at the Foreign Office, Messrs Atkins and Loos - and all the signs are that more ministerial heads will roll. The resignation of the Defence Secretary, Mr Nott, is almost a foregone conclusion. And the future of the Prime Minister, indeed of her government, is far from assured.

The Question of Sovereignty

Before going into the questions of right and wrong, the legitimacy or otherwise, of the Argentine action, it is important to look at the question of sovereignty over the Falklands in the proper historical perspective. Mrs Thatcher claimed the other day in Parliament that Argentina *"has not a shred of justification nor a scrap of legality"*. The British bourgeois press and media have put forward the same viewpoint, painting Britain as the victim of an unprovoked aggression. Here are a few salient facts appertaining to the history of the Falkland Islands.

Both Spain and Britain claimed title to these Islands by discovery, the former through Vespucius and the latter through Drake and Hawkins. The French seem to have landed a party on these islands in 1764 and were only turfed out by the Spaniards. The French called the Islands *Les Isles Malouines* (after the sailors who came from St Malo) and the Spanish called them) *Las Islas Malvinas.* In 1767 the French transferred their rights to the Spanish. In 1770 the Spaniards ejected a British landing party. A year later in 1771, for some unknown reason, the Spaniards relented and allowed the British back. However, the climate proved stronger than the collapsing Spanish Empire, and the British settlement packed it in three years later. The British withdrew leaving behind a British flag and a lead plaque saying that the Islands were *"the sole right and property"* of George III.

Thereafter the Islands went through many vicissitudes of claims to their sovereignty and periods of internal disorder. Spanish occupation ensued until 1810 followed by occupation by the government of Buenos Aires. In 1820 the newly-independent Republic of Buenos Aires announced that it had inherited the rights once exercised by Spain, and started to develop a colony on the Islands. The poor Argentinean colonists made the mistake in 1831 of seizing 3 American sailing vessels for taking their stocks. The Americans, wielding their big sticks as has been their wont since then, organised a sharp naval assault which laid waste the Islands and declared them to be "free of all governance". The British government saw in this Argentinean misfortune and re-occupied the Islands with a military force in January 1833, expelling the local Argentineans from the Islands.

Since then, though Britain has hung on to these Islands which gave it domination of the strategic South Atlantic and Cape Horn routes, Argentina never forgot and never gave up its claim. In 1965 the General Assembly of the United Nations voted by 94 votes to nil, with Britain abstaining, that the two sides should hold talks to resolve the issue peacefully. Since then talks have been held between the two sides, interrupted by several naval confrontations, and the breaking off of diplomatic relations between 1975 and 1979. The British government employed the tactics of delay and procrastination and in the end the Argentine patience ran out and they took what was theirs by force since they could not get it on the negotiating table.

From the above facts it is clear that the Argentines were forced to leave by the superior force of arms at a time when the British Navy really ruled the waves; it is clear that the Argentinean population of these Islands, the *Malvinas,* was expelled by the same superior power of the day. If history has turned round and played a joke on the British ruling class, why should the latter complain even if what has happened is not much to their liking? What was conquered by sword and fire has been taken back by those who had legitimate claim to it, and who have never dropped this claim even if they were hitherto powerless to press it militarily. Much is being made of the undisturbed occupancy for the last 150 years by the British of these Islands, but then much has always been made of such occupancy by all the colonial powers. Did not France make such a lot of its occupancy of Algeria and other countries? Did she not regard her colonies as mere provinces of France? Did Britain herself not make similar claims -with regard to the territories that once constituted her vast empire? It is also said that the people of Falklands do not wish to be part of Argentina, that they are passionately British - more British than the British themselves. That is undoubtedly true, but that is no fault of the Argentinean people, who were as much the victims of British colonial expansion as were the people of British descent on these Isles who were brought there on the understanding - false as it turns out - that these isles were British forever. These Islands were British for as long as the British might of arms was in a position to sustain this. This has in fact been implicitly recognised over the decades by the successive British governments who have conducted negotiations with the Argentine government over the question of sovereignty to these Islands. And if these isles are British and their sovereignty is unquestionable, what then is there to negotiate about with the Argentineans?

The fact of the matter is that the 1700 Islanders are not worth a farthing to our government. What has made these Islands now such a bone of contention are the rich fishing stocks and oil deposits around these Islands. People have never mattered very much to our ruling classes but considerations of strategy and profits have always done so.

One has only to contrast the present demands of some Tory and Labour MPs for governmental blood over letting the people of the Falklands down, with their deafening silence over the expulsion in 1968 of 1300 inhabitants of the island of Diego Garcia, to realise the utter hypocrisy of these jingoistic lickspittles and flunkeys of monopoly capitalism.

Jingoist hysteria

For the first time in more than 25 years the House of Commons sat on a Saturday on the 3 April. During the debate on the Islands, it has to be admitted the Tory Right-wingers and Labour Left-wingers vied with each other in jingoist hysteria. During the debate was born the Leader of the Opposition. So jingoist was Mr Foot's performance that the *Daily Telegraph* gave him a kiss of death by describing his performance as the best ever, adding that this was *"the language of gut patriotism"*. And further *"The furrowed, white-haired old pacifist was leading nothing less than an opposition drum-roll for war". "It was Labour at its patriotic, flag-waving finest"*. Such is always the fate of social-chauvinism!

And *The Times* in its editorial of 5 April, full of sabre-rattling and patriotic fervour, i.e., imperialist jingoism (we shall shortly return to this editorial) commented on Labour's performance in the following terms *"The time may come when the unilateralist Left will look back on its Churchillian posture on Saturday with amazement and regret. For the present it is enough to welcome the prodigal's return"*.

Large Task Force

On Saturday 3 April the House of Commons gave a near unanimous mandate to the government to dispatch a formidable naval task force, composed of 36 ships, including the Aircraft Carriers *Invincible* and *Hermes* as well as guided missile destroyers, frigates and nuclear-powered submarines, for the purpose of *"liberating the Islands from Argentinean rule"*. This force is already on its way and there is every prospect at the moment of a bloody battle over these Islands. It is of the utmost importance that we make our attitude to this impending battle clear. The bourgeois attitude has been outlined by the government, by the Opposition and by the press. Not a single one of these has, not surprisingly, said or done anything that is in the interests of the working class of this country. In the circumstances the working class and its leadership must in the interests of its own class make its attitude clear. Our attitude is that the Falklands belong to Argentina and not to Britain. We have no wish to forcibly take other people's territory or loot other people's wealth. Our demand should be that our government desist from all military action against Argentina and conduct negotiations with the Argentine government on the single issue of securing the lives and well-being of the 1700 Islanders. We should refuse to be fooled by the hysterical leader-writers of the imperialist press, and we should treat their outbursts with the contempt that they deserve.

In its editorial, referred to above, *The Times* tries to compare the Falkland invasion with the Nazi invasion of Poland, and with a racist tinge adds: *"The Poles were Poles; the Falklanders are our people. The Falklands are British territory. When British territory is invaded, it is not just an invasion of our land, but of our whole spirit. We are all Falklanders now"*.

As a matter of fact there are two spirits living side by side in Britain - one imperialist and the other proletarian. To the former all other people's territory is 'our' territory, to the latter it is not so. To the former it is an invasion of 'our' spirit when we cannot plunder other people. To the latter it is not so. We are not all Falklanders, and if the British bourgeoisie wish to go and fight it out, let them do their own dirty work. We in the working class have no wish to shed a single drop of blood for protecting the interests of British imperialism.

The Argentine Fascist Junta

It is now being claimed that we should knock the hell out of Argentina and oppose the latter's claims to the Falklands because it is ruled by a fascistic military dictatorship. Says The Times: "It is the misfortune of the Argentine people to live under a fascist dictatorship as they have done many times over in their turbulent, truculent, unstable 150-year history. *The people of Argentina are again today on their knees under the rifle butts of a military tyranny which has introduced a sinister new idiom to their language - 'the disappeared ones'. The disappearance of individuals is the junta's recognised method of dealing with opposition. We are faced now with a situation where it intends to make a whole island people - the Falklanders - disappear"*. (ibid.)

There is not the slightest doubt that the Argentinean government is fascistic and its rule the most bloody most nasty and most sordid, it is true that more than 12,000 Argentines have disappeared since this fascist junta came to power. And we congratulate *The Times,* and the rest of the British media as well as Her Majesty's Government and Opposition, for having made this belated discovery. Some of us have correctly characterised the Argentinean junta as fascist right from its inception. Over the years *The Times* and most of the other newspapers, who today wax eloquent over the disappearances, kept silent. The British government and British big business were doing good business with Argentina and making jolly good money out of the misfortune of the Argentine people, as they have done out of the misfortune of the South African, the Chilean, the Salvadoran and countless other peoples. The fact of the matter is that these nasty, bloody, fascist regimes would not last a day if it were not for the financial, political and military support afforded them by the various imperialist countries, Britain included. It is indeed ironical that the Royal Navy will be facing in a couple of weeks' time some of the sophisticated hardware provided to the Argentine fascist junta by the benevolence of the British government. These facts ought to be remembered by those who are now calling upon the working class to make sacrifices in a futile and unjust cause, as well as by the working class.

The fact that Argentine people are under the heel of fascism should in no way blind us to the national rights of the Argentinean people over the Falklands. Nor should this fact lead us into the camp of British imperialism and into the defence of its interests. We should not be fooled by the crocodile tears of the age-old apologists of British colonialism and imperialism such as *The Times*. These tears are not shed over either the misfortune of the Argentine people nor that of the Falklanders, these are tears shed over the humiliation and misfortune presently afflicting British imperialism. No doubt the Falklands question is a popular issue in Argentina and the fascist generals need it to distract the attention of the Argentinean people and to retard the latter's resistance to their fascist rule. No doubt that temporarily the generals will gain some popularity. But in 6 months' time this will no longer be the case; there will be no more Malvinas to inflame national feelings. Then the people of Argentina will still be under the heel of the fascist junta and they will doubtlessly get rid of it by waging revolutionary war against it.

National Issue

"Falklands is a national issue and no regrets about the past or anxieties about the future should be allowed to conceal from Argentina Britain's total resolution .... What matters in the next few weeks is that the government should have the fullest possible backing for a combined military and diplomatic operation which calls for nerve and skill on an unusual scale." (Ibid.).

So says *The Times*, expressing the desires, wishes and interests of British imperialism. For our part we, expressing the desires, wishes and above all the interests of the working class, say that Falklands is not a national issue. The issues that matter to us are those concerned with getting rid of unemployment (3 million at present), housing shortages, inadequate social services, of racialism, of war - indeed getting rid of not only the present nasty government but the whole nasty system of production that ever reproduces these problems. We are concerned with conquering these real problems rather than conquering other people's territories. This is the line of thought and policy which must permeate every working-class organisation.

LALKAR February/March 1991

London Demonstrations Show British People Opposed to Gulf War

On Saturday 12 January 1991, the last weekend before the UN deadline ran out, over 200,000 people attended a massive and militant anti-war demonstration in London, which started from Hyde Park and ended with a Rally in Trafalgar Square, where a number of militant speeches were made. Outstanding among these was that of Bernie Grant M.P. who spoke of the right of the Arab people to determine their own destinies. The main slogan of the demonstration 'No Blood for Oil', showed that most people there understood the real nature of this war - that it was not a war for the democratic rights of small nations but a war over who should control Middle East oil, the people of the region or the big imperialist-owned oil companies. Moreover *Lalkar* was bought by large numbers of people, many of whom expressed their appreciation of the firm stand that *Lalkar* is taking on this issue and the guidance it is giving on the nature of the imperialists' machinations.

Anticipating their role as the propaganda arm of the British government, the media reported the demonstration as only being attended by 42,000 (according to the police). The *Sunday Express* outdid all its rivals by claiming only 13,000 people had been there. Maybe it only counted the *Sunday Express* readers. Bernie Grant's speech, and even his presence, went unreported.

Ignoring public opinion in Britain and in America, where the peace movement is even more militant and widely supported, the governments of the imperialist countries decided to go ahead anyway, launching their first bombing strike on the night of Wednesday 16 January. As a result the following Saturday, the 23rd January, there was another demonstration - this time of 20,000 people - held to protest against the war.

It will be noted that the immediate effect of declaration of war has been to cause a certain decrease in the number of people prepared to voice their opposition to war. In particular the 'Labour' Party, which had in a half-hearted way opposed entry into the war, promoted with some success the petty-bourgeois line that we must support 'our' forces. Certainly when working-class young men are herded off to give their lives in an unpleasant and brutal war, it is hard to have to tell them that their cause is unjust. Nevertheless, brutal though the truth may be, much less pain is caused in the long run if the truth is faced rather than attempts made to hide it.

It is extremely important that we develop a consistent strategy to oppose this war. It is our firm conviction, based on facts and not sentiment, that the present war waged by the US-led imperialist coalition is an unjust predatory war for controlling the Arab people's fabulous oil wealth, preventing revolution and protecting medieval and feudal regimes who are nothing but stooges for the attainment of the above two nefarious aims.

In the light of this strategy we wish to review very briefly the stands taken by some of the participants in the anti-war movement.

As we noted above, Labour Party support for the anti-War movement has plummeted since the war began. The Labour Party supports imperialism to the hilt, and its leadership's only opposition to war was tactical - i.e., it claimed that the war could still be waged in a few months' time when Iraq had been weakened by sanctions, as a result of which 'our boys' would suffer fewer casualties. Probably if the Labour Party had been in power rather than in opposition, not even that much 'opposition' to the war would have been forthcoming. Robert Harris of the *Sunday Times* of 13 January, who was demanding war as soon as possible, dismissed the Kinnock line with the contempt that it (and almost all other Kinnock lines) richly deserved when he wrote:

"There is a famous joke ... which seems to sum up the Labour party's position on the war in the Gulf. A man angrily demands of his son if he has cut down the family's apple tree. 'Father, I cannot tell a lie,' replies the boy, solemnly. 'Maybe I did, and maybe I didn't.'

"The opposition's policy on the restoration of Kuwait, as set out last week by Neil Kinnock and Gerald Kaufman, has the pithy brilliance of an Oscar Wilde epigram: Labour does not support the use of force in the immediate future; but if force is used in the immediate future, Labour will support it.

"That nicely covers just about every eventuality ...

"Labour is properly doing its duty as a loyal opposition: supporting the government when British lives are at stake, but giving voice to the widespread unease which should properly be represented in parliament. Its policy is ... utterly fallacious.

"The fallacy is sanctions; more particularly Labour's refusal to put a time

limit on how long it would be prepared to wait for sanctions to work... I have yet to hear a proponent of sanctions indicate, even in vague terms, when that point will come...

"In these circumstances sanctions ... serve ... as a sort of moral escape hatch: a funk hole for those who lack either the wit or the courage to make up their minds."

Frankly we could not have put it better ourselves.

The Campaign for Nuclear Disarmament, too, is coloured with a strong pro-imperialist streak, which tends to divert it from its aims. Hence its 'anti-war' position, trying to please both the pro-imperialists and those who genuinely oppose war, ended up with the absurdity of opposing the war while at the same time opposing withdrawal of the imperialist troops from the Gulf. Obviously if there are troops in the Gulf they are there to be used. The Campaign was prepared to go along with the imperialist line that the cause of the war was aggression by Saddam Hussein against Kuwait, and totally failed to appreciate that it was imperialism's moves to stifle the Arabs' right to control the oil situated on their own territories that had precipitated the crisis. Nevertheless, there are within the Campaign many honest people who will sooner or later reject with disgust the efforts of some of its big leaders, like Bruce Kent, to herd them into the imperialist camp, and thus mobilise them FOR war rather than AGAINST it.

Similar attempts to accommodate both imperialism and opposition to the war at the same time are made by various Trotskyite groupings as well as the Anarchists of Class War. With earsplitting militancy they condemn both imperialism and Saddam Hussein. In this way they help imperialism by neutralising those who cannot stomach being on the imperialist side. At least they do not go over to the side of the oppressed and exploited people of the world who are struggling for freedom. Whenever REAL confrontations take place between imperialism and the people of the world, these 'ultra-revolutionaries' find all kinds of reasons for undermining the freedom struggles, which are never revolutionary enough for their tastes. Forget that, they say, until you get a chance to fight an ideal fight that is uncontaminated by reality. Class War put out a leaflet which really comes over as a caricature of this line, though we believe they actually meant it to be taken seriously. This leaflet thunderously concludes:

"When it comes down to it, Bush, Thatcher and Saddam are all on the same side - the side of the rich and powerful. We have no interest in fighting their battles for them. The only war worth fighting is the class war to get rid of these scumbags for good. In Iraq, *Britain and everywhere else working class people face similar problems (war, dangerous jobs, increasing poverty, etc.) and have the same enemies. By fighting together in a social revolution we can sweep away all the warring states and build a classless world human community in their place, a world where human needs are what counts, not money."* Well, what is wrong with supporting the Iraqi people now against 'our' imperialist masters? Why don't we all get Bush and Thatcher (or Major) now while the going is good? For the moment Saddam is doing a good job against world imperialism. Can't we worry about him later?

The most disgusting leaflet was the one distributed by the Committee Against Repression for Democratic Rights in Iraq (Cardri). Its authors, unable or unwilling to make a distinction between the right and struggle of the Iraqi people for a democratic regime in Iraq on the one hand and the just struggle of the Iraqi people against imperialism on the other hand, give succour to the imperialist forces waging war against Iraq in the following terms:

"The continued intransigence of the Iraqi regime, its continued deliberate policy of sabotaging peace efforts by various international and Arab quarters, and refusal to comply with the UN resolutions, have exposed the utter contempt of Saddam's dictatorship for international values and norms. It demonstrates once again its preparedness to gamble with the fate of the Iraqi people in order to hold on to political power at any cost."

One has to be wilfully ignorant to blame Iraq for the present crisis which even some bourgeois analysts admit has been in preparation ever since the Iran-Iraq war. Cardri reveals its truly reactionary and treasonable role by saying: *"Cardri supports the call by all the main forces of the Iraqi opposition, made at a press conference in Beirut on 29 December 1990, for a peaceful solution to the conflict through intensifying the pressure on Saddam's regime to withdraw unconditionally from Kuwait."* Every intelligent observer of the political developments in the Middle East and in Europe knows that the so-called forces of the Iraqi opposition who gave their call from Beirut on 29 December 1990 are acting as despicable tools of the CIA and intelligence agencies of other imperialist countries, and are being carefully groomed to take over the government of Iraq after, as is the hope of imperialism, the overthrow of the Iraqi regime by the NATO aggressors. In the next issue of *Lalkar* we shall give detailed proof of this assertion of ours.

The most entertaining leaflet was produced by Richard Burns under the title 'We are the wimps against war'. From this extremely hilarious long leaflet we reproduce just one sentence which is Mr Burns' panacea to cure all ills of our society, which he calls a 'phallocracy': *"I believe the only basis for peace is the voluntary surrendering of all arms and their destruction, the practice of pacifism, sustained arguments against patriarchy and a woman-led worldwide peace movement."* One can guess at the hilarity contained in the rest of the leaflet from this single sentence.

As the war progresses into bloody confusion, we are convinced that British working people, like working people the world over, will rapidly learn the true nature of imperialism, will lose their illusions and their faith in imperialist leaders and will start forming themselves into the mighty force that will soon be wiping imperialism off the map forever.

Appendix

LALKAR June 1984

SCARGILL NAILS BOURGEOIS LIES

As we go to print the mineworkers have been on strike for nearly 12 weeks. During this time the strikers, representing 85% of the entire membership of the NUM, braving police violence on the picket lines, hardship caused by the Government's denial of social security payments to miners' families (treatment not even meted out to the families of common criminals and murderers), the Judge Jeffreys-type decisions dished out by the ever compliant judiciary, the denial to strikers of their already-earned holiday entitlement etc., have shown rock-like unity, unflagging morale and a grim determination to win. So the NCB, the Government and Fleet Street have all coalesced their not inconsiderable resources and unleashed a campaign of lies, distortions, misrepresentations and half-truths in an effort to isolate the miners from the rest of the working-class movement and pressurise the strikers into a drift back to work.

To counter this malicious campaign Arthur Scargill, the President of the NUM, has recently put out a brief statement containing the true facts about the coalmining industry and the issues at stake in this strike. We publish Arthur Scargill's statement in full so that our readers may arm themselves with the true facts and not the libellous lies that emanate from our "free" press.

"Britain's miners are fighting to save their industry, pits and jobs. They are fighting against the Coal Board's pit closure programme, which threatens to close over 70 collieries and units, wiping out between 70,000 and 100,000 jobs in the next few years.[1]

"It was Coal Board Chairman Ian MacGregor's announcement on March 6th that at least 20,000 jobs would disappear, and over 20 pits close, this year, that sparked off strike action in the coalfields.

"All of our members have, of course, been involved in national industrial action since last November, when the Union began an overtime ban following the NCB's breaking off of wage negotiations and the continued run-down of our industry.

"We know the British industry is worth saving and it's worth fighting for. No redundancy payment in the world can match the value of a job passed on to the next generation.

"There is no bribe big enough to compensate for lifetime wasted without employment. There is no cash hand-out stunning enough to make up for the loss of a vital na-

---

[1] At the time, Arthur Scargill was accused by the Government and the bourgeois media of scare-mongering. As a matter of fact, if anything, he was guilty of a gross underestimate, for today there are just 7,000 miners - and the coal industry passed into private hands at the beginning of 1995 almost unnoticed (note to present edition)

tional asset: Coal.

"The Coal Board's closure programme is frightening in its implications for the British people - and the British economy. What is also frightening is the way in which the NCB has lied to the miners and to the general public about its plans.

"Ian MacGregor claims that in closing 20 pits and axing 20,000 jobs this year, the NCB will only remove about four million tonnes of coal capacity ... , this is untrue.

"The Coal Board budget for 1984/5 is 97.4 million tonnes. That is 8.2 million tonnes less than the 1983/4 budgeted output of 105.6 million tonnes. The truth is, that more than 40,000 jobs could go over the next year, and the Board could close double the number of pits indicated on March 6th.

"Indeed, the NCB Chairman said less than 12 months ago - on June 14th, 1983, at an industry consultative meeting - that it was the Board's intention to take 25 million tonnes of capacity out of the industry as new capacity such as that from the new Selby coalfield came on stream.

"To phase out 25 million tonnes capacity means eliminating six times the amount publicly stated by the Board, and it is equal to the closure of between 70 and 100 pits, with a drop in manpower from 180,000 to 100,000.

"No coalfield area is safe from the American butcher, Ian MacGregor, and his closure programme.

"If the closure plan was implemented, it would mean the death of half the collieries in Scotland, 60 per cent of those in the North East, 70 per cent of those in South Wales, and a 40 per cent reduction in the Midlands.

"It would wipe out 50 per cent of the pits in the North West, and close 20 of Yorkshire's mines and 20 in North Nottinghamshire. The Coal Board is on record as stating - at an industry joint policy meeting - that 50 per cent of all pits in South Nottinghamshire and North Derbyshire are ear-marked for closure.

"When the Coal Board claims that there will be no compulsory redundancies, its spokesmen are not telling the truth.

"When, on March 6th, Ian McGregor announced the closure programme, he told the Union that he could not guarantee there would be no compulsory redundancies. The truth is that the Board's closure programme will leave miners without work, and families without a livelihood.

Communities will suffer: related industries will be badly hit, and unemployment in the coalfield areas will rocket. The regional poverty which is now a standard feature of 1984 Britain will intensify.

"What is the purpose behind this butchery? What is point of decimating an industry that in fact produces the cheapest deep-mined coal in the world?

"The policies of this Government have nothing to do with what the British people need. Our nation is built upon an island of coal - enough for 1,000 years ahead.

"Coal to meet our industrial needs. Coal for heating hospitals, schools, community institutions. Coal which will outlast oil and gas. Coal instead of terrifyingly unsafe nuclear power. Coal, liquefied into oil.

"Coal, which, used to provide combined heat and power schemes, would give an efficient, effective and clean system with warmth for all our elderly during winter months.

APPENDIX

"Coal is the fuel of the present AND the future. And ours is the cheapest deep-mined coal in the world.

"The cost of producing a tonne of British coal in 1983, before the NUM overtime ban began, was only £38, and that makes British coal, before subsidies, cheaper to deliver to any power station in the nation than deep mined coal from Eastern or Western Europe, the United States of America or Australia.

"Even the NCB hasn't seriously tried to deny that ours is the cheapest coal produced in Europe (East AND West).

"The Board does, however, distort our production costs when compared with those in selected parts of the United States (such as Appalachia) and Australia (New South Wales). But one can't make comparisons on that basis. We would never claim that Selby coal, for example, at £14 a tonne, is typical of British production. In using New South Wales to represent Australia, the NCB says nothing about areas such as Queensland., where deep-mined coal, at £43 a tonne, is £5 more expensive than the coal produced last year in Britain.

"The only honest and sensible comparison is that of like with like: the British coal industry as a whole with that of any other mining industry as a whole, taking all factors into account.

"The truth is that other nations, the U.S. and Australia included, pay large subsidies to their coal industries, thus enabling them to sell their output - which cost a lot more than ours to produce - at a cheaper price than ours.

"We know that the NCB claims that Australian and US coal are not subsidised - BUT THEY ARE. In the United States, there are Government subsidies of over £1,330 million a year, covering research, development and industrial disease. And in Australia there are similar arrangements.

"The West German government gives £2,472 million a year to their coal industry, while in Belgium, coal receives a subsidy of £96 per tonne. But in Britain, we're given only £4 per tonne - and then we're expected to compete!

"If other nations withdrew their subsidies, Britain could sell all the coal she produces - and, on the other hand, if we received the same level of subsidies as our competitors, we would now be developing our industry, and expanding rather than talking in terms of contraction.

"We have a second handicap which is just as crippling. Interest charges of nearly £400 million per year, coal stocking charges of over £200 million per year and other payments result in the NCB paying the Government over £2 million a day!

"Far from pouring money into our industry, this Government is intent on bleeding it to death.

"The Coal Board, the Government and the media accuse the NUM of not wanting to negotiate and of not being prepared to compromise. I've already pointed out that the Coal Board broke off negotiations with our Union last autumn.

"We've consistently made it clear that all they have to do is pick up a phone, and we'll meet them any time and anywhere within the agreed procedures of the industry's conciliation scheme.

"There is an agreement - signed by Government, Coal Board, and the mining unions - which lays down the programme to be followed by our industry. Drawn up 10 years ago, it's called 'Plan for Coal'.

"Plan For Coal recognised the need to expand and develop Britain's mining industry, and the need to prepare a massive investment programme which would enable the mining industry to meet the energy demands of the twenty-first century.

"It recognised coal as the fuel on which the nation's economy could depend, and it laid down the conditions in which Britain could get the best possible returns on its investment in coal.

The Conservative Government accepted the Plan For Coal when elected in 1979, and (more importantly) re-affirmed its support as recently as 1981.

"The miners have adhered scrupulously to the spirit and the letter of the Plan. We have improved coal face production by well over 5 per cent per year during the past 10 years. We have also witnessed and accepted during this time the rapid introduction of new technology - more rapid and far-reaching than anywhere else in the world.

"**Plan For Coal states very clearly that pits will be closed only on grounds of exhaustion - a point which the NUM has never, ever disputed.**

"The Plan envisaged output rising up to 150 million tonnes by 1985, and to 170 million tonnes by the end of the century. The Coal Board chairman at that time - Sir Derek Ezra - believed output would exceed 200 million tonnes by the turn of the century.

"What has happened ? The truth is that the NCB, under Government directive, has been steadily reducing output, cutting capacity, closing pits and axing jobs. The planned budget for 1984/5 is only 97.4 million tonnes - that's nearly 53 million tonnes less than the output projected in the Plan For Coal !

"Under the Plan's terms, Government agreed to provide assistance if this proved to be necessary in order to counter the effects of fluctuation in demand.

"In other words, Plan For Coal provided for subsidies similar to those given to our international competitors, including those within the EEC. This is part of an overall programme of expansion and development for our industry.

But Plan For Coal did not envisage a Government intent on dragging this nation away from a coal-fired energy programme towards an inefficient and frighteningly dangerous nuclear one.

"The CEGB has in fact admitted during the course of the Sizewell Public Inquiry that it intends, on the basis of a high nuclear profile, to be 90 per cent dependent on nuclear power by the year 2020.

"Such a complete reversal of policy can only happen with Government blessing, and such plans to build up the nuclear programme can only be carried out if the coal industry is decimated.

"The NUM calls upon the Coal Board and the Government to honour the Plan For Coal, signed in 1974, for which the Government re-affirmed its support in 1979 and 1981.

"If that is done, no pits will be closed other than on grounds of exhaustion, and we shall have an expanding and developing industry, bringing on stream modern new pits capable of meeting Britain's energy demands now and through the next century.

"We know there's a need for British coal and it's in the interests of the British people to develop it.

"The miners' strike is biting, and it's biting hard. One indication of this is the extraordinary outcry by the Department of Energy and the NCB about the state of coal stocks, in particular those held by the CEGB. Confidential information received from within the Electricity Generating Board itself reveals that at the beginning of April, it held 20 million tonnes of coal, and it was conceded that without any additional supplies it had a total endurance time of 12 weeks. That was over five weeks ago.

"The NUM's predictions about coal stocks related to normal levels of coal burn have been absolutely accurate.

"Coal stocks, of course, have been and are being affected by the CEGB switching from coal to oil, and by the decision to increase oil-fired electricity from 5 per cent to 27 per cent at a cost to the British taxpayer of over £20 million per week.

"In addition, the CEGB **is keeping nuclear power stations operating beyond the dates they would normally close for safety checks - a decision which holds its own dangers.**

"These measures indicate the lengths to which the Government will go in trying to force its pit closure programme upon the miners and the nation. Money - taxpayer's money - is no object. The dispute in our industry (the dispute brought on by Ian MacGregor's closure programme) has thus far cost the taxpayers £1,350 million - enough to keep all our threatened pits open for the next 10 years.

"To go to such lengths to close pits, to seal away valuable coal, can only be described as a criminal act. It's criminal to be thus prepared to destroy jobs, to take the economic heart out of communities, to throw people - especially young people - on the scrap heap.

"It's criminal to press ahead with a pit closure programme which, if implemented, will cost the taxpayer £4.3 billion - while to subsidise our industry, to keep pits open and jobs safe will cost £2 billion: less than half the cost of closures.

"This dispute started on November 1, when the NUM began its overtime ban. That national action is still in operation.

"During the past nine weeks, over 80 per cent of the British coalfields have been on strike, and had it not been for our Nottingham colleagues continuing to work, the power stations would not have received any coal supplies, and would now be close to exhaustion.

"So far the dispute has lost the Coal Board over 24 million tonnes of production, and already industries are beginning to feel the pinch. Towns throughout the mining areas have suffered as a result of the MacGregor philosophy. Whole communities which depend on mining are feeling the effects of this, the longest dispute since 1926.

"The hysteria of the Government, the NCB and the media should demonstrate to any miner that we are winning.

"Our hope is that our colleagues in the Nottinghamshire coalfield will join us and bring this dispute to a swift and successful conclusion.

"There should be no doubt in anyone's mind about the policy of Ian MacGregor - he was sent into British Steel to butcher that industry, and in three years he slashed the workforce from 166,000 down to 81,000, while increasing the corporation's LOSS per worker from just over £3,000 to over £4,700.

"Mrs Thatcher has now appointed him to carry out the same ruthless exercise in the coal industry, and we believe that in defending our "right to work" we are standing firm for all workers against the vandalism of a Tory Government intent on destroying Britain's industrial base[1].

"We have witnessed tremendous solidarity from other trade unions, and in particular from the transport unions, which have been absolutely magnificent.

"They understand that an attack upon our industry is an attack upon them, and for that reason they have responded swiftly and decisively to this situation.

"We have also seen the development of women's support groups all over the British coalfield. Women recognise the threat not just to pits and miners' jobs, but to all mining communities.

"Our young people, above all, have been magnificent throughout this dispute.

"The miners know that to keep pits open is right: it makes sense - economically, socially, and politically.

"We call on Ian MacGregor and the Government to withdraw the pit closure programme now. We ask them to adhere to the Plan For Coal to which both Government and Coal Board are signatories.

"We ask that our industry be developed and expanded, not merely in the interests of miners, but in the interests of the taxpayer and the British nation as a whole".

---

1 This, of course, is inherent to the imperialist stage of the capitalist system, which is characterised by export of capital (note to present edition).

LALKAR November 1984

Lalkar interviews Malcolm Pitt 6th October 1984

Harpal Brar (HB): Comrade Malcolm Pitt, I welcome you, on behalf of the Indian Workers' Front, to Southall. We are very pleased and honoured that you have found time to come to this Rally, which is in support of the NUM and the strike that has been going on for 7 months.

Now that the strike has been going on for 7 months and there has been a lot of comment that the miners, perhaps because of hardship, will go back to work, could you comment on that and tell us what the determination of the mining community is?

MALCOLM PITT (MP): In fact the opposite is absolutely the case, because the government-inspired NCB campaign to get a return to work has failed miserably. Only a handful of miners have actually decided to go back to work, for a variety of (mainly individual) reasons. We have professional blacklegs, such as Mr McGibbon at Betteshanger, who has a long history of association with anti-trade union organisations, but as far as the overwhelming majority of our members is concerned, the determination is now even more solid to continue through to final victory. In fact, I was talking to one of our members a few nights ago and we were discussing Christmas. He said to me: 'We continue at whatever cost now to a final victory, because we have been out so long - the sacrifices have been so great - that as far as we are concerned, victory is the ONLY outcome.'

HB. One issue that is at present hanging over the NUM leadership is the contempt proceedings flowing from Judge Nicholls' judgment declaring the strike in Derbyshire and Yorkshire to be unofficial and that the Union had no right to discipline those members who went to work. I would like to ask you to comment upon two things: (a) What is your position as regards the strike being declared unofficial - how do you maintain that it is official? and (b) What is going to be the response that you would give in the NUM if the leadership of the NUM were put in jail? I know that the Union Executive Committee has unanimously decided not to appear in court and to treat with contempt the contempt proceedings.

MP. As far as the original issue of the official nature of the strike is concerned, first of all, we are not bothered if a court, or any organisation outside the NUM, decides our strike is official, unofficial or whatever. As far as we are concerned it is a decision made by the miners through their own democratic procedures. As far as the strike itself is concerned, it is not so long ago, under Joe Gormley's presidency, that a ballot of the membership threw out an incentive scheme. But because the NCB were so keen on this incentive scheme, it was introduced into one area and endorsed under Rule 41 (just as the present strike has been). That decision was tested in the courts, and Lord Denning ruled that it was quite legitimate for the Union, for the National Executive that is, to endorse the action in one area. That is precisely what has happened in the present strike: despite all the allegations that Scargill had called a political strike to bring down Margaret Thatcher, and similar press statements, the strike itself started quite spontaneously in the Cortonwood colliery in Yorkshire. It spread to other areas, was endorsed by the area leaderships, and was put to the National Executive for endorsement under Rule 41. As far as we are concerned the strike has been conducted through the normal procedures of the Union, whereby areas have taken strike action and their action has been made official by our National Executive and also by Special Conference of the Union. Furthermore, we also feel that, in a situation where people's jobs are at stake, we will not concede to any man or woman the right to put a cross on a piece of paper to vote somebody else out of a job. We believe that it is a fundamental right of our members to be able to fight for their jobs, and that's where we stand.

In regard to the court action, it is fairly clear that there are now serious divisions within both the ruling class and the government about how far they are going to take this dispute. They are uncertain because they have met the solid resistance of the miners and increasingly broad sections of the trade-union movement. The decision of the court to give Arthur another week to decide on whether he should appear before the court is a symptom of their uncertainty as to which way to go. But if they decide they are going to put the leadership of the Union in prison, then I think we can say to them that they will have to start opening the football stadiums to take all the miners who will stand with the national leadership. In that situation we would demand, as of right, the solid support of, and action from, the entire trade-union movement. In the event of the courts taking such a decision I am certain we would receive that support from the entire trade-union movement, whatever people like Mr Hammond and various other defeatists or strike-breakers in the trade union might have to say about the matter.

HB. You have already partly answered the question that I am about to ask you, namely, the question of the ballot. There has been such a hullabaloo on the part of Fleet Street and government ministers, and even of some people who call themselves part and parcel of the labour and trade union movement - people in the Labour Party, people like Eric Hammond, Chapple & Co - who say that miners have not held a ballot and conclude the strike is 'undemocratic'. Recently the *Daily Express* published an opinion poll that found that if the miners were to be balloted they would vote overwhelmingly in favour of strike action. What possible objection could the NUM have to holding a ballot?

MP. It is not an objection. The other fact which came out of that opinion poll was that the majority of our members feel it is totally unnecessary and irrelevant to hold a ballot. You do not start talking about holding a ballot to take strike action seven months after the strike has begun. The question really will be, when this government comes to its senses and recognises that it has already been defeated, how we decide democratically whether or not the settlement is good enough. Then, maybe, a ballot may be considered. It is not a question of our objecting to a ballot. The strike started on the basis of area decisions endorsed by our national union executive. Therefore, as far as we are concerned, the decision to go on strike is past history. It is ironical that people like Chapple and Hammond are demanding a ballot and talking about democracy: in their own union if you happen to be a member of the Communist Party you are not even allowed to hold office! These are not the people to lecture the NUM on questions of democracy!

HB. The next question relates to yet another aspect of the propaganda that has ceaselessly been conducted against the NUM and that is that it is only violence and intimidation on the part of the miners on the picket lines which sustains this strike. The majority of people would otherwise go to work. Can I have your comments on that please?

MP. It is an old myth that it is possible for trade union leaders with a small group of supporters to intimidate the membership of a huge national union with strong traditions of democracy. The miners have traditionally always been extremely cautious about taking strike action, but one thing that has always happened when they actually do so is that they have done so solidly and have exhibited a determination to see the dispute through to a settlement satisfactory to the membership. There is no way that Arthur Scargill, or area officials, with a small group of supporters could intimidate the overwhelming majority of the membership. The members - and not just the members, their wives and families also - have demonstrated every day their support for the Union. There is no way that you could sustain a strike for over 7 months if the majority of members were against such an action.

HB. We are very concerned about the hardship that the mining families have suffered. The men have suffered, but the families especially have suffered tremendous hardship. I would like to know two things: first, is money coming in to sustain them in reasonable conditions, and what more can we do, in addition to holding social evenings such as this one[1], collecting money at work, etc.? Secondly, how has the continuation of this strike affected the morale of the families? Are they more determined than ever before? Or are they beginning to weaken because of the hardships that it has caused, particularly in view of the contemptuous actions on the part of the DHSS, where they have been refusing even funeral expenses for children who have died, on the grounds that their father happened to be a striker?

MP. Let us go back to the original question about the attitude of the members themselves. What has become quite clear is that our members have been in dispute for long and hard bitter months. They are quite convinced of the correct leadership of the Union in regard to the fight against pit closures. One of the dramatic aspects of this strike has been the organisation of the women. Unlike previous strikes in other industries, where women have been organised to break the strike, the 1984 miners' strike will stand out historically as the strike in which the women openly said: 'We are not going to be used as strike breakers. We are going to join the strike because the men are fighting for our livelihoods and our communities. Therefore we have not just a duty but a right to be with them on the picket lines and on the demonstrations. We will see this strike through to the end'. One of the remarkable aspects of the women's movement has been that the women, far from standing behind the men, or even shoulder to shoulder with the men, have often now taken the lead. Often you hear a wife say: 'If my husband went back to work without a proper settlement then we would be on the picket lines stopping the men going to work, so that WE could secure a proper settlement'. I have heard that said on several occasions in different parts of the country. Also the children are coming out to protest - against scabs and so on - to protest in defence of what they are beginning to see as a battle for the family, for the community and, of course, for their own jobs in the future.

HB. You mention the word 'scabs'. Could I ask you who are the people who pay the very heavy legal expenses and the expenses of staying in 5-star hotels of those min-

---

1   The Southall branch of the IWA(GB) held several social evenings during the Coal Strike to canvas political support and raise money for the strike. The Southall branch alone was able to collect upwards of £2,000 which was handed over to the Kent miners.

ers who really are scabs, but who are held up as freedom-loving democrats who want democracy in the Union? Who is actually behind Foulstone and Taylor, and people like that? Who finances them?

MP. It is no secret, because it has been reported in the press, that Silver Birch - or Weeping Willow or Dutch Elm Disease or whatever you like to call him - is already receiving quite large contributions from big companies. We have a similar animal in our own coalfield called McGibbon who, a few years ago, was working at the British Leyland Works in Cowley where he organised against the Transport and General Workers Union. He attempted to break the organisation of the union there, until he was forced to leave. He then came into the Kent coalfield to practise his old tricks there. We know, and it is accepted by Norris McWhirter from the 'Freedom Association' (which as everybody knows is an anti-trade union organisation financed by big business) that there is close liaison between Mr McGibbon and that organisation, as indeed with 'Aims of Industry' and all these various reactionary organisations. We have evidence too that the National Front is also involved, feeding financial support to the strike-breaking elements. This is only one part of the operation which has been organised by the government over several years. The trade union movement has to wake up to the fact that the government, and the people who sustain this government, i.e., big business on an international scale, are people who think ahead. They plan and prepare. Part of their operation has been to organise strike-breaking elements not only within the British coalfields, but within other sections of industry also. The British trade-union movement must wake up to that fact and must equally begin to plan, prepare and have perspectives on struggle. If we do not, then we are going to be always following the initiatives of opposition. This planning is important, not only nationally but internationally as well.

HB. You mention the involvement of the National Front on the side of the strike-breakers, yet the fascists always claim that they are for British workers. Most of the workers in the NUM are British workers, they are white workers, and yet the National Front is involved in strike-breaking. We in this country, as workers and as black workers, try to make a small contribution towards supporting the trade union and labour movement throughout our stay in this country, and have been doing so ever since the Second World War. We have been particularly keen to support the miners because we think they are fighting for every one of us. Can you tell me - and we would like nothing short of the truth, no patronising recognition of our great contribution - whether you have generally been satisfied with the contribution that black workers have made by way of help. Has it brought the black and white workers closer together during the struggle?

MP. Every NUM member who has been involved in the solidarity campaign has been aware of the tremendous response they received from black workers. In the May Day celebrations in London, when our lads were out marching and collecting, many of them noted the fact that if they asked a black worker for a contribution then it was normally given, whereas often from white workers it was not given. Yes, there has been that response, and it has been recognised.

In our own coalfield we have established a link with Southall and the community in Southall, and I think that is valuable. We have to face the fact that racism is something which has been fed into the British working class over several generations. It is not easily overcome. In the mining communities, particularly as miners live in villages which are often isolated, the reactionary attitudes on the question of colour and race often prevail. But I know people in Elvington, who would no doubt have had racist ideas at one time, but whose attitudes changed completely after the visit of the Southall community:

they recognised that they had friends. They discussed the issues of police harassment, and they realised they were suffering the same as black people had suffered over several years. I believe the foundations are being laid for solidarity which will extend far beyond the strike. This is a dimension to the strike which I think the government itself must fear. What has happened during the strike is that large numbers of young people, large numbers of women, and trade-unionists in general have become politically radicalised. People who previously had no involvement with the trade union movement, no real appreciation of socialist ideas, have now, because of their experiences in this strike, begun to develop political consciousness. They are talking about capitalism, about socialism and about the issue of race and our relationship with the black communities.

For instance, people are now beginning to look at the whole situation in Ireland differently: some Yorkshire miners have been across to Belfast and they have experienced what is happening over there. Thus an issue which the trade union and labour movement has for many years tried to hide and to avoid is now coming into people's consciousness and being recognised as something which has to be discussed. We are in a common battle against common enemies - maybe fighting on different fronts, but just the same it is one battle against one major enemy.

HB. The government started this dispute, prepared for it, provoked it, at a time it considered propitious to its strategy of defeating the NUM as a means of defeating the entire trade union movement, subjugating it and castrating it. Some people who, like Jimmy Reid, have really become renegades in our view, go along with that. They say that as a result of this strike the NUM will come out of the strike bleeding and probably finished for the rest of the century. They also say that the price of the NUM strike will have to be paid by the rest of the labour movement and that the Labour Party's fight to get into office will be greatly hindered by this strike. What do you have to say on that?

MP. Well, it is palpable nonsense. I would not expect anything else from Jimmy Reid. It is a tragedy that someone of his stature should have been bought over by the opposition. His is the same sort of argument we have heard in every major social confrontation... No doubt the same sort of argument was heard in Nazi Germany: as long as we did not fight then maybe we could protect our organisations and somehow they would not notice us. But as we know, every defeat of the working class, particularly if it is brought about by the failure of working-class organisations to fight, leads to further attacks by the ruling class. I would look to the fact that over a long period of time we have had mass unemployment; we have had attacks on various sections of the trade-union movement; many of the gains of 1945 in regard to the National Health Service, Social Security and all the other things we have fought for have been lost. There was a general atmosphere of defeat and demoralisation throughout the movement. All that has now changed dramatically - because of the miners' strike. Sections of the trade-union movement, which no doubt would have accepted some of the measly terms which had been offered by the government - the teachers, the railmen, etc. are now coming on. What the NUM has done is to instil confidence in the working-class movement, which will be the foundation (as the 1972 strike was) for a period of working-class advance. I certainly do not see this strike as one isolated incident. We have got a few problems, which will have to be sorted out after the strike is over, concerning certain areas. But I believe that the victory itself will be the means of sorting out that particular problem. We must see this strike as the beginning of a process which not only embraces the immediate industrial issues - such as pit closures or wages or pensions, etc., but beginning to seek a new perspective for society, to think in terms of, and to work towards, the socialisation of the means of production.

HB. The NUM strike has quite rightly dominated both the TUC Conference at Brighton in early September and the Labour Party Conference last week. Even those who would have wished to oppose the NUM had no option but to go along with it and give it full backing - at least in the form of resolutions. What are the chances of these resolutions being implemented? If the government starts moving coal from pitheads, what is going to be the response of other workers in the unions who are committed to supporting TUC policy? Chapple has said (although he demands a ballot from you!) that he does not want to abide by the decisions of the entire labour movement - such is his democratic nature! There have been the power engineers who have also said this. Also lorry drivers do not always follow the instructions of the T & G. What do you think is going to happen in these circumstances? What is going to be the general response of working people?

MP. If we left it to leaders such as Chapple and Gavin Laird and Basnett then obviously we would be waiting for a very long time before we saw any concrete implementation of the TUC decision. We must recognise first of all, though, that in regard to the power industry and the unions involved in the power industry, the EEPTU and the engineers are a minority, and we have got the support of the majority of the trade unions in the power industry! After Hammond's speech at the TUC, Arthur Scargill was informed that six power station electricians had already taken decisions, in protest at Hammond's statements, that they would refuse to move coal which had come through picket lines. I have faith in the rank and file of the trade-union movement in what is becoming ever more clear as a basic class issue in a battle for the survival of trade unions and working class organisations. We will see increasing support in terms of solidarity in power stations, in the docks and elsewhere. I believe that if the government does escalate the dispute to the extent of using troops to take coal from the pitheads to the power stations, there will be a response from power workers and from the entire trade-union movement. I do not think we should rule out, at this time, a movement towards a general strike if in fact the government does decide to escalate the dispute.

HB. Can I assume from your answers that the NUM will be victorious in its battle to ensure that the pit closure programme is withdrawn, that the five collieries that are threatened under the present programme will no longer be threatened, and that you will achieve the main purpose of this strike?

MP. I always said from the beginning of the strike that victory was gained once the miners took up the challenge of the government and the NCB. The battle came after a whole period of divisive tactics by the NCB in regard to redundancy, in regard to trying to take on one area at a time, and all the divisions that created. Our problem was to get a national unity which was capable of taking action on a national scale against the government and the NCB. We achieved that, and I believe that was the victory. Since then I have been absolutely confident that the miners are not waiting for victory: we have already won the dispute. It is a question of the terms of the settlement, and I am absolutely confident, with the leadership we have got, that the settlement will be satisfactory to the members and that we will see a total victory.

HB. Do you have any other remarks to add, because there may be questions on which you want to say something, which I have so far not been able to ask you?

MP. There is one question I did not answer, which was what more could be done by the black community in regard to the strike. The issue of continuing collections is important, because it is quite possible that a political decision will be taken in the law courts to freeze our assets. Therefore it is absolutely vital not only that the present level of financial support should be maintained but that it should be further increased because we are going to need that. At the present time the major task is to implement the decisions taken by the TUC, to ensure that people do go out and fight to win the hearts and minds of the members of trade unions so that we actually do see a developing movement of solidarity with the miners. We have already seen a major step forward with the NACODS decision, by an 82% majority, based not only on the question of payment for not crossing picket lines, but actually on the more fundamental issue of pit closures.

This itself is indicative of the breadth of support that the movement is generating. It is at the same time a warning to the ruling class that new forces are coming into the field. There are indications that members of BACM, the management union itself, are extremely concerned at the length of the dispute and the way the NCB's policies - or rather the government's policies, i.e., the destruction of a large section of our industry - are really becoming much clearer. We are looking forward to victory.

HB. Comrade Malcolm Pitt, on behalf of the Indian Workers' Front, which is the Southall Branch of the Indian Workers' Association (GB), I would like to thank you very much for coming here and answering some of the questions which I deliberately put in a hostile manner. The hostility is not on our part: we are very sympathetic, of course, to your struggle. But these are the questions which ordinary people are raising because they are constantly being bombarded by Fleet Street, the TV, the ministers, even by some people in the labour movement. I am very, very, glad that you have clarified these issues. We will send you a copy of our newspaper and the interview will be published in the November issue of *Lalkar*. Thank you ever so much for coming.

LALKAR December 1984

Kent NUM Leader's Speech at IWF Rally

Last month we printed a brief report of the social evening on 26th October, organised by the Indian Workers Front (Southall) in support of the miners. Cde Malcolm Pitt, Secretary of the Kent NUM, was the guest speaker. We are pleased to be able to publish below Cde Malcolm Pitt's most excellent speech to the rally.

Comrade Chairman, Comrades, I bring you the fraternal greetings of the Kent miners, and also all striking British miners. The Chairman has already referred to the fact that the speakers at this meeting come from the Southall community. I feel that, after the visit of the Southall community to Elvington and our many visits to Southall, I am, in a sense, already part of the Southall community. One of the tactics of imperialism, and particularly British imperialism, has been to divide and rule, to always create divisions, so that they can maintain their exploitation. We ought to thank Mrs Thatcher for laying on the 1984 miners' strike, because one of the positive sides of the strike is that it has brought together many different sections of the working-class movement and many different communities.

I believe that in future, instead of representing the spectre of the police state (and, by God, we have seen some of the police state in operation this year!) 1984 will be seen as the glorious year of the great miners' strike, when the miners and the trade union movement won the greatest victory in our history and turned back the tide of mass unemployment and police terror in this country [applause].

Further, there is no question that we have already won this dispute. The miners have taken the front line on the battle against unemployment. We've said that we will not accept ghost towns in the British coalfields; we have said that we will not accept that our sons and daughters will be put on to a permanent dole queue; and we've also said that we will banish forever the fear and depression which has pervaded the trade-union movement over these last 5 years or so of Tory recession and Tory reaction. And as a previous speaker has said, the miners strike has injected a new spirit in the British working-class movement. We have seen dockers, railwaymen, printers, transport men, we have seen every section of the working class, with all the defeats they have suffered, come together and rally around the call of the NUM for solidarity. And that is why we won the overwhelming support of the Trade Union Congress, and also, at their Conference, the Labour Party. And we welcome those decisions and we look forward to their implementation in terms of concrete action, I would like to say, though, I do wish Neil Kinnock would get off that particular fence in regard to violence on the picket lines. I think it is worth while suggesting that if anybody decides to walk down the middle of the road in between the miners' picket on one side and the police on the other, the only thing that he is liable to get in that confrontation is a sore head. And, in fact, in this situation we need to know which side he is on. I believe that is the issue which faces every activist and every member of the trade-union movement and Labour Party [applause].

But we have also caught the imagination of the world. What we are seeing now is a movement of solidarity of international proportions. A week ago I had the privilege of representing our Union in Athens to put the message of the British miners to Greek workers. And I'm pleased to say that their response was immediate. The dockers of Piraeus said: *"we only have to have the word and we will black every British ship that comes into Piraeus harbour"*. Now that is the sort of tide of solidarity which I would believe is irresistible [applause].We've won a magnificent victory already. 80% of our members have voted with their feet, and with bitter sacrifice over 8 months of a long and hard struggle, their solidarity with the Union and its leadership. Confronted with the obscenity, and that's the only word which can describe it, the obscenity of mass unemployment, the obscenity of seeing whole mining communities destroyed by the McGregor axe, our members said: *"we don't need ballots, we will take action to stop this murder"* [Applause]. We do not believe that any man or woman has a right to put a cross on a piece of paper and vote somebody else out of a job. That is our position and we will stand through to the end of the strike on that position. And when we talk about ballots and votes we certainly will not accept or concede the right to the people of this Government to call a ballot, because these are the people who have denied the people of London the right to vote in the Greater London Council; these are the people who gerrymandered and organised the constituencies of Belfast and Derry to secure the domination of British rule in Ireland, the very people who have denied the majority of Irish people the right to nationhood; and these are the people who for over 200 years have ruled half the peoples of the world and kept them in the thrall of imperialism These are not the people that can lecture the National Union of Mineworkers on the virtues of democracy! And when we talk about a political strike in a country where the judges now decide the rule-book of trade unions, where a government minister can say that the miners' strike is a worthwhile national investment, in a country which can threaten a trade-union leader with imprisonment for standing by the democratic decisions of a union, then every single strike is a political strike, every action by the working class in an employers' country against an employers' state is a political action. And we ought to say so. But the victory is also more than the fact that we have managed to rally the miners, to rally the trade-union movement. We've won an important ideological victory. And I believe that it is necessary to pay tribute to the role of Arthur Scargill. I don't normally play the cult of the individual, but I think it is necessary in the case of Arthur Scargill, because that man has come under the vilest attacks which any trade-union leader has come under in the press in this country. It is because of his consistent leadership that we've won the ideological victory against the cancer of voluntary redundancy - selling a job, which in fact attacks the very foundations of our trade union movement - because our young men are not grovelling to the Coal Board for a cheap hand out to sell their job. Not so long ago the *'Guardian'* carried articles which suggested that the young miners were paid so much money, they had mortgages, they had cars on hire-purchase, they had holidays on the Costa Brava, they had joined the middle classes, they were lost to the trade-union movement, they were not the men to stand with the union in the fight for jobs. But haven't our young miners proved them wrong! (and also proved wrong the defeatists in the labour movement itself who said much the same thing). Our young miners have become the front-line troops on the picket lines. When the *'Guardian'* writes a leader and suggests that the young miners are *"Scargill's Red Guards"*, I think they intend it was some kind of an insult, but I believe that our young miners have taken it as a compliment. We welcome the turn of a new generation of class fighters in this country, we are proud of them.

We are also proud of the women of the British coalfield. The media, this society, has said that women's place is in the home, the kitchen, never in the front-line of the battle. When our men were arrested on the picket lines, and put under bail conditions which prevented them from going on those picket lines, the women organised themselves and said: Our job is not just to cut the sandwiches, and stay in the background; our right and our duty is to be on the front line with the pickets and in the demonstrations. As in the Paris Commune, in Petrograd and in the *Sierras* of Cuba, in every great social upheaval, the women have come forward not as a reserve of militancy, but as front-line members in a common battle for a common objective. I believe that that is a magnificent victory for our entire class. I believe it is a victory that will never be reversed.

Of course, that is why the Tories and their masters within the board-rooms of the international monopolies hate the miners so much and that is why they are willing to throw the full force of the state against us. It has already been said that they have sunk so low that they will take money from miners' wives and children in a vain attempt to starve us back. We have seen our members sent to prison because they failed to pay their rates. We have had men and families with their electricity and gas cut off in petty victimisation. We have also seen large numbers of our members sacked because they have dared to occupy pits to prevent the entry of scabs. We have also seen the whole apparatus of police terror thrown into the British coalfields, thousands of police have occupied the coalfields, whole villages have been cordoned off, a state of virtual curfew exists in many of our mining communities; horses have been used in cavalry charges against unarmed boys in plimsolls and tee-shirts; dogs have been unleashed against women; army personnel, we know, are being used on picket lines in police uniforms, and we have been told by Eldon Griffiths that the time will come when we will suffer plastic bullets against miners pickets. We have seen that 5 of our members died in this dispute - 2 of them murdered on the picket line. Young Davey Jones was found with his chest broken in. They said: *"He must have run into a lamp post"*!! Jo Green was run down by a scab lorry. The driver's name has never been published, no charges have ever been made against him. Apparently in 'democratic' Britain in 1984 it is legal to kill miners' pickets. Yes, there is indeed blood on the coal.

What we have experienced is, of course, what the people of Ireland and your own black communities have suffered for many many years. I have to say that many times we have turned our backs on these uses of state violence, many times we have looked the other way as a labour and trade-union movement. I can say now that the miners have learnt the lesson at the hard end of a police baton. I can pledge, on behalf of my members, that when those weapons are used against other sections of the working class - like the black communities - then we will stand with you.

We have also seen them use the Courts - the 'impartial' British Courts. We have seen them take away the funds of the Welsh miners, even to the extent of freezing the money collected to feed miners' wives and children. We now see another bewigged clown come out and say that Arthur Scargill is in contempt of court. On this one, it seems, they have got cold feet, because when Arthur Scargill said he'd got a Conference to attend and it's rather more important than going to the High Court, they said we'll give him another week to see if wiser counsels will prevail. I hope wiser counsels will prevail with them! If they put Arthur Scargill in prison they will have to open up the football stadiums to put the rest of the British miners in too.

It must sicken everybody: A Government now stands for *"law and order"* and we have a Home Secretary like Leon Brittan. I don't think it's any secret that not so long ago the Government had to issue D-notices to prevent a public scandal about a Cabinet

Minister, to prevent a prosecution. That shows the hypocrisy of the British Government. They protect a Cabinet Minister against a scandal, but they put miners in prison for carrying out their legitimate right to fight for work. We should expose this across the length and breadth of this land. Britain has never known such shame.

But I do not believe that the Thatcher Government in anyway stands for the voice of the British people; I believe that Mrs Thatcher has become merely the mouthpiece of the executive committee of the international monopolies which dominate the world. Those monopolies, which are buying up coal reserves in Australia, South Africa and America, are the same monopolies which are in fact urging this Government on against the miners, to break our Union, so they can get their greedy hands on the rich coalfields of Selby and Vale of Belvoir. This struggle is not an isolated industrial dispute. It is one battle in an international class war and we have to get that message through to the ranks of the entire international working-class and trade-union movement. The crisis of their system can no longer be contained in the far reaches of the Third World, where we can look at India and Palestine from the comfort of our TV screens and see it as something which has nothing to do with us. That crisis has now come home to their own backyard. That is the final note of doom, not only for this Government but also for the system which sustains it. We believe that the true voice of British people is the voice of organised labour. We alone stand from generation to generation, consistently, for what is just and decent in our society. It is the labour movement which organises the aspirations of our people. I believe we ought to take this opportunity in this year of commemoration of the Tolpuddle Martyrs, which began the real history of the international trade-union movement, to pledge ourselves to secure a victory for the miners, but also again to the task of our times which is the emancipation of labour and the winning of a socialist society in this country.

I believe we have already won the dispute. It is only a matter of the time when we will settle the terms of our victory. We have been on strike for 7 -nearly 8 months. We have actually seen the entire labour movement come back to life. I believe we ought to say this is not the end of the struggle, it is the beginning of our struggle for our people to change the conditions of our society. But I believe that is part of our international struggle, so, as I quoted in Elvington the first time that we met, in the words of Che Guevara, in his last letter to Fidel Castro, the Argentinean who fought in Cuba and died in the fight for the liberation of Bolivia *"We are living magnificent days"*. We believe that if we stand together we will not only write a glorious page in the history of our class and the entire international working class, but we will begin that process whereby we will see one of the lesser-known objectives of the NUM in its constitution, Rule 3f. To join with other organisations with the view to the complete abolition of capitalism.

VICTORY TO THE MINERS!
LONG LIVE THE SOLIDARITY OF THE BRITISH MINERS AND THE PEOPLE OF SOUTHALL!
LONG LIVE THE INTERNATIONAL SOLIDARITY OF THE WORKING CLASS!

LALKAR April 1985

LESSONS OF THE NUM STRIKE -

Malcolm Pitt talks to Lalkar

On 9th March 1985, on the occasion of a rally in Southall in support of the miners, Harpal Brar, on behalf of LALKAR, interviewed Malcolm Pitt, President of the Kent miners.

LALKAR: On behalf of the IWA(GB) we welcome you to this Rally. The first question that I would like to ask you is: What do you feel about the outcome of the NUM strike?

MALCOLM PITT: Obviously we are disappointed. I believe this was the greatest opportunity that the trade-union movement has had to turn back the tide of unemployment in this country. I think that many trade-union leaders and many trade-unionists should look to what has taken place with a certain amount of shame, for not giving the sort of support that was necessary. On the other hand, I still think that a major victory has been achieved against the Government and against the ruling class of this country. What we have seen is the mobilisation of over 150,000 men, their wives and families, against the Government policy to close pits, and also really against the system itself. Many of our people have now become aware of what exploitation really means and the methods whereby that exploitation is sustained by the establishment. So when we look at the miners' strike of 1984-85 we will be seeing those young miners that were not looking for an easy way out with redundancy, were not looking for an easy way out to leave the coalfields, but were willing to go onto the picket lines and face the most terrible police violence and harassment that has been seen in this country for many, many years.

Also, I think we need to look at the women who, in many of our communities, have been regarded as second-rate citizens. They came to the fore and fought for their right to participate in the dispute. They have been very much the back-bone of the strike. What we have seen is the rebirth of militant trade-unionism in this country. For many years, the trade-union leaders thought that the way forward was wheeling and dealing with the employer and whatever government was in power. We have been through the experience of the 'social contract'. We've been through the new realism. The miners' strike of 1984-85 said that that is not enough; that is not the way forward. The way forward is militant action. Far from seeing the end of the strike as a defeat for the working class, an end of militant trade-unionism, I believe this is the beginning of an overall process whereby working people begin to challenge not just one employer, but the whole society under which they live.

LALKAR: Would you think that one of the lessons of this particular strike was that in economic struggle alone capital is stronger than the working masses? Therefore if the working class want to be victorious, in the ultimate analysis, it must raise the question of power, as to who rules society and in whose benefit, rather than just trying to solve the crisis of the coal industry, or indeed of the entire British industry, within the conditions of capitalism, no matter how heroic the struggle?.

MALCOLM PITT: I think that is definitely one of the great lessons. I suppose that the biggest mistake that Thatcher made was that she taught that lesson to hundreds and thousands of people, not just in the mining industry, but also in other sections of the trade-union movement that did respond to our appeals. The NUM, when it was founded, enshrined in its constitution one of those early demands of the South Wales miners which called for the Union to support all other groups in the fight for the abolition of capital. There has always been that strong political perspective in our Union. Sometimes it has been submerged by right-wing leaders like Joe Gormley but it's come out very clearly in the last few months. I believe that that itself will be reflected in other trade unions, whereby workers begin to say industrial action is, by itself, not enough. What we have to be talking about is political action on a broad front in terms of the entire class against the system of exploitation which keeps us in a situation where men and women have to face the arbitrary nature of the state and society, whereby they lose their jobs and communities. In the end, one of the great lessons has been, particularly for many of our young men, that they understand now the nature of the state, they have experienced it at the hard end of a truncheon. They know what the state (the police, the courts, etc.) is about. They are now beginning to question the very basis of this society. I think in that sense, Mrs Thatcher has done us a great service.

LALKAR: To what extent is your disappointment at the outcome of the struggle attributable to the role, which in our view is despicable, of the TUC and the Labour Party leadership?

MALCOLM PITT: From the beginning there have been Labour Party members who have been active in support of the NUM. The position of the leadership, particularly Neil Kinnock, has been quite diabolical. The ambiguity he took about initially supporting the strike, the way he got involved in the issue of the ballot, which was a diversion from the major issue; the way that he got himself into a position of condemning pickets for violence which had been produced by the militarisation of the picket line by the masses of police, are all things that worked very much against us. The TUC, despite the fact that we won, overwhelmingly, Congress to give total support to the miners, came out very clearly as seeing its role as trying to fix some sort of shabby compromise between the leadership of the NUM, on the one hand, and the Government and the NCB, on the other hand. It is quite evident that, in the period we are going into, we don't need fixers in Congress House, we need militant trade-union leaders who are willing to use the full industrial strength of the working class to achieve our legitimate aims in terms of our own industries and also on the broader issues facing the working-class movement.

LALKAR: But even in cases where the trade-union leadership of individual unions was supporting you, not only in words but in deeds, we found that they were unable to deliver their membership, which is a serious weakness in the working-class movement. What are the steps you feel we can take in order to rectify that position? The membership were taken in, not just by the propaganda, but also by the large amounts of money that they could make by scabbing - for instance, the scabbing lorry drivers.

MALCOLM PITT: This raises the elementary question of trade-union organisation, education and propaganda. What we have seen for many, many years is people taking our organisations for granted, using them as vehicles for careers rather than for active work at building shopfloor organisation. To a large extent, many of our trade unions have been bluffing. They have used resolutions as a substitute for action. It was inevitable that the Government would call their bluff. That is what has happened. We've discovered that we've been using up the credit of the work which has been done many years ago, particularly in the period of the 30s, when people actually recognised the need to build up shopfloor organisation. Go back to the sacking of Derek Robinson. Previously people had always said that you could never sack a shop steward without very serious repercussions, but they were able to sack a leading convenor, for no reason, and it did not receive the response that was necessary. From then on the Government has probed and probed our organisations and found them wanting. We have got to get back to the basics. That is going to face the miners now. We have got to go back to the pits and our first priority is to rebuild our own organisation. We are now fighting for elementary issues such as union recognition, the right to negotiate freely and to oppose victimisation. All these very basic issues are now in the forefront of our minds. That is an issue that has got to be confronted by the whole movement, otherwise it leaves us in a dream world which will always be shattered when the opposition put their forces into the field. To me, the main task is getting back to the basics of trade-union organisation. We must get back to the shop floor and win our people to recognise the need for organisation.

LALKAR: Might I suggest that the trade-union leadership that we have got has been found wanting, not every one of them, but the vast majority, because they are the product of the old school when conditions were quite all right for imperialist exploitation and there was a lot of money about.

When high super profits were coming in, the trade union leaders were able to reach some decent, or shabby, compromise (whichever way you look at it), with the workers getting some rise. But now that the conditions of international competition among various imperialist powers are getting much harder, they cannot carry on in the old way. The only way they can carry on is by making British industry efficient in terms of the conditions of imperialism. That really means a major onslaught on the British working-class. Therefore, the working-class movement has to learn through hard slog, to produce and throw up new types of leaders which can actually cope with the new situation, rather than the Willises and Murrays and Kinnocks of this world.

MALCOLM PITT: I think Lenin's analysis of imperialism clearly laid out the basis on which reformist trade unions have been built. That has always been on the basis of superprofits and the crumbs from the master's table. That situation has quite evidently changed. But, what we have got is the leftovers of that whole period. Then as long as a person carried a trade-union card and paid his contributions that was enough as far as the organisation of the union was concerned. But it is quite evidently not enough. Now in this period of crisis, as you so clearly put it, where capitalism itself is having to solve its own crises at the expense of working people, that type of organisation, that type of attitude, that type of perspective is severely limited. It is inadequate for the tasks which confront the class. We are going through a similar period to that which we went through at the end of the nineteenth century and also in the 1920's when once again the working-class movement has got to reorganise, to develop new perspectives, new tactics and a clear political objective.

LALKAR: Would I be right to conclude, in the light of the NUM strike, which I think was one of the most glorious chapters in the annals of the British working class, that one of the things that stands today, politically speaking, in the way of the victory of the British working class is actually the rotten Labour Party?

MALCOLM PITT: No, I don't take that position. My own position is that the great strength of the Labour Party is the fact that it was created by the trade-union movement. It was a clear issue of the representation of working people in parliament through their organisation. I don't think it is a question of the organisation itself, because it is like the TUC. Some people compare the TUC unfavourably with the CGT or other trade union bodies. But one of the strengths of the Labour Party is the unity of the movement. Within it, the major battle is for the political orientation of the leadership. I still think that the prime objective is to develop a leadership of the trade-union and Labour movement which has a clear socialist objective and to develop a socialist consciousness which is necessary for the advance of the class[1].

LALKAR: After the Delegate Conference at the TUC last Sunday, 3rd March, which decided to call off the strike, Jack Collins, Secretary of the Kent miners, said that this was a decision that the trade-union movement and the NUM would live to regret. He called people who voted to call off the strike traitors to the working class. What is your view on that?

MALCOLM PITT: I hesitate to use the word traitors, because people sometimes misjudge situations, take decisions under pressure, which weakens the advance. I think that the decisions that were taken were a catastrophe as far as the strike was concerned. There was no question that there was still a majority of miners that were willing to rally to the Union on the straightforward issues which were presented to them - particularly the issues of an amnesty and going back together. The slogan of 'No Victimisation' has always been basic. It was an unnecessary attack upon the Union's strength for the South Wales leadership to put forward the resolution calling the strike off. I believe it was possible to win the National Union and to win the membership to fight particularly on the issue of no victimisation.

We felt very bitter about it. Our action following the Conference was to try and sustain the strike. We are now extremely isolated and have had to bite the bullet. Today, the Kent miners, almost unanimously, agreed that they would return to work on Monday. But we are very, very clear that the battle continues. We are still unbroken[2]. We will continue to fight and rebuild our organisation. Maybe the flame has to be picked up by some other section of the class for a period, but I can assure everybody that the resilience of the miners is still there. I am sure we will be playing a leading role in the movement in future battles.

LALKAR: Can I take it that the attempt of the bourgeois press and the entire bourgeoisie to put a cross against the NUM is rather premature, and that practice will show that the NUM is stronger than ever before, notwithstanding all the disappointments in connection with the outcome of the present strike?

MALCOLM PITT: The miners have suffered defeats in the past. We suffered the great defeat of 1926. Men were forced back to work, again through starvation. But the Union came back. Maybe the next battle will be smaller, but the fighting spirit will still be there, and, in addition, we have now got the experiences of the present battle, experiences that are never lost. Even if we go through a process of closures, which we may

---

1 Notwithstanding his militant role in the NUM strike, Malcolm Pitt was either unwilling or incapable of breaking free from the shackles of social democracy, which is hardly surprising, since so many self-proclaimed 'communists' and 'revolutionaries' are unable to make this leap.

2 Most regrettably, the strike broke Comrade Pitt, as it probably did many others. He has given up his earlier socialist views and now works for a religious charity.

find difficult to resist, over the next period, those militants that leave our industry and go into other industries will be carrying the experience of the great miners' strike of 1984 with them. I think that that will have an effect throughout the whole movement. Certainly it would be very premature to write the NUM off.

LALKAR: Is the NUM, not just you personally, and its leadership fairly pleased with the support they have received from especially oppressed sections, like black workers in this country?

MALCOLM PITT: I have been asked this many times. I can honestly say, without any form of patronising, that the support of the black community has been quite exceptional. When our people first came to London, they actually remarked upon the fact that when they had collecting buckets out in the street, it was black people who were the first to respond. Certainly the relationship that has been developed between Southall and the Kent coalfield and my own pit in particular, Tilmanstone, is a relationship that will continue for many years to come. That can only be a major advantage and benefit to the entire working-class movement.

LALKAR: Thank you Comrade Pitt. We would like to assure you that we have an abiding sense of loyalty to the miners because, by putting up the struggle that they have, they have restored the old-style honour and fighting spirit to working people whatever their colour, religion or beliefs. We shall never forget this struggle. Many thanks indeed.

LALKAR June 1985

Miners' strike 1984-5: Malcolm Pitt sums up.

We reproduce below extracts from the speech made by Cde Malcolm Pitt, President of the Kent NUM, on the occasion of a Rally in Southall which honoured the victories of the miners' struggle. Since the Rally, which was reported in the April issue of *Lalkar*, took place on the 9th of March, just after the National Conference of the NUM had voted for a return to work, the excellent speech made by Cde Malcolm not only sums up the miners' strike but also draws lessons for the entire working-class movement. After a hero's welcome and a standing ovation, he began his speech:

I was thinking of the various words we use in the movement to address meetings. I think tonight in Southall the best means of address is "brothers and sisters". Certainly over the last 12 months we have become brothers and sisters in struggle.

A Great Victory

Tonight, in one sense there is a sadness. Today, we had a meeting of 1,000 of our members in Ramsgate, and sadly we had to pass a resolution that we would return to work this Monday. Last Sunday the Kent area of the NUM did not agree with the position taken by the majority at our National Conference. We believed it was still possible to rally the British coalfields on the issue of amnesty for those of our members who had been sacked. We tried to hold those of our Union nationally who would stand on that issue. Well, we were not successful. Today we took the decision, with sadness, that we would go back on Monday. But I must say that that meeting was one of the most inspiring meetings that I have ever attended: there was no air of defeat, there was no air of despondency, there were no bowed heads. They were men who were proud of what they had achieved in staying in struggle for a year against terrible forces. They were also determined that the struggle would continue through the difficult months and years ahead. This meeting tonight must not be a requiem, a funeral service, it has got to be a celebration of a victory, a great victory (applause), a victory where ordinary men and women have stood against a Government, a ruling class, an establishment, for the right to work, the right to organise, the right to the dignity they deserve as human beings.

A few years ago at our pit we had a Bolivian tin-miner's wife come to Tilmanstone. She was part of a women's delegation in Europe who were going around winning support for their own struggle back in Bolivia. While she was in England, she had a report that their mining village had been surrounded by troops, martial law had been established and her husband and 3 children had disappeared. She said to us I know that I will never see them again. We said: What are you going to do? She said: I am going to continue with this delegation, I am going to win support for the continuing struggle. And that is the message tonight: the battle continues, *Venceremos*, we will win that victory (applause).

The miners are proud that we have been in the front-line of the battle against unemployment. We are proud that we have been able to set an example, and, I believe, a shining example. I will not be modest tonight. I believe that it is a shining example to the whole working-class movement of this country on how we must conduct ourselves in the next few years, because one thing is absolutely certain: there is no way that, in the crisis of this system, we can resolve our problems by creeping round to the back door of Downing Street or meeting in secret venues to work out some shabby form of compromise with the employer or the government. The only way forward for working people is to struggle, and that is the great victory of the miners' strike of 1984-85. That is the victory for which 150,000 of our members, for 12 months, with their wives and families, were willing to give the sacrifice day by day, the terrible hardship, the broken families, the broken marriages, even the suicides.

We managed, also, and I am again proud to say it, not to fall for all the propaganda that the only way that working people can express themselves is by signing pieces of paper and putting crosses on pieces of ballot paper. What the miners said, and will still say again, is that no human being, no man or woman, has the right to put a cross on a piece of paper and vote somebody else out of a job (applause). I believe that the miners' strike will go down as the greatest example of working-class democracy, because men and women voted with their feet every day over twelve months on the issue of the right to work. That is the true democracy which we all stand for.

Tribute to Arthur Scargill

I would like to pay tribute to the leadership of Arthur Scargill. No doubt over the next few weeks, when various people in Fleet Street begin to analyse the miners' strike, more and more of them will begin to level their attacks upon Arthur Scargill. We will see the criticisms begin to develop that he should not have done this, and he should not have done that, but I believe that, despite all the press campaign to persuade miners that now is the time to rid themselves of this "Marxist wrecker", this Arthur Scargill, the British miners will respond to that with even more support. They recognise that Arthur Scargill, unlike almost every trade-union leader in this country, has actually done what he said he would do (applause).

Organisation against tremendous odds

When we talk of victories: What we have seen over the last 12 months is the latent, hidden power of working-class people to organise themselves to struggle against tremendous odds. When we went into this strike we knew it was going to be a long one. As Arthur himself said, you have to expect it to be a long strike because we are not fighting just on the issue of keeping open our pits and protecting our communities. What we are, in reality, doing is challenging the very principle of the system which says that one or two men or women who happen to have been born into positions of power and wealth have the right to put millions of people on the dole. We attacked the principle of that system, and we believe that that itself is not something which we can win by ourselves, but it is in fact the historic task of our entire class.

Of course, as the months went by, and as the hardships developed, people had to organise themselves. I am so proud, in my own coalfield, of what was done to organise the community to survive. Look at our logging teams - the only people that were not getting coal during the great miners' strike were miners. So we had to find a substitute. The men organised themselves into teams for log collection. It has led to virtually the deforestation of large parts of south-eastern England, but it was certainly successful! That is what struggle is about - it is about survival.

We also organised our food, our distribution centres. We had one of the biggest and most successful wholesale and retail food distribution systems in S.E.England. We established our communal kitchens - the food varied from the most plain and simple to the most exotic. We also became experts in how to import food into this country and overcome all the problems of getting across the customs. We also organised our own travel agency. British miners' children now, I would think, are the most well-travelled children in the world. If you want to go to West Berlin and cross East Germany with a passport which quite specifically states that it is not valid in East Germany, then come and see the Kent miners because we will tell you how to do it! We organised shows. We organised many different events to keep our people together. But the main thing about it was that the organisation, which as I have said came out quite spontaneously from the community, is a blazing sign of our ability as working people, not only to organise ourselves in struggle, but to organise society itself - in OUR interests and not in the interests of the few born to wealth and privilege. That is the lesson of the miners' strike.

What we have seen is a whole community coming to life. For many years people were beginning to talk about the end of organised labour in this country. They stood in universities and said that young miners would never fight for their jobs; they said that working-class people were now being bought into a soft life which meant that they would never struggle; there were the privileged workers with jobs and there were the unemployed; they used to say Scargill would never win the hearts of the young miners, who would never struggle. But our young miners have done us proud. Our young miners did not go to the management grovelling for a few pounds to sell their jobs. They stood firm with the union, they stood on the picket lines in the fiercest violence that we have seen this century and they stood firm. They do not deserve the criticism of so-called leaders of the trade-union and labour movement in relation to picket violence. Let us say now: they were and they are our heroes, working-class heroes .

A Tribute to Women

Let us pay tribute to the women. The women of the British coalfields took the decision very early on that they were not going to be reduced to just cutting pieces of bread to make sandwiches for the men. They said that they had a right, they had a duty, to come out with the men and take up the battle themselves. The liberation of the women of the British coalfields was not achieved by academic debates about the rights of women, it was won by class struggle, and that advance will never be reversed. I believe it is a step forward, not only for the women themselves, but it is a step forward for the menfolk because now we are twice as strong as we were before (applause).

Our Lesson on the State

We have learnt some great lessons. We drew on the experience of 1972 and 1974, those great victories, not only of the miners but of the British trade-union movement. This time we have suffered a reverse, but, by God, we have learned many lessons. Those lessons will be put into practice in the next few months and the next years. They are not just the experience of the miners, they are the experience of many working men and women throughout the length and breadth of this country.

After the 1984-5 coal strike, nobody needs to tell a miner that the state is organised oppression by the ruling class over the exploited. We have learned that lesson, we have learnt it the hard way, we have learnt it under the hooves of horses and on the rough end of a policeman's truncheon, we learnt it in the courts. Miners are no longer mystified by the man sitting with a wig on and trying to pretend that he is a different race to them. They are not bemused or scared by prisons, because they have been through that experience. I believe that that itself is a victory, because now we know what the true enemy is, and now we are beginning to see what the solution to our problem is.

We remember, in our experience, that we have lost members. We have had 5 of our members killed, two of them murdered on the picket lines. Their blood itself is a seal on our knowledge of where the police and the state machinery stands. But also let us not forget that these political courts took political decisions when they sent young Terry French to prison for 5 years, when they sent miners to long prison sentences. I say tonight, those miners in prison are political prisoners and they must not be forgotten in the same way that Des Warren and the Shrewsbury pickets were not forgotten (applause).

The Betrayal

We have also seen betrayal. When we won the overwhelming support of the TUC and also the Labour Party Conference, we believed we had the weapon, the instrument, to build up a mass movement of industrial support around our legitimate claim to the right to work. But we were betrayed and that is the only word we can use. The Kinnocks and the Willises betrayed the greatest working-class movement we have seen this century. That is something we must take on board. We have got to say now in the crisis of this system, when there are not all the crumbs which we can squeeze out of India, Africa and the rest of the world, to pay off British workers, that in that situation it is no longer possible to work out the nice little deals which allow employers and trade-union leaders to sit down and drink tea together. We do not want fixers in Congress House; we need leaders of the working class in this country who are willing to lead and willing to struggle, because that is the only way forward (applause).

Socialism - the only way forward

We have seen it all. But what I can say now is that the miners are not going back defeated. Ernest Hemingway said: A man can never be defeated, only destroyed. Well, they have not defeated us and they certainly have not destroyed us. We will be going back on Monday, not cap in hand to the employer, but we are going to go back fighting. We are going back to that pit to say: This is our pit and we are still going to continue the fight for its existence, for its survival. We have learned the lesson.

I remember the words of a great French revolutionary when he said: The great only appear great because we are on our knees. Let us arise! I say tonight, let us together arise! Let us take this world, which is of our making, into our hands to use it for our own needs. That is the only solution for working men and women. I believe that we have got to lift men's and women's eyes to that gleam of gold in the future. The industrial struggles that we go into today are aimed at one objective: to take this society and give it back to the people who produce wealth. That is our objective and that is the only solution to our problem.

Thank you again for your wonderful support.

LALKAR May/June 1994

Can the Labour Party bring us our economic salvation?

In the midst of the deepest economic crisis since the 1930s, as unemployment figures soar, wages stagnate, working conditions deteriorate, and living standards plummet, the question which everybody expects politicians to be able to answer is: how can this crisis be reversed? How can we return to the relative prosperity that we have been used to? How can unemployment be ended?

The answers that a Marxist will give to these questions are often not very welcome. Marxists expect the crisis to get a great deal worse before it gets any better, and expect the deterioration of living conditions of the workers in imperialist countries to be permanent until such time as they have made a revolution in order to be able to control their own destinies. Bourgeois politicians, hoping for votes in elections, besides being responsible for keeping workers' minds off the idea of revolution, will always sound a note of false optimism and tend a tiny flame of false hope.

Lalkar has always found the views of the Marxists in this matter utterly convincing. Only the blind could fail to see that the present crisis is a crisis of 'overproduction', i.e., it is caused by the fact that sufficient buyers cannot be found for the mass of even essential products that the capitalist enterprises produce. The lack of buyers is not caused by lack of need, but by lack of purchasing power: the potential buyers - ultimately the vast masses of working people of the world - have been so impoverished under the capitalist system that they cannot buy. Every step taken to improve the situation only makes it worse, for the only way of 'improving' the situation under capitalism is to close more factories, make more staff redundant, pay less for longer hours, increase the automation of production in order to be able to lay off more staff - in short, to impoverish the working class as a whole even more than it already has been.

This is a system fault in capitalism that periodically causes the kind of devastation that we are now witnessing. The system will only start building up again when so much of the wealth of society has been destroyed that once again there are profits to be made in production.

Workers in imperialist countries are not only seeing their livelihoods disappear because of this inherent design fault of the capitalist system, they are also facing the unavoidable consequences of having tolerated the super-exploitation of the third world - for now third-world workers are competing for jobs with the workers of the old industrialised countries, prepared to work at wage levels that presuppose a standard of living way below that which any West European or North American worker could begin to tolerate. Computing jobs are going to Delhi where people are prepared to work for £3,000 a year to do a job for which English workers would want at least four or five times the salary. Much light industrial production has moved to the Pacific Rim, where workers produce under practically slave conditions, for appalling wages. US car parts production has moved to Mexico, where the workers earn $1.70 an hour - a fraction of what an American worker would have to be paid. Japanese and Hong Kong manufacturers are even setting up plants in Honduras. Why? Because they find that the wages they have to pay in South Korea too high! In these conditions, what possible hope is there for maintaining in Britain, under capitalism, a standard of living which provides good food, good clothes, good housing, good education, good medical care and good cultural facilities?

To some extent the standard of living Western workers have got accustomed to was only allowed to them as a way of discouraging them from following the Soviet Union and creating a decent standard of life for themselves in their own working-class state. Now that the Soviet Union has fallen, the Western bourgeoisies are reasonably confident that the anti-Sovietism and anti-communism they have always propagated has such a firm hold in people's minds that they will not, for the time being at least, seriously attempt to follow the example of the October Revolution, notwithstanding all the misery they are increasingly being forced to endure.

The Labour Party as the major force defending capitalism in the working-class movement.

One of the major factors that prevents workers realising these facts of life is the pleasant little dreams they are fed of recovery being round the corner, a little unpleasant medicine being sure to lead to an all-time cure, and other assorted illusions. The Labour Party is a major peddler of such illusions. It, along with every Trotskyite hanger-on who sceptically refuses to accept that the working class can and will seize state power and build socialism proper, likes to create the illusion that these problems are not due to capitalism itself but to the 'Tories', who are variously presented as incompetent, greedy, anti-working class, etc., the clear implication being that Labour (the so-called party of the working class) would do better. This amounts to denying that there is anything wrong with capitalism itself. It's only those who happen to be managing it that are the problem.

Yes, the Tories may well be incompetent, greedy and anti-working class, but so must anyone be if they are wanting to manage capitalism, especially at the present time. Workers must clearly understand that the Labour Party is NOT offering any alternative - a fact which is apparent, if nothing else, from their political propaganda, some of which we now propose to examine in some detail. The working class cannot deal with the problems that confront it without prising off the deadly clutches of social-democracy, either of the Labour Party type, or of the type of its 'leftist' appendages: those who sing glory to the Labour Party's working-class credentials in the kind of demented chorus more appropriate to toothpaste advertisements.

Here is how Gordon Brown, the Labour Shadow Chancellor, described Britain's economic problems in *Tribune* of 14 May 1993:

"The underlying problem is Britain's long-term failure to invest. Manufacturing investment in the UK is now no higher than in 1979. We invest 1 for every 6 of gross national product: Japan invests one-third of its GNP and, in the burgeoning economies of the Pacific rim, investment is proportionately even greater. In the recovery years of 1993 and 1994, the Organisation for Economic Co-operation and Development predicts that Britain will have the lowest increase in business investment of all 22 OECD *countries, with the exception only of Iceland*.

"*Our shrinking capacity is such that our productivity is 30-35 per cent below the* world's best, with skills levels 40 per cent lower and investment per manufacturing worker a shaming 50 per cent less than that of the world leaders. In 1993, the deficit on manufactured trade will almost double and the overall trade deficit will increase from £12,000 million to £17,500 [million].

"One of our worst investment gaps is in investment in people. In the skills league, Britain comes 20th out of the OECD 22. Only 3 per cent of employees are working towards a National Council for Vocational Qualifications certificate. Two-thirds of our workers have no vocational or professional qualifications, compared with one-quarter in Germany. The skills gap is widest not at degree or higher-technician level but at the level of lower-technician and craft qualifications. It is worst in engineering, in which Germany and France produce twice as many qualified entrants as Britain. Our real expenditure on off-the- job training and vocational education *has fallen in the past five years.*

"Labour's strategy for success starts from a clear analysis of the Tories' failures and a clear set of principles. We believe in mobilising the power of the community in order to invest in individual economic opportunity for all, realised by new instruments for investment. We want not just employment and skills programmes but new tax incentives to foster training, new social security rules that offer pathways out of poverty, new employment and training opportunities and a new university for industry - in other words, a comprehensive programme aimed at creating a modern, productive, full-employment society." (Investment is the Key).

This kind of seductive talk amounts to a lethal dose of bourgeois propaganda aimed at killing off those with genuine concern for the well-being of the working class. The poison is well hidden in wholesome-looking criticism of the system. But the liberal sprinkling of impressive-sounding statistics, proving points that no sane person disputes, are simply there to help pass off as 'scientific analysis' the highly unscientific message that capitalism itself is OK. It works very well in lots of other countries. Things are only bad in Britain because the Tories are so incompetent. If elected the Labour Party will be able to put things right. They will spend money on training (don't worry where the money will come from, or that the relatively small number of people we are training even now can't get jobs) and everything will be all right.

This trick of inundating readers with pages of facts they are likely to agree with, only to slip in (by unavoidable implication rather than completely explicitly) the outrageous claim that there's nothing wrong with capitalism itself is repeated time and time again in all the Labour Party's economic propaganda. An example is the following quotation from their 1993 pamphlet *Making Britain's future:*

"Two out of every five jobs that existed in manufacturing in 1979 have since disappeared. If unemployment statistics were still collected in the same way as in 1979 they would soon register more people out of work than at work making goods ...

"The years since 1979 are marked by historic milestones in Britain's decline. They include the two deepest recessions in post-war history, the largest number of long-term unemployed this century, and the first deficit in manufactured trade for three centuries. We cannot continue this decline."

Well yes, how could anyone disagree? Under capitalism, however, there is not a lot anybody can do about these effects, which are caused both by the worldwide economic crisis as well as by Britain's decline as an imperialist power *relative* to the United States, which is using its military muscle to take, from an imperialist point of view, more than its 'fair share' of the loot emanating from the oppressed countries, leaving

European imperialists, particularly Britain, a great deal worse off than they might otherwise have been. That being so, and bearing in mind that even after expropriating the lion's share of imperialist loot the US is also experiencing economic decline, how does the Labour Party propose to deal with the situation? It certainly does not start by analysing what the problem is. All it does is describe its effects. And its solution?

"Britain needs an urgent change of direction. This must be more than a short-term recovery in consumption, but must be a permanent improvement in our capacity to produce ... The task is now to restore more industrial companies to the front rank of international innovation, productivity and profit."

In other words, empty words. The implication is that manufacturing output has fallen because the Tories adopted a policy of killing off manufacturing. While it may be true that British capital, as far as investing in Britain is concerned, found financial investment abroad more lucrative than industrial investment at home and therefore neglected the latter, this is not due to Tory policy but to the realities of capitalism. Capital always seeks maximum profit. It cannot do otherwise if it does not want to be wiped out by the competition. There is no point in investing in manufacture if the markets are so glutted with cheap goods that no more can be sold. If workers had jobs, and therefore pay packets, more could be sold: but in that context there is no particular reason why a job in the industrial sector is any more advantageous than a job in the financial sector.

The Labour Party claims to be able to control the market

The Labour Party claims to believe, however, with a realism worthy of King Canute, that the laws of the market are not laws at all, but merely the outcome of 'policies', which, of course, can be changed:

*"If we are to reverse the historic decline in our industrial base we must develop an industrial strategy that measures up to the scale of the challenge. It must be a strategy which recognises that government has a key role and rejects the mistake of present ministers in believing that the best role of government is to do nothing lest they spoil the perfection of the market. **There are compelling reasons why government must have a strategy to correct disorders of the market and to promote the health of industry.***

"The market can determine short-term priorities of consumption but often works less well in dealing with long-term strategic judgements. Government has a responsibility in the national interest to take a longer-term view and to encourage investment in research and development that look beyond the short-term horizon of the market.

"Rational market behaviour today by each individual company does not necessarily add up tomorrow to the best outcome for the economy as a whole. Every company has an incentive to avoid its share of training the next generation of the workforce in the hope that its rivals will pick up the burden. Government has a duty to ensure that the country does invest in the skills industry needs and that the cost of that investment is fairly shared.

"Markets can be disrupted by bottlenecks which prevent companies expanding or taking advantage of new opportunities. Government has a leadership role in the co-ordination that can anticipate barriers to growth and help resolve them through co-operation across sectors and between suppliers.

"When the market fails and companies in distress look for a lifeline, government inevitably comes under pressure to intervene. A clear industrial strategy would help de-

fine the circumstances in which intervention would be in the national interest and when government should take the initiative in putting together a rescue package."

Actually, every bourgeois government in the present era of monopoly capitalism plays exactly this role, notwithstanding occasional 'free market' rhetoric. Despite their playing this role, and, to some extent because they play this role, the crisis deepens. There would never be enough money to rescue all the companies that have been sent to the wall because of the general crisis of capitalism. To the extent that governments do spend money in bailing out ailing industries, it is money that has to be found from somewhere - ultimately by taxing surviving industries, thereby threatening their competitiveness. Every attempt to control the market by plugging one hole simply causes an equally violent leak to spring up elsewhere. It is no more controllable than the tide.

Investment in the future

The official Labour Party line on how we are going to get out of these little difficulties is that we are going to beat the Japanese at their own game: we are going to invest in modern industry, in research and development for greater productivity in the new high-tech industries. We are not going to earn less than we have been used to because we are going to produce more competitively than anybody else, make larger profits and thus be able to continue to have the living standards to which we have grown accustomed. Thus page 1 of *Making Britain's Future* says:

"The future belongs to the nations that possess new technology and can turn it into products other nations want to buy. That requires a vigorous and expanding manufacturing section. ...

"The challenge for Britain is to raise the general performance of our manufacturing industry to compete in the global economy. ...

"If we want to compete successfully and add to our living standards, then we must come up with goods that have higher added value, more technology content and better design than those of our competitors. However, [our people] have no chance of competing successfully with other nations unless they are backed by the same investment in machinery, in training in skills and in co-operation from government."

This is the kind of pipedream that the Labour Party uses to try to persuade people to forget reality. Quite frankly, this is the kind of fairy tale that is worthy of small children only.

In this dream, billions of pounds are going to appear out of nowhere to fund research and development: If there is money to be made, why are these billions of pounds not forthcoming now? Why do the Tories not produce these investments? The answer is that nobody is prepared to invest in this superior technology, or in the quest to develop it, because in the impoverished state of the world there is an insufficient guarantee of profits. It would be money down the drain - a speculation which has little chance of a successful outcome. If one needs proof of this, one has only to consider the fact that the most efficient industries of the world, i.e., those of Japan, who can undercut all their competitors, are currently also affected by overproduction and are having to cut back. Unemployment, which was practically unknown - having remained at a steady 2.2% for years - has now risen to the unheard of figure of over 5%, with a corresponding rise in the suicide rate, which is now the highest in the world. If the highest-tech of all high-tech countries are in trouble, why should we assume that high-tech can solve our problems, even if we could find the means to finance it?

Furthermore, as even the Labour Party is forced to admit, these high-tech industries employ very few people. The whole point of technology under capitalism is to become more competitive by cutting costs, particularly labour costs. In present conditions, enormous investment produces very few jobs. So even if one were able to produce some very high-tech industries which were able to find a market for their products despite the recession, the only ones to benefit would be a handful of specialist workers and, of course, an even smaller handful of rich capitalists. The economic miracle that would save the whole country would not be there.

It should be noted that the workers in question would have to have some very special skills - skills that are not to be found in low-wage countries like India - for otherwise 'our' capitalists would have no choice, in order to maximise their chances of making profits, but to go where wages were lowest for people with those particular skills. If India has been able to train an army of computer programmers, why would it, or some other third-world country, or the former Soviet Union, or Eastern Europe, not be able to produce equally talented workers in any other field at much lower cost?

Lord Desai, the Labour Party's former House of Lords economics spokesperson, was removed from that position last year for suggesting that the Labour Party might increase income tax in order to finance industrial recovery. His idea was that the heavy burden of tax should be alleviated in the case of poorer people by larger welfare benefits, but that the burden should fall mostly on those earning over £25,000 a year. Of course, if industrial recovery could indeed be brought about by these proposals, it would be cheap at the price. In fact, everybody knows that there would be no industrial recovery, and all those who receive no welfare benefits would, at the prospect of higher taxes, become even more indifferent and apathetic to the Party's fortunes than they already are. Hence Lord Desai's summary dismissal.

He also suggested that there was no reason why efforts should not be made to encourage foreign investment in Britain, on the basis that so long as we have jobs, why should we care whether the capitalists who employ us are English, German, Japanese, or whatever. In this he is merely advocating what the Conservatives are already doing. Glossy brochures are produced by the British government to attract foreign investment to Britain by issuing glowing reports of how tame and low-paid British workers are. If these brochures have little success when issued by the Conservatives, why should they be more successful if a Labour government issues them? The fact is that British workers are still not cheap enough even if they have been tamed. It is to Mexico and Honduras that the greedy eyes of international capital are turned - and how can we compete with them?

Our Ken's patent remedies

The populist Ken Livingstone also has a patent remedy for curing the economy. His idea is that public spending on the military should be reduced in favour of public spending on things people need, like hospitals and schools, and a classic public works programme to put demand back into the economy. Nevertheless, much as we are in favour of reducing expenditure on the military whose only purpose is to suppress working people, it should be pretty obvious that no extra demand is going to be put into the economy if spending in one area is shifted somewhere else. More nurses and road builders would be employed, but fewer soldiers and munitions workers.

If Ken Livingstone were able to deliver on this suggestion - that less should be spent on the military so that more could be spent on hospitals - then it would well be worth voting for him, not because he would cause the economy to recover, but because what little resources there still were would be used to the greater advantage of working people. However, even he must know that he could never deliver on a promise of that kind. A government which runs capitalism, as the Labour Party has always done and will always do, cannot in a period of economic crisis reduce expenditure on the military, since the military may be needed at any time to put down the rebellion of the working people against their own impoverishment and misery - be it at home or abroad.

Ken Livingstone can only make these 'left-wing' promises because he is not in a position of power in the Labour Party. Should he ever become its leader, as we are sure he intends to, then this left-wing rhetoric will be put an end to PDQ - as it was in the case of Harold Wilson, Michael Foot, Neil Kinnock, etc., who all made their mark in the Labour Party with their fine 'left-wing' rhetoric, because the Party faithful did so much like to hear their siren songs. Ultimately the necessities imposed by the capitalist system constrain everybody. Bryan Gould showed the beginnings of a realisation of this when he wrote in the *Tribune* of 7 May 1993:

"We have made no effective attack on the Tories throughout three years of the recession for the simple reason that we agree with them. We and the Tories accept, so it seems, that [there are] matters beyond political debate and action. We and the Tories are agreed that the bankers know best."

Bryan Gould concludes by saying:

"We have a government which so little understands what it is doing that it is busily reversing the very policy changes which allowed us to escape from recession. ...

"Do we agree with the direction of Tory policy ... ? If we do, whatever happened to the smack of firm opposition? If we don't, why don't we say so?"

Since writing the above article for Tribune, Bryan Gould *has resigned his shadow cabinet post and gone off to New Zealand, the country of his origin, to take up an academic post.*

Bibliography

Attlee, C., *The Labour Party in Perspective*, Gollancz, London, 1937.

Branson, N., *History of the Communist Party of Great Britain 1927-1941*, Lawrence & Wishart, London, 1985.

Callaghan, J., *Socialism in Britain*, Blackwell, London, 1990.

Callinicos, A., and Harman C., *The Changing Working Class*,

Chiozza-Money, Sir L., *Riches and Poverty*, 1905, cited in Cox, I., *Empire Today*, Lawrence and Wishart, London, 1960.

Cliff, T., and Gluckstein, D., *The Labour Party - a Marxist History*, Bookmarks, London, 1988.

Clough, R., *Labour - a Party Fit for Imperialism*, Larkin Publications, London, 1992.

Clynes, Rt.Hon.J.R., *Memoirs*, Vol II (1924-37), Hutchinson, 1937

Cross, C., *The Fascists in Britain*,

Engels, F.,

(All references to Collected Works are to the Lawrence & Wishart 1980s edition of the Collected Works of Marx and Engels).

Anti-Dühring, Foreign Languages Publishing House, Moscow, 1954.

Condition of the Working Class in England in 1844, with a Preface written in 1892, George Allen & Unwin, London, 1892.

The English Elections, 22 February 1874, see Marx and Engels *On Britain*.

History of Ireland, May-July, 1870, Collected Works Vol 21.

Letter to Bebel, 30 August 1883, see Marx and Engels *On Britain*.

Letter to Kautsky, 12 September 1882, see Marx and Engels *On Britain*.

Letter to Kautsky, 4 September, 1892, see Marx and Engels *On Britain*.

Letter to Marx, 7 October 1858, see Marx and Engels *On Britain*.

Letter to Sorge, 7 December 1889, see Marx and Engels *On Britain*.

Letter to Sorge, 18 January 1893, see Marx and Engels *On Britain*.

Letter to Sorge, 11 November 1893, see Marx and Engels *On Britain*.

Origin of the Family, Private Property and the State, in Marx and Engels Selected Works, Lawrence & Wishart, London, 1968.

Preface to *The Peasant War in Germany*, in Marx and Engels Selected Works, Lawrence & Wishart, London, 1968.

Gupta, P.S., *Imperialism and the British Labour Movement, 1914-1964* Cambridge, 1975.

Joseph Rowntree Foundation, *Inquiry into Income and Wealth*,

Klugmann, J., *History of the Communist Party of Great Britain*, Vol 1, Lawrence & Wishart, London, 1969.

Lee, F., *Fabianism and Colonialism - the life and thought of Lord Sidney Olivier*, Defiant, 1988.

Lenin, V.I.,

(All references to Collected Works are to the Progress Publishers, Moscow, edition of the mid 1960s).

British Liberals and Ireland, 12 March 1914, Collected Works Vol 20.

A Caricature of Marxism and Imperialist Economism, Aug.-Oct. 1916, Collected Works Vol. 23.

The Collapse of the Second International, May-June 1915, Collected Works Vol. 21.

Debates in Britain on Liberal Labour Policy, October 1912, Collected Works Vol. 18.

Exposure of the British Opportunists, 16 July 1913, Collected Works Vol 19.

Greetings to the Hungarian Workers, 27 May 1919, Collected Works Vol 29.

Imperialism, the Highest Stage of Capitalism, 1916, Collected Works Vol 22.

Imperialism and the Split in Socialism, October 1916, Collected Works, Vol 23.

Imperialism and the Split in the Socialist Movement, (another name for the previous article in *Lenin on Britain*, Lawrence & Wishart, London, 1934).

'Left-Wing' Communism, an Infantile Disorder, Collected Works, Vol 31.

Liberal-Labour Policy, October 1912, see above *Debates in Britain on Liberal Labour Policy*.

Notes on the Dictatorship of the Proletariat in the Conditions Prevailing in England, in *Lenin on Britain*, Lawrence & Wishart, London, 1934.

Opportunism and the Collapse of the Second International, end of 1915, Collected Works Vol 21.

Preface to the first edition of *State and Revolution*, 1917, Collected Works Vol 25.

Preface to the French and German Editions of *Imperialism, the Highest Stage of Capitalism*, 6 July 1920, Collected Works Vol 22.

Socialism and War, Jul-Aug 1915, Collected Works Vol 24.

Speech at the Second Congress of the Comintern, 23 July, 1920, Collected Works, Vol 31.

The State and Revolution, 1917, Collected Works Vol 25.

War and Revolution, May 1917, Collected Works Vol 24.

Marx, K.,

(All references to Collected Works are to the Lawrence & Wishart 1980s edition of the Collected Works of Marx and Engels).

Capital, Vol I, Foreign Languages Publishing House, Moscow, mid-1950s.

The Civil War in France, Marx and Engels Selected Works, Lawrence & Wishart, London, 1968.

Class Struggles in France, 1850, Lawrence & Wishart, London, 1936.

Critique of the Gotha Programme, Marx and Engels Selected Works, Lawrence & Wishart, London, 1968

The Eighteenth Brumaire of Louis Bonaparte, Marx and Engels Selected Works, Lawrence & Wishart, London, 1968

Letter to Engels, 10 December, 1869, in Marx and Engels *Ireland and the Irish Question*, Progress Publishers, Moscow, 1971.

Letter to Kugelmann, 29 November, 1869, see Marx and Engels *On Britain*.

Letter to Kugelmann, 12 April, 1871, Marx and Engels Selected Works, Lawrence & Wishart, London, 1968

Letter to W. Liebknecht, 11 February 1878, see Marx and Engels *On Britain*.

Value, Price and Profit, Marx and Engels Selected Works, Lawrence & Wishart, London, 1968

Marx and Engels,

On Britain, Foreign Languages Publishing House, Moscow, 1953.

The Communist Manifesto, Marx and Engels Selected Works, Lawrence & Wishart, London, 1968

McKibbin, R., *The Evolution of the Labour Party 1910-24*, Oxford, 1973.

Miliband, R., *Parliamentary Socialism*, Merlin, London, 1972.

Milne, S., *The Enemy Within*, Verso, London, 1994.

Nabudere, D., *The Political Economy of Imperialism,*, Zed Press, London, 1975.

Ovendale, R. (ed), *The Foreign Policy of the Labour Government 1945-51*, Leicester University Press, Leicester, 1984.

Palme Dutt, R.,

The Crisis of Britain and the British Empire, Lawrence & Wishart, London, 1953.

India Today, Gollancz: Left Book Club, London, 1940.

Pollitt, H., Preface to *Lenin on Britain*, Lawrence & Wishart, London, 1941.

Porter, B., *Critics of Empire - British Radical Attitudes to Imperialism in Africa 1895-1914*, Macmillan, London, 1966.

Saklatwala, Sehri, *The Fifth Commandment*, Manchester Free Press, Manchester, 1991.

Snowden, P,

An Autobiography, Vol II, Nicholson & Watson, London, 1934.

Labour and the New World, Waverley, London, 1921.

Stalin, J., *British General Strike, 1926*, Works, Vol 8, Foreign Languages Publishing House, Moscow, 1954.

Tracey, H., *The British Labour Party*, Vol I, Caxton, London, 1948.

Webb, S., *Labour and the New Social Order*, 1918

Index

affiliation, 41, 62 - 63, 112 - 115
Africa, 73, 422
agent of the bourgeoisie, 278
Algeria, 385
All-Ireland Referendum, 372
Allende, Salvador, 156
alternative welfare system, 281
amnesty, 277, 419
Amnesty Bill, 285
Amsterdam Federation of Trade Unions, 54
Anarchists, 147, 391
anti-trade union legislation, 98, 116, 196, 274
apartheid, 74, 252
Argentina, 387
aristocracy of labour, i - iii, v, vii - viii, 66, 74, 80, 82, 97 - 98, 118 - 119, 121, 126, 128, 130 - 131, 221, 278, 327, 335
armaments, manufacture of, vi
armed forces, 157
Ashdown, Paddy, 295
ASLEF, 199
Association of Communist Workers, xiii
Atkins, Humphrey, 367
Attlee, Clement, iv, 69, 71 - 76, 88, 133

Baker, Kenneth, 345
balance of trade, viii
Baldwin, Stanley, 63, 100
Balkan War, 1912, 25
ballot, 201, 239, 359, 361, 415, 420
Basnett, David, 263, 281, 408
Bechuanaland, 74

benefits, 98
Bengal Special Ordinances, 49
Benn, Tony, 71, 90 - 91, 102, 107, 117, 278, 285, 292, 356
Bernstein, Eduard, 145
Bevin, 71
Biffen, John, 356
Bill of Rights, 117
Birmingham 6, 76
'Black Circulars', 63
black community, 418
Blair, Tony, 75 - 76, 85, 87, 89 - 96, 103, 106, 115 - 118, 120, 122 - 123, 125, 360
block vote, 85
Blunkett, David, 288, 338, 342, 344, 360 - 361
BNP, 361
Bolivian tin miner, 419
Bolshevik Party, 118, 269, 348
Bolshevism, 84, 93, 103, 133
Bonaparte, Louis, 143
bourgeois labour party, 8, 14
bourgeois legality, 351
bourgeois media, 282
bourgeois parliamentarism, v, 140
break-away union, 284
'British Road to Socialism', 159
British Anti-War Council, 64
British Coal, 297
British Rail, 214
British Railways Board, 211
British Socialist Party, 41
British Steel, 401
British Steel Corporation, 221
British Union of Fascists, 69

Brittan, Leon, 197, 285
Brown, Gordon, 424
Buckton, Ray, 263
Bush, George, 391
Butler, Gordon, 243
Byrne, Tony, 341, 345
Callaghan, James, 76, 122, 235
Campbell, J.R., 51
Canterbury, Archbishop of, 248
Cape Horn, 384
capital exports, vi, 127
Carrington, Lord, 383
Cawnpore, 48, 66
CEGB, 401
CGT, 417
Chapple, Frank, 240, 281, 408
Chartism, ii, 5
Chartist Party, 5
Chiang-Kai-shek, 58, 154
child slavery, 293
Chile, 155, 252
Churchill Cabinet, 69
Churchill, Winston, 68, 75 - 76, 119
CIA, 190, 252, 392
Citrine, Walter, 57, 69, 124
Clarke, Kenneth, 253
class collaboration, 165
class harmony, 152, 165
class struggle, 421
class war, 280, 285
Clause IV, 75, 82 - 87, 89 - 91, 93 - 95, 98, 101 - 104, 106, 115, 117, 120, 122 - 123, 133 - 134
Clay Cross, 165
CND, 102, 391
Coal Board, 78
Coal Industry Bill, 285
coal strike of 1984-85, x, 103, 124, 265, 267 - 268, 274, 278 - 279, 286, 299
coal-fired power stations, 304
Coalition Cabinet, 68
Collins, Jack, 417
Colombian coal, 293
Combined Cycle Gas Turbine power stations, 305
Comintern, 92
Committee for Middle East Trade, 253
Committee: 1922, 216
common ownership, 117
Communist Liaison, 101
Communist Party of Britain, 95, 97, 101, 105, 108
Communist Party of Chile, 156
Communist Party of Great Britain, 61 - 63, 69, 112, 114 - 115, 124, 139, 149, 157, 166, 233, 278, 284
Communist Party of India, 48
Communist Unity Convention, 41
Connolly, James, 373
contempt of court, 243
Cook, Robin, 88, 119
Cortonwood Colliery, 283
Corvalan, Luis, 155
COSHE, 315
council house repairs, 334
council house sales, 88
courts, 278, 415
CPSA, 131
CPSU, 3
craft mentality, 326
craft outlook, 5
craft privileges, 5
craft unions, 7
'creative accounting', 341 - 342

cretinism, 241
crisis of overproduction, vii, 265, 280, 321, 423
Crosland, Anthony, 173
Cuba, 286
cuts in benefits, 69
Dawes Report, 51
Dean, Brenda, 351, 358
'defence of the fatherland', 26, 98, 117
degradation, 279
Democratic Republic of Viet Nam, 75
Demonstration for miners, 291
Denning, Lord, 244
Desai, Lord, 428
dialectics, 97
dialectrical and historical materialism, 104
Dictatorship of the proletariat, 96 - 97, 108, 113, 145, 188, 347
Diego Garcia, 385
Diplock Special Courts, 368
discrimination, 282
dockers, 214, 221, 244
domestic investment, vii
Dubbins, Tony, 327
Dutch imperialism, 73
East African British passport holders, 76
Easter Rebellion, 35
Eastern Europe, 428
Eccles, Jack, 263
economic crisis, 105
economic depression, 274
economism, 92, 125, 274, 322, 332
Edinburgh eligibility clause, 43
education, v, 106, 117, 129, 334, 342, 344, 360, 425
education 'reforms', 98
EEPTU, 78, 228, 350,
Egypt, 68
Election, 1918, 45
Election, 1922, 45
electoral liability, 285
Electoral Reform Act, 6
Emergency Powers Act, 50
enemy within, 216, 218
Engels, Frederick, i, 109, 277, 284, 331, 354, 369, 378
entryism, 83
Ethiopia, 286
European Decency Threshold, viii, 98
European Workers Anti-Fascist Congress, 64
Ezra, Sir Derek, 400
Fabian Society, 18
Falkland Islands, 383, 387
Falklands, 78
Falklands/Malvinas War, 235, 279, 348, 383,
fascism, x, 63, 124, 388
fascist dictatorship, 63, 387
fascist violence, 282
fascists, 356
Fleet Street, 210, 215, 324
Foot, Michael, 127, 348, 372, 385, 429
foreign investment in Britain, 428
France, 385
franchise, 84
franchise reform, 154
'Freedom Association', 406
Freedom of Information Act, 117
French Revolution, 1848-51, 143

Friends of Soviet Russia, 56, 64
full employment, 116, 132, 321
functional underclass, ii
Gaddaffi, 80, 251
Gaitskell, Hugh, 87 - 88
Galbraith, J.K., ii
Galtieri, General, 195, 217, 275
Gandhi, 64 - 68
GCHQ, Cheltenham, 79, 196, 274
General Election, 1929, 64
General Election, 1935, 63, 68
General Election, 1951, 72
General Election, 1992, 77
General Strike, 61, 408
General Strike, 1926, xii, 123, 199, 276, 299
George, Lloyd, 44, 83, 373
Germany, iii, 70, 110, 425
Ghana, 72
Gill, Ken, 127
GMBATU, 263
Gold Coast, 72
Gollan, John, 150, 152
Gormley, Joe, 403, 415
Gould, Bryan, 429
Grant, Bernie, 389
Greater London Council, 411
Greek liberation struggle, 73
Grunwick, 282
Guildford 4, 76
Gulf War, 78 - 79

H-block hunger strike, 366
Hain, Peter, 117, 119
Hammond, Eric, 78, 240
Hardie, Keir, 22
Hart, David, 79
Hattersley, Roy, ix, 223, 276
Hatton, Derek, 338, 344

Heath, Edward, 205, 268
Heathfield, Betty, 281
Heathfield, Peter, 80, 243, 263, 265, 275, 281, 287
Hegel, 331
Henderson, Arthur, 35, 84, 103, 175, 374,
Heseltine, Michael, 294
High Court, 218
Hitler, 75
Hodges, Frank, 43
homelessness, xiii
Honduras, 424, 428
Hungary, 190
Hunger March, 1936, 69
Hunger Strike, 1981, 78
Hurd, Douglas, 253
Hussein, Saddam, 391
Immigration Act, 1968, 76
Imperialist World War, First, 83, 86, 121, 299
improvement grants, 336
'In Place of Strife', 77, 163
incomes policy, 77
Independent Labour Party, iii, 16, 66, 118
India, 64, 66, 68, 124, 413, 422, 428
Indian liberation struggle, 1928-31, 66
Indian National Congress, 64
Indian Workers Association (GB), xiii, 276, 290, 308
Indian working class, 67
Indian working-class movement, 66
Indo-China, 73 - 74
Industrial Relations Act, 163
inflation, 268
International Class Prisoners' Aid,

BIBLIOGRAPHY / INDEX 439

56
International Class War Prisoners' Aid, 56
International Federation of Trade Unions, 57
International Labour Defence, 64
International Marxist Group, 85, 139, 187
International Miners' Organisation, 287
International Socialists, 92, 139, 177
International Working Women's Day, 282
International, Labour and Socialist, 36
International, Second, 54
    Basle Congress, 25
    Berne, 36
    Copenhagen Congress, 25
    Stuttgart Congress, 24
International, Two-and-a-half, 36
Iran, 73
Iran-Iraq war, 392
Iraq, vii, 68, 78, 392
Ireland, xii, 92, 117, 124
Ireland, troops sent in 1969, 76
Irish people, struggle for self-determination, 76
Irish workers, 282
Iron and Steel Trades Confederation, 78
Israel, 252

Japan, 424
Jenkin, Patrick, 339 - 341
Jenkins, Clive, 127, 320
Jenkins, Rev.David, 229
Johnson, Lyndon, 75
Jolly George, 36

judiciary, 277 - 278
Kaufman, Gerald, 390
Kautsky, Karl, vi, 109, 132
Kent miners, 417
Kent, Bruce, 391
Keynesian consensus, iii, 97, 132, 134
Keys, Bill, 320
'Kick the Tories out', 106
Kinnock, Mrs, 127
Kinnock, Neil, ix, 75, 78, 88 - 89, 127, 213, 223, 249, 252, 259, 270, 276 - 277, 281, 285 - 286, 333, 338, 344 - 345, 390, 415 - 416, 422, 429
Kitson, Brigadier Frank, 159
Korea, 155
Korean peninsula, partition of, 73
Korean people, war of aggression against, 73
Kronstadt rebellion, 190
Kruschevite revisionism, 124
Kuwait, 391

Labour Government, 1923, 161
Labour Government, 1924, 61, 66
Labour Government, 1929, 161
Labour Government, 1929-31, 64
Labour Government, 1945, 162
Labour Government, 1964, 163
Labour Government, Second, 68
Labour Government, Wilson-Callaghan, 74
Labour Governments, 1945-51, 71
Labour leadership, 81
labour movement, 265
Labour Party, 3 - 4, 61 - 64, 66, 69, 71, 75, 80 - 88, 90 - 92, 94 - 96, 98, 102 - 106, 109 - 111, 113 - 115, 117 - 118, 120 - 122, 124 - 125, 130, 134 -

135, 213, 234, 249, 258, 276, 278, 281, 299, 330, 335 - 336, 338, 362, 372, 416
Labour Party Conference 1984, 259
Labour Party leadership, 415
Labour Representation Committee, iii, 20, 121
Laird, Gavin, 408
'law and order', 98
Lawson, Nigel, 269, 275, 301
League Against Imperialism, 56, 64
Lebanon, 79, 252
'Left' Labour Government, 158
Left-Wing Movement, 56, 64
Lenin, V.I., v - vi, xi, 62, 82 - 83, 92, 97, 108 - 110, 112 - 113, 125, 127, 131, 133, 135, 242, 416
Leninism, 97, 108, 110, 112
Lib-lab alliance, iii
Lib-Lab politics, 12
Liberal commitment to low rates, 336
Liberal Democrats, 103
Liberal Party, iii, 16, 61, 66, 121, 336, 338 - 339
Libya, 80, 251, 261 - 262, 277, 289
Liverpool, 215
Liverpool Council, 333, 341 - 342, 345, 347
Livingstone, Ken, 71, 75 - 76, 117, 428
MacDonald, Ramsey, 63, 65, 67, 89, 161, 175
MacGregor, Ian, 193, 197, 210
Major, John, 134
Malaya, 72
Malayan people, liberation struggle of, 73

Malvinas, 383, 388
Manpower Services Commission, 319
manufacturing industry, 427
manufacturing output, 426
market economy, 116
Marx, Karl, ix, 109, 116, 118, 133, 318, 349, 352, 376
Marxian teaching on the state, 111, 139
Marxism, 109, 133
Marxism-Leninism, ii, 90 - 91, 99, 106 - 107, 114 - 115, 123, 135, 347 - 348
Marxist, 99, 423
Marxist-Leninist, 105
Marxist-Leninist party, 98, 135
Marxist-Leninists, 359
Maxwell, Robert, 80
May Day, 201
McGahey, Mick, 167, 197, 237, 243, 275, 281
McLennan, Gordon, 166
Meacher, Michael, 344
means testing, 69
Meerut trial, 64, 66
Mexico, 423, 428
MI5, 79 - 80
middle class (petty bourgeoisie), ix, 118
Middle East, 68 - 69, 73, 124, 389, 392
Militant, 71, 334, 337, 342, 344 - 346
Militant Tendency, 334, 337
militarism, vi
Mill, John Stuart, ix
miners, xii, 193 - 194, 272 - 274,

276, 280, 283, 339, 417
miners strike of 1984-85, 414, 420
miners' strike, 268, 349 - 350, 354
Minimum Lending Rate, 268
minimum wage, 98, 116 - 117
Minority Movement, 55 - 58, 64, 69
misery, 279
Mondism, 61, 123
Monopolies and Mergers Commission, 269
Monopolies Commission, 193
'Morning Star', 95
Morris, Bill, 119, 292
Morrison, Herbert, 375
Mosley, 69, 124, 375
Murdoch, Rupert, 216, 349 - 350, 352, 354 - 355, 357 - 358
Murray, Len, 281, 319 - 321, 326, 416
NACODS, 230, 246, 262, 266
NALGO, 315
Namibia, 74, 102
'National Working Miners Committee', 260
National Charter Campaign Committee, 64
National Coal Board, x, 193, 196, 201, 205, 212, 220, 246, 265 - 266, 269, 272, 274, 276, 283 - 285, 415
National Council of Labour, 63
National Executive Committee, 85
National Front, 76, 406
National Government, 63, 68
National Health Service, iii - iv, viii, 72, 98, 106, 407
National Reporting Centre, 206, 208
National Unemployed Workers Ctte. Movement, 55 - 56, 69

National Unemployed Workers Movement, 64
National Union of Seamen, 199
National Union of Teachers, 360
Nazi, 4, 386
Nazi Germany, 63, 93
near-Marxian phraseology, 140
Nekrasov, 222
New Communist Party, 105 - 106, 108 - 111, 113 - 114, 120 - 121, 123 - 124, 130 - 132, 134
new technology, 427
New Unionism, 9
New Unions, 12
NGA, 221, 323 - 324, 326, 329, 351
Nicholls, Judge, 243, 261
'No Blood for Oil', 389
'No Victimisation', 417
North Atlantic Treaty Organisation, 73, 78
Nott, John, 383
Nottingham miners, x, 78, 203, 207, 281, 284, 286, 401
nuclear power, 294, 306, 398
nuclear weapons, 78
NUJ, 326, 350
NUM, 79 - 81, 193, 195, 207, 212, 215, 220, 238, 246, 265 - 266, 269 - 277, 279 - 287, 415, 417
NUM coal strike, 1984-85, 78
NUM Conference, 284
NUM leadership, 275 - 276
NUM militants, 270
NUPE, 315

October Revolution, 83 - 84, 118, 424
OECD, 424
opportunism, 110, 132, 278, 285

Orgreave, 208, 354
Pacific Rim, 423 - 424
pacifists, 118
Page Arnot, Robin, 170
Palestine, 68, 79, 252
Palme Dutt, R., 60, 65, 67
Paris Commune, 145, 195
Parkinson, Cecil, 301
Parliament, 122, 278 - 279
parliamentarism, 91
parliamentary cretinism, 158
Parliamentary Labour Party, 63, 69
parliamentary party, 121
parliamentary road to socialism, 108, 111
Pearce, Padraig, 373
pensions, 98, 107
Pentonville Five, 244
People's army, 156
People's Charter, 6
People's Democracies, 3
People's March for Jobs, 311
petty bourgeoisie, v, vii
petty-bourgois opposition, 347
picket violence, 421
Pitt, Malcolm, 403, 414
'Plan for Coal', 266, 285, 400
plastic bullets, 412
Poland, 386
police, x, 278, 356, 415
police harassment, 407
Police Support Units, 208
police violence, x, 78 - 79, 197, 207, 259, 276 - 277, 282, 355, 414
policing the coal strike, 260
political courts, 422
political power, 279
Poll tax, 78

Pollitt, Harry, 36, 60, 62
Popular Unity Government (Chile), 156
Post Office, 116
post-war boom, 97
poverty, 107
power cuts, 247, 270
Prentice, Reg, 165
Prevention of Terrorism Act, 76
printworkers, 349 - 350, 354 - 355, 357 - 359
privatisation, 88, 98, 293
privatisation, coal, 301
privatisation, electricity, 301, 305
privileged layers of the working class, 118
privileged upper stratum, 130
proletarian revolution, ii, 151
propaganda, 276
PSBR, viii
public ownership, 116, 118
public services, 343
public works programme, 428
'put welfare to work', 116

Queen, 278

racialism, 282
racism, 406
railwaymen, 222
Railways, 116
rate capping, 342
rate support grant, 336
rate support grants, 337, 342
re-nationalisation, 98
Reagan, Ronald, 374
Red Flag Union, 64
Red International of Labour Unions, 57
Redgrave, Vanessa, 176

redundancy, 307
Rees, Merlyn, 375
reformism, 95 - 96, 416
reformists, 93
refuse collection, 344
Reid, Jimmy, 134, 233 - 234
Relief Ctte. for Victims of German Fascism, 64
Republic of Buenos Aires, 384
resolutions as substitute for action, 415
revisionists, 72, 83, 88, 96, 102 - 103, 105, 107, 111, 115, 117, 119 - 120, 141, 278
revolution, 108, 110, 142
revolutionary alternative, 112 - 113
revolutionary party, 124
Rhodesia, 74
Ridley, Nicholas, 222
'right to work', 197, 280
right to work, 420
Robinson, Tony, 330
Roman Catholic Church, 190
'Round Table Conference', 65
Royal College of Nursing, 315
RUC, 367
Russell, Bertrand, 133
Russia, 61
Russian Revolution, 90

Saklatwala, Shapurji, 56, 59
sale of council houses, 98
Sands, Bobby, xii, 78, 365
Scanlon, Hugh, 173
Scargill, Ann, 281
Scargill, Arthur, 79 - 81, 90 - 91, 95, 103 - 104, 117, 193, 195 - 196, 202, 205, 210, 215, 237, 243, 246, 268, 270, 272 - 273, 275, 280 - 281, 283 - 287, 292, 294, 298, 300, 344, 357, 420
Scottish parliament, 117
SDLP, 380
SDP, 95 - 96, 234
SDP/Liberal Alliance, 278
Seamen's strike, 163
self-rule, 64
sequestration, 79, 218, 281, 287, 351, 358
Shah, Eddie, 221, 326 - 327
Shaw, G.B., 24
Shaw, Giles, 355
Sheffield Council, 342
Shrewsbury building workers, 166
Simon Commission, 58, 64 - 65
Sirs, Bill, 78
Sizewell, 400
Skinner, Dennis, 292, 296
Smith, Ian, 74
Smith, John, 75
Snowden, Philip, 22, 63, 161, 175
'social imperialism', 72
social benefits, 117
social chauvinism, 109 - 110, 132 - 133
social con-trick, 77
social contract, 77, 330, 414
social democracy, 83 - 84, 88, 90, 92 - 94, 96, 103, 112 - 113, 115, 117, 119 - 120, 125, 133, 347
social democratic, 107
Social Democratic Federation, 20
social democrats, 134
social security, 276, 335, 397
social services, 334
social-democratic cretinism, 107
'socialism in one city', 347

'socialist colonialism', 24
Socialist Challenge, 85
socialist construction, 87
Socialist Labour League, 139
Socialist Outlook, 85, 87 - 91, 139
Socialist Review, 94
Socialist Worker, 93
Socialist Workers Party, 71, 91 - 94, 102, 105, 130, 134, 139
SOGAT, 350 - 352, 358 - 359
Soley, Clive, 356
South Africa, 74, 102, 252
South Atlantic, 384
South Korea, 424
Southall, 418 - 419
Soviet Russia, 84
Soviet Union, 3, 69, 87, 93, 124, 133, 233, 424, 428
Spain, 124, 384
Spanswick, Albert, 315
Spartacist, 90 - 91
Special Patrol Group, 354
Stalin, J.V., 86, 93, 199, 233, 277, 299
state, 415
state capitalism, 30
state control, 116
state machinery, 422
Steel, David, 222, 245
Stockport Messenger, 282, 323
Stormont, 76, 379
strike ballots, 116
student grants, 98, 107
subsidies, 399
Suez Canal, 73, 124, 383
Sun Yat-sen, Dr., 49
superprofits, i, 128, 359, 416
syndicalists, 118

T&GWU, 199, 221, 315
Taff Vale, 21
tax, 98
Taylor, Jack, 243
teachers, 360
Tebbit, Norman, 319
Thatcher, Margaret, iv, 77 - 79, 81, 97, 202, 213, 265, 267, 270, 275, 281, 284, 321, 352, 356 - 357, 371, 391, 415
The state, Marxian teaching on, 141
third world, 423
Thomas, J.H., 47, 63
Tories, 61
Tory, 66
Toxteth, 334
Trade Disputes Act, 22
trade unions, 121 - 123, 125, 134
trade-union & labour movement, 280
trade-union bureaucracy, 331
trade-union card, 416
trade-union leaders, 414, 422
Trade-Union leadership, 78, 415 - 416
trade-union legislation, 117, 319
trade-union membership, 126
trade-union movement, 124, 126, 131, 265, 273, 285, 337, 415 - 416
trade-union organisation, 415 - 416
trade-union rights, 106
trench pacifism, 372
Trethowan, Sir Ian, 370
Trevett, Eric, 105 - 108
'Tribune', 166
Tribune group, 119
Trotsky, L., 94, 233
Trotskyist phrases, 83
Trotskyites, 62, 71 - 72, 83, 86, 88,